D1331203

WHY
FAIRY
TALES
STICK

WHY FAIRY TALES STICK

JACK ZIPES

The Evolution and Relevance of a Genre

Routledge
Taylor & Francis Group
New York London

Routledge is an imprint of the
Taylor & Francis Group, an informa business

Routledge
Taylor & Francis Group
270 Madison Avenue
New York, NY 10016

Routledge
Taylor & Francis Group
2 Park Square
Milton Park, Abingdon
Oxon OX14 4RN

© 2006 by Taylor & Francis Group, LLC
Routledge is an imprint of Taylor & Francis Group, an Informa business

Transferred to Digital Printing 2010

International Standard Book Number-10: 0-415-97781-9 (Softcover) 0-415-97780-0 (Hardcover)
International Standard Book Number-13: 978-0-415-97781-4 (Softcover) 978-0-415-97780-7 (Hardcover)

No part of this book may be reprinted, reproduced, transmitted, or utilized in any form by any electronic, mechanical, or other means, now known or hereafter invented, including photocopying, microfilming, and recording, or in any information storage or retrieval system, without written permission from the publishers.

Trademark Notice: Product or corporate names may be trademarks or registered trademarks, and are used only for identification and explanation without intent to infringe.

Library of Congress Cataloging-in-Publication Data

Zipes, Jack David.
    Why fairy tales stick : the evolution and relevance of a genre / Jack Zipes.
        p. cm.
    Includes bibliographical references and index.
    ISBN 0-415-97780-0 -- ISBN 0-415-97781-9 (pbk.)
        1. Fairy tales--Psychological aspects. 2. Fairy tales--History and criticism. I. Title.

PN3437.Z58 2006
398.201'9--dc22   2006004867

Visit the Taylor & Francis Web site at
http://www.taylorandfrancis.com

and the Routledge Web site at
http://www.routledge-ny.com

To Bill Germano, great editor and
friend, who never failed to give
me the inspiration and criticism
I needed at the right times

Contents

Illustrations

The illustrations have been taken from the following books:

Charles Perrault, *Contes*. Illustrations by Maurice Leroy. Paris: Editions de la Nef D'Argent, 1943.
Grimm's Fairy Tales. Illustrations by Jiri Trnka. London: Paul Hamyln, 1961.
Fairy Tales of the Brothers Grimm. Translated by Mrs. Edgar Lucas. Illustrations by Arthur Rackham. London: Archibald Constable, 1900.
Walter Crane, *Beauty and the Beast*. London: Routledge, 1874. Walter Crane's Toybook.
Charles Perrault, *Les Contes de Perrault*. Illustrations by Gustave Doré. Paris: J. Hetzel, 1867.

Chapter 1: "Little Red Riding Hood"
Illustrator: Maurice Leroy

Chapter 2: "The Foolish Wishes"
Illustrator: Maurice Leroy

Chapter 3: "Cinderella"
Illustrator: Maurice Leroy

Chapter 4: "Snow White"
Illustrator: Arthur Rackham

Chapter 5: "Bluebeard"
Illustrator: Gustave Doré

Chapter 6: "Hansel and Gretel"
Illustrator: Arthur Rackham

Chapter 7: "Iron Hans"
Illustrator: Jiri Trnka

Preface

When we hear or read the phrase "once upon a time," we immediately and naturally think that we are about to hear a fairy tale. We are disposed to listening and reading in a particular way and register metaphors in our brain so that they make sense and so we can replicate them in our own way and in our own time. When we hear or read "Little Red Riding Hood," "Cinderella," "Hansel and Gretel," "Bluebeard," or any of the other putative classical fairy tales, we know immediately what is being implied, even though we may not know the exact, original, or so-called authentic text. It is almost as if certain fairy tales were stored in our brains and have evolved as we humans have evolved. But this is not entirely the case, and not all human beings are predisposed and configured to process the fairy tale as if it were innate. Few people would argue, however, that the fairy tale has become a very specific genre in our lives and has inserted itself in inexplicable ways so that many of us try, even without knowing it, to make a fairy tale out of our lives.

How did this behavior evolve? What is its relevance? How do we make things relevant and special through mental and public representations? Why do particular fairy tales stick with us as replicating memes? What is a meme? Can the evolution and relevance of fairy tales be better understood if we examine them as memes? These are some of the questions that I shall answer in this book.

Why Fairy Tales Stick is a complement to my book *Fairy Tales and the Art of Subversion: The Classical Genre for Children and the Process of Civilization*, which was published in 1983.[1] That book focused on how writers cultivated the fairy tale as a socially symbolic act within an institutionalized discourse of the Western civilizing process to comment on norms, mores, and values. I also tried to analyze the ideological impact of fairy tales as they were conceived and used to socialize children. In the course of twenty-five years I have tended to be critical of the classical tales written by Charles Perrault, the Brothers Grimm,

Hans Christian Andersen, and others because of their conservative tendencies with regard to gender, religion, and social class. In addition, I lamented the manner in which other scholars approached the oral folk tale and the literary fairy tale, collapsing the distinctions and dehistoricizing the genres while generating fuzzy psychological and formalist theories that lead more to mystification than elucidation in regard to the interaction between oral and literary genres.

In *Why Fairy Tales Stick* I have reexamined my own approach to the literary fairy tale, especially the classical tales, by including recent research on relevance theory, social Darwinism, evolutionary psychology, and linguistics. This critical reexamination does not mean that I have abandoned the premise of *Fairy Tales and the Art of Subversion*. I still very much believe that fairy tales have formed a relevant discourse within the Western civilizing process as analyzed by Norbert Elias and more recently by Pierre Bourdieu. But I have found that it is important to know something about genetics, memetics, linguistics, and evolution to explain how the literary fairy tale originated in an oral mode and was formed over thousands of years to stick in our brains in very peculiar ways. In other words, the classical fairy tales that evolved did not become stable and establish their values in the seventeenth century simply because they reinforced the ideological norms of patriarchal societies. They spoke to the conflicts and predicaments that arose out of the attempts by social orders to curb and "civilize" our instinctual drives. The oral and literary fairy tales enunciated, articulated, and communicated feelings in efficient metaphorical terms that enabled listeners and readers to envision possible solutions to their problems so that they could survive and adapt to their environments. The notion of miraculous transformation is key to understanding most of the traditional fairy tales that have stuck in us and with us. Just as we as a species have mutated, often in wondrous ways, so has the oral folk tale transformed itself and been transformed as literary fairy tale to assist us in coming to terms with the absurdity and banality of everyday life. Though canonical tales have been established to preserve male domination, as Pierre Bourdieu might argue, they have also been replicated to question them, explore them, change them, and reutilize them. In fact, we use the classical fairy tales in mutated forms through new technologies to discuss and debate urgent issues that concern our social lives and the very survival of the human species.

In his book, *L'evoluzione della cultura* (The Evolution of Culture), the eminent geneticist Luigi Luca Cavalli-Sforza explains that the first phase of cultural transmission is

> mutation, or transformation that brings about the creation of a new idea. This phase is the phase of creation or invention. If new ideas are not created, there is also the possibility of another kind of mutation—the loss of an idea or a custom. The innovation will not be transmitted unless there is a desire to teach it, that is, to disseminate it and to learn it. One could say that the transmission passes through two phases: the communication of information, of an idea, by a teacher (transmitter) to a student (transmittee), and the comprehension and acquisition of the idea. This is the act of reproduction of the idea that happens when the idea passes from one brain to another. . . . Ideas (even if we do not know exactly what they are) are material objects inasmuch as they require material bodies and brains in which they are produced for the first time and reproduced in the process of transmission: like the DNA they are material objects, even if they are profoundly different from the DNA.[2]

Cavalli-Sforza goes on to explain that an idea is like a circuit of neurons, and once an idea has been formed in our brains, it has the capacity to live for a long time, even for an entire lifetime. Susan Blackmore calls an idea that enters and circulates in our brains a meme, a term that she has taken from Richard Dawkins and that she has radically developed in her book *The Meme Machine*.

> Memes are instructions for carrying out behaviour, stored in brains (or other objects) and passed on by imitation. Their competition drives the evolution of the mind. Both genes and memes are replicators and must obey the general principles of evolutionary theory and in that case they are the same. Beyond that they may be, and indeed are, very different—they are related only by analogy. . . . Memes are no more "mythical entities" than genes are—genes are instructions encoded in molecules of DNA—memes are instructions embedded in human brains, or in the artefacts such as books, pictures, bridges or steam trains.[3]

The fairy tale often takes the form of a meme in our brains, as the input of a public representation, or replicator, and we process it in a module and transmit it in sociocultural contexts. It is difficult to say why we select certain fairy tales over others to disseminate. Blackmore would argue that fairy tales as memes compete for our attention to be imitated. Indeed, there is a selection process that indicates cultural and personal preference of some kind. *Why Fairy Tales Stick* is a modest endeavor to explain how we have selected certain fairy tales as memes and how they have evolved particularly over the past three hundred years in Western civilization. Although my focus is largely on Europe and North America, what I have to say about the oral and literary traditions of fairy tales is applicable to the development of the genre in other cultures as well. After all there has been a great dissemination of Western fairy tales through globalization, and of course, many of the so-called Western fairy tales received impulses from and owe their germination to tales that emanated from the ancient Orient or Africa. The fairy tale is a polygenetic cultural artifact that has spread throughout the world through human contact and technologies invented to bring about effective communication.

The first two chapters of this book, "Toward a Theory of the Fairy Tale as a Literary Genre" and "The Evolution and Dissemination of the Classical Fairy Tale," deal with the theoretical basis of my premises and concern relevance theory, memetics, orality, literacy, and epidemiology. Chapters 3 through 6 are case studies that focus on such classical fairy tales as "Cinderella," "Snow White," Beauty and the Beast," "Bluebeard," and "Hansel and Gretel" to explore how they mutated and stuck in human brains and cultures as we have evolved within the civilizing process. My final chapter, "To Be or Not to Be Eaten: The Survival of Traditional Storytelling," is a critical and dialectical examination of tradition and how necessary it is to further the transformation of the fairy tale and other traditional tales while preserving what is beneficial to our survival.

In the course of conceiving this book over the past five years I have had important discussions with my friends Dan Sperber and Gloria Origgi, who have been most generous in sharing their ideas and works with me. I cannot thank them enough for their inspiration. Dan's work with Deirdre Wilson on relevance theory has been of particular significance to me. I also had the good fortune to meet Ute Heidmann and

Jean-Michel Adam, whose theory of *généricité* (genericity) has had a major impact on my approach to analyzing the genre of the fairy tale. My contacts with Graham Anderson and Jan Ziolkowski have also been extremely beneficial. They have both shed new light on the development of the fairy tale in the ancient and medieval worlds, and I have learned a great deal from their studies. Among my friends and colleagues who have influenced me as I wrote this book, I would like to thank Cristina Bacchilega, Pier Carlo Bontempelli, Nancy Canepa, Giorgia Grilli, Don Haase, Donatella Izzo, Roberta Pederzoli, Luisa Rubini, Charlotte Trinquet, and Marina Warner. My intellectual debts to Norbert Elias and Pierre Bourdieu are clear. In addition, I have benefited greatly by reading the works of such scientists and critics as Susan Blackmore, Luigi Cavalli-Sforza, Richard Dawkins, Ellen Dissanayake, Stephen Pinker, Matt Ridley, Edward Wilson, and Robert Wright, who may not share the same views about evolution and the mind, but they certainly have clarified why an understanding of genetics and evolution is crucial for understanding the development of a literary genre and human nature.

Over the past twenty years I have received wise counsel and help from Bill Germano, my former editor at Routledge, to whom I have dedicated this book. I am now working mainly with Matt Byrnie, another great editor at Routledge, who has been a tremendous support in all my endeavors. As usual Fred Veith has been most helpful in preparing the manuscript for the production process, and Sarah Blackmon and Christine Andreasen have been superb in overseeing the entire project. In addition, Mary Bearden has been exceptional as copy editor. Last but not least, I want to express my gratitude to my wife, Carol Dines, who has graciously tolerated my obsession with fairy tales, and to my daughter, Hanna, who has made certain to ground me in the reality of our lives.

"Little Red Riding Hood"
Illustrator: Maurice Leroy

Chapter 1

Toward a Theory of the Fairy Tale as Literary Genre

A s is well known, there is a classical fairy-tale canon in the Western world that has been in existence ever since the nineteenth century, if not earlier. The tales that constitute this canon are "Cinderella," "Little Red Riding Hood," "Sleeping Beauty," "Hansel and Gretel," "Rapunzel," "Rumpelstiltskin," "The Frog Prince," "Snow White," "Bluebeard," "Beauty and the Beast," "Jack and the Beanstalk," "The Princess and the Pea," "The Little Mermaid," "The Ugly Duckling," "Aladdin and the Magic Lamp," "Ali Baba and the Forty Thieves," and so on. In my previous works I argued that these tales became canonized because they were adapted from the oral tradition of folklore for aristocratic and middle-class audiences as print culture developed in the sixteenth and seventeenth centuries and basically reshaped and retold during this time to reinforce the dominant patriarchal ideology throughout the nineteenth and twentieth centuries. Consequently, the most telling or catchy tales were reprinted and reproduced in multiple forms and entered into cultural discursive practices in diverse ways so that they became almost "mythicized" as natural stories, as second nature. We respond to these classical tales almost as if we were born with them, and yet, we know full well that they have been socially produced and induced and continue to be generated this way through different forms of the mass media.

Although I have always subscribed to the notion that the classical fairy tales tend to be overtly patriarchal and politically conservative in structure and theme and reflect the dominant interests of social groups that control cultural forces of production and reproduction, I have never been able to explain satisfactorily why the canonical tales stick with us and why they are so catchy when there are so many other fascinating and artistic tales that are just as good if not better than the canonical tales we tend to repeat and are predisposed to know. To my mind it is not sufficient now to argue as I have done in the past that the classical tales have been consciously and subconsciously reproduced largely in print by a cultural industry that favors patriarchal and reactionary notions of gender, ethnicity, behavior, and social class. There are other important elements or ingredients in the tales themselves as well as external factors that need more attention, for they might explain more fully how and why particular types are disseminated more than others. What is it in the generic nature of the fairy tale that accounts for its cultural relevance and its attraction? Why do certain tales appear to spread almost like a virus, not only in the Western world but also in the entire world?

MEMETICS AND THE EPIDEMIOLOGICAL APPROACH

In *The Great Fairy Tale Tradition: From Straparola and Basile to the Brothers Grimm* (2001),[1] I began trying to answer some of these questions by formulating more specific questions about origins and by proposing a social biological and an epidemiological approach to understanding the relevance of fairy tales. I asked: How did literary fairy tales originate? How did they spread? How was their great tradition formed? There are numerous theories about the origin of the fairy tale, but none have provided conclusive proof about how the literary fairy tale was formed. This is because it is next to impossible to know because the literary fairy tale is similar to a special biological species that was cultivated slowly in an oral tradition and then suddenly flowered at one point in history with the help of the printing press and new social and technological forms of transmission. By the end of the seventeenth century the literary fairy tale erupted and began to evolve and spread indiscriminately and has continued to transform itself vigorously to the present day.

It may seem strange to compare the genre of the fairy tale to a natural form of species. Yet, there is a virtue to using a biological analogy to make sense of the great tradition of the literary fairy tale. In fact, the literary fairy tale has evolved from the stories of the oral tradition, piece by piece in a process of incremental adaptation, generation by generation in different cultures of people who cross-fertilized the oral tales with the literary tales and disseminated them. If we consider that tales are mentally and physically conceived by human beings as material products of culture, then it is possible to analyze how special forms of telling originated as species or what literary critics call genres.

We know that there were many different kinds of storytelling that existed thousands of years ago in antiquity, and they gave birth to types of "wonder" tales that prefigured the literary fairy tales. We also know that there were many kinds of fantastic and marvelous oral *and* literary tales that served to form the hybrid "species" of the literary fairy tale. As a result, we can trace a historical evolution of many of these tales by examining how bits and pieces of a story accumulated in different cultures and then eventually gelled to form a genre. We cannot say with historical precision when the literary fairy tale began its evolution, but we can trace motifs and elements of the literary fairy tale to numerous types of storytelling and stories of antiquity that contributed to the formation of a particular branch of telling and writing tales. In the Western European tradition this branching occurred some time in the early medieval period (perhaps even earlier) and led to the social institution of a special literary genre (*conte de fée*) in the seventeenth century that today we call the literary fairy tale.

I likened the evolutionary process of the specific form of the oral wonder tale and the literary fairy tale to a process of contamination and contagion—the motifs and plots of stories spread like viruses that eventually formed a clearly identifiable genre, species, or virus that we generally call the fairy tale. At the time that I was trying to develop my ideas, I was already familiar with Dan Sperber and Deirdre Wilson's relevance theory and Sperber's epidemiological approach to culture,[2] but I was unfamiliar with Richard Dawkins's concept of the meme, a cultural replicator that has led to the rise of memetics[3]—a speculative theory that, I believe, complements Sperber's epidemiological approach to culture even though Sperber has misgivings about memetics.[4]

Dawkins maintains that there is one fundamental law of life that he believes is undeniable—"the law that all life evolves by the differential survival of replicating entities. The gene, the DNA molecule, happens to be the replicating entity that prevails on our own planet. There may be others. If there are, provided certain other conditions are met, they will almost inevitably tend to become the basis for an evolutionary planet."[5] Indeed, Dawkins argues that there is another new replicator that he calls a meme, a unit of cultural transmission.

> Examples of memes are tunes, ideas, catch-phrases, clothes fashions, ways of making pots or of building arches. Just as genes propagate themselves in the gene pool by leaping from body to body via sperms or eggs, so memes propagate themselves in the meme pool by leaping from brain to brain via a process which, in the broad sense can be called imitation. If a scientist hears, or reads about, a good idea, he passes it on to his colleagues and students. He mentions it in his articles and his lectures. If the idea catches on, it can be said to propagate itself, spreading from brain to brain. ... memes should be regarded as living structures, not just metaphorically but technically. When you plant a fertile meme in my mind you literally parasitize my brain, turning it into a vehicle for the meme's propagation in just the way that a virus may parasitize the genetic mechanism of a host cell. And this isn't just a way of talking—the meme for, say, "belief in life after death" is actually realized physically, millions of times over, as a structure in the nervous systems of individual men the world over.[6]

Much to Dawkins's surprise, his speculative remarks in the last chapter of *The Selfish Gene*, first published in 1976, led to the flowering of memetics, which has become one of the more controversial scientific theories in the twenty-first century.[7] The theory of memetics generally maintains that a meme is an informational pattern contained in a human brain (or in artifacts such as books or pictures) and stored in its memory, capable of being copied to another individual's brain that will store it and replicate it. Susan Blackmore contends that a meme's major trait is its capacity to be imitated and to replicate itself, and it is also what makes human beings different from all other animals. We copy and change all the time, and we are disposed to copying memes that want to be copied. "Memes spread themselves around indiscriminately without regard to whether they are useful, neutral, or positively harmful to us."[8] The memes battle each other for a secure place in the brain, and in order for a meme to survive, it must exhibit three major characteristics: fidelity, fecundity, and longevity. A meme must be capable of being copied in a faithful way; it must be shaped or formed in such a way that many copies can be made; and it must be able to survive a long time so that many copies will be disseminated. In time some memes form a memeplex, which is a group of memes that facilitates replication and can be likened to a genre. According to Blackmore, memes coevolve with genes, often influencing them, or are influenced by them. The dynamics will depend on the environment.

At a June 1999 convention of biologists, zoologists, geneticists, psychologists, linguists, anthropologists, and social scientists in Cambridge, England, the status of the meme was critically debated by the participants.[9] Many questions were raised about the differences between genes and memes, whether memes can operate without constraints, how the brain filters memes, whether memes can be viewed as discrete identifiable units, and what happens psychologically when a meme is processed by the brain. Many of the social scientists rejected the notion of a meme as irrelevant for the study of culture, and many others regretted that there were no examples of "applied memetics."

One possibility to apply memetics would be through a study of the evolution of the oral wonder tale and literary fairy tale. Indeed, a good example of a meme is a fairy tale, but not just any fairy tale, an individual fairy tale and its discursive tradition that includes oral and literary tales and other cultural forms of transmission such as radio, film, video, and the Internet. For example, "Little Red Riding Hood" has become a meme that has stuck in people's minds since at least the seventeenth century and has replicated and propagated itself throughout the world. Clearly this one classical fairy tale has managed to catch and plant itself in brains practically everywhere in the world, as I demonstrated in my 1983 study, *The Trials and Tribulations of Little Red Riding Hood*, which I revised in 1992 and which has since then been followed by more recent studies such as Sandra Beckett's *Recycling Red Riding Hood* (2002), Catherine Orenstein's *Little Red Riding Hood Uncloaked: Sex, Morality, and the Evolution of a Fairy Tale* (2003), Allesandra's Levorato's *Language and Gender in the Fairy Tale Tradition A Linguistic Analysis of Old and New Story Telling* (2003), Anne-Marie Garat's *Une faim de loup: Lecture du Petit Chaperon rouge* (2004), and Walter Fochesato, *Lupus in fabula* (2004),[10] not to mention numerous other essays on the topic. Even this scholarly discussion is memetic, that is, it is bound up with the transmission of memes that only survive if they are relevant or made relevant and stabilized through cultural institutions.

But it is perhaps too easy to accept memetics, a catchy theory, which is becoming more and more popular, when there is no conclusive scientific evidence that proves how memes are either biologically absorbed or transmitted to our brains and retained so that we become disposed to replicate them. There are other psychological, cultural, and social factors that need to be considered if we are ever to have a judicious and credible theory about the origin and transmission and "stickiness" of fairy tales. Nevertheless, the concept of the meme, which needs to be qualified, is, I believe, a valid term and starting point for considering the evolution and relevance of the fairy tale as a genre, and I shall use the term meme here in a broad sense to indicate a public representation or cultural replicator.

At this point I want to turn to Sperber's epidemiological approach because it offers a sounder theory of cultural communication and transmission than Dawkins's notion of the meme's transmission, while not totally dismissing memetics. In his book *Explaining Culture* (1996) and several essays such as "Culture and Modularity" written with Lawrence Hirschfeld and "Why a Deep Understanding of Cultural Evolution Is Incompatible with Shallow Psychology,"[11] Sperber has spelled out in great detail what he means by an epidemiological approach to culture. He begins with the premise that

> Members of a human group are bound with one another by multiple flows of information. (Here we use "information" in a broad sense that includes not only the content of people's knowledge, but also that of their beliefs, assumptions, fictions, rules, norms, skills, maps, images, and so on.) The information is materially realized in the *mental representations* of the

people, and in their *public productions*, that is, their cognitively guided behaviors and the enduring material traces of these behaviors. Mentally represented information is transmitted from individuals to individuals through public productions. *Public representations* such as speech, gestures, writing, or pictures are a special type of public productions, the function of which is to communicate a content. Public representations play a major role in the information transmission.[12]

The fairy tale as public representation (meme) must also be understood as relevant. That is, when the fairy tale is articulated in a communication of some kind, it is made relevant through the brain that operates efficiently and effectively to draw the attention of the listener/reader to the inferred meaning of the communication. A fairy tale as meme wants to be understood in a particular relevant way, otherwise it will not stick in the recipient who is *intended* to replicate it. Sperber and Deirdre Wilson elaborate this process in their book *Relevance* (1986) in great detail, and in a recent article, they explain:

> The central claim of relevance theory is that the expectations of relevance raised by an utterance are precise enough, and predictable enough, to guide the hearer towards the speaker's meaning. The aim is to explain in cognitively realistic terms what these expectations of relevance amount to, and how they might contribute to an empirically plausible account of comprehension.[13]

I shall return to relevance theory later when I discuss "Cinderella" in Chapter 3. What I want to insist on at this point is that a meme must be made relevant to stick, and as a fairy tale it has been made relevant in an evolutionary process.

With regard to the evolution of the literary fairy tale, we can consider its generator as the oral folk tale, in all its generic forms, as a meme that carries vital information for adaptation to the environment. In the process of gathering information in the brain, storing it, making it relevant, and then sharing it, humans tended and still tend to privilege certain data and to use them in specific circumstances. Recently, two European scholars have presented very useful explanations of how memes, when competing with other memes, are processed to become effective replicators. In his essay, "What Makes a Meme Successful? Selection Criteria for Cultural Evolution," Francis Heylighen maintains:

> To be replicated, a meme must pass successfully through four subsequent stages: 1) assimilation by an individual, who thereby becomes a *host* of the meme: 2) retention in that individual's memory; 3) expression by the individual in language, behavior or another form that can be perceived by others; 4) transmission of the thus created message or *meme vehicle* to one or more other individuals. This last stage is followed again by stage 1, thus closing the replication loop.[14]

Heylighen carefully outlines the mechanics of the replication process, and what is most important is his emphasis on subjective criteria that Blackmore and other memeticists neglect. Novelty, simplicity, coherence, and utility form some of the criteria that might influence the recipient's selection, as well as intersubjective criteria that determine to what extent the meme will fit group conditions and expectations. At the same time, the meme has its own criteria of self-justification, self-reinforcement, intolerance, and proselytism without which it would not be fit for replication. Both the stages and criteria can, I believe, be applied to how a particular fairy tale is processed and replicated by an individual or groups of individuals when they hear, read, or see a fairy tale. In addition, there are other sociocognitive mechanisms to be considered.

In Cristiano Castelfranchi's essay, "Towards a Cognitive Memetics: Socio-Cognitive Mechanisms for Memes Selection and Spreading," he pays special attention to the role of norms in meme spreading, the role of social identity and membership, and intergroup differentiation.[15] He argues that a decision is made by the individual (agent) who hosts a meme:

> A cognitive agent activates, selects, prefers, pursues, gives up goals on the basis of what it believes. In other words, it has "reasons" for what it does; a cognitive agent is a goal-directed agent (endowed with intentions, planning, and deliberation abilities, ...); its behaviour is in fact "action" aimed at certain anticipated results (mental representations) and is controlled and motivated by them (these representations).[16]

According to Castelfranchi, there are three mechanisms for meme adoption and replication: the practical problem-solving mechanism, the normative character of cultural transmission, and the social identity mechanism. In other words, the spread or contagion of a meme (fairy tale) does not depend solely on the meme itself, but also on decisions dependent on subjective and external (environmental) factors.

Castelfranchi and Heylighen provide qualifications about the operations of memes that reveal how much more complex a meme is. Imparting knowledge through language and artifacts is an efficient and relevant mode that contributes to the formation and continuity of groups and societies and their specific cultural rites, norms, and customs. We tend to shape and form information as a public representation in special ways that can be categorized socially and aesthetically, and as the human species has evolved, we have cultivated specific art forms linguistically, cognitively, and physically to express and communicate our beliefs and also our wonder about reality and the supernatural.

In her book *What Is Art For?* Ellen Dissanayake discusses the significance of "art as a behavior: making special as behavioral tendency that is as distinguishing and universal in humankind as speech or the skillful manufacture and use of tools."[17] Her notion of making something special to designate art can be related to Sperber and Wilson's notion of relevance or how the human mind functions linguistically and psychologically through modules in the brain to make something relevant and meaningful. Dissanayake states:

> Making special implies intent or deliberateness. When *shaping* or giving artistic expression for an idea, or *embellishing* an object, or recognizing that an idea or object is artistic, one gives (or acknowledges) a specialness that without one's activity or regard would not exist. Moreover, one intends by making special *to place the activity or artifact in a "realm" different from the everyday*. In most art of the past, it would seem, the special realm to be contrasted with the everyday was a magical or supernatural world, not—as today in the advanced West—a purely aesthetic realm. In both, however, there is a sort of salvation of quantum leap from the everyday humdrum reality in which life's vital needs and activities— eating, sleeping, preparing or obtaining food—occur to a different order which has a different motivation and a special attitude and response. In both the functional and nonfunctional art an alternative reality is recognized and entered; the making special acknowledges, reveals, and embodies this reality.[18]

Certainly the conception and use of the folk tale as an oral art form constituted a special manner of public representation in which value was enunciated—value was placed on content and selected to be communicated as a symbolic act. The stories told, in fact, were socially symbolic acts, as I have argued elsewhere,[19] using Frederic Jameson's notion of the individual literary work as a symbolic act, "which is grasped as the imaginary resolution of real contradiction."[20] However, a story may not resolve any or every thing; it is more a communication with words as symbols that impart meaning in sentences and gestures. As Jean Aitchison has pointed out, "language possesses the property of *generativity*—the use of a finite number of elementary parts to produce a potentially infinite number of forms and sentences. Generativity may be a basic property of the human mind: 'The generative nature of language is probably parasitic on the generative nature of human cognition.'"[21] Specific forms of language regenerate themselves. If a form of telling became highly special and relevant, it was remembered and passed on. If the contents were crucial for adapting to the environment, they too were disseminated time and again in forms that were recalled and transformed. Imitation and transmission are, indeed, key for understanding the evolution of a specific form of oral folk tale that was picked up by a print culture in Europe and gave rise to the institutionalization of the literary fairy tale.

Sperber has carefully explicated how the transmission of a meme or public representation, which can be equated with a particular tale, occurs. According to his theory, there is a language faculty or module[22] in the brain that enables humans to acquire language and other inputs, to copy and process them, and then to reproduce them in communication with other humans who share and can decipher their linguistic codes and cultural meaning. All this occurs in a causal chain of culture, which Sperber and Hirschfeld outline in "Culture and Modularity":

> The basic structure of the causal chains of culture consists … [of] an alternation of mental and public episodes. How can such an alternation secure the stability of the contents transmitted? Two main types of processes have been invoked: imitation and communication. Imitation decomposes into a process of imitation of observation and a process of public of re-production of the behavior or of the artifact observed. In

between these two processes, there must be a third, mental one, that converts observation into action. Communication decomposes into a process of public expression of a mental representation and a process of mental interpretation of the public representation. Between these two processes, there must be a third environmental process whereby the action of the communicator impinges on the sensory organs of the interpreter. Ideally, imitation secures the reproduction of public productions (behaviors of artifacts) while communication secures the reproduction of mental representations. Imitation and communication may overlap or interlock when the imitator acquires a mental representation similar to that which guided the behavior imitated, or when the interpreter reproduces the public representation interpreted.[23]

It is important to stress that imitation and communication are *not* simple copying mechanisms in the causal chain of culture. Whatever the brain acquires through a stimulus is remembered, interpreted, adopted, and reproduced to contribute to the formation of a community and culture. For instance, a tale that draws a person's attention and is recorded in his or her brain will not be told again as a communication, whether oral or written, in exactly the same way, but the person will tell it because he or she feels it is relevant in a certain sociocultural context. It will also not become part of a cultural tradition or canon unless it is vital to the survival of a community and the preservation of its values and beliefs. When members of a community "latch on" to a folk tale and conserve it so that it sticks, they do so because it provides relative stability for the community and its culture, and they will continue to retell it and transmit it in a variety of ways. As Sperber and Hirschfeld argue:

> [T]he contents of cultural representations and practices must remain stable enough throughout a community for its members to see themselves as performing the same ritual, sharing the same belief, eating the same dish, and understanding the same proverb in the same way. We are not denying, of course—in fact we are insisting—that culture is in constant flux and that its stability is often exaggerated. Still, without some degree of stability, nothing cultural would be discernible in human thought and behavior. In fact, a wide variety of representations, practices, and artifacts exhibit a sufficient degree of stability at the population scale to be recognizably cultural. ... Anthropologists (and, today, also "memeticists" developing the suggestions of Richard Dawkins) take generally for

granted that human imitation, communication, and memory abilities are sufficiently reliable to secure a faithful enough reproduction of contents through communities and generations. "Faithful enough" does not mean absolutely faithful, of course; it means faithful enough at the micro level to explain the relative stability we observe at the macro level.[24]

Stability is key to understanding why fairy tales stick. But a particular tale such as "Little Red Riding Hood" does not remain fixed in the brain nor will it last forever. Its condition is relative and determined culturally and biologically in a historical evolutionary process that reveals how we value things through mental and public representation. Sperber suggests that we can understand how memes are produced and transmitted if we view the modular organization of the brain as constituted by a variety of domain- or task-specific cognitive mechanisms called modules. There are innate learning modules that are "biological adaptations that perform their functions by drawing on cognitive inputs to generate acquired modules. Acquired modules have an innate basis and have derived biological functions and direct cultural functions. With cognitive adaptations and modules articulated in this manner rather than equated, the massive modularity thesis should become much more plausible and acceptable."[25]

In the case of the oral folk tale, an acquired module, derived from an innate learning module, has developed in the brain that enables us to determine first what kind of artifact the mind is recording and then enables us to begin to distinguish it. The innate learning module helps us classify and comprehend the tale, but if the tale acquires a certain cultural significance through repetition or special attraction, it may generate an acquired module that recognizes certain formal conditions that an input has to meet. For instance, in the case of "Little Red Riding Hood," it may have at one time simply been recognized by the brain as a folk tale with certain distinguishing features such as a wolf that attacks and devours a girl. But as the tale acquired cultural significance and was repeatedly told, printed, and reproduced in other artistic forms, the brain was stimulated through a particular innate module or even through two or three innate modules working together to recognize the memetic quality of the tale through an acquired module. As long as the tale continues to fulfill both cultural and biological conditions for recognition and relevance, it will regularly be transmitted to provide relative stability to a culture.

Oral tales, as I have already stated, are thousands of years old and it is impossible to date and explain how they were generated, but they must have become vital for adapting to the environment and changes in the environment as soon as humans began to communicate through language. Whether there was such a cultural artifact as an oral wonder tale or fairy tale as we know it today in an oral form cannot be determined, although we do know through all kinds of archaeological evidence such as cave paintings, pottery, tombs, parchments, manuscripts, and scrolls that tales with fantastic creatures, magical transformation, and wondrous events were told and disseminated in tribes, groups, communities, and societies. As many of the tales became irrelevant and anachronistic, they were forgotten. But those that continued to have cultural significance were "imitated" and passed on, to be sure, never in the exact way they were first told. Bits and pieces, what we may call motifs, characters, topoi, plots, and images, were carried on and retold during the rise of early European civilization in Latin and vernacular languages and in many cases written down mainly by male scribes, many of them religious. Gradually, as tales were used to serve specific functions in court entertainment, homes, and taverns, on public squares, fields, and work places, and during rituals such as birth, marriage, death, harvest, initiation, and so on, they were distinguished by the minds of the members of a community and given special attention. Engendered as cultural artifacts they formed generic traits that made them appropriate for certain occasions. The cultural requirements were never so strict to prevent the tales from mixing with one another, becoming mixed, or borrowing from one another. There was never a pure oral wonder tale, myth, legend, or fable. But as humans became more discerning and their brains developed the cognitive capacity to recognize, refine, and retain specific narratives that spoke to the conditions in their environment about survival, they began to group, categorize, and shape diverse stories artistically to make better and more efficient use of them. All of this occurred long before print culture came to dominate artistic production in Europe.

Clearly, the generic nature of the literary fairy tale is related to the general evolution of oral folk tale types. Numerous scholars have set their studies of oral and literary tales in a sociohistorical context to arrive at definitions, categories, and types of the fairy tale. The focal points of these studies and their conclusions vary a great deal, and some even contradict one another; yet, they all *historicize* the conception of the fairy tale as a literary genre. Though it is clear that it is virtually impossible to date the "birth" of the literary fairy tale and to ascertain one single oral *Urform* that gave rise to it, we can certainly grasp those crucial social factors that contributed to the rise of the literary fairy tale as genre. This was the primary purpose of my early book *Fairy Tales and the Art of Subversion*, in which I made use of Norbert Elias's ideas in *The Civilizing Process* to demonstrate how the literary fairy tale assumed a socializing function within the development of social codes, norms, and values. And this function can be considered one of its major generic attributes up to the present and may in part account for the fairy tale's widespread dissemination. However, I did not explore how the genre developed as a speech act or how it was stamped by "textual communities" during the Renaissance and baroque period in Italy, which may account for the consolidation of certain fairy tales as memes. I want to here return to the "origins" of the genre and consider its place in the civilizing process via insights provided by Mikhail Bakhtin, Tzvetan Todorov, Brian Stock, Jean-Michel Adam, and Ute Heidmann in an effort to contribute toward a theory of the literary fairy tale as genre that has in part been constituted by memes, depending on the cultural relevance of particular tales. Though it might be more prudent to use the term public representation to talk about the classical fairy tales, I shall continue to use the term meme in the broadest possible sense to denote a particular fairy tale that has been canonized in the Western world and become so memorable that it appears to be transmitted naturally by our minds to communicate information that alerts us to pay attention to a specific given situation on which our lives may depend.

At the heart—or should I say—brain of my theory is the proposition that the literary form of the fairy tale derives from speech acts that became significantly conventionalized and encoded within a community of like speakers who appropriated oral narratives in their own interest to explore and discuss the rational bounds of social constructs of their own making that curb their instincts and to voice their desires and social and political concerns. As we shall see, the symbolic order established by literary fairy tales is not static, but it is certainly marked continually by recognizable recurring motifs, topoi, and conventions and has been framed by male hegemonic concerns. Within the borders of the oral and written frame there is a dialogue concerning gender-oriented rituals, social initiations, or the appropriate manner of behavior in specific situations. A product of civilization, the literary fairy tale, in contrast to the rough and raw folk tale, is very "civil." Paradoxically, the fairy tale creates disorder to create order and, at the same time, to give voice to utopian wishes and to ponder instinctual drives and gender, ethnic, family, and social conflicts. In doing so, it reflects upon and questions social codes to draw a response from readers/listeners. It communicates information. It selects that which has become relevant in a community to inform members of that community what has become crucial for adaptation to the environment in the most effective manner possible that might be entertaining and instructive. The writers/speakers of this genre knowingly play upon a scale of memorable and notable motifs, conventions, and topoi to engage the audience in a dialogue that harks back to a tradition of oral folk tales and literary fairy tales and refers to present and future social conflicts. The fairy tale acts through language to depict all kinds of issues and debates that concern socialization and civilization. Once a fairy tale has gelled or been artistically conceived so that it is ostentative, it seeks to perpetuate itself indiscriminately. Like the selfish gene, a fairy tale as meme is concerned with its own perpetuation and will adapt to changes and conflicts in the environment. Conditioned by fairy tales, we insist that the fairy tale act out these conflicts through conventionalized language and codes that stimulate a play with ideas.

We act as though fairy tales have always been with us. But this is not the case. There was a point in time when literary fairy tales were not expected and used in the manner that we expect and use them. To understand why this is the case means understanding the history of the genre, and it is at this point that I would like to turn to Bakhtin, Todorov, and Stock to clarify my position and to prepare the ground for an examination of "genericity," or "*généricité*,"[26] a term conceived by Jean-Michel Adam and Ute Heidmann, and its possible value in studying classical fairy tales in relation to genetics, memetics, and material culture.

MIKHAIL BAKHTIN

In his essay, "The Problem of Speech Genres," Bakhtin explains that "each utterance is individual, of course, but each sphere in which language is used develops its own *relatively stable types* of these utterances. These we may call *speech genres*."[27] Any speech act or utterance has the potential to develop into a genre depending on the social context and usage. Bakhtin makes a distinction between primary (simple) and secondary speech genres (complex). "Secondary (complex) speech genres—novels, dramas, all kinds of scientific research, major genres of commentary, and so forth—arise in more complex and comparatively highly developed and organized communication (primarily written) that is artistic, scientific, sociopolitical, and so on. During the process of their formation, they absorb and digest various primary (simple) genres that have taken form in unmediated speech communion. These primary genres are altered and assume a special character when they enter into complex ones."[28]

For example, in the case of the literary fairy tale (a secondary speech genre) we can detect how it has absorbed everyday speech in the dialogues, proverbs, and idiomatic expressions that lose their direct relation to reality and contribute to the formation of the literary fairy tale as a socially symbolic act and a literary artistic event.[29] Therefore, it is crucial to study the manner in which the fairy tale has been derived from simple speech genres in concrete historical circumstances if we are to appreciate its aesthetic and ideological relevance in our own time and how it continues to unfold, making use of simple speech utterances and other complex genres.

Bakhtin insists that "the difference between primary and secondary (ideological) genres is very great and fundamental, but this is precisely why the utterance should be revealed and defined through analysis of both types. ... The very interrelations between primary and secondary genres and the process of the historical formation of the latter shed light on the nature of the utterance (and above all on the complex problem of the interrelations among language, ideology, and world view)."[30] Of course, we can never ascertain exactly how and why the primary genre took its form because, in the case of literary history, we can only know the primary speech genre through the secondary. Yet, this is the value of a secondary genre like the literary fairy tale: it preserves elements of the primary speech genre and enters into a dialogue with it as it transforms itself into something new and more complex. The literary fairy tale can only be grasped as a genre with memetic attributes if we analyze the manner in which its speakers/writers appropriated vernacular forms and patterns of speech and entered into a dialogue with what was told, heard, and written in order to address a specific audience. As Bakhtin states:

> [T]his question of the concept of the speech addressee (how the speaker or writer senses and imagines him) is of immense significance in literary history. Each epoch, each literary trend and literary-artistic style, each literary genre within an epoch or trend, is typified by its own special concepts of the addressee of the literary work, a special sense and under-standing of its reader, listener, public, or people. A historical study of changes in these concepts would be an interesting and important task. But in order to develop it productively, the statement of the problem itself would have to be theoretically clear.[31]

In the case of the origination of the literary fairy tale in Italy, we know that its evolution was dependent on the manner in which the writer situated him- or herself within a speech community. From Giovanni Boccaccio's *The Decameron* (1349–50) and Giovanni Sercambi's *Novelle* (1390–1402) in the fourteenth century through Pompeo Sarnelli's *Posili-cheata* (An Outing to Posillipo, 1684) at the end of the seventeenth century, there are clear indications of the relationship of the writer to the community that enable us to propose some theoretical principles. Each of these authors used a frame tale in which storytellers shared their tales with listeners, who were also tellers, and all their tales were intended for a community of readers and tellers. In addressing a particu-lar speech community, writers seek to use, explore, and validate their own speech acts as they assume a conceptual and aesthetic whole. The validation can only occur through the recognition of fictional and real listeners/readers, who are part of a community. To the extent that a given group of readers/listeners/tellers wants to acknowledge and seek to reply to the artwork, they contribute to the formation of a genre. In commenting on *The Thousand and One Nights* and other cycles of framed folk and fairy tales, Stephen Benson astutely remarks, "Every teller is in turn a listener in the *Nights*, as is to be expected from a text that grew out of oral storytelling, and it is in the representation of the commonplace act of narration, including the telling of tales about tales, that this paradigm of the framed story cycle self-consciously manipulates what later came to be proposed as the structural properties of narrative."[32] In the case of the literary fairy tale in Italy, Giovan Franceso Straparola, Giambattista Basile, and Sarnelli, the three major Italian propagators of fairy tales during the Renaissance, framed their works around speech communities with the obvious desire to stimulate some kind of response and initiate further discussion about the ideological, social, and biological issues raised by their tales. Within the frames of their cycles of tales, Straparola's *Le piacevoli notti* (The Pleasant Nights, 1550–53), Basile's *Lo cunto de li cunti* (The Tale of Tales, also known as The Pentamerone, 1634–36), and Sarnelli's *Posilicheata* (1684), they chose a particular primary speech genre, the oral folk tale, in order to expand upon it and have it approved and acknowledged as a socially acceptable vernacular and literary mode of communication. Therefore, we must ask, if we want to understand the beginnings of this literary genre, what constituted the fairy tale as a secondary speech genre? What must our focus be if we are to understand the historical origins and development of the literary fairy tale?

Bakhtin suggests three organic aspects of the utterance that will enable us to understand its wholeness: (1) the semantic exhaustiveness of the theme; (2) the speaker's plan or speech will; (3) the typical compositional and generic forms of finalization.[33] In particular, he emphasizes that the most important factor is constituted by the stable *generic* forms of the utterance:

> [T]he speaker's speech will is manifested primarily in the *choice of a particular speech genre*. This choice is determined by the specific nature of the given sphere of speech communication, semantic (thematic) considerations, the concrete situation of the speech communication, the

personal composition of its participants, and so on. And when the speaker's speech plan with all its individuality and subjectivity is applied and adapted to a chosen genre, it is shaped and developed within a certain generic form. Such genres exist above all in the great and multifarious sphere of everyday oral communication, including the most familiar and most intimate.[34]

With regard to the literary fairy tale, the *choice* to produce written compositions made by various authors at particular points in history is crucial for grasping how the fairy tale took form as a genre. As a primary genre, the oral folk tale circulated hundreds, if not thousands, of years before it came to be *registered* in script and was formed and shaped according to semantic and syntagic rules and audience expectations. When authors began writing the tales, however, the narratives did not become *fully* generic and memetic as a literary genre because a literary genre is also an institution. To be *fully* developed a genre has to be instituted in a society; that is, it must be accepted and used by different groups as a specific mode of entertainment, communication, and socialization. It must also have effective modes of publicity, dissemination, and reception that will enable the genre to take root in society.

TZVETAN TODOROV

Like Bakhtin, Todorov believes that a genre begins as a speech act and undergoes various transformations before becoming institutionalized. He makes this point clearly in his insightful essay, "L'origine des genres."[35] As an institution, however, the genre does not remain static and can only be defined relatively in a sociohistorical context.

> A new genre is always the transformation of one or many older genres: by inversion, by displacement, by combination. A contemporary "text" (this word designates also a genre in one of its senses) owes just as much to 'poésie' as to the "novel" of the nineteenth century just as the "comédie larmoyante" combines traits of comedies and tragedy of the preceding century. There has never been a literature without genres. It is a system in the process of continual transformation, and the question of the origins can never leave historically the terrain of the genres themselves.[36]

The basic question, then, becomes: How do transformations come about? For Todorov, everything is connected to a systematic development of genres, which he defines as "classes of texts" (*classes de textes*). He maintains that a discourse is made up of enunciated sentences or enunciated words, and like Bakhtin, he argues that its meaning depends on the context of enunciation. In other words, a discourse is always by necessity a speech act (*un acte de parole*) constituting a text. If one designates genres as classes of texts, this designation occurs in a meta-discourse about genres in history that has, as its aim, the establishment of properties, traits, and laws of the text. In other words, genres are nothing but the codification of discursive properties. These properties reveal the semantic aspect of the text (meaning), the syntactic aspect of the text (relation of the parts to one another), the pragmatic aspect of the text (the relation among users), and the verbal aspect (all that concerns the materiality of the signs).

According to Todorov, genres exist as institutions that function like the horizons of expectation (*horizons d'attente*) for the readers and models of writing (*modèles d'écriture*) for the authors. It is through their institutionalization that the genres communicate with the society in which they are currently developing. "Each epoch has its own system of genres that is in touch with the dominant ideology. Just like any other institution the genres give testimony about the constitutive traits of the society to which they belong."[37] Todorov explains that there is a reason why not all speech acts become genres, and this is because "a society chooses and codifies the acts which correspond most closely to its ideology. This is why the existence of certain genres in a society, their absence in another, reveals a great deal about this ideology and permits us to establish it with more or less great certainty."[38]

BRIAN STOCK

In its literary form, the fairy tale as genre did not really begin to assume an existence until the fourteenth century in Italy, and even then its existence was precarious because there were very few writers and readers of fairy tales. Certainly, fairy-tale motifs can be found in ancient Indian,

Chinese, and Arabic scripts, the Bible, and Greek and Roman literature, and there are numerous fairy-tale features and themes in medieval
literature, especially in the Latin poems and stories, courtly romances,
lais, legends, fabliaux, primers, and exempla. However, there was no distinct and distinguishable genre in literature called the fairy tale until
the seventeenth century, first in Italy and more importantly in France,
because there was no *textual community* to cultivate and institutionalize
it and because the vernacular languages had not yet fully developed into
literary languages. Without the appropriate conditions of reception and
transmission in large groups of textual or literate communities, the fairy
tale could not have established itself as a genre. Within these communities, the oral performance, recitation, and communication continued to
play a major role.

According to Brian Stock, a textual community is a microsociety organized around the common understanding of a script. As he explains:

> [T]he rise of a more literate society in the eleventh century automati-
> cally increased the number of authors, readers, and copiers of texts
> everywhere in Europe, and, as a consequence, the number of persons
> engaged in the study of texts for the purpose of changing the behav-
> ior of the individual or group. This, *in nuce*, was the rationale behind
> much reformist and some orthodox religious agitation, to say nothing
> of communal associations and guilds. These textual communities were
> not entirely composed of literates. The minimal requirement was just
> one literate, the *interpres*, who understood a set of texts and was able
> to pass his message verbally to others. By a process of absorption and
> reflection the behavioral norms of the group's other members were even-
> tually altered. The manner in which the individuals behaved toward
> each other and the manner in which the group looked upon those it
> considered to be outsiders were derived from the attitudes formed during
> the period of initiation and education. The unlettered and semilettered
> members thereby conceptualized a link between textuality, as the script
> for enactment of behavioral norms, and rationality, as the alleged rea-
> sonableness of those norms.[39]

Although it is clear that there were numerous types of "oral communities," which shared and used many kinds of folk narratives performed
at court and at the hearth and in other distinct places where tales were
exchanged, and that these communities were later to serve as models

or frames for the conception of literary fairy tales, textual communities concerned with fairy tales were not formed until the sixteenth century, and it was really not until the end of the seventeenth century in France that full-fledged textual communities emerged and solidified the institution of the literary fairy tale as genre in Europe. Of course, I am using Stock's helpful notion of "textual community" in a modified form.

It is with the rise of textual communities, court entertainment, schools, reading societies, academies, literary associations and institutions, and salons and the interaction with oral traditions of storytelling that the formation of the fairy tale as genre took place. And this formation made the tale linguistically malleable, accessible, and purposeful as a memetic linguistic formation that carried relevant information about the survival of the species, in particular, the survival of individuals, and representatives of different social classes who are bent on improving their status and condition in society. The form and information constitute its psychological appeal and explain why the brain gradually recognized basic fairy tale types through a cognitive module. As memes (cultural replicators or public representations) particular fairy tales were endowed with and recognized as having great value in communities and societies. Their memetic value resides in their potential to assist human beings to become more alert to particular signs, to improve their situations, and to adapt more successfully in a changing environment. Fairy tales as memetic forms can only be successful if they can copy themselves and are interpreted and revised successfully to address a society's cultural needs and demands. Moreover, they will only be effective if they can mutate and blend in altered and adapted forms that respond to environmental transformations.

Dawkins maintains that "co-adapted meme-complexes evolve in the same kind of way as co-adapted gene-complexes. Selection favours memes that exploit their cultural environment to their own advantage. This cultural environment consists of other memes which are also being selected. The meme pool therefore comes to have attributes of an evolutionarily stable set, which new memes find it hard to invade."[40] Like genes, memes are selfish and seek their own advantage. They will mutate and affect the brain so they can be effectively reproduced to maintain their relevance. This leads to a troubling problem. Again, to quote Dawkins:

> However speculative my development of the theory of memes may be, there is one serious point which I would like to emphasize once again. This is that when we look at the evolution of cultural traits and at their survival value, we must be clear *whose* survival we are talking about. Biologists, as we have seen, are accustomed to looking for advantages at the gene level (or the individual group, or the species level according to taste). What we have not previously considered is that a cultural trait may have evolved in the way that it has, simply because it is *advantageous to itself.*[41]

This last point is important because Dawkins does not believe that we are totally determined by our genes, and that his position in the nurture versus nature debate is a judicious one. If we know that genes and memetic linguistic forms are selfish, and if we recognize what they are and how they influence us, we have the power to select them, "rebel" against them, and change them so that the human species and the environment might be transformed in such a way to make civilization itself more humane. At the very least we can endeavor to "map out" our individual destiny and common destiny and seek alternatives to change ourselves and our environment. Fairy tales provide us with hope that some relevant transformation is possible.

JEAN-MICHEL ADAM AND UTE HEIDMANN

One way we do our choosing, despite the selfishness of genes and memes, is through cooperation. Put another way, even a gene recognizes the importance of cooperation for its own sake. A gene cannot reproduce itself and proliferate without the assistance of other genes. Neither can a meme, and the fairy tale cannot be understood as genre if we do not take into account the manner in which it interacts with and depends on other genres. This is the underlying principle behind Jean-Michel Adam and Ute Heidmann's theory of *généricité* (genericity).[42] They argue:

[T]he concepts of genericity and the *effects of genericity* have as their goal to think simultaneously about the discursive frame and reading/interpretation as complex processes. ... Genericity concerns ... the placement of a text in relation to open generic categories. This relationship is based on the production and/or the recognition of the *effects of genericity*, inseparable from the effect of textuality. As soon as there is a text—that is, the recognition of the fact that a series of enunciations form a complete communication—there is an *effect of genericity*, that is, an inscription of this series of enunciations into a particular practice of discourse. The genericity is a socio-cognitive necessity that relates each text to the inter-discourse of a social formation. A text does not in itself belong to a genre, but it is placed in relation to one or many genres at the point of production as well as at the point of reception-interpretation.[43]

Adam and Heidmann demonstrate that a particular fairy tale as literary text touches on other genres and may have even been constituted in its formation by other genres. It is best defined by its relationship to other genres as it keeps mutating. For instance, tales such as Perrault's "Bluebeard" or "Little Red Riding Hood," which incorporate elements of tragedy, initiation rituals, warning tales, and motifs from other genres such as animal fables and morality plays, form and are informed by a genre called the fairy tale, which is constantly in the process of defining and redefining itself. Using the categories of transtexuality, peritextuality, and intertexuality developed by Gérard Genette in *Palimpsestes*,[44] Adam and Heidmann argue that genres are always in direct relationship with the sociodiscursive formations and the interdiscourse process that they constitute.

Each text develops its own dynamic by activating centrifugal and centripetal forces, a dynamic that is important to analyze in itself before comparing it to another text that has its own dynamic. Through a comparative and textual discourse analysis, we mean the comparison of the respective dynamic of the textual and trans-textual forces of two or more texts. This type of comparison differs from the use of comparison in the studies of folklore and literature in that it does not approach the texts through their static characteristics (the occurrence of motifs, genetic traits, intertextual traces, etc.) but relatively through the dynamic of their textual and transtextual forces.[45]

Adam and Heidmann's notions of genericity are very fruitful for an understanding of how and why canonical fairy tales continue to appeal to us and stick with us, particularly because they emphasize the relative and dynamic nature of the genre of the fairy tale and stress the significance of appropriation and comparison within a historical context. If we draw and build upon their ideas, we can see that to analyze a literary fairy tale and the genre of the fairy tale entails: (1) determining the text and its place in a sociocognitive discursive formation; (2) comparing it with other fairy-tales texts of its period; (3) comparing it with texts of other generic formations; (4) understanding the linguistic elements that constitute its proper forces and constitute its dynamic force within the genre of the fairy tale; (5) analyzing its transformation beyond its original publication, that is, to study its reception in different sociohistorical contexts as well as new texts that are produced and interrogate the original text; (6) recognizing the mediation of oral and literary tales that interact with one another to bring about mutations. In general, the approach of Adam and Heidmann is an explicit critique of how folklorists have tended to approach literature or tales that have become literary:

> According to our discursive concept of text, the meaning of written tales is generated by this complex interaction of textual forces such as thematic-semantic configuration, textual composition and microlinguistic texture, with text-*transcending* forces such as genericity, intertexutality, paratextuality and cotextuality. The literature of written tales informed by folklorists' research on oral tales tends to neglect the textual and transtextual dimensions, precisely what we see as crucial for their meaning and interpretation. Folklore studies put the main focus on the examination of motifs and themes, i.e. on the thematic contents of the tales, but fail to take into account the specific context of their utterance, let alone their textual and transtextual strategies. We argue that the complex meaning of a written tale is produced by the specific linguistic, textual and discursive *articulation* of the chosen motifs and themes, while folklore studies often assume that the meaning of a tale is simply inherent in a universal grammar of motifs and symbols.[46]

If we accept the notion that all genres must be understood as constituting a dynamic process, that is, as part of a genericity, we can learn more about canonical tales as public representations and replicators that become memes connected to the civilizing process and how they settle in our brains and are elaborated by our minds. Certain fairy-tale texts have become formative and definitive, and they insert themselves into our cognitive processes, enabling us to establish and distinguish patterns of behavior and to reflect upon ethics, gender, morality, and power. As the fairy-tale genre formed itself and was formed by myriad tellers and writers, they (and their publishers, listeners, readers) brought their tales in relation to other fairy tales and genres, and they made some of them special, or took a special interest in tales that we have made canonical. They copied them and changed them, and as they took hold of these tales, the tales took hold of them. The tales have evolved in response to changes in the environment, its own linguistic properties and potential, and the particular social institutions of diverse cultural groups throughout the world. To a certain extent, it is impossible nowadays to speak about the fairy tale, especially a canonical tale, narrowly as a printed text, for it has transcended both the oral and literary in iconic formations that depend on the technology of the radio, cinema, advertising, Internet, and so on. Canonical fairy tales are complex memes that are a result of the conflicting forces of cultural production. They are special and relevant because we cultivate them as special and relevant in our speech and in our writings and images.

If we analyze the *généricité* of a particular fairy tale to determine how it has become memetic, we shall see that it often assumes a contradictory role in the transformation of culture and in the behavior of human beings. Before looking at a specific tale, "Little Red Riding Hood," as an example, I want to make some general remarks about the fairy tale and the Darwinian notion of selection and adaptation because I believe that the fairy tale as genre is intricately related to the way we have evolved and developed thought processes and behavioral patterns in response to our changing environment, in particular, to the problems we have caused by trying to dominate nature and at the same time deny our very own nature. Very few folklorists and critics have examined fairy tales from an evolutionary psychological perspective, despite the fact that fairy tales deal opulently with evolution of the human species under particular cultural conditions that often engender crises. For instance, let us consider some of the situations that the heroines and heroes in the fairy tale confront: a mother dies and her daughter is persecuted; a stepmother tries to kill another young girl so that her own daughter will become rich; a young girl is threatened with murder if she does not work hard enough to produce yarn; a young man is left nothing by his father and will starve if he doesn't kill a cat; children are abandoned in a forest where they will probably die; a young woman is compelled to live with a beast or her father will die; a young man leaves home and becomes a thief because there is nothing else for him to do; a poor discharged soldier is given next to nothing by a king and left to his own means to survive; an ugly duckling is almost killed by other animals in a farm-yard; a cat eats a mouse; a tailor must kill a giant or beasts, otherwise he will be killed himself; a daughter must flee the incestuous desires of her father; a woman's children are killed or taken from her because she does not show the proper behavior; a man is transformed into a beast because he is not compliant; a young girl is raped and killed by a wolf. All of these situations incite similar questions: What must an individual do to adapt to a new and unexpected situation? Does a person become heroic through a special kind of adaptation? How will the heroine or hero survive? What does a person have to do to maintain power so that she or he can survive? How must one protect oneself in a dog-eat-dog world? Are there alternative ways of living and reproducing the species that do not involve the transgression of other bodies?

In some respects I believe that we have been attracted to fairy tales because they are survival stories with hope. They alert us to dangerous situations, instruct us, guide us, give us counsel, and reveal what might happen if we take advantage of helpful instruments or agents, or what might happen if we do not. They communicate the need to be oppor-tunistic, to exploit opportunities, to be selfish so we can survive. They have arisen out of a need to adapt to unusual situations, and many of these situations are similar the world over so that many of the same types of tales have arisen and been disseminated and transformed so that new generations will learn to adjust to similar situations in chang-ing environments. All tales want to stay alive in us, and they compete for our attention. However, only certain ones remain with us, catch on, attach themselves to our brains so that we will remember them and propagate them—of course, never in the exact same way that the tale originated, but we are urged to articulate or respond to the tale when the need arises. We choose a particular metaphorical tale to be more precise and effective in what we want to express. Yet, each tale in its mutated form must articulate why it is still necessary and relevant in a changed environment and whether its impact is positive or negative.

The Trials and Tribulations of Little Red Riding Hood Once Again

"Little Red Riding Hood" is a tale about rape and the survival or non-survival of a rape victim. It is a tale about predators and how to deal with them. In my book *The Trials and Tribulations of Little Red Riding Hood*, I demonstrated that the origin of the *literary* fairy tale can be traced to male fantasies about women and sexuality and to conflicting versions with regard to the responsibility for the violation in the tale. In particular, I showed how Charles Perrault and the Grimm Brothers transformed an oral folk tale about the social initiation of a young woman into a narrative about rape in which the heroine is obliged to bear the responsibility for sexual violation. Such a radical literary transformation is highly significant because the male-cultivated literary versions became dominant in both the oral and literary traditions of nations such as Germany, France, Great Britain, and the United States, nations that exercise cultural hegemony in the West. Indeed, the Perrault and Grimm versions became so crucial in the socialization process of these countries that they generated a literary discourse about sexual roles and behavior, a discourse whose fascinating antagonistic perspectives shed light on different phases of social and cultural change. In discussing this development, however, I did not examine how it might be a linguistic and memetic form related to evolutionary theories about instincts, adaptation, and survival. Therefore, I should like once more to summarize my arguments about the sociopsychological implications of the changes made by Perrault and the Grimm Brothers and conclude by considering how the tale has evolved up to the present and why it is still so popular.

Before I focus on the literary texts, however, I want to discuss some oral and literary tales from antiquity and the ancient world that more than likely contributed to the formation of the key motifs of the canonical "Little Red Riding Hood": the girl with a red hood or cap; her encounter with a wolf/werewolf/ogre in the forest; the predatory wolf's deception that leads to the grandmother's murder; the girl's rape or rescue that concludes the story. None of these motifs, it must be borne in mind, are particular to the times of Perrault and the Grimms, or to our very own times of rabid violence and violation. Nor are they the sole "properties" of "Little Red Riding Hood." That is, they can be found in other genres during different time periods in various societies, and these genres may have contributed to and helped form the literary fairy tale. For instance, Graham Anderson, in his significant study, *Fairy Tale in the Ancient World*, demonstrates that there were numerous tales, references, and allusions to these motifs in antiquity:

> It seems clear enough that, despite the absence of a name for the heroine in Pausanias' story of Euthymus and Lykas, we do have one good clear "take" of the traditional Red Riding Hood in antiquity; and a whole dossier of other partly converging hints surrounding a girl with a "flame-red" name and associations; the circumstantial evidence of a "Heracles and Pyrrha" version is likewise strong. The available materials offer us two things: the skeleton of a story in which a child, male or female, is threatened, raped or eaten by a figure with wolf or ogre associations, then disgorged or otherwise reconstituted with or without the substitution of a stone, while the wolf-figure is drowned or killed, and a "flame-girl" (in whatever sense) survives the drowning to see new life brought from stones. The tally of Red Riding Hood tales is quite impressive.[47]

Anderson argues convincingly that, because of prejudices against folk tales and fairy tales in antiquity and prejudices held by contemporary classicists and folklorists, the literature and lore of ancient Greece and Rome have not been sufficiently studied so that we can grasp their "genetic" connection to the fairy tale. Therefore, we have been prevented from gaining a deeper understanding of the fairy tale's evolution. Thanks to his exhaustive study of tales and motifs in the ancient world, however, we now have a much more comprehensive grasp of the memetic and epidemiological formation of canonical fairy tales. In discussing the motif of "a ring swallowed by a fish," Anderson asks the question whether any society can afford to forget such a remarkable and "memorable" story, and he argues that, when a tale becomes so special, a society generally will incorporate it as an oral and literary tale of its culture.

> If we accept the latter premise, then we can accept the hypothesis of widespread diffusion of folktale, with deviant and misrecollected versions by forgetful or inaccurate storytellers easily corrected by those with better memories. What we should guard against is the idea that tales will be reinvented in more or less identical form by different societies as they proceed through progressive stages of civilization, a fantasy of nineteenth-century proto-anthropology, or that because a large number of popular tales use a finite number of motifs, then oral storytellers simply shuffle the motifs around to make new tales. There are indeed instances where two convergent tales can become confused, or where one tale seems to borrow from another, but on the whole[,] hybrids, common as they are, still remain marginal in the process of diffusion of tales. The more examples of any given international tale-type we study, the more clearly we can see the integrity and logic of the tale.[48]

As tales were told and written down, one could argue, particular motifs were retold and rewritten as if they needed to be set in a plot that would enable their survival and enable them to become highly communicative and memorable. They gradually had to be congealed in a stable form to become canonical, so to speak, and though one cannot precisely detect each step in the formation of a classical literary tale, the more information we gather about the spread of the motifs the more light we will shed on why and how a tale becomes memetic. Though it might be misleading to discuss Egbert of Liège's Latin verse tale in "The Richly Laden Ship" (*Fecunda ratis*, 1022–1024) as a direct result of the Greek and Roman tales and motifs connected to them—nor do I want to insist on a direct diachronical development of a particular tale type—the appearance of Egbert's tale, sometimes referred to as "Little Red Cap and the Young Wolves,"[49] is significant because it is another indication that the motifs of the canonical "Little Red Riding Hood" were still mutating and had not yet found a memorable formation. In his superb study of medieval fairy tales, *Fairy Tales from Before Fairy Tales: The Medieval Latin Past of Wonderful Lies*, Jan Ziolkowski writes that, "although Egbert drew extensively upon the Bible and patristic writings [for "The Richly Laden Ship"], he also relied heavily, by his own admission, on the rich oral traditions that circulated in his region, a border zone between Germanic and Romance language and culture groups. In it he incorporated many Latin translations of vernacular proverbs. Because many of the proverbs originated among the uneducated countryfolk, Sigebert of Gembloux (ca. 1030–1112) referred to the poem as a book 'in metrical style about the sayings of peasants.'"[50]

Egbert's tale, "About a Girl Saved from Wolfcubs" ("De puella a luppelis seruata") is short and apparently straightforward:

About a Girl Saved from Wolfcubs

What I have to relate, countryfolk can tell along with
me,
and it is not so much marvelous as it is quite true to
believe.
A certain man took up a girl from the sacred font,
and gave her a tunic woven of red wool;
sacred Pentecost was [the day] of her baptism.
The girl, now five years old, goes out
at sunrise, footloose and heedless of her peril.
A wolf attacked her, went to its woodland lair,
took her as booty to its cubs, and left her to be eaten.
They approached her at once and, since they were
unable to harm her,
began, free from all their ferocity, to caress her head.
"Do not damage this tunic, mice," the lisping little girl
said,
"which my godfather gave me when he took me from
the font!"
God, their creator, soothes untame souls.[51]

Since Egbert wrote this tale for pedagogical and religious purposes, it is not surprising to learn, according to Ziolkowski, that he "Christianized" a popular oral tale to instruct young readers of Latin how to avoid the devil (wolf) through baptism. It is not clear what the oral source of the Latin literary tale was, but it was more than likely *not* filled with references to baptism, Pentecost, and the miraculous powers of the Christian God.

As Ziolkowski notes, "Whether or not the common people of Egbert's day—the peasants—recounted a girl-and-wolf story in which the liturgical color and baptisms of Pentecost figured prominently is beyond our ken." However, "it is imaginable that Egbert, the cleric, Christianized a non-religious story of a little girl in a red garment who was rescued miraculously from being devoured by a wolf: aware that the redness of the garment was too familiar an element in his sources to allow for its omission, he made a virtue of a necessity by coordinating the color with the symbolism of the liturgy. If Egbert imposed Christian features in this fashion, then the redness in the story told by the common people could have had a general apotropaic significance that the Latin poet particularized with a religious dimension when he appropriated it."[52]

We shall never really know all the conditions under which Egbert wrote his verse tale, but what becomes clear from his appropriation of oral materials and from many other instances of appropriation in the early medieval period is that each time an oral tale was written down to be preserved, either as a form of communication, entertainment, or education, it had an ideological dimension that indicated a transformation of the contents and motifs of the story. Among the motifs there is often a special germ to every canonical fairy tale, and in the case of "Little Red Riding Hood," it is rape (violation, the devouring of a little girl or boy) that is at the heart of the discursive formation. When a tale evolves through the discursive appropriation of oral and literary transmission, this germ remains and is at the heart of its memetic appeal. Whenever tellers and writers told or wrote a variant of "Little Red Riding Hood" before it was "stabilized" in Charles Perrault's published text of 1697, they were intent to make it their own story first as a mental representation before they produced their public representation. Their versions of "Little Red Riding Hood," often without a title, were interventions in the evolution of the tale. It is the constant interaction between what Bakhtin called primary and secondary speech genres that constituted the epidemiological dissemination of this canonical fairy tale and all the other canonical narratives. By the time the tale about a girl raped by a wolf reached tellers and writers in the seventeenth century, it had undergone many transformations and had incorporated ancient mythic and religious elements while articulating ideological views about gender and the causes of violation and how to survive it.

Here it is important to refamiliarize ourselves with a rendition of the oral tale as it was probably disseminated in France during the seventeenth and eighteenth centuries before Charles Perrault refined and polished it according to his own taste and the conventions of French high society in King Louis XIV's time.[53]

The Story of Grandmother

There was a woman who had made some bread. She said to her daughter:

"Go carry this hot loaf and bottle of milk to your granny."

So the little girl departed. At the crossway she met *bzou*, the werewolf, who said to her: "Where are you going?"

"I'm taking this hot loaf and a bottle of milk to my granny."

"What path are you taking," said the werewolf, "the path of needles or the path of pins?"

"The path of needles," the little girl said.

"All right, then I'll take the path of pins."

The little girl entertained herself by gathering needles. Meanwhile the werewolf arrived at the grandmother's house, killed her, put some of her meat in the cupboard and a bottle of her blood on the shelf. The little girl arrived and knocked at the door.

"Push the door," said the werewolf, "It's barred by a piece of wet straw."

"Good day, Granny. I've brought you a hot loaf of bread and a bottle of milk."

"Put it in the cupboard, my child. Take some of the meat which is inside and the bottle of wine on the shelf."

After she had eaten, there was a little cat which said: "Phooey! ... A slut is she who eats the flesh and drinks the blood of her granny."

"Undress yourself, my child," the werewolf said, "and come lie down beside me."

"Where should I put my apron?"

"Throw it into the fire, my child, you won't be needing it anymore."

And each time she asked where she should put all her other clothes, the bodice, the dress, the petticoat, and the long stockings, the wolf responded:

"Throw them into the fire, my child, you won't be needing them anymore."

When she laid herself down in the bed, the little girl said:

"Oh, Granny, how hairy you are!"

"The better to keep myself warm, my child!"

"Oh, Granny, what big nails you have!"

"The better to scratch me with, my child!"

"Oh, Granny, what big shoulders you have!"

"The better to carry the firewood, my child!"

"Oh, Granny, what big ears you have!"

"The better to hear you with, my child!"

"Oh, Granny, what big nostrils you have!"

"The better to snuff my tobacco with, my child!"

"Oh, Granny, what a big mouth you have!"

"The better to eat you with, my child!"

"Oh, Granny, I've got to go badly. Let me go outside."

"Do it in bed, my child!"

"Oh, no, Granny, I want to go outside."

"All right, but make it quick."

The werewolf attached a woolen rope to her foot and let her go outside.

When the little girl was outside, she tied the end of the rope to a plum tree in the courtyard. The werewolf became impatient and said: "Are you making a load out there? Are you making a load?"

When he realized that nobody was answering him, he jumped out of bed and saw that the little girl had escaped. He followed her but arrived at her house just at the moment she entered.[54]

It is obvious from this oral tale that the narrative perspective is sympathetic to a young peasant girl (age uncertain) who learns to cope with the world around her. She is shrewd, brave, tough, and independent. Evidence indicates she was probably undergoing a social ritual connected to sewing communities:[55] the maturing young woman proves she can handle needles, replace an older woman, and contend with the opposite sex. In some of the tales, however, she loses the contest with the male predator and is devoured by him. There is no absolute proof that the above synthetic tale pieced together by the astute French folklorist Paul Delarue was told in the exact same form in which he published it. However, most scholars, anthropologists, and critics who have studied nineteenth-century French variants of "Little Red Riding Hood" agree that some form of "The Story of Grandmother" existed before Perrault made the tale memetically unforgettable, or that the tale made itself memetically memorable through him.

Perrault revised some kind of oral tale that featured a young girl endangered by a predatory wolf to make it the literary standard-bearer for good Christian upbringing in a much more sophisticated manner than Egbert or oral storytellers. Moreover, his fear of women and his own sexual drives are incorporated in his *new* literary version, which also reflects general male attitudes about women portrayed as eager to be seduced or raped. In this regard, Perrault began a series of literary transformations that have caused nothing but trouble for the female object of male desire and have also reflected the crippling aspect of male desire itself.

What are the significant changes he made? First, she is donned with a *red* hat, a *chaperon*,[56] making her into a type of bourgeois girl tainted with sin since red, like the scarlet letter A, recalls the devil and heresy. Second, she is spoiled, negligent, and naive. Third, she speaks to a wolf in the woods—rather dumb on her part—and makes a type of contract with him: she accepts a wager, which, it is implied, she wants to lose. Fourth, she plays right into the wolf's hands and is too stupid to trick him. Fifth, she is swallowed or raped like her grandmother. Sixth, there is no salvation, simply an ironic moral in verse that warns little girls to beware of strangers, otherwise they will deservedly suffer the consequences. Sex is obviously sinful. Playful intercourse outside of marriage is likened to rape, which is primarily the result of the little girl's irresponsible acts.

We need not know the exact oral tale on which Perrault based his version of "Little Red Riding Hood" to understand that he had gathered together motifs from tales he heard or read to conceive his compact, startling tale about a girl who should have known better than to talk to a wolf in the forest. What is important to know is: (1) there were similar oral tales circulating during Perrault's time; (2) there had been similar literary tales about persecuted heroines in Latin and vernacular European languages; (3) the production of this tale has to be understood within context of the debates about the social place of women and the "quarrels" about ancient and modern literature in which Perrault was engaged with Nicolas Boileau; (4) there was a virtual wave or vogue of fairy-tale writing during the 1690s in France and that Perrault, influenced by Cartesian thought, took issue with other writers about the logic of fairy-tale writing; (5) this tale and others he wrote were probably read out loud in social settings.

During the eighteenth century Perrault's text circulated on the continent in different forms. His book *Histoires ou contes du temps passé* was reprinted in French many times and also in adulterated chapbook versions with woodcuts. It was translated into English by Robert Samber in 1729 and into other European languages. It was sometimes printed by itself and sometimes in books with titles such as "Mother Goose Tales." Since most educated people in Europe knew French, Perrault's "Little Red Riding Hood" was easily accessible to them. By the end of the eighteenth century the tale was so well known that Ludwig Tieck, one of the great German romantic writers of fairy tales, wrote a play titled *The Life and Death of Little Red Riding Hood* (*Leben und Tod des kleinen Rotkäppchens*, 1800).

In 1812, the Brothers Grimm delivered the second classic version of "Little Red Riding Hood," based on an oral German version they had heard from a middle-class young woman of Huguenot descent. The Grimms made further alterations worth noting. Here the mother plays a more significant role by warning Little Red Riding Hood not to stray from the path through the woods. Little Red Riding Hood is more or less incited by the wolf to enjoy nature and to pick flowers. Her choice symbolizes her agreement with a devilish creature whom she has already directed to her grandmother. Instead of being raped to death, both grandma and granddaughter are saved by a male hunter or gamekeeper who polices the woods. Only a strong male figure can rescue a girl from herself and her lustful desires.

The Perrault and the Grimm versions became *the* classical stories of Little Red Riding Hood and have served as the models for numerous writers of both sexes throughout the world who have amplified, distorted, or disputed the facts about the little girl's rape. Why, we must ask, did the Perrault and Grimm versions become the classic ones and not the "The Story of Grandmother," the oral tale, which is more "feminist," so to speak? What is it that made the oral tale so catchy that it was picked up by Perrault and made even "catchier" in his version so that it replicated itself and was reproduced by thousands or hundreds of thousands of authors, storytellers, dramatists, educators, publishers, illustrators, filmmakers, and many other kinds of tellers of the tale? What constituted its memetic quality? Once more, I want to suggest that the key idea of "Little Red Riding Hood" is that women are responsible for their own rape, an idea not central to the oral tale. I also want to suggest that, while the oral tale caught on, it, too, was changed by the Perrault version, which was modified by the Grimms' tale as memes tend to be, and today the dominant classical version is an amalgamation of Perrault's and Grimms' tales.

If memes are selfish, as Dawkins has declared, the persistence of a story that presents rape relevantly in a discursive form to indicate the girl asked to be raped, or contributed to her own rape, can be attributed to the struggle among competing memes within patriarchal societies that tend to view rape from a male viewpoint that rationalizes the aggressive male sexual behavior. Given the control that males have exercised in society at large and in the cultural domain, it is not by chance that the meme of "Little Red Riding Hood" has taken hold and spread. Yet, it is not entirely negative as a meme, and it is a meme that has mutated, especially in the past thirty-five years, under strong ideological influences of the feminist movement.

Originally, as I suspect, the tale in the oral tradition, told from the perspective of women, opened up questions about the predatory nature of men and how to avoid rape or violation to survive. Perrault did not dispute the fact that men tend to be predatory, but he shifted the responsibility of physical violence and the violation of the body to the female, and since his communication fit the dominant ideology of his times shared by many women (and perhaps ours), his story competed with all others and became the dominant meme and remains so to this day. As dominant meme, it does not simply convey the notion that women are responsible for their own rape, but it also conveys a warning about strangers in the woods, the danger of violation, and an extreme moral lesson: kill the rapist or be killed. Used or transformed as a warning tale, it reveals that the tale is open to multiple interpretations and also has a positive cultural function. However, it is a contested meme and contested in such a manner by numerous feminist artists and writers who view "Little Red Riding Hood" in a negative light about a woman's responsibility for her own rape that I am more prone to think the meme's selfish qualities have more to do with a gendered discourse within the civilizing process that tends to skew discourses to rationalize uncontrollable and irresponsible male behavior that can be changed, just as the meme itself can mutate. Certainly, it is very difficult to change sexual behavior. In a very long and provocative chapter on gender and rape in his book *The Blank Slate*, Steven Pinker discusses Randy Thornhill and Craig T. Palmer's *A Natural History of Rape* and claims that feminists have focused on the wrong issue of power to explain the causes of rape. Pinker believes, along with Thornhill and Palmer, that rape concerns the male's desire to propagate his genes, a desire for sex, and a capacity to engage in pursuit of violence.[57] These instinctual drives are so powerful that they may take hundreds of years and complex genetic and social changes if rape is to be diminished throughout the world. At times, Pinker minimizes the connection between sexual drives, social reinforcements, and social power that still enable males to exercise their domination in various ways, but he also fortunately recognizes the significance of the feminist challenge to the way rape is displayed, transmitted, and narrated in Western society.

> If we have to acknowledge that sexuality can be a source of conflict and not just wholesome mutual pleasure, we will have rediscovered a truth that observers of the human condition have noted throughout history.

And if a man rapes for sex, that does not mean that he "just can't help it" or that we have to excuse him, any more than we have to excuse the man who shoots the owner of a liquor store to raid the cash register or who bashes a driver over the head to steal his BMW. The great contribution of feminism to the morality of rape is to put issues of *consent* and *coercion* at center stage. The ultimate motives of the rapist are irrelevant.[58]

And they are just as irrelevant in the fairy tale of "Little Red Riding Hood," which has, however, remained relevant because it continues to raise moral and ethical questions about sex and power.

I want to close with some brief remarks about a remarkable film that reflects upon the possibility for cultural transformation or change. I am referring to Matthew Bright's brilliant film *Freeway* (1996), which depicts the trials and tribulations of a semiliterate teenage girl named Vanessa, whose mother is a prostitute and whose father abandoned her. She is picked up on a highway by a serial rapist and killer, and because she is so street smart, she manages to turn the tables on him, grab his gun, and shoot him. She then takes his car but is arrested because the rapist miraculously survives. Two detectives interrogate her, but largely due to their male prejudices, they do not believe her story about attempted rape. In prison Vanessa succeeds in escaping while the two detectives follow leads from people they interview that convince them that the rapist was really lying. The rapist flees to Vanessa's grandmother's house, kills her, and awaits Vanessa. When she arrives, she bravely beats him to a pulp, and the astonished detectives, who had wanted to help her, show up only to witness how Vanessa can easily take care of herself.

I mention this film because the mass media's dissemination of images through commercials, films, video, and news stories tends to follow Perrault and continues to suggest that women lure and seduce men and ultimately are responsible if anything happens to them. The contested representations suggest that there is another way of viewing desire, seduction, and violation. If there are really such things as memes— and I am convinced there are—and if memes can influence us and be changed as our behavior is transformed, it is important that we take the theory of memes and fairy tales themselves more seriously. As we know, tales do not only speak to us, they inhabit us and become relevant in our struggles to resolve conflicts that endanger our happiness.

"The Foolish Wishes"
Illustrator: Maurice Leroy

Chapter 2

The Evolution and Dissemination of the Classical Fairy Tale

For a long time it has commonly been assumed that our classical fairy tales were representative of particular cultures. Charles Perrault's tales are considered very French, the Grimms' collection is regarded as genuinely German, and Hans Christian Andersen's stories are certainly Danish. Although there is some truth to these assumptions, they conceal the deep cross-cultural and multilayered origins and meanings of these pan-European tales that also have fascinating connections to northern Africa and the Orient, including the Middle and Far East. Of course there can be no denying that the tales are culturally marked: they are informed by the languages that the writers employed, their respective cultures, and the sociohistorical context in which the narratives were created. In this regard one can discuss the particular Italian, French, German, or English affiliation of a tale and also make regional distinctions within a particular principality or nation-state. Nevertheless, the tales have a great cross-cultural appeal that transcends their particularity: they contain "universal" motifs and experiences that writers borrow consciously and unconsciously from other cultures in an endeavor to imbue their symbolical stories with very specific commentaries on the mores and manners of their times. They also address common instinctual drives and social problems that arise from the human attempts to "civilize" these drives.

Fairy tales have always been "truthful" metaphorical communications and reflections of personal and public experiences, the customs of their times, and the civilizing process; that is, they regard the private and public interrelations of people from different social classes seeking power to determine their lives. The truth value of a fairy tale is dependent on the degree to which a writer is capable of using a symbolical linguistic code, narrative strategy, and stereotypical characterization to depict, expose, or celebrate the modes of behavior that were used and justified to attain power in the civilizing process of a given society. Whether oral or literary, the tales have sought to uncover truths about the pleasures and pains of existence, to propose possibilities for adaptation and survival, and to reveal the intricacies of our civilizing processes.

HISTORICAL BACKGROUND

For the past three hundred years or more scholars and critics have sought to define and classify the oral folk tale and the literary fairy tale, as though they could be clearly distinguished from each other, and as though we could trace their origins to some primeval source. As I have stated in the previous chapter, this is an impossible task because there are very few if any records with the exception of paintings, drawings, etchings, inscriptions, parchments, and other cultural artifacts that reveal how tales were told and received thousands of years ago. In fact, even when written records came into existence, they provided very little information about storytelling among the majority of people, except for random information that educated writers gathered and presented in their works. It is really not until the late eighteenth and early nineteenth centuries that scholars began studying and paying close attention to folk tales and fairy tales, and it was also at this time that the Brothers Grimm, and many others to follow, sought to establish national cultural identities by uncovering the putative "pure" and natural tales of their so-called people, the folk, and their imagined nations.

From a contemporary perspective, the efforts of the Brothers Grimm— and the numerous projects that they helped to inspire developed by Peter Christen Asbjørnsen and Jørgen Moe, *Norwegian Folktales* (1841), Johann Wilhelm Wolf, *German Fairy Tales and Legends* (1845), George Stephens and H. Cavallius, *Old Norse Fairy Tale: Gathered from the Swedish Folk* (1850–99), Ludwig Bechstein, *German Fairy Tale Book* (1845), Friedrich Wolf, *German Popular Tales and Legends* (1845), Ignaz Vinzenz and Joseph Zingerle, *Children and Household Tales from Tyrol* (1852), Aleksandr Afanas'ev, *Russian Fairy Tales* (1855–63), Georg Widter and Adam Wolf, *Folk Tales from Veneto* (1866); Otto Sutermeister, *Children and Household Tales from Switzerland* (1873), Vittorio Imbriani, *Florentine Tales* (1871), Giuseppe Pitré, *Popular Sicilian Tales, Novellas, and Stories* (1875), Jeremiah Curtin, *Myths and Folk-lore of Ireland* (1890), and Joseph Jacobs, *English Fairy Tales* (1890), to name but a few[1]—have led to a misconception about the nature of folk tales and fairy tales: there is no such thing as a "pure" national folk tale or literary fairy tale, and neither genre, the oral folk tale or the literary fairy tale—if one can call them separate genres—is a "pure breed"; in fact, they are both very much mixed breeds, and it is in the very way that they "contaminated" each other historically through cross-cultural and intercultural exchange that has produced fruitful and multiple variants of similar social and personal experiences.

Naturally, the oral folk tales that were told in many different ways thousands of years ago preceded the literary narratives, but we are not certain who told the tales, why, and how. We do know, however, that scribes began writing different kinds of tales that reflected an occupation with rituals, historical anecdotes, customs, startling events, miraculous transformations, and religious beliefs. The recording of these various tales was extremely important because the writers preserved an oral tradition for future generations, and in the act of recording, they changed the tales to a greater or lesser degree, depending on what their purpose was in recording them. As I have already shown in the previous chapter, the literary fairy tale, which is a genre that only became popular after the advent of the printing press in the fifteenth century, has deep roots in the oral tradition; motifs and elements that became part of the literary fairy-tale tradition were disseminated thousands of years ago and were gradually shaped in the early medieval period through the repeated transmission of tales that were written and retold and that mutually influenced one another. There is no evidence that a separate oral wonder-tale tradition or literary fairy-tale tradition existed in Europe before the medieval period. But we do have evidence that people told all kinds of "fantastic" tales about gods, animals, catastrophes, wars, heroic deeds, rituals, customs, and simple daily incidents in antiquity and in non-European cultures. Graham Anderson has performed a great service for folklorists and serious scholars of the fairy tale by demonstrating how Greek and Roman myths contributed to the generic development of the literary fairy tale by studying oral and literary sources in the pre-Christian ancient world.[2] What we call folk-tale or fairy-tale motifs are indeed ancient and appear in many pre-Christian epics, poems, myths, fables, histories, and religious narratives.[3] As Derek Brewer remarks:

> [T]he survival of a story orally delivered depends on the memory of the audience. It does not seem that folktales, including fairy tales, are memorized in verbal detail but according as they deal with matters of concern to the community, and in terms of stereotyped characters and narrative patterns. The pattern has its own internal logic which does not necessarily depend on material probability or a plot with strict cause and effect, as does the novel, at least in theory. The general pattern must satisfy the common desire for a marvel and a satisfactory outcome.[4]

However, the formation of the narrative structure common to the oral wonder tale and the literary fairy tale only began to take clear recognizable shape in Europe sometime first during the early medieval period because it was at this time that writers were prompted to recognize it as memorable and wrote it down. How this occurred, where it occurred, and exactly when it occurred are difficult questions to answer with precision because the tales developed as a process largely through talk, conversations, and performances that caught the imagination of people from different social milieu and were gradually written down first in Latin and then eventually in different vernacular languages, when they became more acceptable in the late Middle Ages.[5] Clearly, the literary fairy tale developed as an appropriation of a particular oral storytelling tradition that gave birth to the wonder tale, often called the *Zaubermärchen* (magic tale) or the *conte merveilleux* (marvelous tale). As more and more wonder tales were written down in Latin and vernacular languages from the twelfth to the fifteenth centuries, they constituted the genre of the literary fairy tale, and writers began establishing its particular conventions, motifs, topoi, characters, and plots, based to a large extent on those developed in the oral tradition but altered to address a reading public formed largely by the clergy, aristocracy, and the middle classes.[6]

Though the peasants were excluded in the formation of this literary tradition, their material, tone, style, and beliefs were also incorporated into the new genre, and their experiences were recorded, albeit from the perspective of the literate scribe, writer, monk, or priest. The tales that were told cut across different classes and segments of a particular society—rural, urban, and court. The wonder tales, which often carried implicit notions of "might makes right" and transformation, were always considered somewhat suspect by the ruling clerical and educated classes. The threatening aspect of wondrous change, turning the world upside down, was something that these classes always tried to channel through codified celebrations like Carnival and religious holidays.[7] In discussing how the wonder tale about Cockaigne (the world turned upside down, or Cuckoo Land) developed, Herman Pleij remarks:

> In any case, toying with the idea of an obviously nonexistent dreamland is as old as literature itself. This must mean that the Cocaigne material belongs to the oldest of oral traditions, otherwise it would not have been written down as soon as man started wielding the pen. ... This early evidence in writing of an already abundantly present Luilekkerland [Cocaigne] is an important indication that such dreams of plenty inevitably belong to the fantasies of humankind in its early condition. Their ingredients—consisting of formulaic elements, individual motifs, and stock themes—are part of a widespread oral culture that has continued to the present day. In addition, details of this oral tradition continue to crop up in written literature, which then forms its own traditions, sometimes—but not necessarily—interacting with the oral transmission of these same stories.[8]

Indeed, writers staked out political and property claims to wonder tales as they recorded and created them, and official cultural authorities sought to judge and control the new genre as it sought to legitimate itself. The establishment of literacy was, among other things, a way to police the use of language through schooling, religion, and legislation of laws.

It is extremely difficult to describe what the oral wonder tale was because our evidence is based on written documents, and there are many types of wonder tales with diverse plots and characters, bound intricately with customs and rituals, that are often inexplicable. General theories about the origin and spread of the folk tales leading to the formation of the literary fairy tale were first conceived at the beginning of the nineteenth century and have been elaborated and contested up through the twenty-first century. The Brothers Grimm believed that fairy tales were derived from myths that had been religious at one time, but storytellers had gradually discarded their religious connotations, and the tales became secular wonder tales. Their views were expanded by Theodor Benfey (1809–81), a scholar of Sanskrit, who argued in his introduction to the Indic *Pantscha Tantra* (1859) that the genre of the fairy tale originated in ancient India as an oral wonder tale and spread first to Persia and then to the entire Arabic-speaking world.

Eventually, the oral wonder tales were transmitted to Europe via Spain, Greece, and Sicily through trade, migration, and the Crusades. The Grimms and Benfrey believed that there was one point of origin or one place of birth (monogenesis) that led to the formation of the folk tales. In contrast, Joseph Bédier (1864–1938), a French folklorist, opposed their views and developed his notion of polygenesis in *Les Fabliaux* (1893); he maintained that the tales originated in different places and were cultivated by gifted storytellers. The notion of polygenesis was also at the basis of the British anthropological scholars Edward Burnett Tylor (1832–1917), Andrew Lang (1844–1912), and James George Frazer (1854–1941),[9] who maintained that, since the human species was similar throughout the world, humans responded to their environment in similar ways, giving rise to identical tales that varied only according to the customs they developed. They differed from Bédier in that they believed that the common people as well as gifted storytellers cultivated the tales in their rituals and customs. The oral wonder tale was one among different types of tales that were cultivated throughout the world, often with similar plots and themes. Many other folklorists such as Giuseppe Pitrè in Sicily and Frederick Thomas Crane in America supported these views. The anthropological approach stimulated the research of Aarne Antti in *The Types of the Folktale* (1913), which fostered the historic-geographical method of tracing the origins of a tale type, and of Johannes Bolte and Georg Polívka in *Anmerkungen zu den Kinder- und Hausmärchen der Brüder Grimm* (Annotations to the *Children's and Household Tales* of the Brothers Grimm, 1913–32), a work that contained variants and more information about the texts collected by the Grimms.

A common assumption made by almost all folklorists and anthropologists in the nineteenth and early twentieth centuries was that the fairy tale was part of an oral tradition thousands of years old. However, in *Versuch einer Theorie des Märchens* (Attempt at a Theory of the Fairy Tale, 1931), Albert Wesselski (1871–39) dismissed the notion altogether that the literary fairy tale emanated from an oral tradition. Instead, he argued that, despite the existence of oral folk tales in antiquity, there was no such thing as a fairy tale, and the fairy tale as a genre was really the creation of individual writers, who forged the genre in the fifteenth and sixteenth centuries and its basis is literary. His ideas were soundly rejected and answered by, among others, the Danish folklorist Bengt Holbek, whose thorough and thoughtful work *Interpretation of Fairy Tales* (1987) demonstrates clearly that some forms of the fairy tale have existed in the oral tradition for millennia. His ideas have been explored and supported by numerous folklorists and literary historians, while a small group, largely made up of German academicians, has lamely tried to support Wesselski's views.[10]

In the United States, Ruth Bottigheimer has endeavored to reignite the debate by arguing that folk and fairy tales were mainly spread by books.[11] However, she ignores the fact that most people in the medieval and Renaissance periods could not read, that Latin was the dominant script and print language,[12] that the early collections of tales include storytellers from different classes within the frames, and that there is a great deal of evidence in pre-Christian societies that all kinds of tales, including wonder tales, circulated by word of mouth. She even maintains that people did not have the capacity to remember tales accurately, despite the fact that many cultural groups such as the Somalians cultivated their tales only through oral transmission up through the late twentieth century. Moreover, she tries to set up a false debate between so-called oralists and herself as though there were a clear divide, and argues that only published books provide accurate evidence for the origins, existence, and spread of fairy tales. Her positivist approach to oral history recalls the elitist manner in which the upper classes treated popular culture and negated their customs and forms of entertainment. Scholars who have used a more inclusive and expansive approach that focuses on the interaction between elite and popular cultures and the interplay between orality and literacy reveal the narrow confines of her argument.

Forms and Contents of the Oral Wonder Tale and the Literary Fairy Tale

The debate about the origin and transmission of the fairy tale as oral wonder tale, while significant and productive, can be misleading and distracting when we consider that the spoken language existed long before writing systems were developed, and when we take into account that it is impossible to determine when and how certain types of tales evolved. What we do know, as Jan Ziolkowski has pointed out, is that:

> Europe has had writing systems for thousands of years. Clay, stone, metal, bark, papyrus, wax, parchment, and paper are only a selection of the materials that have been used for this purpose. Tales have been told during those millennia, but most tellings have not been set down in writing or otherwise recorded. Part of the reason is the sheer practical one that it has been happily impossible to capture in writing all the words people have spoken. ... Of course, the dearth of premodern folktales results not only from a lack of means for writing but even more from a decision not to record them on the part of the men who controlled those channels. Some types of literature were written down again and again, while others failed to receive official approval, either explicit or tacit, which was an indispensable prerequisite for being memorialized in literature.[13]

If we accept the premise that most "simple forms"[14] of narrative such as the fable, myth, anecdote, proverb, animal tale, exemplum, fabliau, and fairy tale owe their origins to oral transmission that cannot be dated, and if we also accept the premise that the interaction of oral modes of telling with writing systems brought about the development of literary genres, we can achieve a greater understanding of how and why the literary fairy tale took root as literacy developed and how certain tales become memetic. In Vladimir Propp's now famous study, *The Morphology of the Folk Tale* (1928), he outlined thirty-one basic functions that constitute the formation of a paradigm, which was and still is common in Europe and North America. Though I have some reservations about Propp's categories because they are based on an exclusive analysis of the Russian wonder tale, and because he does not discuss the social function of the wonder tale or its diverse aspects, his structuralist approach can be helpful in understanding plot formation and the reasons why certain tales have become so memorable.[15] By functions, Propp meant the fundamental and constant components of a tale that are the acts of a character and necessary for driving the action forward. The plot generally involves a protagonist who is confronted with an interdiction or prohibition that he or she violates in some way. Therefore, there is generally a departure or banishment and the protagonist is either given a task or assumes a task related to the interdiction or prohibition. The protagonist is *as-signed* a task, and the task is a *sign*. That is, his or her character will be stereotyped and marked by the task that is his or her sign.

In sociological terms, each character is to act out what Pierre Bourdieu calls a *habitus*,[16] that is, the characters occupy the whole complex of thinking, acting, and performing of a position within the family and society: names are rarely used in a folk tale; characters function according to their status within a family, social class, or profession; and they often cross boundaries or transform themselves. It is the transgression that makes the tale exciting; it is the possibility of transformation that gives hope to the teller and listener of a tale. Inevitably in the course of action there will be a significant or signifying encounter. Depending on the situation, the protagonist will meet either enemies or friends. The antagonist often takes the form of a witch, monster, ogre, or evil fairy, while the friend is a mysterious and supernatural individual or creature, who has unique powers and gives the protagonist gifts. Sometimes there are at first three different animals or creatures that test the protagonist to see whether he is worthy of their help. Whatever the occasion, the protagonist must prove him- or herself and acquire gifts that are often magical agents, which bring about a miraculous or marvelous change or transformation. Soon after, the protagonist, endowed with gifts, is tested once more and overcomes inimical forces. However, this is not the end because there is generally a peripety or sudden fall in the protagonist's fortunes, which is only a temporary setback. A miracle or marvelous intervention is needed to reverse the wheel of fortune. Frequently, the protagonist makes use of endowed gifts (and this includes magical agents and cunning) to achieve his or her goal. The success of the protagonist usually leads to marriage; the acquisition of money; survival and wisdom; or any combination of these three. Whatever the case may be, the protagonist is transformed in the end. The functions, which move the action and constitute the plot, provide the conditions for a "marvelous" transformation.

Propp's analysis works well for a particular type of oral wonder tale, but it is not applicable for many other types of the wonder tale. Nevertheless, his theory helps us understand that the structure of oral tales depends heavily on memory, repetition, and resolution. The significance of the paradigmatic functions of wonder tales and their distinct characters, identified through their social class and habitus, is that they facilitate recall for teller and listeners. Over hundreds of years they have enabled people to store, remember, and reproduce the plot of a given tale and to change it to fit their experiences and desires because of the easily identifiable characters associated with particular social classes, professions, and assignments. The characters, settings, and motifs are combined and varied according to specific functions to induce *wonder* and *hope* for change in the audience of listeners/readers, who are likely to marvel or admire the magical changes that occur in the course of events. At the center of attraction is the survival of the protagonist under difficult conditions, and the tales evoke wonder and admiration for oppressed characters, no matter who they may be. It is this earthy, sensual, and secular sense of wonder and hope that distinguished the wonder tales from other oral tales such as the legend, the fable, the anecdote, and the myth; it is clearly the sense of wonder that distinguishes the *literary* fairy tale from the moral story, novella, sentimental tale, and other modern short literary genres. Wonder causes astonishment, and as marvelous object or phenomenon, it is often regarded as a supernatural occurrence and can be an omen or portent. It gives rise to admiration, fear, awe, and reverence. In the oral wonder tale, we are to marvel about the workings of the universe where anything can happen at any time, and these *fortunate* and *unfortunate* events are never really explained. Nor do the characters demand an explanation—they are instinctively opportunistic and hopeful. They are encouraged to be so, and if they do not take advantage of the opportunity that will benefit them in their relations with others, they are considered either dumb or mean-spirited.

The tales seek to awaken our regard for the miraculous condition of life and to evoke profound feelings of awe and respect for life as a miraculous process, which can be altered and changed to compensate for the lack of power, wealth, and pleasure that most people experience. Lack, deprivation, prohibition, and interdiction motivate people to look for signs of fulfillment and emancipation. In the wonder tales, those who are naive and simple are able to succeed because they are untainted, naturally good, and can recognize the wondrous signs. They have retained their belief in the miraculous condition of nature, revere nature in all its aspects, and accept their own natural inclinations. They have not been spoiled by conventionalism, power, or rationalism. In contrast to the humble characters, the villains are those who use words and power intentionally to exploit, control, transfix, incarcerate, and destroy for their own benefit. They have no respect or consideration for nature and other human beings, and they actually seek to abuse magic by preventing change and causing everything to be transfixed according to their interests. The marvelous protagonist wants to keep the process of natural change flowing and indicates possibilities for overcoming the obstacles that prevent other characters or creatures from living in a peaceful and pleasurable way.

The focus on the marvelous and hope for change in the oral wonder tale does not mean that all wonder tales, and later the literary fairy tales, served and serve a radical transforming purpose. The nature and meaning of folk tales have depended on the stage of development of a tribe, community, or society and the evolution of the human species. Oral tales have served to stabilize, conserve, or challenge the common beliefs, laws, values, and norms of a group. The ideology expressed in wonder tales always stemmed from the position that the narrator assumed with regard to the relations and developments in his or her community; and the narrative plot and changes made in it depended on the sense of wonder, marvel, admiration, or awe that the narrator wanted to evoke. In other words, the sense of the miraculous in the tale and the intended emotion sought by the narrator are ideological. Narrators sought to use language and the art of communication to make their utterances special and relevant so they would catch on and stick in the ears and brains of their listeners.

Since these wonder tales have been with us for thousands of years and have undergone so many changes in the oral tradition, it is difficult to determine the ideological intention of the narrator; and when we disregard the narrator's intention, it is often difficult to reconstruct (or deconstruct) the ideological or historical meaning of a tale and its reception. In the last analysis, however, even if we cannot establish whether a wonder tale is ideologically conservative, radical, sexist, progressive, and so on, it is the celebration of miraculous or fabulous transformations in the name of hope that accounts for its major appeal. People have always wanted to improve or change their personal status or have sought magical intervention on their own behalf. The emergence of the literary fairy tale during the latter part of the medieval period bears witness to the persistent human quest for an existence without oppression and constraints. It is a utopian quest that we continue to record through the metaphors of the fairy tale, even today.

Two more important points should be made about the oral tradition of transmission that concern the magical contents of the tales and the mode in which they were disseminated. It has often been assumed that the magical properties and gifts in the tales along with the supernatural and incredible events could only have been believed by the gullible and superstitious "folk" (i.e., the peasantry and children). Over the years the wonder tales and the fairy tales were gradually associated with untruths or silly women's tales. Allegedly, only an old goose or gossips would tell them.[17] But this notion of what constituted the meaning of a wonder tale or fairy tale for people of the past is misleading, if not fallacious, and that is perhaps the case today as well. During the Middle Ages, most people in *all* social classes believed in magic, the supernatural, and the miraculous, and they were also smart enough to distinguish between probable and improbable events.[18] The marvelous and the magical in all their forms were not considered abnormal, and thus all genres of literature that recorded marvelous and supernatural incidents were not judged to be absurd or preposterous. On the contrary, they were told and retold because they had some connection to the material conditions and personal relations in their societies. To a certain degree they carried truths, and the people of all classes believed in these stories, either as real possibilities or parables. Magic and marvelous rituals were common throughout Europe, and it is only with the gradual rise of the Christian Church, which began to exploit magic and miraculous stories and to codify what would be acceptable for its own interests, that wonder tales and fairy tales were declared sacrilegious, heretical, dangerous, and untruthful. However, the Church could not prevent these stories from being circulated; it could only stigmatize, censure, or criticize them. At the same time, the Church created its own "fairy-tale" tradition of miraculous stories in which people were to believe and still do believe. This is true of all organized religions and continues to be the case today. The magical tales of the Bible and religious texts have always been compelled to compete with the secular tradition of folk and fairy tales for truth value.

Aside from displacing oral wonder tales and fairy tales or replacing them with their own myths since the early Middle Ages, organized religions, their schools, and their believers began "feminizing" the tradition of wonder and fairy tales and thereby dismissing it as not relevant to the "real world" or the true world of belief. If women were regarded as the originators and disseminators of these tales, then the texts themselves had to be suspicious, for they might reflect the fickle, duplicitous, wild, and erotic character of women, who were not to be trusted. Thus, their stories were not to be dismissed as trivial. The association of women with the fairy tale, Mother Goose, the gander, the nursery, bedtime, and the unbelievable belies how tales were told and disseminated in

Europe and North America from the Middle Ages to the present. (Incidentally, this association was often coupled with children, that is, the folk were regarded as simple children, and their tales were thus belittled as simplistic, ignorant, and crude by the upper classes and the clergy.) We have absolutely no proof that women were the "originators" or prime tellers of tales, the primeval spinners, or that they told their tales primarily to children. Tales were told in walks of life in the Middle Ages and during the Enlightenment, as they are today, and both sexes contributed to and continue to contribute to the tale-telling tradition. Troubadours, professional court storytellers, kings, queens, merchants, slaves, servants, sailors, soldiers, spinners, weavers, seamstresses, woodcutters, tailors, innkeepers, nuns, monks, preachers, charcoal burners, and knights carried tales as did children. It would be an exaggeration to insist that everyone in society told tales or that they were good and interesting tale tellers. But we must imagine that everyone was interested in news from afar, local events, and entertaining tales to pass the time, and we know that the original terms for fairy tales stemmed from terms like "Mär," "cunto," or "conte," which simply meant a tale about something newsworthy, any kind of "novel" or exotic tale, and a tale that was special for the listeners and worth repeating. These tales were often embellished, or they were ritual tales that brought the members of a community closer together. Since we cannot prove one way or another how frequently and by whom the tales were told, we must be cautious in making generalizations about who the "caretakers" of the tales were. But one factor is clear: the folk were not just made up of the peasantry or the lower classes. The term folk should be considered an inclusive term when used to describe a "folk tale" because everyone told tales during the medieval and Renaissance periods, and the tales were the property of everyone and anyone. The great majority of people in the Middle Ages up through the beginning of the nineteenth century were nonliterate, and thus everyone participated in one way or the other (as teller or listener) in oral traditions. Everyone was exposed to some kind of storytelling, and nobody can claim "true authorship," despite many claims made in the name of the mythological "folk," the common people, or peasantry, which the Grimms and many other folklorists romanticized and idealized in the nineteenth century. Even when the tales were read, they tended to be recited and transmitted orally in all social classes or across social classes, depending on who could read.[19]

When it comes to the literary tradition of the fairy tale, however, the situation is different because men were privileged when it came to education, and the literary tradition, though it consisted of appropriated tales from women and men alike, was firmly in the hands of men.[20] The motifs, characters, topoi, and magical properties of the literary tradition can be traced to tale collections from the Orient that pre-date Christianity. They are apparent in Indian, Egyptian, Greek, and Roman collections of tales, myths, and legends and in the texts that constitute Oriental and Occidental religions. However, they were never gathered or institutionalized in the short forms that we recognize in the West until the late Middle Ages. Then male scribes began recording them in collections of tales, epics, romances, and poetry from the tenth century onward. Most of the early work was in Latin, and the interactions between the Church and lay people and between orality and literacy help us understand how the fairy tale evolved and was disseminated. As Rosmarie Thee Morewedge has maintained:

> [W]e must rely on the wealth of tale collections that have come to us from medieval and pre-medieval sources, that were told by the tale-tellers; it must be remembered that tales did not stop being part of an oral tradition just because they were written down by vagrants, preachers, merchants, crusaders or other literati. Recognizing the need for secular oral entertainment that had been and continued to be met by tale-tellers, and recognizing that people wanted and needed to be amused, the church in effect attempted to improve on the popular tale-telling that took place in medieval secular communities by providing the greatest oral entertainment in magically illuminated mega-cathedrals (with illustrations of *Heilgeschichte* in stone, glass, and canvas) that resonated to the beauty of the priest's voice proclaiming the word of God? Who would not thrill to hear tales heard in the village retold in the grandeur of the cathedral, articulated by a trained preacher/tale-teller/entertainer? Which talented priest would not want to serve the missionary thrust of the church by collecting tales heard in childhood, read in school, heard on travels and in various monasteries?[21]

The Latin literary and oral tradition helped pave the way for the vernacular development of the fairy tale. In Italy fairy-tale motifs can be found in the anonymous thirteenth-century *Novellino* (*The Hundred Old Tales*), Giovanni Boccaccio's *Decameron* (1349–50), Giovanni Sercambi's *Novelle* (*Novellas*, 1390–1402), Poggio Bacciolino's *Facetiae* (c. 1450), Luigi Pulci's *Morgante* (1483), Matteo Maria Boiardo's *Orlando innamorato* (*Orlando in Love*, 1495), Ludovico Ariosto's *Orlando Furioso* (1516), and Ser Giovanni Fiorentino's *Il Pecorone* (*The Big Sheep*, 1564); in France, in Marie de France's *Lais* (c. 1189), Chrétien de Troyes's *Yvain, or the Knight of the Lion* (c. 1190), *Perceval* (c. 1195), and *Les Cent Nouvelles Nouvelles* (*The Hundred Tales*, 1456–61), and François Rabelais's *Gargantua and Pantagruel* (1532–64); in Germany, in the anonymous *König Rother* (c. 1150), the thirteenth-century verse novella *Asinarius*, Wolfram von Eschenbach's *Parzifal* (c. 1210), Hartmann von Aue's *Erek* (1180–85), *Armer Heinrich* (*Poor Henry*, 1195), and *Iwein* (c. 1205), the anonymous *Fortunatus* (1509), Martin Montanus's *Wegkürtzer* (1560), Andreas Strobl's *Ovum Paschale Novum* (1694), and Johann von Grimmelshausen's *Simpliccismus* (1669); in England, in *Beowulf* (eighth century), *Sir Gawain and the Green Knight* (fourteenth-century poem), Geoffrey of Monmouth's *Vita Merlini* (c. 1150), Geoffrey Chaucer's *The Canterbury Tales* (c. 1387), Sir Thomas Malory's *The Death of Arthur* (1469), Edmund Spenser's *The Faerie Queene* (1590–96), William Shakespeare's *Midsummer Night's Dream* (1595–96) and *The Tempest* (1611), and Ben Jonson's *The Alchemist* (1610); in Spain, the Oriental influence was important in such translated works as *Disciplina Clercalis* (c. twelfth century), *Sendebar* (1253), and *Kalila e Dimna* (thirteenth century), and in the chivalric novels *Cavallero Zifar* (1300) and *Amades de Gaula* (1508). In general, Oriental tales were spread in Europe both through oral retellings and translations into various European languages. Some key works that influenced European writers of fairy tales are *The Fables of Bidpai* (The Persian/Arabic adaptation of the Indian *Pancatantra*), *Navigatio Sancti Brendani*, and Christoforo Armeno's *Peregrinaggio di tre giovani figliuoli del re di Seren* (*Voyage of the Three Young Sons of the King of Ceylon*, 1557). In addition, such works as the thirteenth-century *Gesta Romanorum* (*Deeds of the Romans*) and *Legenda aurea* (*The Golden Legend*), written by Jacobus de Voraigne, were used as primers for young children and contained folklore and fairy-tale motifs as did many of the sermons and instructional books that were published from the fifteenth century onward. It is interesting to note that one of the tales in the *Gesta Romanorum* probably spawned the oral and literary dissemination of the remarkable *Fortunatus* (c. 1509), a medieval bestseller, published by the editor Johann Otmar in Augsburg, which was responsible for hundreds of different versions up through the twentieth century.[22]

The basic plot of this story reveals just how prevalent the fairy tale had become in both oral tradition and in print by the end of the fifteenth century. In brief the tale concerns a young man named Fortunatus on the island of Cyprus. His father squanders the family's wealth, and consequently Fortunatus decides to set out on his own to seek his fortune. After he joins the entourage of the Earl of Flanders, he travels to Flanders and wins a tournament, but jealous rivals and the threat of castration cause him to flee to London, where he leads a life of decadence and then returns to the Continent. Destitute, he wanders about Brittany and becomes lost in a forest. A kind fairy or Dame Fortune takes pity on him and grants him either wisdom, strength, long life, wealth, health, or beauty. He must select one of them. Fortunatus chooses wealth, and she gives him a magic purse that will always provide money for him. After wandering about Europe for a while, he returns to the island of Cyprus and finds that his parents are dead. However, with his magic purse, he is able to restore the family name and marries a young lady from a noble family. After two sons are born, he begins traveling again and eventually procures a magic cap that transports him to any place he wishes once he puts it on his head. Before he dies as a respected member of society, he bestows his gifts on his two sons who lose them because of their greed and carelessness.

There were many variations of this plot, and sometimes, instead of just one hero named Fortunatus, there were three young protagonists and three fairies. Sometimes the gifts are different. Fortunatus also makes use of an invisible cloak. In a significant essay about the origins of *Fortunatus*, Luisa Rubini has shown that the German folk book of *Fortunatus* was more than likely preceded by Spanish and Italian versions.

> If we assume that the German *Fortunatus* was produced at the turn of the 15th to the 16th century in the Augsburg region, the possibility cannot

be ruled out that the German author was acquainted with the Italian chapbook (or had heard it being narrated), but this does not mean that the character of the German original novel of the 15th and 16th centuries is being called in question. Lively economic and cultural relations, contacts and exchange between southern Germany and (northern) Italy are amply documented for that period, and the presence of Italian literature, both serious and popular (also in the form of cheap prints) in German libraries provides further evidence.[23]

The rise and spread of Fortunatus is significant because it is only one of many examples that indicate how widespread the fairy tale was in Europe by the beginning of the sixteenth century and the important role played by Italian culture in both oral and print traditions. Another good example is the wonder tale about the grateful dead that can be traced to pre-Christian antiquity and spread widely throughout Europe in the medieval period. Its dissemination has been amply studied by Gordon Hall Gerould in *The Grateful Dead: The History of a Folk Story* (1908). In Italy, the rise of the literary fairy tale as a short narrative form stemmed from the literary activity that flourished in Florence during the fourteenth century and led to the production of chapbooks and various collections of *novellas* in Italian and Latin under the influence of Boccaccio's *Decamerone*. The novella, also called *conto*, was a short tale that adhered to principles of unity of time and action and clear narrative plot. The focus was on surprising events of *everyday* life, and the tales (influenced by oral wonder tales, fairy tales, fabliaux, chivalric romances, epic poetry, and fables) were intended for the amusement and instruction of the readers. Before Boccaccio had turned his hand to writing his tales, the most famous collection had been the *Novellino* written by an anonymous Tuscan author in the thirteenth century. But it was Boccaccio who set a model for all future writers of this genre with his frame narrative and subtle and sophisticated style. It was Boccaccio who expanded the range of topics of the novella and created unforgettable characters, which led to numerous imitations by writers such as Ser Giovanni Fiorentino, Giovanni Sercambi, Franco Sachetti, Piovano Arlotto, and Matteo Bandello, to name but a few.

GIOVAN FRANCESCO STRAPAROLA

It was undoubtedly due to Boccaccio's example and the great interest in the novella that Giovan Francesco Straparola came to publish his collection, *Le piacevoli notti* (*The Pleasant Nights*, 1550–53) in two volumes.[24] Straparola is a fascinating figure because he was the first European writer to include approximately fourteen fairy tales in his collection of seventy-four novellas and because we know next to nothing about him.[25] Straparola was probably born about 1480 in Carvaggio, but there are no records that confirm this as a fact, especially since his surname "Straparola," which means the loquacious one, may have been a pseudonym. We only have information from the first volume of *Le piacevoli notti* that he was born in Carvaggio and that he was the author of another work *Opera nova de Zoan Francesco Straparola da Caravazo* (1508), a collection of sonnets and poems, published in Venice. Nor are we certain of his death in 1557. Most likely he had moved to Venice as a young man, and it is clear from his collection of novellas, which he called *favole* (fairy tales), that he was very well educated. He knew Latin and various Italian dialects, and his references to other literary works and understanding of literary forms indicate that he was versed in the humanities. Whoever Straparola may have been, his *Piacevoli Notti* had great success: it was reprinted twenty-five times from 1553 to 1613 and translated into French in 1560 and 1580 and into German in 1791.

The allure of his work can be attributed to several factors: his use of erotic and obscene riddles,[26] his mastery of polite Italian used by the narrators in the frame narrative, his introduction of plain earthy language into the stories, the critical view of the power struggles in Italian society and lack of moralistic preaching, his inclusion of fourteen unusual fairy tales in the collection, and his interest in magic, unpredictable events, duplicity, and the supernatural. Similar to Boccaccio, Straparola exhibited irreverence for authorities, and the frame narrative itself reveals a political tension and somewhat ironic if not pessimistic outlook on the possibilities of living a harmonious happy ever-after life.

In the opening of the book that sets the frame for all the *favole*, Straparola depicts how Ottoviano Maria Sforza, the Bishop-elect of Lodi (most likely the real Sforza, who died in 1540) was forced to leave Milan because of political plots against him. He takes his daughter, Signora Lucretia, a widow, with him, and since her husband had died in 1523, it can be assumed that the setting for the *Nights* is approximately some time between 1523 and 1540. The bishop and his daughter flee first to Lodi, then to Venice, and finally settle on the island of Murano. They gather a small group of congenial people around them: ten gracious ladies, two matronly women, and four educated and distinguished gentlemen. Since it is the time of Carnival, Lucretia proposes that the company take turns telling stories during the two weeks before Lent, and consequently, there are thirteen nights in which stories are told, amounting to seventy-four in all.

As was generally the case in upper-class circles, a formal social ritual was followed, one that was clearly modeled on real court entertainment during Straparola's time. Each night there was a dance by the young ladies. Then Lucretia would draw five names of the ladies from a vase, and those five ladies would tell the tales that evening. But before the storytelling, one of the men had to sing a song, and after the song a lady told a tale followed by a riddle in verse. Most of the riddles were examples of the double entendre and had strong sexual connotations, especially those told by the men. The object was to discuss erotic subjects in a highly refined manner. During the course of the thirteen nights, the men were invited every now and then to replace a woman and tell a tale. In addition, Lucretia herself told two tales.

To a certain extent, the fictional company on the island of Murano can be regarded as an ideal representation of how people can relate to one another and comment in pleasing and instructive ways about all types of experience. The stories created and collected by Straparola are literary fairy tales, revised oral tales, anecdotes, erotic tales, buffo tales of popular Italian life, didactic tales, fables, and tales based on writers who preceded him such as Boccaccio, Franco Sacchetti, Ser Giovanni Forentino, Giovanni Sercambi, and others. In the second volume he translated and adapted many Latin tales that he passed on as his own. In the fairy tales, as well as in most of the other narratives, Straparola focuses on power and fortune. Without luck (magic, fairies, miracles) the hero cannot succeed in his mission, and without knowing how to use the power of magic or taking advantage of a fortuitous event or gift, the hero cannot succeed. Though wicked people are punished, it is clear that moral standards are set only by the people in power. Thus Galeotto can kill his brides at will, and fathers can seek to punish or sleep with their daughters at will. The majority of the tales center on active male protagonists who are heroic mainly because they know how to exploit opportunities that bring them wealth, power, and money. Straparola begins most of his tales in small towns or cities in Italy and sends his protagonists off to other countries, realms, and, of course, into the woods or onto the seas. His heroes are adventurers, and there is a sense that the fairy tales have been gathered from far and wide. It is apparent in almost all his tales that he was influenced by oral storytelling and social rituals. It was common for young courtiers during this period to spend a year or so traveling when they reached a certain age and to prove themselves during their "exotic" voyages. There were tumultuous changes throughout Europe, and the motif of transformation, common in many folk tales, was emphasized even more in the fairy tales of Giambattista Basile. The pursuit of change and greater pleasure and power in life, improving one's social status, had always been important in oral folk tales. In the literary fairy tale, this motif had to pass the test of censors, and the metaphors and language had to be honed to meet audience expectations.

If Straparola did indeed spend most of his life in Venice, it would not be by chance that the tales he read and heard came to this port city from far and wide and that he was obliged to hone them to meet the expectations of the reading public. Venice was a thriving and wealthy city in the sixteenth century,[27] and Straparola would have had contact with foreigners from all over Italy, Europe, and the Orient. Or he would have had news about them. This real "news," perhaps also rumors and gossip, formed the basis of the *favole* in his collection that traveled far and wide. Though there are no records of how his tales were disseminated, they would have been read aloud at courts and in reading societies and repeated, and, of course, they were reprinted several times in the course of the sixteenth century. But the collection's significance for the development of the literary fairy tale in Europe has generally been neglected. Of course, he alone did not trigger the development, but there are clear signs that his tales circulated throughout Europe through print and by

word of mouth and had a considerable influence among educated writers: Basile was apparently familiar with his book,[28] and it is obvious
that Mme. d'Aulnoy, Mme. de Murat, Eustache Le Noble, and Jean de
Mailly adapted his tales in France at the end of the sixteenth century,
and through them they spread to Germany and were eventually noticed
by the Brothers Grimm, who wrote about Straparola and Basile.[29] In
short, Straparola, steeped in folklore, storytelling customs, and literature, played a crucial role in the formation of the genre of the literary
fairy tale in Europe, and though it would be misleading to talk about a
diachronic history of the literary fairy tale with a chain reaction that
begins with Straparola, leads to Basile, then the French writers of the
1690s, and culminates in the work of the Brothers Grimm, I would like
to suggest that, together, the works of these authors form a historical
frame in which the parameters and genericity of the early literary fairy
tale were set, and within that frame there was an institutionalization
of what we now call fairy-tale characters, topoi, motifs, metaphors, and
plots, and such institutionalization could have only developed with the
technology of printing, the improved distribution of printed materials,
and the approval and recognition of the educated classes. The quasi-
acceptance of the genre—quasi because the censors did not fully accept
it—enabled numerous writers to experiment and produce highly original fairy tales. These writers were also tellers, for the split between oral
and literary narrators was never as great as we imagine it to be, and their
familiarity with the folklore of their respective societies played a role in
their literary representations in the fairy tale. Giambattista Basile's work
is a case in point. I want briefly to sketch the further development of
the literary fairy tale beginning with Basile, then moving to the French
writers of the 1690s, and concluding with the Brothers Grimm.

GIAMBATTISTA BASILE

In contrast to Straparola, we know a great deal about Basile.[30] Born in
the small village of Giugliano near Naples in about 1575, he came from
a middle-class family, and in 1603 he left Naples and traveled north,
eventually settling in Venice, where he earned his living as a soldier

and began writing poetry. By 1608 he returned to the region of Naples and held various positions as administrator and governor in different principalities and courts while pursuing a career as poet and writer until his death in 1632.[31] Though he became well known for his poems, odes, eclogues, and dramas, written in Tuscan Italian, and helped organize court spectacles, his fame today is due to his astounding collection of fifty fairy tales written in Neapolitan dialect, *Lo cunto de li cunti* (*The Tale of Tales*, 1634–36), also known as the *Pentamerone* (*The Pentameron*), published posthumously thanks to the efforts of his sister Adriana, a famous opera singer.

There is no clear proof that Basile knew Straparola's tales, but it is more than likely he was acquainted with them in some form, especially since he had spent about three years in Venice, where Straparola's tales had been published and were still in circulation. However important Straparola might have been for Basile's conception of his fairy tales, he was a pale light in comparison with the fiery imaginative Basile. To my mind, Basile is the most original and brilliant writer of fairy tales in Europe until the German romantic E. T. A. Hoffmann came on the scene in 1814. Not only did Basile draw on an abundance of literary and historical sources to create his hilarious ironical tales, but he was deeply acquainted with the folklore of a vast region around Naples and was familiar with Oriental tales. His command of the Neapolitan dialect is extraordinary, for he managed to combine an elevated form of the dialect with vulgar expressions, metaphors, idioms and brilliant proverbs,[32] many of which he created himself. The frame narrative (following Boccaccio, of course) is fascinating in and of itself. His "tale of tales" sets the stage for forty-nine marvelous stories that stem from the oral tradition. In this frame tale, Zoza, the daughter of the King of Vallepelosa, cannot laugh, and her father is so concerned about her happiness that he invites people from all over the world to try to make her laugh. Yet, nobody can succeed until an old woman, who attempts to sop up oil in front of the palace, has her jug broken by a mischievous court page. The ensuing argument between the old woman and the page, each hurling coarse and vulgar epithets at one another, is so delightful that Zoza bursts into laughter. However, this laughter does not make the old woman happy, and she curses Zoza by saying, "Be off with you, and may you never see the bud of a husband unless it is the Prince of Camporotondo!" To her dismay, Zoza learns that this prince named Tadeo is under the spell of a wicked fairy and is in a tomb. He can only be wakened and liberated by a woman who fills a pitcher that is hanging on a nearby wall with her tears.

In need of help, Zoza visits three different fairies and receives a walnut, a chestnut, and a hazelnut as gifts. Then she goes to Tadeo's tomb and weeps into the pitcher for two days. When the pitcher is almost full, she falls asleep because she is tired from all the crying. While she is sleeping, however, a slave girl steals the pitcher, fills it, wakes Tadeo, and takes the credit for bringing him back to life. Consequently, Tadeo marries her, and she becomes pregnant.

But Zoza, whose happiness depends on Tadeo, is not about to concede the prince to a slave girl. She rents a house across from Tadeo's palace and manages to attract the attention of Tadeo. However, the slave girl threatens to beat the baby if Tadeo spends any time with Zoza, who now uses another tactic to gain entrance into Tadeo's palace. On three different occasions she opens the nuts. One contains a little dwarf, who sings; the next, twelve chickens made of gold; and the third, a doll that spins gold. The slave girl demands these fascinating objects, and Tadeo sends for them, offering Zoza whatever she wants. To his surprise, Zoza gives the objects as gifts. Yet, the final one, the doll, stirs an uncontrollable passion in the slave girl to hear stories during her pregnancy, and she threatens Tadeo again: unless women come to tell her tales, she will kill their unborn baby. So, Tadeo invites ten women from the rabble known for their storytelling: lame Zeza, twisted Cecca, goitered Meneca, big-nosed Tolla, hunchback Popa, drooling Antonella, snout-faced Ciulla, rheummy Paola, mangy Ciommetella, and diarretic Iacoba. The women spend the day chattering and gossiping, and after the evening meal, one tale is told by each one of the ten for five nights. Finally, on the last day, Zoza is invited to tell the last tale, and she recounts what happened to her. The slave girl tries to stop her, but Tadeo insists that Zoza be allowed to tell the tale to the end. When he realizes that Zoza's tale is true, Tadeo has the slave girl buried alive pregnant, and he marries Zoza to bring the tale of tales to a "happy" conclusion.

Unlike the narratives by Boccaccio and Straparola, Basile's tales, which are told during banquets with music, games, and dance, are entirely fairy tales and are told by lower-class figures in dialect—evidence of a storytelling tradition among the common nonliterate people. There are constant local references to Naples and the surrounding area and to social customs, political intrigues, and family conflicts. Basile was an astute social commentator, who despaired of the corruption in the courts that he served and was obviously taken with the country folk, their surprising antics, and their needs and drives for change. As Michele Rak has observed:

> [I]n the case of the *Cunto* the plots are all filled with the same theme: the change of status. The situation of each tale evolves rapidly to bring wealth and beauty to some of the characters and poverty and ruin to others. This change is only realized amidst conflict, foremost in the interior of the minimal social unit—the family about which there are many stories of fathers, mothers, stepmothers, sons, brothers—and then in the elementary reports of relations in the family—about which there are many stories about marriages and above all about unequal marriages between princes and shepherdesses. The change of status of these fairy-tale characters can be read as a metaphor of a much broader change: the acceleration of the time and mode of the cultural process characteristic of this phase of the modern era. In the *Cunto* the most evident signs of this transformation of the cultural regime are registered explicitly: the emergence of symbolical traditions, the opening of new dimensions of communication, the restructuring of the system and hierarchy of family relations, a broader literacy, the amplification and identification of the types of readers who also read the new novel, the client of the literature of celebration, the participant at the feasts and the theatricalization of public life.[33]

In his most recent work, *Logica della fiaba* (2005), Rak argues that Basile's *Cunto de li cunti*, more than Straparola's *Le piacevoli notti* or any other baroque collection of tales, paves the way for the establishment of the literary fairy tale in Europe. According to him, the *Cunto* was a highly unusual and sophisticated work that became known and spread through many different channels. Basile's tales were not read and used like literary works; they were not censored and were rarely cited by the elite readers. The tales were recited at courts and functioned like a canvas upon which other listeners, readers, writers, and tellers could manipulate the figures as they desired.[34] Rak explains that there is a clear logic to all the tales that sets a model for most of the literary fairy tales that immediately followed the publication of the *Cunto*, a model that also influenced the formation of the oral wonder tale. The type of fairy tale (*il racconto fiabesco*) conceived by Basile

> produced a literary genre, and its stories produced other texts that had a great circulation because the fairy tale used stories that stemmed from the heritage of Mediterranean culture and because a model was prepared through its structure that proved itself to be stable: it repeated its com-munications (*avvisi*) to readers in a regular cadence set up also in the secondary stories. With this model it was possible to construct many diverse tales that were adaptable to various circumstances as the numer-ous variants and versions have proven.
>
> The *Cunto* stabilized a formula that became a current in the Euro-pean tale. Its literary value depends in part on its inter-textuality and pan-culturalism (it assimilates local traditions that are very diverse); on its flexibility (it adapts to circumstances that vary a great deal); on its order (it permits an identification with a register [repertoire of characters and motifs] that is part of a European heritage and consents to have it used.[35]

To be precise, Rak maintains that there are several components that determine the Basile model: fairies, ogres, the game, the court, fortune, the whimsical journey, transformations, the body. Each tale in the *Cunto* was told to entertain a court society as a sort of a game, a dangerous game, because the storyteller could lose his life if he uttered the wrong words or was indiscreet and offended the nobility. The goal of the story-teller was to make the audience laugh, and laughter itself was a relief and escape for the storyteller who used metaphors to test and perhaps sub-vert the conventions of the court (i.e., civility). Each tale involves some kind of journey into the woods, onto the sea, or to another city. This journey reflected the trip that a courtier generally took when he came of age so that he might see the world or test himself. Along the way his survival would depend on fairies and ogres, who arbitrarily choose to help or destroy him. Fortune plays a momentous role. The episodic and unpredictable movement within the logical structure of the tale reflects the turmoil and exploration of the seventeenth century. Bodies are enmeshed in the plot. They are beautified, tortured, demolished, rejuvenated, and transformed as the protagonist seeks to survive at all costs and improve his social status in the ever-changing world.

Similar to Straparola, Basile shared a concern with power, sex, and transformation and was fascinated by the wheel of fortune and how Lady Fortuna intervened in people's lives to provide them with the opportunity to advance in society or to gain some measure of happiness. Of course, he also depicted how Lady Fortuna could devastate people and cause destruction. Again, like Straparola he was not overly optimistic about establishing social equality and harmonious communities. Conflict reigns in his tales in which a usually demure Cinderella chops off the head of her stepmother and a discreet princess virtually liquidates a seducer in a battle of the sexes. Nevertheless, his tales exude mirth because of the manner in which he turns language inside out and creates a carnalvesque atmosphere. Just as the frame tale leads to the exposure of the stealthy slave girl with no holds barred, all the narratives seek to reveal the contradictory nature in which all members of society pretend to comport themselves according to lofty standards but will stoop as low as they must to achieve wealth and happiness. Basile takes great delight in minimizing the differences between coarse peasants and high aristocrats, and certainly if his tales had been written and published in Italian, they would have found their way to the Church's Index.

The Institutionalization of the Fairy Tale in France

As it was, Basile's tales were—remarkable to say—reprinted several times in the seventeenth century despite the difficulty of the Neapolitan dialect and, through translations into Italian and then French, they became fairly well known in Italy and France. We do not know all the channels of transmission and dissemination, but there are clear signs that Basile's and Straparola's tales were picked up and passed on by storytellers and writers because they were memorable and spoke relevantly to the needs and interests of people from different backgrounds. In France, it is apparent that Mlle. Lhéritier was very familiar with his tales, and three of hers, "The Discreet Princess," "The Enchantments of Eloquence," and "Ricdin-Ricdon," depend heavily on three of his stories. In fact, the Italian influence in France during the 1790s was much more profound than scholars have suspected. At least six of Mme. d'Aulnoy's fairy tales can be traced to Straparola's *favole*; two of Mme. de Murat's tales owe a great debt to Straparola; and three of Mailly's tales and two of Le Noble's are very imitative of Straparola's works. Finally, almost all of Perrault's tales have models in the collections of Straparola and Basile. The Italian influence was certainly there,[36] and it is not necessary or even important to undertake an assiduous philological comparison to prove theft, imitation, or appropriation, for clearly word about Straparola and Basile was spread through books, storytelling, and conversations. What is significant and fascinating is the manner in which French writers began in about 1790 to be attracted to oral folk tales and literary fairy tales and created a vogue[37] of writing that was to last approximately a century and brought about the institutionalization of the fairy tale as a literary genre in Europe and North America.

Perhaps I should say French women writers, or to be even more specific, Mme. d'Aulnoy, because she and they almost single handedly transformed the Italian and Oriental tales as well as oral tales into marvelous fairy tales that were serious commentaries on court life and cultural struggles at the end of the eighteenth century in Versailles and Paris. As Patricia Hannon has remarked:

> [W]hether denigrated by learned men such as Villiers or praised by the modernist *Mercure*, tale writing was considered a group phenomenon largely because the majority of narratives were published by salon women who displayed their authorial identity through interior signings and intratextual references to each other's work. At the end of the century when … French women were writing in heretofore unprecedented numbers, the *salonnières* Aulnoy, Bernard, Lhéritier, and their colleagues transformed what Erica Harth has described as the salon of space of conversation into the space of writing.[38]

It was Mme. d'Aulnoy who began the vogue by incorporating a tale "L'Isle de la Félicité" ("The Island of Happiness") into her novel *L'Histoire d'Hipolyte, comte de Duglas* (1790) through the means of conversation. Talk and the oral tradition in all its forms are key to understanding the rise and institution of the literary genre. Interestingly the tale does not end happily because the protagonist Adolph does not follow the commands of Princess Felicity and is whisked away by Father Death, not unlike many folk tales in which Death always gains the upper hand. As a consequence, the disappointed Princess Felicity does not show herself on earth any more, and perfect happiness is unattainable. Mme. d'Aulnoy went on to write another sixteen tales published in *Les Contes de Fées* and *Contes Nouveaux ou les Fées à la Mode* between 1696–98. She along with Henriette Julie de Murat coined the term "conte de fèe," a term that stamped the genre and indicated the narrative power of women, for the fairies and writers/tellers of these texts are in control of the destinies of all the characters. These tales are intricate, long discourses about the importance of natural love and tenderness (*tendresse*), subjects dear to her heart. In addition, they tend to embody a critique of the conventional court manners from an aristocratic woman's perspective that is further enhanced by the dialogues in the narrative frames in which her tales are installed. The conversations surrounding her tales are very important because the tales themselves grew out of literary entertainment and parlor games that had become common in many of the literary salons in France by the 1690s. It was in the salons and elsewhere that the French literary fairy tale was conventionalized and institutionalized. Marie-Jeanne Lhéritier, Catherine Bernard, Charlotte-Rose Caumont de La Force, Henriette Julie de Murat, Jean de Mailly, Eustache Le Noble, Charles Perrault, and other writers frequented many of the same salons or knew of one another. Interested in participating in a social discourse about the civilizing process in France, modern culture, and the role of women and aware of the unique potential that the fairy tale possessed as metaphorical commentary, these writers produced remarkable collections of tales within a short period of time: Mlle. Lhéritier, *Oeuvres meslées* (1695); Mlle. Bernard, *Inès de Cordoue* (1695), a novel that includes *Riquet à la houppe*; Mlle. de la Force, *Les Contes des contes* (1697; Charles Perrault, *Histoires ou contes du temps* passé (1697); Chevalier Jean de Mailly, *Les Illustres Fées, contes galans* (1698); Mme. de Murat, *Contes de fées* (1698); Paul-François Nodot, *Histoire de Mélusine* (1698); Sieur de Prechác, *Contes moins contes que les autres* (1698); Mme. Durand, *La Comtesse de Mortane* (1699); Mme. de Murat, *Histoires Sublimes et Allégoriques* (1699); Eustache Le Noble, *Le Gage touché* (1700); Mme. d'Auneuil, *La Tiranie des fées détruite* (1702); and Mme. Durand, *Les Petits Soupers de l'année 1699* (1702).

Though the quality of the writing varied among these authors, they all participated in a notable modernist movement, for this was the period of French cultural wars when Nicolas Boileau and Perrault debated the merits of classical Greek and Roman models versus new French innovative art in the famous *Querelle des Anciens et des Modernes* (*Quarrel of the Ancients and Moderns*, 1687–96) and when the "infamous" *Querelle des femmes* (*Quarrel about Women*) pervaded various aspects of French culture. This was not an official debate, but it still raged in public during the latter part of the seventeenth century, as men continued to publish tomes about the proper role of women and how to control their bodies and demeanor, if not their identities.[39] The transformation of literary and oral tales into *contes de fées* was not superficial or decorative. The aesthetics that the aristocratic and bourgeois women and men developed in their conversational games and in their written tales had a serious aspect to it. As Patricia Hannon maintains:

> [W]omen at once embrace and manipulate modernist *mondain* ideology. Ostentatiously adopting the consecrated aristocratic aesthetic of negligence, the *conteuses* cultivate a positive class and gender identity in order equally to write beyond it. Claims of frivolity, amusement, amateurism, all found in women's metacommentaries on their chosen genre, at once denote their own ambivalence in crossing over into the "masculine" territory of writing and publishing, and ensconce them safely in an ideological social frame which their fictional narratives will at times challenge. If the notion of the female author came of age during the last years of the century, it is perhaps because the salon appears to have conflated the notions of conversation and composition.[40]

Though they differed in style, perspective, and content, the writers of fairy tales, female and male,[41] were all anticlassical, and their narratives were implicitly written in opposition to the leading critic of the literary establishment, Boileau, and his followers. As Lewis Seifert has made clear:

> [T]he use of the marvelous in the *contes de fées* differs from that in both the mythological and the Christian epic. ... By contrast, the *contes de fées* do not reduce the marvelous to allegorical systems of aesthetic, moral, or religious plausibility. Although they do have recourse to a moraliz-ing pretext with the use of interspersed maxims and/or appended final morals, these serve to motivate the representation of individual charac-ters or traits that are thereby plausible, and not the marvelous setting as a whole, which remains *invraisemblable*. Even further, the fairy tales make deliberate use of the marvelous and are thus deliberately implau-sible. This self-conscious and playful use of both the supernatural setting and the moralizing pretext distances any real belief in fairy magic, but also contributes to the readability of the text.[42]

In this regard, the French writers continued the remarkable experi-mentation with the marvelous that the Italians, namely Straparola and Basile, had begun many years before them, but they were able to ground and institutionalize them as a genre more effectively than the Italians had done through the salon culture and advances made in literacy and in printing. Like Straparola and Basile, they exploited the marvelous in conscious narrative strategies to deal with real social issues of their time. Paradoxically, the more implausible they made their stories, the more plausible and appealing were their hidden meanings that struck readers as truthful and have not lost their truth content today. The accomplishments of the French writers were many: (1) They reacted to social and political events with great sensitivity, and since this was a period of Louis XIV's great wars that devastated the country and also a period of famine, there was great discontent with his reign and with the court that was palpable in many of the tales. (2) They were ingenious in the manner in which they combined the salon conversations and games into their tales and at the same time refined the "vulgar" folk idiom to address their concerns that covered the role of precocious women, the relations and condition of court society, tender and natural love, war, duplicity, class status, taste, morality, and power relations. (3) Almost all the marvelous realms the writers created, whether they were male or female, were governed by fairies and had little if any reference to Greek,

Roman, and Christian allegorical systems. Fairies were omniscient and omnipotent and ruled their universes, and there was no explanation why or how they had achieved such great power. Clearly, however, their "feminine" reign was in opposition to the mundane reign of Louis XIV and the Church. (4) Sex, desire, and gender relations were prominent topics in their tales that were often expositions on the need for natural love and tenderness versus cruelty and violence; (5) The cross-cultural connections—the motifs they wove into their tales—are vast and stem from Italy, the Orient, the French urban and rural settings, and other European cultures. Although the French language and particular cultural references stamp these tales as French, they are also filled with and enriched by a pan-European and Oriental tradition that formed them.

During and after the vogue, the fairy tales that began to be transfigured and crystallized as classical fairy tales were mainly those written by Perrault. This may be due to the fact that he was the most famous among the French writers who published fairy tales. It may also be due to the fact that they were short and exquisitely written. The brevity of the tales, many of which were modeled on Basile's works and oral folk tales, certainly made them more memorable as potential memes. Perrault had always frequented the literary salons of his niece Mlle. Lhéritier, Mme. d'Aulnoy, and other women, and he had been annoyed by Boileau's satires written against women. Thus, he wrote three verse tales, "Griseldis" (1691), "Les Souhaits Ridicules" ("The Foolish Wishes," 1693) and "Peau d'Ane" ("Donkey Skin," 1694), along with a long poem "Apologie des femmes" (1694) in defense of women. Whether these works can be considered pro-women today is another question, for Perrault extolled the intelligence and capabilities of women while maintaining that they should be put to use in the domestic and social realms. This contradictory perspective can be seen in most of his fairy tales. However, Perrault was definitely more inclined to respect women than either Boileau or Racine, and his poems and tales make use of a highly sophisticated style and folk motifs to stress the necessity of assuming an enlightened moral attitude toward women.

In 1696, Perrault embarked on the ambitious project of transforming several popular folk tales with all their superstitious beliefs and magic into moralistic tales that would appeal largely to adults and demonstrate a modern approach to literature. He had a prose version of "Sleeping Beauty" ("La Belle au Bois Dormant") printed in the journal *Mercure Galant* in 1696, and in 1697 he published an entire collection of tales titled *Histoires ou contes du temps passé* (*Stories or Tales of Times Past*), which consisted of a new version of "Sleeping Beauty," "Le Petit Chaperon Rouge" (Little Red Riding Hood"), "Barbe Bleue" ("Blue Beard"), "Cendrillon" ("Cinderella"), "Le Petit Poucet" ("Tom Thumb"), "Riquet à la Houppe" ("Riquet with the Tuft"), "Le Chat botté" ("Puss in Boots"), and "Les Fées" ("The Fairies").

Numerous critics have regarded Perrault's tales as written directly for children, but they overlook the fact that there was no children's literature per se at that time, and that most writers of fairy tales were composing and reciting their tales for their peers in the literary salons. Certainly, if Perrault intended them to make a final point in the "Quarrel of the Ancients and the Moderns," then he obviously had an adult audience in mind who would understand his humor and the subtle manner in which he transformed folklore superstition to convey his position about the "modern" development of French civility. Perhaps the most important development at this time is that his tales stuck, not only in Europe, but they were also about to catch on throughout the Western world.

The first French vogue was not a vogue in the sense of a fad, for shortly after the turn of the century it gave rise to a second phase that included Oriental tales and diverse experiments that consisted of farces, parodies, innovative narratives, and moral tales for the young. Perhaps the most momentous event was the publication of Antoine Galland's *Les Milles et une nuits* (*The Thousand and One Nights*, 1704–17) in twelve volumes. Galland had traveled and lived in the Middle East and had mastered Arabic, Hebrew, Persian, and Turkish, and he was also thoroughly familiar with the first vogue of fairy tales since he lived in Paris. After he published the first four volumes of *The Thousand and One Nights*, the tales became extremely popular, and he continued translating them until his death. The final two volumes were published posthumously and contained tales for which there are no manuscripts. Galland did more than translate. He actually adapted the tales to suit the tastes of his French readers, invented some of the plots, and drew material from an Arabic informant to form some of his own tales. His example was followed by

Pétis de La Croix (1653–1713), who translated a Turkish work by Sheikh Zadah, the tutor of Amriath II titled *L'Histoire de la Sultane de Perse et des Visirs. Contes turcs* (*The Story of the Sultan of the Persians and the Visirs. Turkish Tales*) in 1710. Moreover, he also translated a Persian imitation of *The Thousand and One Days*, which borrowed material from Indian comedies. Finally, there was the Abbé Jean-Paul Bignon's collection *Les Aventures d'Abdalla, fils d'Hani* (1710–14), which purported to be an authentic Arabic work in translation but was actually Bignon's own creative adaptation of Oriental tales mixed with French folklore. All of the Oriental collections had a great exotic appeal to readers of fairy tales, not only in France. European readers had a strong interest in other "exotic" countries and cultures, and the tales, though highly implausible and marvelous, attracted readers because they appeared to represent these "other" diverse and strange people through obvious wish-fulfillments and escape fantasies. In addition, the material, motifs, settings, and plots of the tales furnished European writers and storytellers with a greater repertoire and stimulated their imaginations for centuries to come, for the Arabian tales in particular were translated in hundreds of editions and many different European languages. Among them "Sinbad the Sailor," Aladdin and the Magic Lamp," and "Ali Baba and the Forty Thieves" have become part of the Western classical tradition. Like most of Perrault's tales, they have stuck with us up through the twenty-first century.

By 1720 the literary fairy tale was firmly entrenched in France, and its dissemination was to increase throughout the eighteenth century in different forms. Perhaps the most significant way was through the chapbooks of the Bibliothèque Bleue, a series of popularized tales published in a cheap format in Troyes during the early part of the seventeenth century by Jean Oudot and his sons Nicolas and Pierre Garnier. These collections (later translated and imitated in Germany as the Blaue Bibliothek and introduced in England as chapbooks) were at first dedicated to the Arthurian romances, lives of saints, and legends. They were carried by peddlers to towns and cities in the country and made works originally written for an upper-class audience available for all classes. It was not until the later part of the eighteenth century that Oudot, Garnier, and other publishers began including fairy tales and other stories in the

Bibliothèque Bleue format. By this time there were over 150 publishers in approximately 70 different places that were printing series of chapbooks.[43] Most of the fairy tales were abridged, and the language and style were changed so that they became comprehensible for all readers including the young. They were read aloud and appropriated by the lower classes, which, in turn, changed them in the oral tradition, and their "folk" versions would filter back into the literary tradition through writers who heard them in some form or another. In addition to the popularization of the literary fairy tale through chapbooks and the oral tradition, the original texts by d'Aulnoy, Perrault, Lhéritier, and others were read by numerous French writers who grew up with fairy tales of the first vogue; their attitude toward the tradition became more satirical. As Mary Louise Ennis remarks: "the Comte de Caylus, himself the author of the *Contes orientaux*, commented that one hardly read anything else but fairy tales in his youth. In fact, so obsessed was the public by 1755 that Frédéric-Melchior Grimm opined that just about everyone had put his hand to one. Fairy tales and Oriental intrigues became so popular that they influenced aristocrats and commoners alike. Accordingly, parodists could count upon the public's recognition of primary texts to decipher the encoded humor of their rewritten tales."[44]

Among the more important French writers of fairy tales during the first half of the eighteenth century were Philippe de Caylus (*Féerie novelles*, 1741 and *Contes orientaux tirés des manuscrits de la bibliothèque du roi de France*, 1743), Marie-Antoinette Fagnan (*Kanor, conte traduit du turc*, 1750; *Minet bleu et Louvette*, 1753; *Le Miroir des princesses orientales*, 1755), Antoine Hamilton (*Le Bélier*, 1705; *L'Histoire de Fleur d'Epine*, 1710; *Quatre Facardins*, 1710–15), Louise Cavelier Levesque (*Le Princes des Aigues*,1722 and *Le Prince invisible*, 1722), Catherine Caillot de Lintot (*Trois nouveaux contes de fées avec une préface qui n'est pasmoins serieuse*, 1735), Marguerite de Lubert (*Sec et Noir, ou las Princesse des fleurs et le princes des autruches*, 1737; *La Princesse Camion*, 1743; *Le Prince Glacé et la princesse Etincelante*, 1743), Henri Pajon ("Eritzine & Parelin," 1744, "L'Enchanteur, ou la bague de puissance," 1745, and "Histoire des trois fils d'Hali Bassa," 1745), Gabrielle-Suzanne de Villeneuve (*La jeune Amériquaine et les contes marins*, 1740 and *Les Belles solitaires*, 1745), and Claude-Henri de Voisenon (*Zulmis et Zelmaïde*, 1745 and *Le Sultan Mispouf et la Princesse Gismine*, 1746).

Although not all these writers wrote parodies, they were so well versed in the conventions of fairy-tale writers that they enjoyed playing with the motifs and audience expectations. Consequently, their tales often bordered on the burlesque and even on the macabre and grotesque. The fairies did outrageous things with their power. Humans were turned into talking fish and all kinds of bizarre animals. Sentimental love was parodied. Numerous tales abandoned morality for pornography and eroticism. Thomas-Simon Gueullette endeavored to make his collection of *Les Mille et un quarts d'heure* (*Thousand and One Quarter Hours*, 1715) like Galland's *Thousand and One Nights*, just as he had sought to give a folklore aspect to *Soirées bretonnes* (*Breton Evenings*, 1712). Most of the tales in the second wave have clear textual references to a literary genre that had established itself, but it should not be regarded as separate from the oral tradition, for conversation, talk, discussions, and readings often formed the basis for literary production, no matter what the social class of the author was.

In 1741 Charles Duclos, Philippe de Caylus, and Claude-Henri de Voisenon were challenged by Mlle. Quinault in her salon to write a tale based on designs by Boucher, and the result was not only Duclos's acerbic fairy tale, *Acajou et Zirphile* (1744), which poked fun at fairy-tale conventions and criticized a libertine society, but probably Jean-Jacques Rousseau's "La Reine Fantasque" (1758), which ridiculed monarchy and satirized women. Rousseau attended Mlle. Quinault's salon, and it has generally been assumed that he participated in the wager to see who could write the best tale based on Boucher's engravings. The tales by de Caylus and de Voisenon have not survived, but their other collections of comic fairy tales such as *Contes orienteaux* and *Zulmis et Zelmaïde* reveal to what extent they were familiar with written and oral versions of tales and discussions about them.

French fairy-tale writers of the eighteenth century were very conscious of how talk and conversation formed the basis of their tales and continually embedded their tales within frame narratives that highlighted the exchange of literary fairy tales and dialogue. Two of the most famous versions of "Beauty and the Beast" function as exemplary tales within a storytelling frame narrative. Mme. de Villeneuve's *La jeune Amériquaine et les contes marins* (1740) recounts the voyage of a young girl returning to Saint Domingue, where her parents are plantation owners, after finishing her studies in France. During the trip, the girl's chambermaid is joined by everyone on board in telling stories. This volume contains two fairy tales, "Les Naïades" and "La Belle et la Bête," and it is notable that de Villeneuve's long and complicated version of "Beauty and the Beast"—it is close to two hundred pages in its original publication—indicates a familiarity with Mme. d'Aulnoy's narratives and at the same time presents an elaborate discourse on blood lines, social class, and the merits of the bourgeoisie that reveal how she sought to interject her ideas of the civilizing process into the debates about appropriate marriages and the morals of her time. This is even more clearly the case in Mme. Leprince de Beaumont's version of "Beauty and the Beast" (1757). It is to her credit that she was one of the first writers to compose eminently didactic fairy tales for young readers, particularly girls, to improve their social status. The influence of the British writer Sarah Fielding's *The Governess or, Little Female Academy* (1749), which contains two moralistic fairy tales within a frame story involving a governess telling stories to young girls, is clear. Mme. Leprince de Beaumont was herself a governess in England for many years, and she published *Le Magasin des enfans* (1757) in the form of a series of dialogues that a governess holds with her young pupils ranging in age from five to twelve. Interspersed with lessons in geography, history, and religion are about eighteen fairy tales that are metaphorical accounts of how proper moral and ethical behavior can bring about happiness for a young ladies. Although Mme. Leprince de Beaumont advocated more equality and autonomy for women in society, her tales are contradictory insofar as they depict how girls should domesticate themselves, support men, and prove their worth by demonstrating industriousness and good manners. It was through reading, dialogue, and lessons that girls could socialize themselves to advance their status in society, and Mme. Leprince de Beaumont's "faith" in the power of reading the right materials would have a widespread effect on how fairy tales for children would be composed and shaped in the later part of the eighteenth century and through the nineteenth century.

THE RISE OF THE LITERARY
FAIRY TALE IN GERMANY

The French influence on the development of the literary fairy tale for young and old was prevalent throughout Europe and culminated in Charles-Joseph Mayer's remarkable forty-volume collection, *Le Cabinet des fées* (1785–89), which brought together a good deal of the most important fairy tales, including many of the Arabian tales by Galland, published during the past one hundred years in France. Discreet if not prudish, Mayer excluded the erotic and satirical tales. Nevertheless, his collection, which was reprinted several times, had a profound influence because it was regarded as the culmination of an important trend and gathered tales that were representative and exemplary for the institution of a genre. Ironically, its most immediate impact was in Germany, where the literary fairy tale had not been flowering, but thanks to the French influence, it began to flourish in the last three decades of the eighteenth century. As Manfred Graetz has indicated in his significant study, *Das Märchen in der deutschen Aufklärung. Vom Feenmärchen zum Volksmärchen*,[45] the German educated class was largely fluent in French and could read most of the French works in the original. However, German translations of numerous French fairy tales helped German writers to form their versions in their own language to establish the "German" literary genre in German-speaking principalities. It should be noted that most of these early translated tales were very free and could be considered adaptations. The first translations began as early as 1710, and they were based on Galland's *Thousand and One Nights*. Some of the other more important translations were Friedrich Eberhard Rambachs's *Die Frau Maria le Prince de Beaumont Lehren der Tugend und Weisheit für die Jugend* (1758), based on Mme. Leprince de Beaumont's *Le Magasin des enfans*; Wilhelm Christhelf Siegmund Mylius's *Drei hübsche kurzweilige Märlein* (1777), three fairy tales by Hamilton; Justin Bertuch's *Ammen-Mährchen* (1790), based on Perrault's *Histoires ou contes du temps passé*; and *Feen-Märchen der Frau Gräfin von Aulnoy*, 4 volumes (1790–96), fairy tales by Mme. d'Aulnoy that appeared in *Die Blaue Bibliothek*. Most significant was the publication of the *Cabinet der Feen* (1761–66) in nine volumes translated by Friedrich Immanuel Bierling. This collection provided the German reading public with key French fairy-tale texts and sparked imitations of different kinds. The work of Martin Christian Wieland was in part inspired by the French fairy tale, and he in turn was crucial as a cultural mediator. A famous German novelist and poet, closely associated with Weimar culture, Wieland published an important collection of tales titled *Dschinnistan* (1786–90), which included adaptations from the French *Cabinet des Fées* as well as three original tales "Der Stein der Weisen" ("The Philosopher's Stone"), "Timander und Melissa," and "Der Druide oder die Salamanderin und die Bildsäule" ("The Druid or the Salamander and the Painted Pillar"). Typical of all these tales is the triumph of rationalism over mysticism. Among his other works that incorporated fairy-tale motifs are *Der Sieg der Natur über die Schwärmerei oder die Abenteuer des Don Sylvio von Rosalva*,[46] (*The Victory of Nature over Fanaticism or the Adventures of Don Sylvio von Rosalva*, 1764), *Der goldene Spiegel* (*The Golden Mirror*, 1772), and *Oberon* (1780). In addition he wrote "Pervonte" (1778–79), a remarkable verse rendition of Basile's "Peruonto," which concerns a poor simpleton, whose heart is so good that he is blessed by the fairies and thus rises in society. Minor writers (Friedrich Maximilian Klinger, Christoph Wilhelm Guenther, Albert Ludwig Grimm, Friedrich Schulz) as well as major writers were influenced by the French vogue, German translations, and Wieland's works. Though Johann Karl August Musäus called his important collection of fairy tales *Volksmärchen der Deutschen* (*Folk Tales of the Germans*, 1782–86) and Benedikte Naubert titled her volume *Neue Volksmärchen der Deutschen* (*New Folk Tales of the Germans*, 1789–93), these works and others were pan-European and were also influenced by translations of Oriental tales into French and German. One of the first important collections for young readers, *Palmblätter* (*Palm Leaves*, 1786–90), four volumes edited by August Jakob Liebeskind with contributions by Johann Gottfried Herder and Friedrich Adolf Krummacher, had the subtitle "erlesene morgendländische Erzählungen" ("selected Oriental stories"), and one of the key romantic texts by Wilhelm Heinrich Wackenroder had the title "Ein wunderbares morgendländisches Märchen von einem nackten Heiligen" ("A Wondrous Oriental Tale of a Naked Saint," 1799).

In fact, by the time the German romantics came on the literary scene, the fairy tale had been more or less well established in Germany and the Austro-Hungarian empire, and they could abandon the conventional structure and themes and begin to experiment in a vast number of ways. All the major romantic writers, Ludwig Tieck, Novalis, Clemens Brentano, Achim von Arnim, Joseph von Eichendorff, Friedrich de la Motte Fouqué, Adelbert Chamisso, and E. T. A. Hoffmann, wrote fairy tales that revealed a great familiarity with the French and Oriental literary tradition as well as the oral tradition and folklore in Germany. Tieck composed a series of fairy-tale plays, *Der gestiefelte Kater* (*Puss in Boots*, 1797), *Die verkehrte Welt* (*The Topsy-Turvy World*, 1799), *Der Blaubart* (*Bluebeard*, 1797), *Rotkäppchen* (*Little Red Riding Hood*, 1800), *Däumling* (*Thumbling*, 1812), and *Fortunat* (1816) that were based largely on Perrault's stories. However, his plays are more extraordinary parodies that toyed with audience expectations and combined motifs from the literary and oral tradition in unconventional ways. His "Little Red Riding Hood," which the Grimms knew, was turned into a serious tragedy with an apparent commentary on the French Revolution. Almost all the romantic tales reflected social conditions during the Napoleonic Wars and French occupation of Germany. Clemens Brentano, a good friend of the Brothers Grimm and a staunch German patriot, began experimenting with Basile's *Pentamerone*, the new title of *Lo Cunto de li cunti*, about 1805 and planned to adapt twenty or more tales in German. He succeeded in rewriting only eleven. Some were published separately during his lifetime, and after his death they appeared as *Italienische Märchen* (*Italian Fairy Tales*) in 1845.

THE BROTHERS GRIMM

Brentano, who was also a talented lyric poet, is a pivotal figure in the development of the Grimms' collection. In 1805 he published *Des Knaben Wunderhorn* (*The Boy's Wonder Horn*), an important book of German folk songs, with Achim von Arnim, and he wanted to produce a similar book of folk tales and sought help from various contributors. In 1806 he turned to the Brothers Grimm, who, by that time, had collected a great deal of material pertaining to German folklore. They agreed to save tales for Brentano, and between 1807 and 1812 they gathered approximately forty-nine tales from oral and written sources. Ironically, the tales did not come directly from the "simple folk," but from educated aristocratic and middle-class informants familiar with the oral tradition. For instance, in Kassel there was a group of young women from the Wild family (Dortchen, Gretchen, Lisette, and Marie Elisabeth) and their mother Dorothea, and young women (Ludowine, Jeanette, and Marie) from the Hassenpflug family. They gathered together regularly to relate tales that they had read or heard from their nursemaids, governesses, and servants. In 1808 Jacob formed a friendship with Werner von Haxthausen in Westphalia, and he and Wilhelm visited the Haxthausen estate and recorded tales from a group of young men and women. Other important informants in Kassel were Dorothea Viehmann, a tailor's wife, and Johann Friedrich Krause, an old retired soldier. Many of the tales that the Grimms collected were French in origin because the Hassenpflugs were of Huguenot ancestry and spoke French at home. In addition, the French occupied the Rhineland during this time, and there was a strong French influence throughout this region. In short, from the beginning, the Grimms did not make careful distinctions with regard to the "nationality" of their tales, nor did they rule out literary tales. Their "folk" included every social class of people. Just as the formation of the literary genre emanated from the mutual influence and interchange of the oral and literary tales that circulated in the medieval period, the Grimms' collection was drawn from the same "fountains," so to speak.

In 1810, Brentano requested that the Grimms forward the tales they had gathered to him, so they copied forty-nine stories that were in rough form and kept a copy for themselves. By this time, they were skeptical of Brentano's project and feared that he might tamper with the tales and change them into poetic literary versions. Ironically, Brentano had lost interest in compiling a collection of folk tales, whereas it was the Grimms who transformed the tales into exquisite literary narratives. Through some kind of oversight, Brentano left the forty-nine tales in the Ölenberg Monastery in Alscace, while the Grimms destroyed their manuscript after using it as the basis for the first edition of the *Kinder- und*

Hausmärchen (*Children's and Household Tales*), published in two volumes in 1812 and 1815. Therefore, it is thanks to Brentano that we can understand how the Grimms altered the tales. His copy of the manuscript, now known as the Ölenberg manuscript, was first rediscovered in 1920 and published in different editions in 1924, 1927, and 1974.[47]

The first two volumes of *Children's and Household Tales* contained 156 tales and copious notes in the appendixes and were not at all intended for children. It was not until 1819, when the second edition appeared in one volume with 170 texts—the notes were published separately— that the Grimms decided to cater to young readers as well as a growing middle-class reading audience of adults. After the publication of the second edition five more editions were produced until 1857 as well as ten printings of a smaller edition of fifty tales.[48] The final edition of 1857 contained 210 tales, which had been carefully stylized by Wilhelm so that they reflected what he and Jacob considered a popular if not natural "folk" tone[49] and genuine customs and beliefs that the German people had cultivated. Like Basile, they made ample use of proverbs, for they felt that the truth of experience was to be found through the sayings and rituals of the folk and their metaphorical narratives.

The folk, as we know, is an imagined corpus just like the notion of a nation, and though the Grimms deceived themselves by believing there was something essentially German about their tales, their endeavor to create a body of tales through which all Germans, young and old, could relate and develop a sense of community was admirable and led to the production of tales that laid the foundation for the classical fairy tale used throughout the world. This was a result of their utopian and idealistic program in the name of democratic nationalism. At the same time they came to realize that their tales were very pan-European and contained strong Oriental influences. Just a look at their notes published separately in 1856 reveals how knowledgeable they were about the historical development of the fairy tale. There are important entries in the "Literatur" section on Straparola, Basile, Perrault, Mme. d'Aulnoy, and the entire French school as well as short commentaries on the fairy tale in Spain, England, Scotland, Ireland, Greece, Sweden, Denmark, the Slavic countries, and the Orient. The Grimms saw in the tales from other countries numerous parallels and similarities that they could trace in their "German tales."

Little did they know that these "foreign" ingredients would help their collection become the most famous anthology of fairy tales throughout the entire world. Indeed, the appeal of their tales may have something to do with the history of their cross-cultural connections.

In 1823 Edgar Taylor translated a selection of the Grimms' tales as *German Popular Stories* with illustrations by the gifted George Cruikshank. The book was an immediate success, and there was a second printing in 1826. From that time on there have been hundreds if not thousands of translations of the Grimms' tales in English and other languages throughout the world. In 1868, John Ruskin, whose quaint fairy tale "The King of the Golden River" was greatly influenced by the Grimms, wrote an introduction to an enlarged edition of *German Popular Stories*, in which he stated:

> For every fairy tale worth recording at all is the remnant of a tradition possessing true historical value;—historical, at least in so far as it has naturally arisen out of the mind of a people under special circumstances, and risen not without meaning, nor removed altogether from their sphere of religious faith. It sustains afterwards natural chances from the sincere action of the fear or fancy of successive generations; it takes new colour from their manner of life, and new form from their changing moral tempers. As long as these changes are natural and effortless, accidental and inevitable, the story remains essentially true, altering its form, indeed, like a flying cloud, but remaining a sign of the sky; a shadowy image, as truly part of the great firmament of the human mind as the light of reason which it seems to interrupt. But the fair deceit and innocent error of it cannot be interpreted nor restrained by a wilful purpose, and all additions to it by art do but defile, as the shepherd disturbs the flakes of morning mist with smoke from his fire of dead leaves.[50]

This is a curious statement from an author who used his art willfully to transform what he believed to be folklore from the Grimms into one of the most well-known and imaginative fairy tales of the Victorian period, namely *The King of the Golden River* (1851). But, despite its contradiction, Ruskin put his finger on what lies behind the constant transformation and transmission of fairy tales. Historically specific they have indeed arisen out of the minds of human beings in search for the truth of their experiences, and they have been passed on through word of mouth and the written word. With each repetition through the oral and literary traditions that mutually influenced each other, diverse cultural experiences became intertwined and interlaced with the instinctual drives of the human species to survive, and they formed the foundations of the Grimms' collection and other collections to follow.

The Grimms' *Children and Household Tales* was not the culmination of the oral and literary traditions, but it did bring together representative tales in a style and ideology that suited middle-class taste throughout Europe and North America, and the subsequent value of the tales has been determined by the manner in which people throughout the world have regarded them as universal and classic. If we trace the canonization of particular fairy tales, we can see that their versions of "The Frog Prince," "Little Red Riding Hood," "Cinderella," "Snow White," "Sleeping Beauty," "Rapunzel," "Rumpelstiltskin," "The Golden Goose," "The Bremen Town Musicians," and others developed memetic qualities and reinforced some basic ostensive and relevant features of these tales that we can find in the works of Straparola, Basile, d'Aulnoy, Perrault, and others. Disseminated through print and other cultural institutions by word of mouth, these tales were changed and replicated in a gradual process that has affected the way our minds receive this material and reiterate it.

Although it is difficult to gather accurate figures, the Grimms' tales (along with certain Perrault versions) are probably the most reprinted and best known in the world and serve as reference points for all kinds of cultural productions for opera, theater, radio, cinema, mass media, and advertising. The metaphorical manner of our speech communication and modes in which we reflect upon ourselves incorporate fairy-tale lore as we frequently seek to make our lives like fairy tales. Though we do not realize it, we bring ourselves closer to people from many different cultures through the cross-cultural connections of the tales, even though we endow them with our own specific individual and cultural meanings as we appropriate and replicate them in diverse ways. There was never such a thing as a "pure" folk tale or a "pure" fairy tale, and the evolution of the fairy tale must be understood within the framework of Adam and Heidmann's genericity and Sperber's epidemiology.

At the beginning of the nineteenth century the function of the fairy tale for adults underwent a major shift throughout Europe, thanks to the German Romantic movement and tales by Novalis, Ludwig Tieck, Adelbert von Chamisso, and E. T. A. Hoffmann, among others, that made it an appropriate medium to carry on a sophisticated dialogue about social and political issues and the civilizing process within the bourgeois public sphere. However, the fairy tale for children in England, Germany, and France remained suspect until the 1820s. This suspicion did not prevent fairy tales from being published and circulated. There were, in fact, various collections of fairy tales published for children in England by John Harris (*Mother Bunch's Fairy Tales*, 1802) and Benjamin Tabart (*Popular Fairy Tales*, 1804–8) along with illustrated chapbooks containing "Little Red Riding Hood," "Cinderella," "Sleeping Beauty," "Jack the Giant Killer," "Beauty and the Beast," and so on. These collections flourished throughout Europe and were read by children and adults, but they were not considered the prime or appropriate reading material for children. Nor were they considered to be "healthy" for the development of children's minds. The majority of the tales and stories for children were sentimental, moralistic, realistic, and didactic, intended to demonstrate and model manners and morals. Even the Brothers Grimm, in particular Wilhelm, began in 1819 to revise their *Children's and Household Tales*, adding Christian sentiments and cleansing narratives of their erotic, cruel, or bawdy passages. However, the fantastic and wondrous elements were kept, and during the 1820s, a change in attitude toward the fairy tale for children could be noted and was signaled in England by the publication of Edgar Taylor's translation of the Grimms' tales under the title of *German Popular Stories* (1823), in Germany by Wilhelm Hauff's *The Caravan* (*Die Karawane*, 1825), and later Ludwig Bechstein's *German Fairy Tale Book* (*Deutsches Märchenbuch*, 1845), in France by reprintings of Perrault's tales and Sophie de Ségur's *Nouveaux contes de fees* (*New Fairy Tales*, 1857), illustrated by Gustave Doré, who also created the great classical illustrations of Perrault's tales, and last but not least, in Denmark by Hans Christian Andersen's publication of fairy tales in 1835, which would soon become the most popular throughout Europe and North America in the nineteenth century. Some of his tales, many based on folk tales, such as "The

Tinderbox," "The Princess on the Pea," "The Emperor's New Clothes," "The Swineherd," and "The Little Mermaid," became canonized.[51]

During the nineteenth century educators and upper- and middle-class parents gradually began to realize, probably due to their own reading experiences, that fantasy literature and amusement would not necessarily destroy or pervert children's minds. On the contrary, children needed amusement—"all work and no play makes for a very dull day"—so they could relax and recharge themselves after a rigid school day. Whether the children were of the middle class and attended school or were of the lower class and worked on the farm or in a factory, they needed a recreation period—the time and space to recreate themselves without having morals and ethics imposed on them, without having the feeling that their reading or listening had to involve indoctrination.

Significantly, it was from 1830 to 1900, during the rise of the middle class, that the fairy tale came into its own for children. It was exactly during this time, from 1835 onward, to be precise, that Hans Christian Andersen began publishing his tales. Almost all his tales were immediately translated and published in England, Germany, and America. Andersen brilliantly combined humor, Christian sentiments, and fantastic plots to form tales that amused and instructed young and old readers at the same time. This was exactly what Sarah Fielding, Mme. Leprince de Beaumont, and Albert Grimm had endeavored to do before him, but the social conditions had not been ripe enough for such tales to spread in Europe, especially because they were so class-specific. By 1830, however, the sociocultural setting in Europe and America had become more propitious to receive the fairy tale, and Andersen opened it up for the proper grooming of good Christian children.

Up until the 1850s, the majority of fairy-tale writers for children, including Catherine Sinclair, George Cruikshank, and Alfred Crowquill in England, Collodi in Italy, Comtesse Sophie de Ségur in France, Ludwig Bechstein in Germany, and Horace Scudder in America emphasized the lessons to be learned in keeping with the principles of the Protestant ethic—industriousness, honesty, cleanliness, diligence, virtuousness—and male supremacy. The fairy tale was intended to play a major role in the socialization process. However, just as the "conventional" fairy tale for adults had become subverted at the end of the eighteenth century, there was a major movement to write parodies of fairy tales for children, to turn them upside down and inside out, to include allusions to sex and desire, to question the traditional value system and suggest alternatives to the endings that appeared to contradict the notion of wonder and transformation that had been so dominant in the wonder folk tale. Writers such as William Makepeace Thackeray (*The Rose and the Ring*, 1855), George MacDonald ("The Light Princess," 1863), Lewis Carroll (*Alice in Wonderland*, 1865), Charles Dickens ("The Magic Fishbone," 1868), Jean Ingelow (*Mopsa the Fairy*, 1869), Juliana Ewing (*Old-Fashioned Fairy Tales*, 1882), Andrew Lang (*Princess Nobody*, 1884), Mary Louisa Molesworth ("The Story of a King's Daughter" 1884), Oscar Wilde (*The Happy Prince and Other Tales*, 1888), Kenneth Grahame (*The Reluctant Dragon*, 1898), Edith Nesbit (*The Last of the Dragons*, 1900), and many others began to experiment with the fairy tale in a manner that would make young readers question the world around them. Their tales did not offer prescriptions for good housekeeping and clean living. Instead, they suggested that conventional living could lead to the imprisonment of the soul and mind, and they offered "utopian" alternatives. The British writers had a great impact on Americans, who began to develop their culturally specific fairy-tale tradition toward the middle and end of the nineteenth century. The firm of John McLoughlin began publishing numerous fairy-tale toy books at midcentury. Writers such as Nathaniel Hawthorne, James Kirke Paulding, Christopher Pearse Cranch, Horace Scudder, Louisa May Alcott, Frank Stockton, Howard Pyle, Catherine Pyle, and others contributed fairy tales to magazines like the *St. Nicholas* in the 1870s and 1880s or published their own collections of tales. There was even a collection of Native American fairy tales, *The Indian Fairy Book* (1869). The major writer of this time was Frank Stockton, who published some unusual book tales like *Ting-a-Ling* (1871), *The Floating Prince and Other Fairy Tales* (1881), and *The Bee-Man of Orn and Other Fanciful Fairy Tales* (1887). While the European fairy tales served as models for the American writers, there was clearly a movement to "Americanize" and establish a genuine *American* literature.

It is not by chance that the most notable and memorable American fairy tale was produced right at the end of the nineteenth century: L. Frank Baum's *The Wizard of Oz* (1900), clearly based on the European fairy-tale structure, which depicts Dorothy's great desire and need to break out of the gray bleakness of Kansas. Her imagination and initiative are awakened so she can ultimately determine her destiny with the assistance of her three helpers. Though Dorothy returns to America, she realizes in the sixth Oz book, *The Emerald City of Oz* (1910), that she cannot stay in a country where farmers are driven to ruin by bankers and exploitation is accepted as the "American way of life." Baum's creation of fourteen Oz books, considered an American fairy-tale saga, is a political and cultural commentary with profound ramifications for the eventual development of the fairy tale as a genre. In fact, Baum set the stage for other fairy-tale novels and series such as those by J. R. R. Tolkien, C. S. Lewis, T. H. White, and Michael Ende. Even Salman Rushdie, author of *Haroun and the Sea of Stories* (1990), has often paid tribute to *The Wizard of Oz*, and numerous books and films continue the Oz tradition through the twenty-first century.

At the same time that Baum made history in America, J. M. Barrie contributed to the imaginative radicalization of the fairy tale with his drama *Peter Pan, or the Boy Who Wouldn't Grow Up* (1904), based on tales he first published in *The Little White Bird*. Barrie's fairy-tale drama, later adapted as a novel, *Peter and Wendy*, in 1911, is a play about nostalgia, sexual longing, and the resistance to conformity and convention, indicating just how important the fairy tale had become for adults, young readers, and spectators. Indeed, during the London premiere of Barrie's *Peter Pan* in 1904, the largely adult audience responded to Peter Pan's question whether they believed in fairy tales with a resounding "Yes!" It was a "Yes" that was repeated the following year in New York and continues to echo in theaters and cinemas up through today. Perhaps more than Baum's Dorothy, Peter Pan on stage and in film has captured the imagination of young and old readers and spectators throughout the world.

By the beginning of the twentieth century, the fairy tale had become fully institutionalized in Europe and North America for adults and children, and its functions had shifted and expanded. The institutionalization of a genre means that a certain process of production, distribution, and reception has become fully accepted within the public sphere of a society and plays a role in forming and maintaining the cultural heritage of that society. Without such institutionalization, any genre would perish. As institution, the genre is involved in the socialization and acculturation of readers. Thus, it is the interaction of writer/publisher/audience within a given society that makes for the definition of the genre in any given epoch. The aesthetics of each fairy tale will depend on how and why an individual writer wants to intervene in the discourse of the genre as institution and to replicate stories in the mind.

By the beginning of the twentieth century, there were three currents in the fairy-tale tradition that existed side by side: the classical or conventional fairy tales of Perrault, the Grimms, and Andersen, which were increasingly sanitized and made more "appropriate" for an idealized concept of childhood when published for children; innovative fairy tales that often parodied the conventional ones from multiple political perspectives and sought to bring about radical aesthetic innovations; and widespread oral storytelling of fairy tales of different kinds in homes, libraries, schools, recreation centers and spaces, and through the mass media. These currents have developed the memetic tradition in fascinating ways that need further exploration.

"Cinderella"
Illustrator: Maurice Leroy

Chapter 3

Once Upon a Time in the Future: The Relevance of Fairy Tales

hy not begin with a true story, an anecdote? It is relevant here.

On March 1, 2000, I spent an hour answering questions about children's literature on the Wisconsin Public Radio program "Conversations" with Kathleen Dunn, and at one point I was discussing why I thought the Harry Potter novels had spread throughout the world and sold in the millions. I went into an elaborate explanation about the power of advertising and media hype as well as myths about J. K. Rowling, the unknown author, who pulled herself up by her bootstraps to become a famous author. But as I finished my explanation, an eager young man called into the program and informed me that I was mistaken. "Your thesis is wrong," he said. "Harry Potter is really Cinderella all over again, and we're always drawn to Cinderella."

Some years ago, in one of the more interesting studies of the fairy tale in German, *Die Zaubergärten der Phantasie: Zur Theorie und Geschichte des Kunstmärchens* (The Magic Gardens of the Imagination: On the Theory and History of the Literary Fairy Tale), Friedmar Apel argued:

[T]he history of the literary fairy tale is also the history of the struggle of the imagination against its increasing suppression by reality. Compared to other poetic forms the possibilities for the elaboration of this problematic are limited for the fairy tale. ... While other genres could preserve their forms in that they continued to tolerate the idea of the unity of world and soul only negatively within themselves, the fairy tale has this conceivability as its prerequisite no matter how much it is relativized. The cessation of this conceivability means for the fairy tale that it must abandon its role as the representative form of the marvelous if it does not want to disintegrate into mere entertainment literature through a pretended harmony and detachment from the processes of life.[1]

Indeed, Apel went so far as to argue that the fairy tale had lost its deeper significance by the beginning of the twentieth century because it had not and could not develop the appropriate forms and means to deal with the torn relationship between the imagination and reality. Beauty and harmony cannot be attained and maintained in reality as absolute values, and it is the incapacity of the fairy tale as genre to deal with the dissonance of modern life that foreshadows its swan song.

Though Apel traces the historical predicament of the genre with great lucidity and concern for its social and philosophical aspects, it appears to me that he was much too rash in dismissing the genre as too rigid to adapt itself to the changing conditions of reality and unsuitable as a genre to be able to reflect critically upon the social and material tensions that constitute our beleaguered modern and postmodern sensibilities. It is not that Apel was wrong in his assessment of the genre's predicament, but he failed to take into account the genre's deeply ingrained adaptability and "evolvability," especially its potential as a meme. He did not consider how its utopian function has actually expanded in the twentieth and twenty-first centuries to include a kind of negative dialectic that has imbued it with a significant self-critical feature and enhanced possibilities for aesthetic variation and experimentation. Moreover, the predicament of the fairy tale since the twentieth century is one that plagues all of modern art, and Apel is aware of this when, in commenting on the great Austrian writer Hugo von Hofmannsthal's fairy tale "The 672nd Night," he states:

The problematic is to be sure not only one that confronts the fairy tale, not only one of Hofmannsthal's early works, but it contains the paradox of all modern art: it wants the beautiful for life, but it withdraws from the beautiful by seeking to hold on to it, otherwise it will reinforce negativity in the portrayal. The diluting of the boundary between imagination and reality appears therefore as guilt in Hofmannsthal's [fairy tale]. The creation of the fairy-tale world, the mastery of the means of a form is not an aesthetic-technical problem, but rather an ethical one, the responsibility of the poet vis à vis life.[2]

Here Apel puts his finger on what I consider the most important problem for all writers and especially writers of fairy tales—the ethical one. Why choose to write a fairy tale? What is involved in the selection process? How does the fairy tale as meme latch on to the writer? What does a writer hope to accomplish in using this genre to address children or adults? What responsibility does a writer bear when construing utopian or dystopian alternatives to our contemporary world? Are writers of fairy tales unethical and irresponsible when they create false happy endings and delude us into believing that harmony is possible in our rapidly changing postmodern globalized war-torn world? Is it unethical to publish fairy tales in all their mass-mediated modes to make as much profit as one can by playing with our utopian desires? Of course, most of the fairy tales produced in the twentieth and twenty-first centuries have become more geared to pure entertainment and are trite retellings of tales told to pass the time away. Yet, overall the fairy tale has not lost its relevance throughout the world. In fact, one might even argue that, with the increase of literacy throughout the world, the literary fairy tale produced as book, hypertext for the Internet, advertisement for commodities, script for film, radio, and television, comic, cartoon, and cultural artifact has grown in relevance.

Why such relevance? Why do we attach so much value to the literary fairy tale for young and old? What is the prognosis for the future of the fairy tale at the beginning of the twenty-first century? How are we being configured to respond to new configurations of the fairy tale? Are the stock phrases that begin and end traditional fairy tales—"once upon a time" and "happily ever after"—empty of all meaning? Is it hopeless and senseless to want to depict and think about our lives as fairy tales?

It is, of course, impossible to answer all these questions, but I would like to explore the moral, aesthetic, and political value of fairy tales for the twenty-first century by discussing some aspects of relevance theory developed by Deirdre Wilson and Dan Sperber and what Sperber calls an epidemiology of representations in his book *Explaining Culture* because they shed light on why the fairy tale is still so significant for American culture, if not for global culture. Then I will present a brief overview of some of the more recent developments in the genre with a focus on the multiple "Cinderella" versions that have been produced within the past twenty years in an endeavor to grasp the significance of this phenomenon. Underlying my analytical exploration is the thesis presented in the first two chapters that the fairy tale as genre has become contagious and spreads like a meme in different strains. It is a strange viral genre because it contains positive and negative effects within socialization processes. As it has evolved and spread, it acts like a meme that undergoes multiple mutations in interaction with the environment. It is encoded and carries relevant information that enables us to know the world and uses this information both to expose and conceal the problematic nature of social relations. It is perhaps this tension between disclosure and closure within the metaphoric conventions of the genre that make it so viable as an appealing form of communication and narration.

RELEVANCE THEORY AND EPIDEMIOLOGY

Ever since the publication of *Relevance: Communication and Cognition* (1986) by Deirdre Wilson and Dan Sperber, there has been a great interest in relevance theory by scholars not only in linguistics and cognitive psychology, but also in literary studies, communication, and philosophy.[3] It is very easy to misunderstand relevance as a theoretical concept, that is, to understand it more as a philosophical concept that pertains to categories of significance and value and determines what is pertinent about an object or expression for the needs of the producer and recipient. But Wilson and Sperber approach relevance in light of advances made in sociobiology and cognitive psychology; they understand human

cognition in relation to a biological function of information process-
ing and seek to understand how parts of the brain work efficiently to
provide us with relevant information to increase our knowledge of the
world. They operate with two governing principles: (1) human cognition tends to be geared to the maximization of relevance, and (2) every
act of ostensive communication communicates a presumption of its own
optimal relevance.[4]

By ostension or ostensive communication they mean an act that
manifests its intention and draws attention to what is relevant. They
insist that relevance is not a commodity, but a "property of inputs to
cognitive processes. It can be a property of stimuli, for example, which
are inputs to inferential processes. Stimuli, and more generally phenomena, are found in the environment external to the organism; assumptions, which are the output of cognitive processes of perception, recall,
imagination or inference, are internal to the organism. When we claim
that human cognition tends to be geared to the maximisation of relevance, we mean that cognitive resources tend to be allocated to the pro-
cessing of the most relevant inputs available, whether from internal or
external sources. In other words, human cognition tends to be geared to
the maximisation of the cumulative relevance of the inputs it processes.
It does this not by pursuing a long-term policy based on computation of
the cumulative relevance achieved over time, but by local arbitrations,
aimed at incremental gains, between simultaneously available inputs
competing for immediately available resources."[5]

Among the ways we try to know the world and ourselves in relation
to our environment, we have used and continue to use the fairy tale as
a metaphorical mode of communication. It is a socially symbolic act of
representation and communication. For centuries we have developed
the oral and literary capacity within our brains to communicate relevant
information about specific conditions and relations in our lives and to
use and change this information as we adapt to our changing environments for survival. There is a domain or module within our brains that
enables us to form and conceptualize information according to vari-
able linguistic conventions, and we have developed a strong genetic disposition to forming and cultivating mental and public representations

within social and cultural institutions that make the fairy tale relevant as a literary genre because it is both efficient and ostensive.

In his book *Explaining Culture: A Naturalistic Approach*, Sperber makes a distinction between mental representations consisting of beliefs, intentions, and preferences and public representations consisting of signals, utterances, texts, and pictures. The fairy tale is both mental and public representation, and certain fairy tales become so significant within a culture that we become disposed to re-representing it in manifold ways in the course of history. We also tend to replicate particular fairy tales, which become "classical" and assume memetic qualities. It is almost as if they were second nature in us. Sperber is interested in the question as to why some representations are propagated and take root, so to speak, in general and in specific contexts, and others do not. To answer this question he developed a theory of an epidemiology of representations to explain how certain ideas or representations become contagious. By no means does he want to suggest that cultural representations are pathological or that they are like viruses that mutate only occasionally. Sperber insists that "representations are transformed almost every time they are transmitted, and remain stable only in limiting cases. A cultural representation in particular is made up of many versions, mental and public ones. Each mental version results from the interpretation of a public representation which is itself an expression of a mental representation."[6]

In Chapter 1 I used a biological model of the evolution of a natural species to explain how the fairy tale as a species originated, evolved, and spread in western Europe,[7] but I did not pay enough attention to human agency in discussing the means by which fairy tales are transmitted and the importance of inferential and intentional transformation. Sperber's theory provides a more substantial basis for understanding why certain fairy tales stick in our lives, and I want to use it to elaborate some of my ideas about the transmission and dissemination of fairy tales to the present. Sperber maintains:

> [A]n epidemiology of representations is not about representations, but about the process of their distribution. In some cases, similar representations—for example, versions of the same myth—are distributed by a repetitive chain of public and mental representations; in other cases,

many different representations, the contents of which do not at all resemble one another, are involved in the same distribution process. In particular, some of the representations involved may play a regulatory role by representing how some of the other representations involved are to be distributed. The distribution of these regulatory representations plays a causal role in the distribution of the other representations in the same complex. Institutional phenomena, I maintain, are characterized by such hierarchical causal chains.[8]

In the case of the literary fairy tale we know that it emanated from and evolved within an oral tradition of storytelling and that the communication and transmission of literary tales gradually became institutionalized through print and word of mouth by the seventeenth century. What is important to bear in mind is that neither the institutionalization of the fairy tale as genre nor the individual tale as text itself has remained fixed, and one of the problems with using structuralist approaches, such as the one developed by Vladmir Propp's *Morphology of the Folk Tale*, to understand the "nature" of the fairy tale as literary genre or the oral tale is that it fails to consider the interrelation between oral and literary traditions and the mutations and variations of the literary fairy tale that has numerous strains. Sperber emphasizes this point:

A process of communication is basically one of transformation. The degree of transformation may vary between two extremes: duplication and total loss of information. Only those representations which are repeatedly communicated *and* minimally transformed in the process will end up belonging to the culture. The objects of an epidemiology of representations are neither abstract representations nor individual concrete representations, but, we might say, strains, or families, of concrete representations related both by causal relationships and by similarity of content. Some of the questions we want to answer are: what causes such strains to appear, to expand, to split, to merge with one another, to change over time, to die? ... The diffusion of a folktale and that of a military skill, for instance, involve different cognitive abilities, different motivations and different environmental factors. An epidemiological approach, therefore, should not hope for one grand unitary theory. It should, rather, try to provide interesting questions and useful tools, and to develop the different models needed to explain the existence and fate of the various families of cultural representations.[9]

If we are to use an epidemiological approach effectively to understand the changing importance and function of the fairy tale at the beginning of the twenty-first century, we need some guiding or operative principles to explain particular representations and phenomena and how and why they continue to spread and to be spread. Therefore, I want to present some theses that may help us grasp why the fairy tale, and in particular why a fairy tale like "Cinderella," remains so ostensively relevant in American and also in British culture, not to mention the continental.[10]

First, there is no such thing as a pure literary fairy tale or a separate literary tradition. The fairy tale developed out of an oral cognitive mode of communication and narration; it was continued and expanded through print, which generated another mode of transmitting relevant information. When fairy tales came to be printed as public representations, they were read privately and publicly, remembered and retold orally, and republished, always with changes.

Often the first texts were printed in Latin, especially in Europe. Rhetorical and linguistic conventions were gradually established through the institutionalization of vernacular languages. Though most of the literary fairy tales published in Italy during the sixteenth and seventeenth centuries tended to be short, anywhere from five to ten pages, there were numerous tales published by French writers at the end of the seventeenth century that were forty pages or more, and by the eighteenth century there were numerous fairy-tale novellas and novels. The literary forms varied depending on what the authors considered to be the most efficient means to transmit their relevant messages, but undoubtedly they remembered basic nodal points and ideas that they may have heard or recorded to write a tale intended to fit generic expectations and outside audience expectations.

Second, from the sixteenth century to the present, fairy tales have been transmitted in different ways, depending on the relevant information they were intended to communicate and on their function within a given social context or institution. For instance, fairy tales were recited at courts for entertainment and social communication about manners, norms, and mores, and they were performed as ballets, masques, operas, and plays. As the bourgeoisie ascended to power in the nineteenth century, the relevant content of the transmissions changed and the cultural, linguistic, and psychological disposition of the people also underwent transformation. The fairy tales were printed as books, broadsides, and chapbooks and read in public and private. They became part of costume balls in which people would assume particular fairy-tale characters. They were part of charades and parlor games. By the end of the nineteenth century the fairy tales were transmitted by radio and film, through advertisements of different kinds, and a plethora of illustrated books and postcards. With the rise of film, cartoons, comic strips, and musical shows at the beginning of the twentieth century, fairy tales became a major staple of all forms of the mass media.

Third, there were different social functions of the literary fairy tale, which was initially *not* intended for the entertainment or education of children, and yet, children had for centuries listened, remembered, and communicated through fairy tales because of their relevance to their lives. Until the mid-eighteenth century most of the fairy-tale publications were produced for adult audiences. It was not until the publication of Sarah Fielding's *The Governess, or Little Female Academy* (1749) and Mme. Leprince de Beaumont's *Le Magasin des enfans* (1757) that fairy tales began to be published specifically for children. The functions of the tales varied, depending on the sociocultural context. For sure, entertainment and instruction were always part of their function, but they were designed to communicate ideas about natural instincts, social relations, normative behavior, character types, sexual roles, and power politics. Their modes ranged from the comic to the tragic, and the mode of transmission depended on the environment and context in particular societies—the court, the fireside, the field, the ship, the dining room, the hearth, the tavern, the nursery, the classroom, the library, the radio, the cinema, and now the computer screen.

Fourth, it is difficult but possible to declare, as Apel has done, that there is something innate or inherent in the fairy-tale genre that endows it with its unique quality. One could ask: Is the fairy tale by its nature disposed toward happiness, hope, and harmony? Is it disposed to informing others as recipients and participants in a civilizing process about pertinent moral predicaments and conflicts and to assisting people to grasp alternatives for resolving them through particular metaphors and motifs? Is this disposition its special appeal and part of its function? Or do human beings have a basic utopian potential, a utopian disposition, somewhat like a natural force, that has been socially cultivated, as Ernst Bloch has argued?[11] Hopes, wishes, and dreams were not always fulfilled in the early fairy tales for adults, but they tended to be fulfilled for young readers. The notion of the happy fairy-tale ending became an ideological notion mainly in the nineteenth century, and even then, many authors such as George MacDonald and Oscar Wilde explored the disappointment of hope and unhappiness in their fairy tales. Are fairy tales part of a nostalgic longing for a happy past that never was? Indeed, fairy tales seem to be about the past but open up future vistas for the possibility of transformation. Fairy tales, even when they are preserved in their traditional and conventional forms, appeal to all audiences because they reinforce the notion of transformation and allow, through condensed and relevant forms, for easy memorization.

Fifth, the transformative and utopian qualities of the fairy tale appeal to young and older audiences and make it both stable and flexible as a literary form. Instituted within the family, schools, cinema, television, and computer in the twentieth century as the acceptable form for readers and spectators of all ages, the fairy tale is flourishing in American and British society in the twenty-first century. If we consider it in terms of Jean Michel Adam and Ute Heidmann's concept of *généricité*,[12] how it refers to other genres and cultural artifacts, borrows from them, mixes them, and cultivates them to enrich itself, we have a better understanding of the durability of the fairy tale in the twenty-first century.

Finally, an epidemiological approach to fairy tales can enable us to understand how strains of fairy tales are formed and spread as types of memetic communication. For instance, if it is relevant to know what dangers and risks a child, especially a young girl, might face when her mother dies, information about the circumstances she may confront will be communicated among people in different forms and will alter as environmental stimuli change. The father of the girl might remarry; he might remarry a woman with children; he might remarry a woman who is jealous of the daughter and may want to advance the cause of her own children; he might neglect and abandon his daughter; he might die and leave the girl without any protection. The girl might feel unwanted, guilty for causing her mother's death and hence want to dirty or besmirch herself, abandoned, longing for the love and protection of her dead mother, desperate for love from someone outside her family. The initial situation, the death of a mother who leaves behind a daughter, gives rise to different predicaments for the child—predicaments that will need cures, and information to bring about the cure once it is communicated. The formation of the cures as relevant stories is computed in the brain, and if a metaphorical mode of signaling to other people what might occur in a given situation becomes effective, it will be chosen over other modes of communication and become a relevant cultural representation. As a metaphorical mode of representation, whether it may be oral, iconic, or written, the fairy tale effectively draws our attention to relevant information that will enable us to know more about our real life situations, and through its symbolical code and flexible structure, it allows for personal and public, individual and collective interpretations. The relative formation of a strain within the fairy-tale genre offers the possibility for contested discourses about the transformation of social and political relations.

Fairy-Tale Transmission

Before turning to "Cinderella" as a case study about the relevance of the fairy tale today, I will provide a brief account of some of the numerous ways in which the fairy tale is transmitted as cultural representation and forms a vital part of the different cultural discourses. I shall focus mainly on texts of different kinds produced during the 1990s and the early part of the twenty-first century, and I shall be more descriptive than critical in order to present a background against which "Cinderella" is being memorialized for future generations. I shall also maintain that the fairy tale has assumed epidemic proportions, and that there are strains of the viral genre that we contain to spread more effectively than others.

Let us begin with the various collections of fairy tales that bring together texts by different authors within specific frames. Perhaps the

most prolific anthologists, aside from Mike Ashley in the United Kingdom, are Ellen Datlow and Terri Windling in the United States. During
the 1990s and early part of the twenty-first century they edited seven
important anthologies: *Black Thorn, White Rose* (1993), *Snow White, Blood
Red* (1994), *Ruby Slippers, Golden Tears* (1995), *Silver Birch, Blood Moon*
(1999), *Back Heart, Ivory Bones* (2000), *A Wolf at the Door and Other
Retold Fairy Tales* (2000), intended mainly for young readers, and *The
Fairy Reel* (2004). Their collections contain works by prominent writers
such as Joyce Carol Oates, Tanith Lee, Neil Gaiman, Charles De Lint,
Gregory Maguire, and Jane Yolen, as well as unknown authors whom
they regard as part of fin de siècle fairy-tale renaissance. As Datlow and
Windling state in the introduction to their most recent anthology:

> In this series, some of the finest writers of mainstream, horror, fantasy,
> and children's literature gather together to explore the many pathways,
> dark and bright, leading to enchantment. The diversity and range of
> their wonderful tales demonstrates our central premise: that classic folk-
> tale motifs still have much to offer fiction writers, and readers, today. ...
> As we move from one century to the next, it is interesting to note that
> the current popularity of fairy tale literature echoes the fairy tale renais-
> sance that occurred at the turn of the last century.[13]

The range of reinterpretations of classic fairy tales in Datlow and
Windling's anthologies is vast, whereas Mike Ashley's three collections of comic fantasy published between 1997 and 1998 bring together
mainly satiric, ironic, and mock versions of fairy tales by well-known
authors such as Terry Jones, Terry Pratchett, Harry Harrison, and others. In addition he has edited one of the better anthologies of unusual
fairy tales from the nineteenth century to the late twentieth century.
All his titles begin with "mammoth"—*The Mammoth Book of Fairy Tales*
(1997) or *The Mammoth Book of Comic Fantasy* (1999)—and they are
indeed mammoth. More specific and smaller are collections such as
Alan Foster and Martin Greenberg's *Smart Dragons, Foolish Elves* (1991);
Ed Gorman and Martin H. Greenberg's *Once Upon a Crime* (1998),
mystery fairy tales by well-known authors; Terri Windling's *The Armless
Maiden and Other Tales for Childhood's Survivors* (1995), stories that deal
with child abuse; Michael Ford's two anthologies, *Happily Ever After:
Erotic Fairy Tales for Men* (1995) and *Once Upon a Time: Erotic Fairy*

Tales for Women (1996); Mike Resnick and Martin Greenberg's *Aladdin: Master of the Lamp* (1992), variations of this one tale from *The Arabian Nights*, which provided the material for Susan Schwartz's anthology, *Arabesques: More Tales of the Arabian Nights* (1988); Denise Little's *Twice Upon a Time* (1999), which contains fairy tales with a new twist; Art Spiegelman and Françoise Mouly's *Little Lit: Folklore and Fairy Tale Funnies* (2000), unusual fairy-tale cartoon strips; Kathleen Ragan's *Fearless Girls, Wise Women and Beloved Sisters: Heroines in Folktales from Around the World* (1998); Jane Yolen and Heidi Stemple's *Mirror, Mirror: Forty Folktales for Mothers and Daughters to Share* (2000); and Martin Greenberg and Janet Pack's *Magic Tails* (2005), contemporary fairy tales and fables about cats. These collections present a variety of viewpoints on particular topics and are different from those volumes by individual authors who have a particular ideological perspective and style through which they wish to convey their message. For instance, there are a number of feminist authors who are more or less successful in revising and subverting traditional patriarchal narratives. Some of the more interesting works here are Francesca Lia Block's *The Rose and the Beast* (2000), Emma Donoghue's *Kissing the Witch: Old Tales in New Skins* (1997), Priscilla Galloway's *Truly Grim Tales* (1995), Virginia Hamilton's *Her Stories: African American Folktales, Fairy Tales, and True Tales* (1995), Katrin Tchana's *The Serpent Slayer and Other Stories of Strong Women* (2000), Nancy Walker's *Feminist Fairy Tales* (1996), and Jane Yolen's *Not One Damsel in Distress: World Folktales for Strong Girls* (2000). Another related and innovative approach to fairy tales can be found in Peter Cashorali's *Fairy Tales: Traditional Stories Retold for Gay Men* (1997). Almost all the rewritings of the traditional fairy tales have a greater awareness of the complexities of sexuality and gender roles and have sought to explore traditional fairy tales with a social consciousness and awareness in keeping with and critical of our changing times. Important here are Adèle Geras's trilogy *The Tower Room* (1990), *Watching the Roses* (1991), and *Pictures of the Night* (1992), Tanith Lee's *Snow White* (2000), Gail Carson Levine's *Ella Enchanted* (1997), *The Princess Test* (1999), *The Fairy's Test* (1999), and *Princess Sonora and the Long Sleep* (1999), Robin McKinley's *Deerskin* (1993) and *Spindle's End* (2000), and Donna Jo Napoli's *The Prince of the Pond* (1992), *The Magic Circle* (1993),

Zel (1998), *Sirena* (1998), *Spinners* (1999), written with Richard Tchen, and *Beast* (2000). These books focus on a single classical fairy tale and are intended for young adults, matched, or perhaps I should say over-matched, by the extraordinary number of picture books for younger readers. Some of the more innovative works are Alma Flora Ada's *The Three Golden Oranges* (1999), Tony Blundell's *Beware of Boys* (1991), Michael Buckley's detective series, *The Sisters Grimm: The Fairy Tale Detectives* (2004), *The Sisters Grimm: The Unusual Suspects* (2005), and *The Sisters Grimm: The Problem Child* (2006), Lauren Child's *Beware of the Storybook Wolves* (2000), Brock Cole's *Buttons* (2000), Sally Gardner, *I, Coriander* (2005), Dom DeLuise's *Hansel and Gretel* (1997), Virginia Hamilton's *The Girl Who Spun Gold* (2000), Charlotte Huck's *Toads and Diamonds* (1996), Lincoln Kisten's *Puss in Boots* (1992), Jonathan Lang-ley's *Rumpelstiltskin* (1991), Susan Lowell's *Little Red Cowboy Hat* (1997), Marianna Mayer's *Baba Yaga and Vasalissa the Brave* (1994), Katherine Paterson's *The Wide-Awake Princess* (2000), Jon Scieszka's *The Frog Prince Continued* (1991), Diane Stanely's *Rumpelstiltskin's Daughter* (1997), Mike Thaler's *Hanzel and Pretzel* (1997), Brian and Rebecca Wildsmith's *Jack and the Meanstalk* (1994), and Paul Zelinsky's *Rapunzel* (1997).

In the United Kingdom during the 1998 national year of reading, the British publisher Scholastic brought out an interesting series of inex-pensive illustrated fairy-tale books by well-known authors who sought to reinterpret classical tales: Henrietta Branford, *Hansel and Gretel*, Berlie Doherty, *The Snow Queen*, Anne Fine, *The Twelve Dancing Princesses*, Alan Garner, *Grey Wolf, Prince Jack and the Firebird*, Susan Gates, *The Three Heads in the Well*, Adèle Geras, *The Six Swan Brothers*, Michael Morporgo, *Cockadoodle-doo, Mr. Sultana!*, Philip Pullman, *Mossycoat*, Alan Temperley, *The Simple Giant*, Jacqueline Wilson, *Rapunzel*, Kit Wright, *Rumpelstiltskin*, and Diana Wynne Jones, *Puss in Boots*. Finally, mention should be made of numerous novels and collections of tales for adults that either make use of fairy-tale motifs, create new forms of fairy-tale telling, or retell a classical fairy tale in highly provocative and innovative ways. Among the more significant works in chronologi-cal order are A. S. Byatt, *Possession* (1990), Sheri Tepper, *Beauty* (1991), Kathryn Davis, *The Girl Who Trod on a Loaf* (1993), Margaret Atwood, *The Robber Bride* (1993), A. S. Byatt, *The Djinn in the Nightingale's Eye*

(1995), Gregory Maguire, *Wicked* (1995), Graham Joyce, *The Tooth Fairy* (1996), Robert Coover, *Briar Rose* (1996), Nancy Springer, *Fair Peril* (1997), Murray Bail, *Eucalyptus* (1998), Stephen Mitchell, *The Frog Prince: A Fairy Tale for Consenting Adults* (1999), Peg Kerr, *The Wild Swans* (1999), Mary Sharratt, *Summit Avenue* (2000), Tanith Lee, *White as Snow* (2000), Robin McKinley, *Spindle's End* (2000), Gregory Frost, *Fitcher's Brides* (2002), A. S. Byatt, *Little Black Book of Stories* (2003), Gregory Maguire, *Mirror Mirror* (2003), Shannon Hale, *The Goose Girl* (2003), Robert Coover, *Stepmother* (2004) and *A Child Again* (2005), Aimee Bender, *Willful Creatures* (2005), and Lauren Slater, *Blue Beyond Blue* (2005). Many of these authors have their own websites or are listed on websites on the Internet. In fact, there are hundreds of fascinating fairy-tale websites or hits with hypertexts of varying quality including interactive programs. Among the most interesting are "The Endicott Studio of Mythic Arts," "Folklore and Mythology Electronic Texts," and "Fair e-Tales." There are also publishers like Greenwood, Norton, August House, Oryx, and ABC-CLIO that publish many books that deal with folklore and fairy tales; Tor and DAW produce important fantasy and fairy-tale collections; most large publishers of children's books, especially Scholastic and Penguin in the United States and United Kingdom, will offer a great variety of fairy-tale books; a new journal, *The Fairy Tale Review*, edited by Kate Bernheimer and dedicated to publishing original fairy tales, made its appearance in 2005; scholarly journals such as *Marvels & Tales*, *The Journal of American Folklore*, *Folklore*, *Children's Literature*, *The Lion and the Unicorn*, *Children's Literature Quarterly*, *The Horn Book*, and many popular publications such as *Storytelling World* and *Storytelling Magazine* produce significant articles on fairy tales; and several academic presses, such as Wayne State University Press, Pennsylvania University Press, Princeton University Press, and Indiana University Press, publish monographs concerned with different aspects of the genre.

   If I were to include the large number of advertisements, cartoons, films, videotapes, radio programs, toys, merchandise, and wearing apparel that make use of fairy tales, it would appear that we were living in a fairy-tale universe. Indeed, there may be some truth to this as many of us seek to regulate our lives in keeping with fairy tales or the transmission of fairy tales. The external stimuli of fairy tales are immense; fairy tales act on us in infancy and continue to play a role in our lives through old age. Fairy tales are not just contagious, when considered from an epidemiological perspective, they are injected into our systems almost as a cure for dreaded social diseases.

The appeal of fairy tales still has a great deal to do with utopian transformation and the desire for a better life, and the manner in which we make it relevant in our mental representations will be in reaction to the outside stimuli and to moral codes instituted by hegemonic groups within a respective society. The more social relations make us discontent and feel as though we were objects alienated from our own communities, the more we seek a haven in mental projections of other worlds. But our disposition toward fairy tales is not uncritical. We do not blandly accept the cultural representations of fairy tales without changing or contesting them in our minds and through physical acts that lead to public cultural representations. The fairy tales that become memes are not mechanically replicated. We re-form the "replicators" based on our experience with the world around us and our desire to reshape our lives and environment. More than ever before in history we have fairy tales about fairy tales, or fairy tales that expose the false promises of the traditional fairy tales and leave open the question of a happy ending or even end on a tragic note. Some never end. In fact, the fairy-tale experimentation is overwhelming, and there are now particular strains within the fairy-tale genre, the so-called canonical tales, that have produced their own discourses. In other words, as I demonstrated in my book, *The Trials and Tribulations of Little Red Riding Hood*, a particular fairy tale comes to embody a discourse that becomes culturally relevant, and it is over the body of a particular constellation or figure such as Little Red Riding Hood that writers articulate positions regarding aspects of that tale. In the case of "Little Red Riding Hood," I argued—and still argue—that ostensive communication concerns relevant information about rape or violation of the body. The tale has become culturally relevant through the narrative means and strategies that we have metaphorically and socially construed to constitute its relevant quality. As I discussed in the previous chapter, we use the tale pertinently to comment in one way or another on sex and violence as can be seen in such recent and different cultural representations as Matthew Bright's cult film *Freeway* (1996), Todd Edwards's animated film for children, *Hoodwinked* (2006), Francesca Lia Block's short story "Wolf" (2000), Patricia Santos Marcantonio's *Red Ridin' in the Hood and Other Cuentos* (2005), and the picture books *Ruby* (1990) by Michael Emberley and *Beware of the Storybook Wolves* (2000) by Lauren Child. Other tales in the classical fairy-tale canon have come to embody and represent other discourses equally important, and they appear to assume a prominent role in the general cultural discourse at critical periods and reflect cultural predicaments and tendencies. "Cinderella" appears to be a good case in point.

"CINDERELLA"

During the last decade of the twentieth century there have been an astonishing number of picture books, novellas, novels, poems, hypertexts, plays, toys, and films that have transformed the representation of that dirty humiliated good girl who proves herself to be beautiful and a winner/survivor despite all the ashes and cinders that are heaped upon her. We recognize her for what she is—a true princess. At the same time, it is very difficult to establish her true identity in the twenty-first century, for she has become totally multicultural in the United States, primarily French or European in the United Kingdom, and in some cases transformed into a dog, penguin, dinosaur, or hog. For example, these are some of the picture books recently published in the United States and United Kingdom: Shirley Climo, *The Egyptian Cinderella* (1989), *The Irish Cinderella* (1996), *The Persian Cinderella* (1999); Jewell Reinhart Coburn, *A Hmong Cinderella* (1996), *Angkat: The Cambodian Cinderella* (1998), *Dormitila: A Cinderella Tale from the Mexican Tradition* (2000); Sheila Hébert Collins, *Cendrillon: A Cajun Cinderella* (2000); Joanne Compton, *Ashpet: An Appalachian Girl* (1994); Jude Daly, *Fair, Brown & Trembling: An Irish Cinderella Story* (2000); Pamela Duncan Edwards and Henry Cole, *Dinorella: A Prehistoric Fairy Tale* (1997); Adèle Geras, *Cinderella* (1996); Vanessa Gill-Brown, *Rufferella* (2000); Diane Goode, *Cinderella: The Dog and Her Little Glass Slipper* (2000); Alvin Granowsky, *That Awful Cinderella* (1993); Rebecca Hickox, *The*

Golden Sandal: A Middle Eastern Cinderella Story (1998); Ellen Jackson, *Cinder Edna* (1994); Nina Jaffe, *The Way Meat Loves Salt: A Cinderella Tale from the Jewish Tradition* (1998); Ann Jungman, *Cinderella and the Hot Air Balloon* (1992); Deborah Lattimore, *Cinderhazel: The Cinderella of Halloweeen* (1997); Adeline Yen Mah, *Chinese Cinderella and the Secret Dragon Society* (2005); Rafe Martin, *The Rough-Face Girl* (1992); Marianna Mayer, *Baba Yaga and Vasalissa the Brave* (1994); Barbara McClintock, *Cinderella* (2005); Frances Minters, *Cinder-Elly* (1994); Bernice Myers, *Sidney Rella and the Glass Sneaker* (1996); Janet Perlman, *Cinderella Penguin or, the Little Glass Flipper* (1992); Penny Pollock, *The Turkey Girl: A Zuni Cinderella Story* (1996); Robert San Souci, *Sootface: An Objibwa Cinderella Story* (1994), *Cendrillon: A Caribbean Cinderella* (1998), *Cinderella Skeleton* (2000), and *Little Gold Star: A Spanish American Cinderella Tale* (2000); Vivian Sathre, *Slender Ella and Her Fairy Hogfather* (1999); Alan Schroeder, *Smoky Mountain Rose: An Appalachian Cinderella* (1997); Judy Sierra, *The Gift of the Crocodile: A Cinderella Story* (2000); Francesca Simon, *Don't Cook Cinderella* (1996); Mike Thaler, *Cinderella Bigfoot* (1997); William Wegman, *Cinderella* (1993); and Arthur Yorinks, *Ugh* (1990). In addition Judy Sierra has published an Oryx multicultural anthology of different versions of "Cinderella" from various countries, and Neil Philip has produced a collection of "Cinderella" versions in *The Cinderella Story* (1989) that date back to the eighteenth century. There are also feminist versions in the works of Donoghue, Block, and Yolen, and there are interesting book-length versions for young and adult readers. For instance, as part of her princess tales series, Gail Carson Levine has published *Cinderellis and the Glass Hill* (2000) for ages seven to twelve and Gregory Maguire has produced *Confessions of an Ugly Stepsister* (2000) for young adults. One of the most important fairy-tale films of the 1990s was *Ever After*, which was also transformed into a book, and of course, Tom Davenport's important work, *Ashpet: An Appalachian Folktale* (1989), produced as a video for public television and classroom use, is one of the more insightful interpretations of the "Cinderella" tradition. Three textbooks—Theda Detlor's *A Fresh Look at Fairy Tales: A Thematic Unit Exploring Gender Bias in Classic Stories* (1995), Monica Edinger's *Fantasy Literature in the Elementary Classroom: Strategies for Reading, Writing, and Responding*

(1995), and Gail de Vos and Anna Altmann's *New Tales for Old: Folktales as Literary Fictions for Young Adults* (1999)—offer effective ways to analyze and use "Cinderella" with young readers. The renascence of storytelling in the United States and United Kingdom has brought about a renewed interest in retelling the classical fairy tales, and in one issue of *Storytelling World*, several well-known storytellers presented the introduction to their different versions with titles such as "Cinder Ellie," "Benizara and Kakezara," "Shmutzie," "Liberating Cinderella," "Words Into Flowers: Les paroles de fleurs," "Cinder Girl," "The Feisty Little Flea," "Pick a Pumpkin," "The Untold Story of a Cinderella," "Walking in Cinderella's Shoes," "Chipper," and "Cinder Elephant."[14] For background reference, there are two informative websites, David K. Brown's "Cinderella Stories" (http://ucalgary.ca/~dkbrown/cinderella.html) and "The Cinderella Project" (http://www-dept.usm.edu/~engdept/cinderella/cinderella.html); both provide links to other sites. Other innovative and fascinating interactive sites such as Joline Blais, Keith Frank, and Jon Ippolito's "Fair e-Tales" (http://www.three.org/fairetales/) provide multiple ways to reread and reinvent "Cinderella," "Little Red Riding Hood," and "Rapunzel."

During the past six years I have assisted filmmaker Joanna Kiernan and artist Joellyn Rock, who developed extraordinary projects related to "Cinderella." In the proposal that she sent to the National Endowment for the Humanities, Kiernan outlined her television program with accompanying digital video disc and website as follows:

> *Cabinet of Spells: Cinderella* will dramatize and comment on versions of *Cinderella* from the 9th century to the present from Germany, Italy, France, Scotland; the Middle East; China; and Nigeria in Western Africa. Fairy Stories are now considered children's Literature, but this is a very recent development, and the program intends to speak to adult and young adult audiences. As well as *Cinderella*, the program will look at two versions of the related story of *Donkey Skin*, a variant of *Cinderella* where the father is the abusive parent, forcing his daughter to flee from his incestuous demands. With over 1000 known variants and many contemporary re-tellings, *Cinderella* is probably the most popular fairy tale in the world, while conversely, the *Donkey Skin* story has been largely suppressed during the last two centuries, its telling once again timely. The program allows the ancient art of storytelling to lead the

viewer into its rich historical material. While the *Cinderella* with the glass slipper and pumpkin coach is known by nearly everyone in the Americas and Western Europe, other variants of the tale are surprisingly unknown. The program will show how the shifting social contexts, performance environments, and multiple re-tellings of the tale have produced a contemporary Cinderella that synthesizes conflicting voices and messages. The result is often a reduction of meaning, and the loss of the vivid testimonial the story offers of women's experience. *Cabinet of Spells* will address that problem by untangling the different voices that lie embedded in the tale, and uncovering startling historical information about the real conditions of women's lives in the past. Through the viewing experience this ubiquitous and still beloved fairy tale will be de-familiarized and deeply enriched.[15]

I shall return later to Kiernan's significant remarks about the relationship between "Cinderella" and "Donkey Skin," and why there is a spreading of one tale and an obfuscation of another, both intimately related to each other, just as the Russian Vasalisa tale is. In her MA thesis proposal at the University of Minnesota–Duluth, Rock wrote:

Storytellers and Graphic Designers occupy a similar role as communicators of cultural iconography and canon. *The Vasalisa Project* will explore the subversive potential of the storyteller/designer by mixing and remixing messages both visually and textually. In its eclectic aesthetic, the project will mine the resources of an artistic network, soliciting writing and imagery via the internet. Through this collaborative process, it will attempt to build a sense of community. In its interactive form, the project will offer its audience a sense of agency. The resulting product will provide an alternative to the tidy packaging of fairy tales by media corporations.[16]

The narrative that she created along with the images was published in *Marvels & Tales* as "Barebones," and it has a distinctly feminist perspective intended to animate a response from viewers. The first part reads:

once there was
and once there was not
a little girl named
vasalisa
vasalisa
vassalissa

wassilisa
she was the sweetest thing,
a really
REALLY
good girl.
Her mother dressed her in the perfect
good-little-girl-little-outfit
with a black skirt and a white apron,
a white blouse and a red vest
all embroidered
and painstakingly
designed.

On her feet, Vasalisa wore little red boots.
On her head:
a scarf
decorated with colorful patterns
that had been passed (with viral ferocity)
from generation
to generation
was tied
babuska-style
beneath her chin.
Her long braids twisted like DNA down her back.
Her mother loved her very much,
doted on her
wished she might stay this
sweet and doll-like forever.[17]

This passage is part of the first node of a series of nodes that constitute the text and images of Rock's version of "Vasalisa the Brave," the good Russian girl, who suffers humiliation after humiliation in her quest for self-respect and autonomy. But does she really gain self-respect and autonomy in a marriage with a prince? Will she be free of abuse in her marriage? Will she be recognized for who she is? Is there truly a happy ending to her suffering? If so, why do we keep revisiting this story? Why is it so infectious?

If we take together all the thousands if not hundreds of thousands of endeavors (many of the oral kind) that pertain to "Cinderella," can we speak of a "Cinderella epidemic" today? Or is it more appropriate to speak about a "Cinderella complex," which Colette Dowling in 1981 called "a network of largely repressed attitudes and fears that keeps women in a kind of half-light, retreating from the full use of their minds and creativity. Like Cinderella, women today are still waiting for something external to 'transform their lives.'"[18] But is Cinderella really passive? If we recall, in two of the earliest literary versions of "Cinderella," Giambattista Basile's "Cat Cinderella" (1634) and Mme. d'Aulnoy's "Finette Cendron" (1698), she did not hesitate to kill to get what she wanted, and even in the Grimms' version, she takes an active role by provoking her discovery through an ostensive act as does the heroine of many of the "Donkey Skin" tales. So, I have my doubts as to whether the thousands or hundreds of thousands of "Cinderella" tales constitute a "Cinderella complex." It might be more pertinent to discuss them in relation to what some psychologists have called the "Cinderella syndrome," in discussing how foster daughters have used the tale to attract attention to their maltreatment by their foster parents.[19] But the question that the Cinderella discourse opens up, perhaps the underlying relevance of the tales from the very beginning, concerns child abuse or infanticide, which many of our canonical fairy tales touch upon—something that really should not come as a surprise to us.

THE TRUTH ABOUT CINDERELLA

In a recent study, *The Truth about Cinderella: A Darwinian View of Parental Love*, Martin Daly and Margo Wilson maintain that there is nothing special about the European tradition of stories about wicked stepmothers and stepfathers who unjustly mistreat their stepchildren. "Innocent children are victimized by vicious, neglectful, exploitative stepmothers and stepfathers all over the world. Cinderella's domestic situation is iconic."[20] Indeed, there is an iconic constellation that pertains to familial relations where there is a stepmother or stepfather. Daly and Wilson demonstrate that there is something about the human condition, a genetic disposition, which explains why biological parents are more inclined to treat their children with more kindness and love than stepparents give their stepchildren. In fact, Daly and Wilson are not afraid to talk about stepfamily dysfunction, and they raise significant questions directly related to the spread of the "Cinderella" tale:

> What are the simple epidemiological facts about problems in one family circumstance versus another? Do children really incur risks of various sorts when one parent dies or departs and the remaining parent takes a new partner? And if so, to what degree: are we talking about a slight elevation of risk, or something more dramatic? These would seem to be rather obvious questions for research, but as we shall see, they have been surprisingly neglected. And that is unfortunate, because it turns out that the risk differentials are immense.[21]

Daly and Wilson explore the behavioral patterns of animals and humans to show that there are certain striking similarities in situations that involve nongenetic parents. Animals, particularly the males, will not exert energy or emotions to look after offspring that are not their own and in some cases will kill the offspring. The major factor that contributes to this abusive behavior is related to the allocation of resources. In the case of humans, parents often resent obligations to children who are not their own, and they generally will not take time and spend energy in guaranteeing their survival, which may threaten their own genetic lineage. For the most part they do not provide them with the same care and love that they would provide their genetic children. Daly and Wilson reveal that the risk factor for child abuse is greater in families with stepparents than in those with two genetic parents, and this situation is widespread and has probably existed for centuries. As they explain:

> Step-parents do not, on average, feel the same child-specific love and commitment as genetic parents, and therefore do not reap the same emotional rewards from unreciprocated "parental" investment. Enormous differentials in the risk of violence are just one, particularly dramatic, consequence of this predictable difference in feelings. The Darwinian process favours attributes that contribute to their own proliferation relative to alternatives. That's *all* that it favours, all it *can* favour. It follows that the motives, emotions, attentional priorities, and so forth—have

been shaped by the process of natural selection to be effective means to the ends of personal and kin reproductive success. In this light, we may expect the psychology of parental solicitude in any species to be designed to allocate parental investment discriminatively, in ways that will promote the individual parent's genetic posterity (inclusive fitness).[22]

Although Daly and Wilson cannot provide absolute "truth" that stepparents and dysfunctional families are at the basis of the Cinderella tales and form a kind of Cinderella syndrome or discourse, they do enable us, I believe, to grasp how and why "Cinderella" is contagious and has spread and will continue to spread in different forms in the twenty-first century. If we accept the notion that humans are genetically disposed toward discriminating in loving and rearing their own biological children, and if we also accept that environmental stimuli such as family formation and cultural representations, in particular, tales about stepchildren and their parents, play a role in the manner in which we store, remember, and retell relevant material for cognition and adaptation, then it is not difficult to grasp why "Cinderella," as mental and cultural representation and part of a relevant oral and literary genre that has been accepted and developed "memetically" over the past five centuries, has such a profound meaning for contemporary society. We live at a time when there are numerous divorces, numerous families with stepchildren and stepparents, numerous dysfunctional families, and a high rate of child abuse. "Cinderella" as imaginative narrative does not mince words but uses words and images to tell things as they are, or as they might potentially develop for stepchildren—with hope that we can understand and overcome abuse. But does it tell the whole story?

As Daly and Wilson point out, most abuse in stepfamilies is caused by the stepfather, not the wicked stepmother. If this is the case, why is the stepmother singled out as the wicked character in the tales? Daly and Wilson suggest that more women died from childbirth before the twentieth century and that there were more families with women as stepmothers. There are also some other reasons. It is well known that the Brothers Grimm changed many biological mothers to stepmothers because they did not want to cast disrespect on their own mother or mothers in general. Moreover, one could also argue that, though the father figure in Cinderella tales up to the present does not physically harm his daughter, he does contribute to her suffering through benign neglect and abandonment. Generally speaking, he does nothing to help her or to protect her. If anything he enables the stepmother and stepsisters to exploit Cinderella and to degrade her. In other words, he contributes to the abuse by absenting himself from his daughter's side. Clearly, though one may interpret "Cinderella" in other ways, its primary theme concerns child abandonment and abuse. The tale asks from the very beginning: What will happen to a child when her mother dies and the father remarries? It is a question that is also asked by the "Donkey-Skin" tales, closely related to the Cinderella discourse, and there, of course, the issue of incest and abuse by the biological father is raised.

If "Cinderella" caught on centuries ago, that is, took root in different ways in the minds of numerous people in Europe, was remembered through word of mouth and print, and became contagious and stuck, it was, I contend, because it was addressing issues of child abandonment, family legacy, sibling rivalry, and parental love. Many of these contested areas or issues remain with us, or they have been transformed in some way. Though the more traditional versions of Perrault's and Grimms' "Cinderella" continue to be replicated, there have been highly significant transformations that signal shifts in perspective with regard to abused stepchildren. Moreover, even the "traditional" Cinderella tales still speak to a predicament in stepfamilies that has not been resolved and perhaps may never be. Consequently, this "strain" of the fairy-tale tradition will continue to spread. But what are some of the alternatives to the Perrault and Grimm versions? Are they more pertinent for the twenty-first century? Do they offer more hope?

CONTEMPORARY CINDERELLAS

There appear to be two distinct tendencies in the transmission of "Cinderella" texts in the 1990s and the early part of the twenty-first century that indicate how writers will continue to transform and adapt the basic plot about an abused or unwanted child as survivor: the picture books and stories included in anthologies for very young readers between five and ten do not alter the traditional narrative very much; the stories and novels for readers ten and above, especially those intended for young adult and adult readers, make dramatic changes in the plot and often focus on aspects unrelated to abuse or they minimize the issue of abuse. Of course, it is difficult to discuss all the texts and illustrations that have been produced during the past fifteen years, and consequently I will comment only on some select examples from the two groups I have mentioned. In each case I will deal with books that are, in my opinion, indicative of tendencies that will have a bearing on the development of the fairy-tale genre as a whole.

In analyzing the recent epidemic of "Cinderella" picture books, the first question that comes to mind is: Why so many when there is so much duplication? The answer here is obvious. The publishing industry is based on a competitive market, and each company, large and small, wants to capitalize on the memetic fame of Cinderella. The result is that there are numerous mass-market cheap "Cinderella" books that repeat the same message. Perhaps the most popular text or icon today is that of Disney's *Cinderella*, which continues to float throughout the world in various viral forms. It is probably not an exaggeration to assert that millions of children will grow up exposed to some form of the traditional "Cinderella" narrative, often a mix of the Perrault, Grimm, and Disney versions, and even the revised texts and pictures that contest or question the conventional plot and forms that rely on the basic motif of the abused stepchild or orphan. Here are some examples of how different books begin more or less the same and end on a harmonious note.

> Once upon a time a sweet pig named Ella lived with her father. Then Father Pig got married again. His new wife and her two daughters were very mean. Father Pig was a traveling salesman and was away from the ranch more days than he was home. So Ella got all the meanness those steppies dished out.[23]
>
> Now lis'en. Smack in the heart o' the Smoky Mountains, there was this old trapper livin' in a log cabin with his daughter. One night, while Rose was fryin' a mess o' fish, the trapper, he starts lookin' dejected-like.
>
> "I reckon it's hard on ye, not havin' a ma," he said. "Tell me, Rose would ye lak me to git hitched again? There's a widow woman with

two daughters down the road a piece. Way I see it, we'd all fit together neater'n a jigsaw."

"I don't mind," said Rose, settin' a plate o' corn bread on the table. "You go a-courtin', Pa, if you think it's best."

So before the huckeberries was fit for pickin', the trapper got himself hitched for the second time. That's when the trouble started a-brewin'.[24]

Long ago in a cabin deep in the shadow of Eagle's Nest Mountain, lived a serving girl called Ashpet. She'd been hired out since she was a young girl to the Widow Hooper and her two daughters, Myrtle and Ethel. All day long the Hooper women thought of chores for Ashpet to do, "After you're done washin' up, there's firewood that wants bustin', and our supper to cook. And don't forget to tend to the animals."

Now Ethel and Myrtle were as ugly as they were lazy, but Ashpet was fresh-faced and regular featured. Those two girls were so jealous that whenever anyone came to their cabin, they stuck Ashpet under a washtub. And they never let her go anywhere.[25]

Once upon a time there lived a fine gentleman who had a beautiful home on St. Charles Avenue in New Orleans. He had one child, a daughter. She was *très belle*! He gave her all that he could buy and spoiled her terribly because she had no mother. The little girl did wish for a mother and her *père* knew this. So he married a woman with two daughters, hoping it would make his *petite fille* happy. The new *belle-mère* had not been married one day when she became very jealous of her husband's child. She gave her stepdaughter all the hard and dirty work to do while her own daughters pampered themselves all day long.[26]

Long, long ago in the land of Cambodia, there lived a lonely fisherman and his daughter, Angkat. Their riverside home in a quiet inlet was sheltered by waving palms. Being dutiful and obedient, Angkat was the joy of her father's life.

Beyond the fisherman's pond there lived a widow and her daughter, Kantok. She was a girl of great beauty but had no redeeming qualities.

While cleaning his fish ponds one day the lonely fisherman and the widow met. They were soon married. The minute Angkat and Kantok became stepsisters the new wife insisted that her daughter be known as Number One daughter in the family. That was the most important of family distinctions.

Angkat protested, "But I am my father's daughter, and I am entitled to be the Number One child!" Discontentment filled the air and in no time at all, there was little peace in the new family.[27]

There once lived a fisherman whose wife had drowned, leaving him with a small daughter named Maha. Nearby lived a widow with her own young daughter. Every day she went to the fisherman's house to care for Maha, and every day she said, "You poor motherless child! I love you like my own."

"Father," begged the girl, "You should marry our good neighbor so you won't have to cook your own food or mend your own clothes, and then I can have a mother and a sister."

Her father stroked her hair. "Ah little one, I shall never marry, for stepmothers are often jealous of another's child."

But Maha continued to beg, and by and by the fisherman and the neighbor were married.

At first all went well, but as time passed the woman saw how much the fisherman loved his daughter. She saw how lovely and clever the girl was, and how pale and clumsy her own daughter seemed in comparison. As the months went by, Maha was forced to do more and more of the work, and during the day when the fisherman was gone, her stepmother fed her nothing but a few dried dates.[28]

Once there was a rancher who married for his second wife the orneriest woman west of the Mississippi. She was meaner than a rattlesnake, and she had two daughters who were the spitting image of her. The rancher also had a daughter, who was just as sweet and gentle as she could be. Her name was Cindy Ellen.

Cindy was a pretty good cowgirl, too. Riding her little gray horse, she wrangled and roped and galloped and loped with the best buckaroos on the range

But as soon as the wedding was over, that snaky old stepmother began to pick on poor Cindy Ellen. She was so good she made her step sisters look bad. So her stepmother made her do all the dirty work around the ranch.[29]

At the far edge of Baba Yaga's forest there lived a mean-spirited woman with her two ill-tempered daughters and her stepdaughter, Vasilisa. Whereas the other girls were cruel and ugly, Vasilisa was kindness itself and beautiful beyond measure.

Vasilisa's mother had died when the girl was quite young. Her father had soon remarried, more for the child's sake than for his own, believing his daughter should have a mother's love as she grew up. But while his intentions were for the good, the results were sadly the opposite.[30]

In two Native American story books, *Sootface: An Ojibwa Cinderella Story* by Robert San Souci and *The Rough-Face Girl* by Rafe Martin, the initial situation concerns a widower with three daughters, and the two eldest maltreat the youngest so that her face becomes marred. In another unusual Native American version, *The Turkey Girl: A Zuni Cinderella Story* by Penny Pollock, an orphaned girl, who does not keep her promise to magical turkeys, is left in rags at the end of the tale. But, for the most part, no matter how extraordinary or ethnic the storybook may be, the abused girl (and sometimes it is a boy) generally triumphs in the end. For instance, in Jude Daly's *Fair, Brown and Trembling*, the tale begins in a similar way to the Native American versions, but in a different setting:

> Once upon a time, high among the green hills of Erin, there stood a castle. In it lived a widower and his three daughters: Fair, Brown, and Trembling. Fair and Brown always wore new dresses to church on Sundays. Trembling stayed at home. "You must do the cooking," said her sisters. But the real reason they would not let her out of the house was because Trembling was very beautiful, and they were terrified she would marry before they did. (1)

Of course, Trembling is helped by the henwife to appear in magnificent array at the church door every Sunday. The Prince of Emania pursues her and defeats some other princes to marry her. The tale ends on this "bright" note: "In time they had fourteen children, and they lived ever after in great happiness. As for Fair and Brown … they were put out to sea in a barrel with provisions for seven years—and were never seen again!" (24–25).

Now whether having fourteen children brings happiness or causing your sisters to die is fair punishment is something for readers to decide. What is interesting is that this "Irish tale," based on Jeremiah Curtin's *Myths and Folk-lore of Ireland*, was written and illustrated by the *South African* artist Jude Daly. Many of the writers of the storybooks have the ostensible objective to recapture and restore some kind of ethnic

and national tradition and will endeavor to legitimate the effort by cit-
ing historical sources at the beginning of narrative or as an afterword.
While the intentions may be sincere, they are misleading, for the writers cannot and do not have the foggiest notion of how and why these
tales were relevant or significant in their original traditions. Nor can
they contribute to an ongoing folk tradition. What the writers are cultivating, however, is a literary, oral, and iconic tradition that focuses on
the treatment of stepchildren, orphans, foster children, or the youngest
child in a family. And their narratives have a bearing on how we will
remember and record the Cinderella-like versions in the future.

The picture books, despite apparent differences, have more or less
the same outline: a widower remarries after his wife dies. He recedes
into the background or vanishes after the marriage and permits his only
daughter to be maltreated by her stepmother and stepsisters. The soiled
girl, often given a degrading nickname, lacks love, protection, and guidance. She seeks help from another powerful female figure (perhaps her
dead mother) who provides her with the resources to regain her self-
respect and establish her true identity through marriage to a wealthy
prince. She can find love and become a beloved object. What is striking
about most of these lovely or humorous illustrated children's books is
that the stepmothers and stepdaughters or sisters are depicted as wicked
and terrifying. The fathers are mostly well intentioned and disappear
from the story. The key agent of power lies with a magical female who
intervenes to assist the downtrodden girl and make her feel loved.

This plot or constellation is altered greatly in most of the works for
young adults and adults, but the writers of stories, novellas, and novels
for older readers assume a deep knowledge of the traditional narrative
about Cinderella. In fact, they depend upon this relevant knowledge
as though it were part of the reading audience's material experiences, as
though they were already disposed to the tale. Therefore, they feel free
to experiment in ways that the producers of storybooks do not feel they
can take poetic license. Here I should like to cite some examples by Gail
Carson Levine, Philip Pullman, Priscilla Galloway, Francesca Lia Block,
Emma Donoghue, Gregory Maguire, and Mavis Jukes.

Levine, Pullman, and Galloway all shift the focus from a girl to a
boy in novel ways. Levine, who has written a series of princess tales for

readers between the ages of seven and twelve, introduces a young farm-hand named Ellis who lives with his two brothers, Ralph and Burt, in an imaginary kingdom of Biddle. Evidently they are orphans, and Ellis is called Cinderellis because one of his inventions with flying powder backfired, and he became covered with soot and ashes from a chimney. Ellis is always trying to win the attention and respect of his two plod-ding brothers, but they neglect him, and he suffers from loneliness, as does Princess Marigold, who has no mother and whose father is always away on quests. Eventually, the father realizes his daughter is ready for marriage, and he prepares a contest to determine what knight might marry her. The king has a glass mountain built, and whoever can climb it on a horse can have Marigold for a bride. With the help of three magi-cal horses and powder, Cinderellis accomplishes the task.

Levine's narrative is comical and not to be taken very seriously. The problem faced by Ellis and Marigold, two humble and innocent char-acters who ooze sweetness, is loneliness and neglect, and once they encounter each other, it is clear they will no longer need their brothers or father to live happily ever after. This is certainly not the case with Roger in Pullman's *I Was a Rat!*, which has more tragic-comic overtones than Levine's trivial story. In this novel, a grubby young boy dressed in a tattered page's uniform appears out of nowhere on the doorstep of a cobbler's shop at ten in the evening. An old couple named Bob and Joan provides him with shelter and care. When he tells them he does not have a name, they are puzzled and explain to him what it means to have a name. Bob and Joan do not realize that Roger, the name they bestow upon him, was once Cinderella's page and had indeed been a rat, but somehow the fairy godmother had not retransformed him into a rat. In his human condition Roger must learn what it means to be civilized, but at the same time, he is bent on proving to Bob and Joan that he truly was a rat. Indeed, he cannot prevent himself from acting like a rat in certain situations. What follows is a series of tragic-comic episodes in which Roger's rodent behavior is greeted with punishment and horror by the adult world. Newspaper reports about his "dangerous" behavior are interspersed in the novel, and they create mass hysteria as they portray Roger as a monster. But he is merely a kind-hearted inno-cent who has great difficulty learning proper English expressions and manners and is completely misunderstood by the world around him. Only Princess Aurelia, who was once Cinderella, can help prove that he is not a subhuman fiend or a venom-dipping beast from the nethermost pit of hell, but just a normal little fellow. In the end, Roger gives up his quest to be a rat again because he might be exterminated by people driven to hysteria by the mass media. Though he says it's difficult being a person, he's willing to become a cobbler/craftsman like Bob. So Roger stays with Bob and Joan, and Pullman ends the novel with sweet irony: "The world outside was a difficult place, but toasted cheese and love and craftsmanship would do to keep them safe."[31]

Safe from whom, one must ask. Safe from society? Safe from the media? Safe from the forces of "civilization"? Roger's tale is very reminiscent of the profound true story of the nineteenth-century Casper Hauser, whose life has been the subject of plays and novels. This young man appeared one day in a German village out of the blue and could not speak or write. He had been mysteriously confined in a house in the woods until his late adolescence. When the well-intentioned people of the town discovered the young "savage," they tried to "civilize" him and eventually caused his death. In Pullman's novel, Roger is ironically a Cinderella figure, who learns that he will be victimized in society for appearing to be different and wanting to prove this difference. He does not triumph in the end. Rather he withdraws and seeks refuge from a world that misunderstands him. He merely survives.

Another male figure in a Cinderella tale, "The Prince," by Priscilla Galloway also feels misunderstood, and he recounts his story in a first-person narrative that reveals just how obnoxious he is. From the very first paragraph it is clear that we are dealing with a highly neurotic and narcissistic character: "Guilt. Guilt. Guilt. My analyst keeps telling me I need to work out my feelings of guilt. Such nonsense. My mother died when I was born. I killed her. My father kept provoking wars so that he'd have to go away and fight them because he couldn't stand the sight of me, and no wonder, always reminding him."[32] In the course of his self-indulgent story we learn that he has had a homosexual affair with Stephen, his tutor, who was put to death by the prince's father because of his disapproval of the relationship. In fact, he orders a ball and commands the prince to choose a wife, or the king will choose one for him.

The prince vows he will not marry, but he dances with a princess with glass slippers, and her toes remind him of Stephen, his former lover, and the foot fetish he had. When the young lady rushes away from him, he is left with a glass slipper and is obsessed with finding her.

Galloway's provocative narrative is concerned with obsession and self-absorption. We learn nothing about Cinderella but all about a pathetic prince. The implications are clear: if this prince is what Cinderella can expect, she will have nothing but trouble for the rest of her life. Galloway's intriguing first-person narrative reveals the ambivalence of the happy ending of most Cinderella narratives. We know nothing about the prince except for his foot fetish.

In Emma Donoghue's "The Tale of the Shoe," we have another first-person narrative, but this time it is Cinderella's voice that we hear, and it is the voice of an awakening and a new beginning. In grief about her mother's death, the unnamed young woman endeavors to deal with her sorrow through work: "Nobody made me do the things I did, nobody scolded me, nobody punished me but me. The shrill voices were all inside. Do this, do that, you lazy heap of dirt. They knew every question and answer, the voices in my head. Some days they asked why I was still alive. I listened out for my mother, but I couldn't hear her among their clamor."[33] Fortunately, one day a stranger appears, a friend of her mother, who describes herself as from her mother's tree, and indeed, she provides the support and comfort that the young woman needs. She enables her to attend three balls until the young girl realizes she is in love with the older woman, and she throws the other shoe that she did not lose at the ball into the woods to leave for home with the strange woman. Donoghue's story is a coming of age fairy tale that celebrates the self-awareness of a young woman and love that she feels for another woman.

This story is repeated with a slightly different emphasis in Francesca Lia Block's "Glass." Told in a third-person narrative, a young woman who is somewhat inhibited and likes to stay at home, clean, and tell stories to her sister, meets a strange woman with red and white hair, young and old, who begins to speak to her in whispers. She said:

> You cannot hide forever, though you may try. I've seen you in the kitchen, in the garden. I've seen the things you have sewn—curtains of dawn,

twilight blankets and dresses for the sisters like a garden of stars. I have heard the stories you tell. You are the one who transforms, who creates. You can go out into the world and show others. They will feel less alone because of you, they will feel understood, unburdened by you, awakened by you, freed of guilt and shame and sorrow. But to share with them you must wear shoes you must go out you must not hide you must dance and it will be harder you must face jealousy and sometimes rage and desire and love which can hurt most of all because of what can then be taken away. So make that astral dress to fit your own body this time. And here are glass shoes made from your words, the stories you have told like a blower with her torch forming the thinnest, most translucent sheets of light out of what was once sand.[34]

This passage reads like a pep talk, and it is, for Block's story is trite: it waxes sentimental about a young woman who incurs the jealousy of her sisters because she dares to come out of herself and win the attraction of a prince. When she realizes that her sisters despise her because of the attention that the prince shows her, she runs away, loses her shoe, and deprecates herself at home. However, the prince pursues because he recognizes her for what she is, and his love for her draws her out for good. So Block's coming of age tale is a more traditional heterosexual version of love than Donoghue's more unusual lesbian version. What is important in each case is that two women authors focus not so much on child abuse but on the need for love. The focus is on the self-affirmation of a young woman, who has been suffering from grief about a dead mother. The intervention of an older, powerful, wise woman in the form of a fairy godmother is the necessary impetus for self-discovery.

Such intervention does not occur in Gregory Maguire's compelling novel, *Confessions of an Ugly Stepsister*, one of the more graphic Cinderella novels about wicked stepmothers and child abuse to have appeared in recent years. Maguire sets his story in the small city of Haarlem in seventeenth-century Holland, and he has a great eye for capturing the customs and living conditions of the time. His narrative concerns the return of the widow Margarethe Fisher from England with her two daughters, Ruth, an awkward but gentle mute, and Iris, a plain but gifted and compassionate girl. Fierce in her determination to protect her daughters and to provide a livelihood for her daughters, Margarethe finds a job as a servant for a master painter and then as head of the van den Meer household, where Irene is giving English lessons to a beautiful and anxious girl named Clara, who had been abducted and saved from her kidnappers when she was a child. Because of this incident, she never leaves the premises, and her mother, Henrika, is overly protective. When Henrika becomes pregnant, her health declines, and she dies in childbirth as does her baby. We later learn that she was poisoned by Margarethe, and of course, it is Margarethe who takes over the household and marries Cornelius van den Meer. From this point on she rules the domestic affairs of the house with an iron fist, and though Clara and her stepsisters are close and mutually supportive, Margarethe treats her with disdain and becomes obsessed with guaranteeing the business success of her new husband and the rise of her own daughters in society. However, everything she does and touches is eventually ruined. Her new husband's business goes bankrupt; Clara rebels against her and becomes an ash girl who refuses to leave the kitchen; Ruth becomes more and more petulant; and Iris becomes torn as she tries to keep the peace in the family and pursue her own interests in painting. When the Dowager Queen of France comes and a ball is held in her honor and the honor of the Prince of Marsillac, Iris convinces the beautiful Clara to attend and help save the family. She succeeds, and while Clara and the prince have a moment of intimacy, Ruth burns a portrait of Clara in a desperate act to help her mother and starts a fire at the ball, a catastrophe that brings an end to her mother's machinations. But this is not a happy ending, for we learn in an epilogue, surprisingly told by Ruth, who was not as slow and vacant as she appeared to be, that Clara leaves Haarlem with the prince and eventually ends up in New York, where she dies. Iris marries a painter and dies at a young age. The wicked mother/stepmother Margarethe, though blind, lives on without remorse.

In fact, Maguire's novel is concerned with the immortality of this stepmother, who is the driving force behind the action of the novel. He is not dismissive of the stepmother figure, nor is he judgmental. The entire narrative, in fact, is construed to represent Ruth's viewpoint, and while her tone is terse and her perspective frank, she has empathy for her mother, as though this was the way life was back then, this was the way my mother acted to enable us to survive if not prosper. Margarethe's motives were no different from those of the others in "good" society.

So, Ruth's "confession" is a true story mainly about her mother and her ambitious striving to make sure that her own genetic daughters would have a better life. She acts out of desperation and tries to overcome poverty by any means she can just as the Dutch merchants ruthlessly deal with one another in the town of Haarlem. It is a dog-eat-dog world that Maguire depicts, and it is no surprise that the crude and domineering Margarethe is not punished in the end but lives on and will haunt future Cinderella tales.

It is clear that stepmothers like Margarethe will continue to haunt Cinderella narratives so long as there is no magical intervention and so long as there is no real intervention in dysfunctional families. In Mavis Jukes's *Cinderella 2000: Looking Back* (1999), a novel for young readers ten and up, we have an instance of intervention by a "fairy godmother" granny, but it represents more of a regressive step than a step forward into the twenty-first century. In this frivolous novel, which takes place in California, fourteen-year-old Ashley Ella Toral, who has lost both her mother and father, is being raised by her zany irresponsible stepmother Phyllis, who has mean and preposterously nasty twelve-year-old twins, Paige and Jessica. Phyllis can control neither the twins nor herself. Ashley is the only sane person in this household, and she is looking forward to ushering in the year 2000 at the Ocean Crest Country Club and beginning a relationship with the handsome Trevor Cranston. The twins, who have no redeeming qualities whatsoever, and Phyllis, who is a caricature of a flighty, well-meaning, but incompetent mother/stepmother, are threatening to ruin Ashley's dreams until Phyllis's mother arrives from Florida and takes Ashley's side. Coincidentally, she has just won the lottery, and she uses her money and wisdom to enable Ashley to drive to a ball in a limousine with Trevor. And so, it appears that life in 2000 will be happy for Ashley.

Yet, such a revision of the Cinderella story does not augur happiness for young girls (or boys) who are seeking to sort out problems with their siblings and parents or to deal with problems of identity and sexuality in the teenage years. Jukes places too much emphasis on material things and money as means that will help Ashley to become more confident and content with her disastrous situation. The arrival of a savvy grandmother who just happens to have extraordinary power and insight into her situation is a deus ex machina that might work in fairy tales, but it is contrived and simplistic in this novel that makes a mockery out of previous endeavors by writers who have seriously explored the ravaging effects that humiliation and abuse might have for a young girl. There is, of course, always a role for parody and comedy in Cinderella revisions, but Jukes's novel is a contrived romance that relies too much on caricature and stereotypical roles so that the humor of the situation falls flat.

Jukes's *Cinderella 2000* is insignificant but not irrelevant. Its relevance is constituted by the motivation of the writer to communicate something new about a disadvantaged fourteen-year-old orphan who must submit to intolerable living conditions with her stepmother and stepsisters; by the intention of the writer to make something aesthetically and ideologically unique out of a narrative that we recognize as belonging to a particular strain of the fairy-tale genre; by the format in which the text is produced and distributed; by the reception of the text among the intended readers; and by the social, aesthetic, and ideological functions it plays within the genre along with other comparable texts.

The irrelevance of *Cinderella 2000* is also relevant. If the text does not take root, does not make a mark, does not catch on, it will indicate that the information that is being communicated and the manner in which it is being communicated do not have a meaning for a particular culture in a certain historical context. This does not necessarily mean that the work of art is lacking, for it could be revived, or perhaps the timing is wrong. The fact that a text becomes a bestseller does not mean that it is a work of great literature. Relevance may have little to do with the intrinsic value of a work of art. What relevance reveals is that at a certain point in time, relevant information necessary for cognition can be considered crucial for understanding social relations, for adaptation to changing conditions, and for changing the environment. The choices that we make when we seek to transform the world are intertwined with ethics, aesthetics, and politics. As we continue to form and re-form fairy tales in the twenty-first century, there is still a glimmer of utopian hope that a better past lies ahead, but more practically, a fairy tale like "Cinderella" replicated as meme reveals to us what we have not been able to resolve and how much more we need to know about the world and ourselves.

"Snow White"
Illustrator: Arthur Rackham

Chapter 4

The Moral Strains of
Fairy Tales and Fantasy

In the new view, human beings are a species splendid in their array of
moral equipment, tragic in their propensity to misuse it, and pathetic in
their constitutional ignorance of the misuse.

Robert Wright, *The Moral Animal* (1994)

I f the genre of the fairy tale has evolved like a virus through oral,
printed, and mass-mediated forms, it has succeeded because it
has developed various memes and strains that make the information within the narratives more relevant, effective, and contagious.
Folklorists generally prefer to discuss the spread of the various strains
of fairy tales by using the Aarne-Thompson tale-type catalog,[1] which is
indeed valuable and functional. But I believe that the descriptions of
the tale types are limited and often misleading. Nor do they indicate
anything about the meaning of the diverse types, why they spread, who
generates and spreads them, and how they become so culturally relevant
in different societies in the evolution of the genre. Instead of talking
about tale types, it is time now in the twenty-first century to take an
epidemiological approach and discuss the discursive strains of the fairy
tale and the moral and political motives behind and within the narratives as they assume various forms. Here I would like to summarize my
theses as I have developed them in previous chapters with an emphasis
on the moral strains of the fairy tale.

The Evolution of the Fairy Tale

Fairy tales have evolved as humans have evolved. I am tempted to say there has been a "survival of the fittest" that we sometimes designate as a classical canon. In the course of the past five centuries, approximately fifty to seventy-five tales have risen to the fore in the Western world and have been repeatedly retold in diverse forms—rarely in the same way, always adapting to the environment and circumstances in which they were generated. But they stick. There appear to be a certain propensity within human beings to reproduce some basic narratives, as though there were a "fairy-tale" gene within us that I have called a replicator, mental representation, or meme. There appears to be modules within our brains that make us more disposed and susceptible to the formation of distinct stories about basic human drives and conflicts. These stories touch our instincts so deeply that we have cultivated them and passed them on from generation to generation to further the reproduction of our species in our own interests and to help us adapt to, know, and transform our changing environment.

It has taken fairy-tale strains hundreds of years to reach a stable form, a kind of equilibrium, and this stabilization occurred in the modern European period between the fifteenth and nineteenth centuries about the time new technologies and the rise of literacy facilitated the dissemination of tales. The evolution of the fairy tale has parallels with the evolution of cultural transformations. This was the period in which the printing press was invented, vernacular languages became standardized, and thus tales could be preserved more efficiently. The oral tales could be marked down. Humans could leave their markings much in the same manner that animals do, except that there was a moral and political relevance to the markings.

In the case of literary fairy tales, it is clear that their hybrid formation was intimately tied to the manner in which human beings sought to articulate their thoughts and feelings about everyday life, crucial information about conflicts, and possible solutions to these conflicts. In this regard, fairy tales have always been part of culture or a civilizing process. They incorporate a moral code that reflects upon the basic instincts of the human being as a moral animal and suggest ways to channel these instincts for personal and communal happiness. This moral component of the fairy tales does not mean that the proposed morals or norms are good. Every moral code in every society is constituted by the most powerful groups in a community or nation-state and serves their vested interests. What the fairy tale does—and it does this perhaps more efficiently and effectively than any other genre—is represent basic human dilemmas in tangible metaphorical forms that reflect how difficult it is for us to curb basic instincts. Fairy tales are all about basic instincts and genetic evolution within a civilizing process.

We have already seen that "Cinderella" reveals and explores the propensity of stepparents or substitute parents to abuse, abandon, neglect, or kill their nonbiological children. This propensity is connected to a basic human drive to invest love, time, and energy in children that are biologically reproduced to carry on one's species. Stepparents and stepchildren—if not society at large—are faced with moral choices when placed in "unnatural" situations, that is, situations that can lead to the undermining of their self-interests. This is why moral codes are important. This is why tales are told to prepare and inform us about the unexpected. And the more universal the style and format of a particular tale type, the greater the applicability and the better the chances that the story will continue to remain relevant. Thus, the narrative kernel of "Cinderella" serves as the basis for a never-ending discursive formation of similar stories retold and reenacted millions of times through word of mouth, print, theatrical performance, radio, cinema, video, toys, and the Internet.

With each retelling the tale touches on basic instincts and moral codes and also adapts itself to the environment in which it is produced. The moral code will influence how a particular artist or group of artists will endeavor to readdress the dilemma of stepparents and stepchildren, for there are multiple ways to live harmoniously in "unnatural" relations. Perhaps the term undesirable would be better than unnatural. No biological parent or child desires to be abandoned or obliged to live with a "stranger." It is extremely difficult to integrate oneself or to be integrated into a family or tribe with which one does not have kinship. We have always been somewhat conflicted about how we are supposed to or ought to conduct ourselves in such a process.

Fairy tales popularize the conflicts we humans have as moral animals. Such tales were always popular. By that, I mean belonging to the *popolo*, the people, rich and poor, educated and non-literate, good and bad. There was never a time in the modern period when these tales or like-tales were not disseminated, although religious castes and ruling classes tried to censor them or distance themselves from these "frivolous" or "crude" tales. But these tales have stuck. Not only have they stuck in our bodies and memories, but they have spread with good reason. They address and readdress the animal/human conflict within us and within a civilizing process that has formed a code of principles and precepts based both on arbitrary rules and practical experience.

What else is "Snow White" about but a stepmother's basic inclination to eliminate a daughter who is not hers and a father's lack of invest-ment in his daughter because she will not necessarily guarantee him the reproduction of his species? Indeed, after the death of Snow White's mother, he has another wife who will bear him offspring and does not have to pay much attention to his daughter. What else is "Beauty and the Beast" about but the molding and grooming of a young woman so that she can (despite danger to herself) pursue a proper mate of quality who will guarantee her the reproduction of her species? Why else does the miller exploit his only daughter but to advance himself and progeny in the eyes of the king? What else is at the bottom of tales such as "How Six Made Their Way in the World" and "Six Servants" but a basic drive for retribution or tit-for-tat because a powerful king has not displayed compassion or the proper altruistic attitude? Put another way by the comic book and film *The X-Men*, how can we use our extraordinary powers to rectify the evil in the world through a display of moral altru-ism? What else is the meaning of tales such as "Belle-Belle" or "Mulan" but a demonstration of how a higher intelligence can unite extraordi-nary natural forces to benefit civilization and humanity?

All these tales are currently being reproduced primarily in the United States and United Kingdom but always with the aim for replication and reproduction on a global scale. There are literally hundreds if not thou-sands produced and adapted for modern human sensibilities. The adap-tations—or perhaps mutations might be the better word—are linked to mutable genetic dispositions and changing social and political orders, and they reveal differences in moral attitudes toward family, the rearing of children, sexuality, and politics that have evolved during the twentieth century, and I also want to focus on some recent adaptations to assess what these tales may signify about the "civilizing" and aesthetic value of fairy tales and fantasy and how we envision possible solutions to a postmodern world that has made a mockery of absolute truths and rightful and righteous behavior. I am interested in examining the discursive strains of the fairy tale, how individual artists are using them for their own self-interests, how the market exploits them for its interest, and how and why young and old readers might favorably receive them as part of their popular culture. There are many works I could choose to study, but to make my argument as concise as possible, I shall deal with a limited number of tales and films that are related to the classical canon of fairy tales: Tanith Lee's *White as Snow*, Donna Jo Napoli's *Beast*, Disney's *Mulan*, and DC Comics' *The X-Men*.

SNOW WHITE

Like "Cinderella," the tale of "Snow White" has engendered a plethora of many different versions in the past ten years including two important film versions, Tom Davenport's *Willa: An American Snow White* (1996) and Michael Cohn's *Snow White: A Tale of Terror* (1997) featuring Sigourney Weaver and Sam Neil as well as an important website by Kay Vandergrift.[2] This tale appears to be similar in its concerns to "Cinderella." After all, a mother dies following childbirth, and her innocent daughter is persecuted by her stepmother. There are, however, too many oral and print versions of this tale that depict a *biological* mother as the abuser of her daughter and introduce different conflicts so that both "Cinderella" and "Snow White" have developed separate discursive strains within the fairy-tale genre. The tale touches on a number of basic issues that reflect universal instinctual struggles among women and grave moral predicaments that originated thousands of years ago. The fierce, primeval conflict between women clearly made this tale relevant for families, tribes, and communities many years before it began to take shape in literary form in the late eighteenth and early nineteenth centuries. Let us recall that the manuscript version of the Brothers Grimm titled "Little Snow White" ("Schneewitchen," 1810) concerned a "godless" mother who seeks to kill her daughter because the child becomes more beautiful than she herself is. Out of a deep-seated jealousy, stirred by a magic mirror, the queen concocts a plot that ends in her own hideous death. Like all the Grimms' classical tales, "Snow White" has been the subject of numerous valid and sometimes insipid interpretations. In my opinion, the most revealing psychological analysis of the tale is the chapter in Sandra Gilbert and Susan Gubar's *Madwoman in the Attic*, because it enables us to grasp why the tale is so contagious and demands rigorous moral thinking on the part of listeners and readers.

Gilbert and Gubar argue that the tale dramatizes "the essential but equivocal relationship between the angel-woman and the monster-woman" of Western patriarchy: "The central action of the tale—indeed its only real action—arises from the relationship between these two women: the one fair, young, pale, the other just as fair, but older, fiercer; the one a daughter, the other a mother; the one sweet, ignorant, passive, the other artful and active; the one a sort of angel, the other an undeniable witch."³ Gilbert and Gubar strongly suggest, as do many other feminists, that the competition between the two women results from a patriarchal culture that pits woman against woman for the favor of a male. In other words, it would appear that women are victimized under social conditions beyond their control. Though there may be a great deal of truth to this point, especially in contemporary society, there is another aspect to the struggle between Snow White and her stepmother that needs to be addressed before turning to Tanith Lee's work, for there are some basic features in the Grimms' tale that reveal instinctual drives in women and infer that they are less victims than very much agents of their own destinies.

In his book, *The Moral Animal*, Robert Wright remarks:

[T]he gauging of a man's commitment does seem to be part of human female psychology. That male commitment is in limited supply—that each man has only so much time and energy to invest in offspring—is one reason females in our species defy stereotypes prevalent elsewhere in the animal kingdom. Females in *low*-MPI [male parental investment] species—that is, in most sexual species—have no great rivalry with one another. Even if dozens of them have their hearts set on a single, genetically optimal male, he can, and gladly will, fulfill their dreams; copulation doesn't take long. But in a high-MPI species such as ours, where a female's ideal is to *monopolize* her dream mate—steer his social and material resources toward her offspring—competition with other females is inevitable. In other words: high parental investment makes sexual selection work in two directions at once: Not only have males evolved to compete for scarce female eggs; females have evolved to compete for scarce male investment.[4]

If we assume that females are deeply concerned with finding the right male for reproduction and with producing children who will carry on the woman's genes, and that they will employ their traits to succeed and survive, we can see how relevant the message of "Snow White" is and how it raises important moral issues for culture. Let us recall the most classical 1857 Grimm version of "Snow White." The tale begins with a queen, who desires to have a child on whom she wants to bestow particular traits that will enable her offspring to survive—"a child as white as snow, as red as blood and as black as the wood of the window frame." She dies, and her child will be set in competition with another female, "a beautiful lady, but proud and arrogant and could not bear being second to anyone in beauty." Within the first two paragraphs, we have the seeds of a story dealing with competition and selection, and the relevance of the tale—the reason why it remains with us today and is passed on in a discursive strain—is marked by the manner in which females cope with one another to select or attract a male whom they consider worthy of their eggs.

In the case of "Snow White," it is clear that the new queen will want to have her own progeny, that she must maintain her status in her family and in the realm as the most beautiful woman, and that she will "naturally" seek to eliminate her competition. Snow White is dangerous competition, not only because her presence devalues the older queen's status, but because she foreshadows what will happen to the queen in a patriarchal society when she will no longer be beautiful and fertile. The queen acts on behalf of her genes, and the adolescent Snow White must be awakened in more ways than one to understand the climate that spurs women to compete viciously against one another for the favor of men. The moral of the story is capital punishment, if you will. But why should the queen be punished for doing what comes natural? One reason, of course, is that she did not comply with the moral code of her times. It is not right to attempt to murder your stepdaughter just because she threatens you. Another reason is that the moral code is predicated on male hegemony and thus ruthlessly punishes women who actively pursue their self-interests. But the morality of the tale has less to do with the punishment than with posing the dilemma that most women *feel* even today. How do you fulfill natural inclinations and attract a partner (either for reproduction or for sexual gratification) without killing off the competition that may undermine your self-interest?

The thousands of "Snow White" retellings and variants since the publication of the Grimms' tale testify to the fact that the dilemma cannot be easily solved and that the environment in which women have sought to adapt their natural inclinations to suit moral codes has not been conducive to minimizing competition. In fact, many writers indicate that the competition has become much fiercer and that younger women are initiating the rivalry and eliminating older women and even their mothers before the latter take the initiative. In Neil Gaiman's "Snow, Glass Apples," we have a provocative narrative told from the perspective of the queen stepmother, who does everything within her power to befriend her stepdaughter, who has demonic powers. Nothing works. So the queen resorts to having her killed and her heart taken from her. Yet, the stepdaughter recovers and returns with a vengeance to have her stepmother baked alive in an oven from which the queen tells her story.

TANITH LEE'S SNOW WHITE

Though the horror and brutality of this tale may seem somewhat exaggerated, it is nothing compared to three different versions by Tanith Lee. In "Red as Blood" (1983) Lee depicted a violent clash between stepmother and daughter that emphasized the raw brutality of the competition; in another short tale, "Snow-Drop" (1993), set in the contemporary period, a woman, who is frustrated in her marriage and frustrated with her art, kills a young circus performer. In both tales, the women appear to be driven by uncontrollable instincts that they do not understand and cannot control. In her most recent deliberation about the "Snow-White" constellation, Lee is even more radical in presenting the rapacious nature of human beings who appear to prey on one another. One has to wonder whether she sees any hope for the future of the species as civilized human beings, for there is very little to comfort readers in the way she weaves an elaborate tale about competition between women and the predatory instincts of men.

Lee's novel, *White as Snow* (2000), though based on the Demeter and Persephone myth and set somewhere in Italy during the first three centuries of the Christian era, concerns contemporary sexual and social relations. Let us not delude ourselves: every fairy tale and every work of fantasy written and published in our times is a metaphorical reflection about real conditions in our own societies, even when it pretends to be about a distant past or realm that has never existed. So it is with *White as Snow* and all the different versions of "Snow White," which inform us about consequences and moral choices that result from very particular behaviors.

In this instance, the initial situation in the novel determines how a mother and daughter relate to each other and to their environment. Arpazia, a young princess of seventeen, is about to be killed or sacrificed by her father because he does not want her to fall into the hands of his enemy, the prince Draco, who is about to besiege and take his castle. However, Arpazia does not want to die, and she is saved by her handmaiden, Lilca, who has made a deal with the enemy and lets them enter the castle through a secret door. But "because Lilca had betrayed the castle, allowing Draco's army in by the secret door, Draco in fact had her hanged. He did not like faithfulness, and in those days sought always to make vivid examples of his moral stance. But to Arpazia, seeing she had been innocent in the matter, he subsequently gave back several of her 'treasures,' as he termed them, a reward for allowing him to sack the castle before her father could burn everything. He even initially forgave her attempt to escape and curse him—evidently neither had worked. He told her, her behavior was not surprising. She was a virgin and virtuous."[5]

As we discover, there is a great deal of irony in this passage. Draco—the name means dragon or ogre—has no real morals whatsoever. He will soon rape Arpazia and pursue his desire to establish his rule in a kingdom in which pagan and Christian divinities are worshiped in bizarre ways. Arpazia gives birth to a daughter named Candacis or Coira, whom Arpazia cannot bring herself to love because the child had been born out of rape. All the characters act out of self-interest, and love—a feeling of compassion, empathy, or altruism—is rarely felt. It is true that Arpazia takes on a lover, but she refuses to have his child and drives him away. In the meantime, her daughter Coira, whom she wants killed, flees with some dwarfs to a mining town where she takes on one of the dwarfs called Hephaestion as her lover. Her crazed mother, however, pursues her and poisons her. Coira recovers only to become the sex object of Hadz, one of the perverse bastard sons of Draco. Eventually, Hadz puts Arpazia to death, and Coira is rescued, not by a charming prince, but by the cunning dwarf Hephaestion. Coira finds herself pregnant, and it is not certain whether the child, whom she wants to bear, has been sired by Hadz or Hephaestion. What is certain is that Hephaestion wants to be a father to a child, and that they sleep under the protection of the stars. Lee ends the novel this way:

> They slept. Stars flew over. The sky grew thin.
>
> Blood, that dye of war and butchery, announced it was also the color of life. It bloomed in Coira's lips. It dazzled in flowers along the wide, adventurous plain.
>
> Soon the watching mirror saw in the East, that always-rising place of renewals, advents, a rightness like itself. The mirror offered neither question nor reply. The mirror's dialogues were done.
>
> And when the sun rose, it rose blood-red.[6]

This is a strange ending! If Lee is trying to indicate that there is a glimmer of hope that will emerge from all the bestial behavior that her characters have not only experienced but also displayed and exhibited themselves, it is a false glimmer and somewhat contrived. Are we to believe that Coira's child will have a better life and that the child symbolizes love and rebirth? Perhaps Lee might want us to believe that the color of blood is ambivalent, but she has shed so much blood in her novel and shown how most of the individuals in her story are bloodthirsty that there is little reason to believe that the princess, the dwarf, and their offspring will have much of a chance in the future, no matter how much they love one another. After all, Hadz and his father Draco still rule. There are no signs that they and the people in their kingdom will change. Moreover, there is no stable moral code. Might makes for right. It appears that cunning and ruthlessness are the keys to survival.

What are we to conclude from this intricate rewritten "Snow White" without an apparent happy ending by one of the foremost writers of fantasy in contemporary England? Should we attribute Lee's pessimistic outlook on the competition between women in this particular fairy-tale discourse to her idiosyncratic perspective, her gloomy outlook, and her penchant for lurid description? But Lee is not alone in revising "Snow White" to open up questions about our lack of morals and how vicious women can be to one another and how men continue to prey upon women to satisfy their lustful desires. There are similar versions by Robert Coover, Pat Murphy, Jane Yolen, and Michael Blumlein, not to mention again the film *Snow White: A Tale of Terror.* Lee, like other writers, uses hyperbole and mythic metaphor adroitly to elaborate a message embedded in the classical constellation of the "Snow White" tale and to make it more relevant. Whereas happiness is more or less guaranteed by the moral choices made by Snow White and the dwarfs in the more traditional tales, Lee suggests that there are no moral choices whatsoever that can be made in a world without morals. The best we can hope for is survival in a mutually beneficial relationship within a barbaric world.

BEAUTY AND THE BEAST

The situation is much different and somewhat more comforting in the recent retold versions of "Beauty and the Beast." This difference may depend on how the cycle of oral tales about the beast-bridegroom evolved. There is strong evidence to suggest that the tale evolved from a ritual concerned with a young woman's coming of age. She must complete three arduous tasks to save a bestial male who must integrate himself into her society. Here the female is a civilizing force searching for a quality male who is chosen to procreate with her. Crucial here is the instinctual desire to select a male who will be the best provider and caretaker of the female's offspring. First and foremost, the young woman must demonstrate courage and perseverance. But in many other beast-bridegroom tales, there is another emphasis: the female is expected to prove how submissive she is, first to her father and then to her future husband the beast. She does not choose her husband-to-be and is expected to save her father and wed a male not of her choosing. In an essay that I published in 1994, I discussed how the classical version of "Beauty and the Beast" by Mme. Leprince de Beaumont was essentially a didactic tale of female domestication that furthered sadomasochistic relations between men and women.[7] The name Belle or Beauty assumes meaning through the behavioral traits that the young woman displays as a good housekeeper and domesticated woman: industrious, diligent, loyal, submissive, gentle, self-sacrificial. Not all these traits are necessarily bad, but in the context of the plot, Beauty's behavior leads to the denial of her own desires. In fact, we never really know her desires, but we certainly know what her father and the Beast want.

Thanks to the feminist movement in the 1970s, we have learned much more about female desire, and thanks to Angela Carter's two superb versions, "The Courtship of Mr. Lyon" and "Tiger's Bride," both in *The Bloody Chamber and Other Stories* (1979), the moral conflict of the "Beauty and Beast" discourse has become more evident, and it centers on how "beauty" or one's physical and mental attributes are to be used: Should a young girl be marketed by her father just so he can survive? Should a young girl sacrifice her body to protect her family? Is it right to oblige a young woman to repress her natural inclinations and live according to the designs of male desire? Are there differences in how we define beauty for women and bestiality for men? Disney's film and Broadway's musical renditions of "Beauty and the Beast" minimize most of the questions and transform the conflict into a power struggle between two macho men who vie for the affection of a pretty petite bourgeois maiden who wants to leave her provincial town and lead a grand and glamorous life. Despite providing her with a touch of feminist feistiness, the Disney screenplay writers did not alter the plot very much: the boys struggle for the charming girl. The right guy wins. She moves up in society, and everyone sings and rejoices.

This is not the case in the more serious contemporary explorations of "Beauty and the Beast." It is certainly not the case with Donna Jo Napoli's recent version. In the past ten years Napoli has rewritten several of the more significant classical tales into psychological novellas that reveal the deep and often dark instinctual drives that motivate the characters to commit devastating crimes. With deliberate care she examines the inner life of her characters and wants to grasp the natural and psychic forces that compel them to break moral codes. In *Beast* (2000) the Persian prince Orasmyn is cursed and transformed into a lion by a pari because he allows a defiled camel to be sacrificed on a high holiday. Told from a first-person narrative in the present tense, Orasmyn's tale is one of flight into himself. As a devout seventeen-year-old follower of the Islam faith, Orasmyn is forced to contend with his basic nature as an animal: he breaks every religious code by copulating with lionesses, killing other animals and eating raw meat, preying on the weak, and exhibiting his raw power. The only way he can be saved is by the love of a woman, and after he has a rude awakening about his animal limitations in India, Orasmyn the lion discovers a book about a rose garden that his mother had wanted him to read, and he decides to travel to France because he had heard that the best roses grow in France and French women give off the perfume of roses. Instinctively he believes he will find the woman who will love him in France.

It is in France that Orasmyn learns to cultivate another side of his personality. Not only does he occupy an abandoned castle, but he begins to grow and cultivate a rose garden. The rest of the story, unfortunately, follows the traditional "Beauty and the Beast" tale: a merchant arrives; he trespasses; the Lion demands his daughter as payment for his sin; Belle arrives; they learn to love each other; she returns from a visit to her sick father and saves the prince. Napoli is not very original in the manner in which she ends the tale. Nevertheless, there is a new emphasis in her version that endows it with a different quality and indicates how male-female relations might be transformed. East meets West in this tale, and the introspective Orasmyn and the extrovert Belle develop mutual respect for each other, and through the act of writing and reading together, they share an understanding of each other's needs and experiences. Orasmyn leads Belle to read Ovid's *Metamorphoses* and the *Aeneid*. She introduces him to a Chinese book that helps him understand her needs. There is also an important passage in Napoli's novel that refers to Ovid and sums up the crux of the moral dilemma experienced by Orasmyn. When Belle arrives at the castle, he observes her unseen while she picks up an almond, dips it in honey, and eats it.

> I think of the Greek myth of Persephone, the girl Hades stole to be his wife in the Underworld. She ate six pomegranate seeds, and thus sealed her fate: She had to live with Hades six months of every year—one month for each seed. Does this woman think she's come to marry the King of the Underworld? Is that almond in her mouth a symbol of resignation to a hideous fate? And now I remember Persephone's downfall in the first place: She wandered away from her friends to smell the sweet narcissus. The young woman before me asked for roses. She smells them now. I feel her heart; she believes she is doomed.[8]

Orasmyn has Belle completely in his power, and he could rape and devour her. But unlike Hades—and unlike Draco and Hadz in Lee's *White as Snow*, which also employs the Persephone myth—he chooses to subdue his instincts and recognize her needs. This is the paradox of the novel: the more he learns about his instincts and how to control them, the more he will be free to love. The male predatory nature is and can be transformed, and this message, spoken through a male narrator, is a message that is rarely heard in popular culture where male hormones run rampant on big and small screens and in print throughout the world.

MULAN AND THE X-MEN

The "moral" challenge to male domination has expressed itself in popular culture in manifold ways, and at the root of some of the more successful films for young and old such as *Mulan* (1998) and *The X-Men* (1999) are folk and fairy tales. Though these films appear to be very original, they both stem from stories told probably hundreds of years ago in somewhat different forms. In fact, though apparently very different, they are very much connected and share some basic roots. *Mulan* seems to be a film that focuses largely on the prowess of young women, who can accomplish extraordinary feats if given the opportunity. *The X-Men* seems to be a film about outcast mutants who seek to save humankind, largely Americans, despite the fact that the Americans maltreat mutants in the name of genetic normality. Both films are indeed about what they seem to be, but they are also more, and they are also more related than they appear.

In an essay on evolution and the work of Stephen Jay Gould in the *New Yorker*, Robert Wright commented:

> [M]any biologists believe that human social organization has also favored genes for intelligence. Our species, for example, has "reciprocal altruism." We are designed to feel warmly toward people who do favors for us, to return the favors, and thus to forge mutually beneficial relationships—friendships. What's more, one kind of favor we swap is social support. That is, we are a "coalitional" species; groups compete with each other for status and influence. Reciprocal altruism takes brainpower—to remember who has helped you and who has hurt you. And the coalitional variety takes more brainpower, since strategic plotting and communication among allies are vital.[9]

The basic appeal of both the *Mulan* and *X-Men* narratives concerns reciprocal altruism and the use of intelligence to bring about justice and in part to guarantee the survival of those humans who do not favor barbarity and will not destroy the world. The plot in both films is driven by a highly intelligent character who brings together other talents or extraordinary traits exhibited in other characters and brings them to bear on a conflict that threatens the survival of family, tribe, community, or nation. Force is thus acceptable and has a moral purpose if it is employed in self-defense or in defense of a particular group to which one belongs. As Matt Ridley has commented in *The Origins of Virtue*, "the virtuous are virtuous for no other reason than that it enables them to join forces with others who are virtuous, to mutual benefit. And once cooperators segregate themselves off from the rest of society a wholly new force of evolution can come into play: one that pits groups against each other, rather than individuals."[10]

The story on which the film *Mulan* is based can be traced back to a Chinese ballad probably composed in the fifth and sixth centuries. It was included in imperial court anthologies as *The Song of Mulan* during the Tang Dynasty (618–907), and it became a popular legend and has remained popular in China up to the present. In fact, during the 1990s two illustrated bilingual editions of the ballad were published for young readers in California, and in 1998 Robert D. San Souci's English-only adaptation of the ballad, *Fa Mulan*, appeared. According to the screen credits, his story served as the basis for the Disney film. No matter who receives "credit," the popularity of this unusual legend, which spread by word of mouth in China, has a great deal to do with reciprocal altruism and coalition building. The ancient ballad is brief and to the point: An enemy invades China. The emperor calls on each family to send one man to defend the country. Hua Mu Lan's father is old and tired. With her father's consent, she dresses in warriors' clothes and represents her family disguised as a man. She will fight not only for China but for her family's honor. She leads troops in a hundred battles for ten years and gains the rank of a general. When the enemy is defeated, the emperor wants to reward Hua Mu Lan with a minister's post and the title to a nobleman's house and land. But she refuses, for she merely wants to return to her father and help him in his old age. Once she returns and is given a warm welcome by her father and mother, she resumes her identity as a female and astonishes some of the comrades with whom she fought. Depending on the version one reads, it appears that she will marry one of the warriors. However, in many instances, she remains single.

San Souci's text adds many historical details and fills in gaps in the ballad. For example, he provides background material about the enemy, the Tartars, who lived in Mongolia and Manchuria, and often invaded China. They were changed to Huns in the Disney version. He also depicts how Mulan developed military skills. However, he does not alter the plot very much, nor is he very original in adapting it. In contrast, the Disney film is highly innovative, and though it may be criticized to a certain extent for not being as "politically correct" as it could be, the book and film adaptation of the Chinese legend is captivating. Obviously, the popularity of *Disney's Mulan*, as the book and film are called, depends very much on Disney's powerful distribution system.

However, this is not the only reason. The Disney producers and artists spent four years conceiving and designing the film, book illustration, and plot line, and as usual, much of the appeal of the film depends on the comic characters such as the cricket Cri-Kee, the guardian dragon Mushu, the three soldiers, Ling, Yao, and Chien-Po, as well as the villainous Hun Shan Yu and the sinister eagle that accompanies him. The landscape and architecture paintings are intricately designed and based on visits to sites in China, and the artists managed to create colorful settings and costumes for each scene based on their research and their actual impressions of ancient Chinese buildings and landscape. Though it is clear that there is a strong feminist message in the Disney version, the success of both film and book emanates, in my opinion, from the basic altruistic impulses and the relations that are formed throughout the fairy tale, implying a virtue in collective action. And we are talking about a fairy tale, a formulaic Disney fairy tale, which the Disney artistic teams, working together, have found effective in communicating relevant messages ever since the first major Disney film, *Snow White*, was produced in 1937.

In *Mulan* the young girl is concerned about the family's name and honor from the very beginning, but she also wants to follow her heart. It is because of her endeavor to work through relations with all those around her—her father, mother, grandmother, dragon, the three soldiers, and of course, the handsome captain Shang—that Mulan assumes a certain moral authority, using force only when it means protecting family, friends, and nation. One of the producers of the film, Pat Coats, remarked, "Everyone contributed to help make Mulan a thinking, feeling human being who acts out of love for other people. She's a completely unselfish hero."[11]

But she also reveals how intelligence can be used to draw together disparate talents to create a more humane and just society and to guarantee the survival of her kin. Her transformation reads like the fairy tale of the young female or male who sets off to rectify a great injustice but needs three to six extraordinary characters or traits to accomplish the task. In the folk and fairy-tale tradition there are numerous tales like this,[12] and one of the most significant is Mme. d'Aulnoy's *Belle-Belle or the Chevalier Fortuné* (1697). It is somewhat stunning that few if any critics have referred to this tale when writing about *Mulan* because the two tales are so similar. It is all the more stunning because d'Aulnoy must have read or heard about the Chinese ballad during her travels in Europe. How else could she have conceived the following plot?

A very good and gentle king is conquered by the Emperor Matapa, his neighbor, who ransacks the kingdom and takes all the treasures back to his realm. The defeated king wants to recapture his wealth and gain revenge. So he issues a proclamation requiring all the noblemen of his kingdom to come and serve him in person or to send a well-armed son. On the frontier of the kingdom, a nobleman, eighty years old and reduced to poverty, is in a quandary because he only has three daughters. However, each one volunteers to disguise herself and join the army, but the first two daughters cannot pass the test of a fairy disguised as a shepherdess. As usual, it is the youngest daughter, Belle-Belle, who gains the help of this fairy, who, in turn, gives her a dashing magical horse named Faithful Comrade, whose extraordinary qualities are enumerated by the fairy: "He eats only once a week, and it's not necessary to look after him, for he knows the present, past, and future. I've had him a long time, and I've trained him as I'd train my own horse. Whatever you wish to know, or whenever you need advice, you need only consult him. He'll give you such good counsel that most sovereigns would be blessed to have ministers like him. Consider him more as your friend than your horse."[3] As if this horse were not enough, the fairy gives Belle-Belle a magic key to a trunk with a large wardrobe and changes her name to the Chevalier Fortuné.

Indeed, Belle-Belle is most fortunate. Hence, her male name Fortuné. On her way to join the king, she meets Strongback, a powerful woodcutter; Swift, an amazing runner; Sharpshooter, a superb marksman; Hear-All, a gifted listener; Boisterous, a powerful blower of windmills; Tippler, a man who can easily drink up lakes and seas; and finally Gorger, who has an insatiable appetite. All of these fantastic men join Belle-Belle, who arrives at the court and is taken by surprise when the king's sister, the queen, falls in love with her, while Belle-Belle becomes enamored of the king. When Belle-Belle as the Chevalier does not return the sister's advances, the queen arranges for Belle-Belle to be sent on the dangerous mission of recapturing the king's treasures. Little does she know that Belle-Belle has the assistance of her horse and the six gifted men, and with their aid, she defeats the sinister Emperor Matapa. When she returns, the queen has her falsely accused of treason, and Belle-Belle is to be burned at the stake. As her shirt is being stripped from her, however, her true identity is revealed. The queen is poisoned, and Belle-Belle marries the king, who is most grateful to her for defeating his enemy.

There are, of course, many notable themes in this complex fairy tale: the cross dressing and androgynous character of Belle-Belle, the rivalry between brother and sister for Belle-Belle's favor, the question of loyalty, and the theme of natural love. But clearly d'Aulnoy's storyline was taken from some oral or written version of the Chinese legend about Mulan, and clearly the tale focuses on the benefits of altruism and the unification of extraordinary forces by a higher intelligence to overcome the rapacity of an evil emperor. In some ways, Belle-Belle, like Mulan, is selfish insofar as she acts to guarantee the perpetuation of her family and kin. But this is the paradox of virtue: if we act with others on behalf of our selfish genes, they will reciprocate and our genes will be replicated.

The Brothers Grimm were drawn to this topic in two tales in their collection of *Household and Children's Tales*—"How Six Made Their Way in the World" and "The Six Servants." In the first narrative, a discharged soldier, unjustly treated by his king, gains revenge with a strong man, a fast runner, a sharpshooter, a blower, and a freezer. Together they defeat the king's daughter in a race, undermine his duplicitous schemes, and share his treasures in the end. In the second narrative, a king's son seeks to marry the beautiful daughter of a powerful sorceress. He recruits a fat man with a belly as large as a mountain, who can eat tons of food; a listener, who can hear everything that happens in the world; a rubber man, who can stretch himself miles on end; a blindfolded man, whose sight shatters whatever he glances at; a weather transformer, who can withstand any intolerable climate; and a sharp-eyed man who can see long distances and throughout the whole world. With these six servants, the prince is able to complete three tasks set by the sorceress, who remains duplicitous after his victory and convinces her proud daughter that she is too good for a commoner. So, the prince must overcome the sorceress a second time and humiliate the princess before he marries her.

It is interesting to observe that "How Six Men Made Their Way in the World" is essentially a political tale about class struggle within a patriarchal realm: a common soldier with the help of six extraordinary common men overcomes a tyrannical king and shares his treasure, and "The Six Servants" is essentially a tale about a dispute among ruling elites that has a sexist bias: a prince wins and abducts an unwilling princess and demeans her until she recognizes her submissive role in the prince's life. But both tales can also be read as narratives about subduing rapacious instincts in human beings and the necessity for establishing a moral code of behavior in the name of civilization. Here we can see the strong connection to "The Ballad of Mu Lan," "Belle-Belle or the Chevalier Fortuné," and the books and film based on the Mulan legend: evil is associated with the invasion of the private and public body by an alien force, the exploitation of one's energies, the lack of altruism, duplicity, the abuse of power; good is associated with kindness, loyalty, compassion, mutual recognition, the use of intelligence to bring together extraordinary forces for a just resolution of conflict. At the heart of all these tales is a paradox: the common good is established through selfish genes. Other important related questions that this tale raises are: How do we determine what constitutes identity and moral character and how can we bring about social relations that allow for individual talents to flourish and work together for the common good?

As usual, the fairy tale and fantasy literature debate these questions, and there is one fairy tale as comic and film that sheds light on the complexity of these questions. I am referring specifically to *The X-Men* in its various mutations, and though it might seem strange to suggest that *The X-Men* is a fairy tale, I believe that the basic plot of the initial popular film reveals just how much it is indebted to the Chinese, French, and German tales: a higher intelligence brings together individual super heroes with fantastic powers to form a coalition to save the human species.

The X-Men have their origins not only in ancient European and Oriental folklore and the literary fairy-tale tradition, but also in American folklore and specifically in the development of popular superheroes in the comic book tradition. This is evident if we trace the evolution of such heroes as Superman, Captain Marvel, Batman, Flash Gordon,

Wonder Woman, and so on. These heroes eventually led to the creation of *The Fantastic Four* in the 1960s that, in turn, generated *The X-Men*. In particular, the appearance of *The Fantastic Four* was significant because this comic book brought about a radical change in storylines and ideology and also harked back to important themes of altruism and intelligence in the fairy tale. As Bradford Wright comments in *Comic Book Nation*:

> The Fantastic Four, and the Thing in particular, reworked the formula for comic book superheroes. These were heroes who reconciled the competing imperatives of individualism and communal responsibility. Although the concept was new to comic books, such character types were actually well grounded in American popular culture, since American audiences had historically shown a marked preference for reluctant heroes who defend the community while maintaining a personal distance from society. The classic archetype, of course, is the Western frontier hero, existing on the border between civilization and the wilderness and championing the best qualities of both. Embodied in the reluctant hero were the celebrated possibilities of American republicanism: virtuous citizens giving to the community without sacrificing their freedom and individuality. The demands of World War II and the Cold War had subverted whatever individuality superheroes like Superman and Batman had once possessed for the sake of the national consensus. Now the Fantastic Four opened the door for reluctant comic book heroes to pose an alternative to that consensus.[14]

By 1963 the X-Men, a group of teen-age mutants, under the guidance of the genial Professor Xavier, began posing radical political and moral questions about the national consensus in America, and they have continued their provocative questioning into the twenty-first century. It is difficult to summarize the story of the X-Men because—similar to the oral origins of classical fairy tales—there is no one story or *Urtext* and because the creators of the X-Men series have changed and also altered their political and aesthetic perspectives. Therefore, I want to refer to the most popular version, the 2000 film, and the books and comics spawned by this cinematic production.

Though the original comics did not begin with the Holocaust as the metasymbol or icon that marks the action of all the stories, the screenplay and all adaptations use it as the haunting signifier that marks the postmodern world. The very first scene is a dark rainy night in Poland during 1944, and the little boy Erik Lehnsherr is torn from his parents by the Nazis and experiences the horrors of the concentration camps. The human brutality that Erik witnesses transforms him later into Magneto, the most powerful mutant in the world along with Professor Xavier. Erik survives World War II and goes to Israel, where he discovers his ability to control magnetism and initially joins with Professor X to combat a high-tech terrorist organization known as Hydra. However, due to his experiences in the concentration camp, Magneto does not trust humans to govern themselves or to treat mutants with human compassion. Consequently, he decides to rule the world. In contrast, Professor X, who is telepathic and has extraordinary mental powers, has faith in human beings and seeks to protect them from Magneto and his gang of evil mutants and educate "normal" humans so that they will tolerate all forms of the human species.

The major conflict in all the X-Men versions from its inception in the 1960s through the twenty-first century is highly ambivalent, and this ambivalence makes for intriguing adventures. Magneto believes profoundly that human beings are evil; he has personally, that is, physically, experienced the sadistic and homicidal tendencies of a group of humans who believe in genetic purity. He is convinced that there is a racist and puritanical impulse in human beings, perhaps exemplified in the person of Senator Robert Kelly, who believes that mutants are dangerous and should be registered so that they can be controlled—the first step toward extermination. Evil resides in the norm of governmental control, intolerance of differences in the species, ethnic cleansing, and racism. However, the goodness of Magneto's attitude toward such sinister intolerance is brought into question because he sets himself up as a dictator and judge of humankind. His moralistic position is tainted by his obsession with power. On the other hand, Professor Xavier recognizes the perversion of good in Magneto's politics, and he seeks to offset this evil by demonstrating the good that mutants can do in the world. This is why he establishes a school for gifted youngsters in his ancestral mansion in Westchester County, outside New York, and forms a special group of mutants to assist him in defending humans so that humans and mutants can live in peace. His school is a place where teenage mutants learn to control and develop their unusual powers to help humanity.

There is a strong indication that the rise of a large number of mutants took place after World War II and might have something to do with the genetic experimentation that German scientists were conducting and that has been carried on by genetic scientists since that time. Whatever the case may be, Professor Xavier has helped and schooled numerous mutants, who have special DNA, sometimes referred to as junk DNA. The most talented remain with him, and in the film, we are introduced only to five: Rogue, a young girl, who is able to absorb the memory and powers of anyone she touches; Storm, also known as Weather Girl, a beautiful African princess, who can control weather conditions; Cyclops, whose optic blasts can destroy anything in his sight; Jean Grey, also known as Marvel Girl, who has telepathic powers that enable her to read minds, stun enemies with mental bolts, and move objects with her mind; Wolverine, a ferocious somewhat bestial Canadian, also called Logan, who has unbreakable steel claws and uncanny senses. They are opposed by Magneto's mutants such as Toad, whose tongue can lash out and kill people, and Sabretooth, who has the powers of a prehistoric animal. The plot of *X-Men* the film is simplistic as are most of the storylines of the comic book sequels. Magneto sees evil in the U.S. government's move toward mutant registration, and he kidnaps Kelly and later Rogue in an attempt to use his powers through them to kill thousands of people and take over the world. With the help of Professor Xavier's brains behind them, the X-Men join together to outwit Magneto and bring about a peaceful outcome without human beings realizing how close they came to extinction. Magneto lives on as Professor Xavier's prisoner, unrepentant and convinced that he has done no wrong.

What is significant in all the X-Men episodes and their popular adaptations—and what constitutes their popularity and contagious appeal—is the manner in which the stories replicate and recapitulate folk and fairy tale narratives in a distinct discursive strain that addresses moral conflicts concerned with genetic survival and altruism. In the cycle of X-Men tales—almost all the heroes and heroines are introduced as teenagers who do not know what to do with their extraordinary genetic powers that make them into mutants and outsiders at the same time.

They are the freaks, nerds, outsiders, and weirdos of society, and at the same time, they are also the saviors of civilization and the human species. It is the great paradox of the X-Men cycle that aberration guarantees the survival of the normative and perhaps enriches it. In the novel Jean Grey explains it to the U.S. Senate this way:

> In recent years ... and for reasons which are still a mystery, we have seen this latent [junk] DNA in our bodies mutating. These mutations manifest at puberty, and are often triggered by periods of heightened emotional stress. ... The new DNA strands caused by the mutations are producing some admittedly startling results. In other words, this previously unused DNA is not "junk" DNA at all, but rather a vast storehouse which contains the almost limitless potential for human advancement ... we are now seeing the beginnings of another stage of human evolution. Not a new race of creatures to be feared, but rather the opportunity to find advancement within us all.[15]

At their best, folk tales, fairy tales, and fantasy literature represent metaphorically the opportunities for human advancement and the conflicts that arise when we fail to establish civilizing codes commensurate with the self-interests of large groups within the human population. The more we give in to base instincts—base in the sense of basic and depraved—the more criminal and destructive we become. The more we learn to relate to alien groups and realize that their survival and the fulfillment of their interests are related to ours, the more we might construct social codes that guarantee humane relationships.

Fairy tales hint of happiness. This hint, what Ernst Bloch has called the anticipatory illumination,[16] has constituted their utopian appeal, which has a strong moral component to it. We do not know happiness, but we instinctively know and feel that it can be created and perhaps even defined. Fairy tales map out possible ways to attain happiness, to expose and resolve moral conflicts that have deep roots in our species. The effectiveness of fairy tales and other forms of fantastic literature depends on the innovative manner in which we make the information of the tales relevant for the listeners and receivers of the tales. As our environment changes and evolves, so too do we change the media or modes of the tales to enable us to adapt to new conditions and shape instincts that were not necessarily generated for the world that we have created out of nature. This is perhaps one of the lessons that the best of fairy tales and fantasy literature teaches us: we are all misfit for the world, and yet, somehow we must all fit together to survive.

"Bluebeard"
Illustrator: Gustave Doré

Chapter 5

The Male Key to
Bluebeard's Secret

On the contrary, I love women but I don't admire them. ... Women are
of the earth, realistic, dominated by physical facts.

Monsieur Verdoux, directed by Charlie Chaplin

ven when Bluebeard's wife opens the door to her husband's
bloody chamber in Charles Perrault's notorious tale, she really
never learns his secret—why he killed his previous wives and
who he really is. The revelation of his crimes does not reveal the secret
that accompanies him when he is killed. There is no investigation afterward. His wife as sole survivor inherits all his wealth and uses part of it
to arrange a marriage for her sister Anne and part to pay commissions
for her two brothers so that they can become captains in the royal army.
"The rest she used for her marriage to a worthy man who made her
forget the miserable time she had spent with Bluebeard." So ends the
story. With the exception of two ironic and contradictory verse morals
added by Perrault, we learn nothing more about Bluebeard, other than
ambiguous messages that playfully conceal Bluebeard's secret. Essentially, the wife's past history with Bluebeard is to be repressed, and yet,
it has become one of the more haunting and baffling fairy tales in the
classical canon, one that keeps rearing its horrific head in all forms of
art and literature when we least expect it.

In the most recent study of many studies of this irresistible horror tale, Maria Tatar concludes her book by remarking:

> Bluebeard has left its fingerprints in many obvious and not so obvious places, and we obsessively return to it to try to understand marital discord, unaware that the story itself has dictated certain cultural terms, in much the way that the biblical account of Eve and the mythical story of Pandora have shaped our thinking. Hence the importance of investigating the story, looking at how it reflects our anxieties as cultural symptom, yet also probing the reach of its cultural effects as it continues to shape our fantasies and desires.[2]

Tatar unlocks many of the mysteries behind our attraction to "Bluebeard" by focusing on the anxieties that arise in marriage when two people wed, do not know each other, and try to create some form of intimacy. According to Tatar, the reason why we may be attracted to this tale is that it communicates important lessons about all that can go wrong in a marriage. "It stands virtually alone among our canonical fairy tales in a negation of a 'happily ever after' ending. It gives us an up-close-and-personal view of marriage, confirming everything we didn't want to know and were afraid to ask about it."[3] This view is true to a certain extent, but it ignores the fact that Bluebeard and his wife never quarrel, that he indisputably sets the laws in his household, that he obviously wants to test her obedience, and that he is not even afraid to punish her in the presence of his wife's sister. Clearly, he had warned her about the rules of the house, and he believes it is his right to kill her—something that she does not contradict. Though he dies because of the intercession of her brothers, Bluebeard does not explain or repent his actions. Nor does it seem that his wife and siblings want an explanation. Everyone profits from his death. Indeed, there is a happy ending, and Bluebeard's wife enters another marriage with a man who makes her forget the past.

One could thus ask: Is this tale truly about marital discord? Are we really attracted to the tale because it tells us what we don't want to know about marriage? Perhaps, but I think that there is much more to this puzzling tale that has intrigued writers, artists, filmmakers, readers, and spectators over three centuries. In fact, we need to review some salient aspects of this classical tale if we are at least to understand the narrative strategy for dealing with women developed by Perrault, how it fit into his notion of civilité and masculine domination, and why it has become so relevant for the civilizing process in the West. Bluebeard, we must recall, is not an aristocrat. If anything he represents the ugly, wealthy nouveau riche, and he may have made his money through criminal and illicit acts. Several critics assume that he is a financier. His wife's family looks down upon him because his "blue beard" makes him ugly and terrifying. But when they visit his country estates and see how rich he is, the youngest daughter overcomes her distaste and marries him for his money, knowing full well that he had things to hide. She is from the upper class and it is possible that this marriage of convenience suits both of them. She gets his money; he gets a connection to an aristocratic family. He wants obedience and respect as the authority of power, but she violates his rules. Knowing full well the possible consequences of her transgression, she had already beckoned her brothers to visit her, and sure enough, they arrive in time to kill Bluebeard, making their sister an heiress to a fortune. Both Bluebeard and his wife are calculating individuals. Neither marries for love but for social or financial advancement. In sociobiological terms they select mates who will best propagate their genes, so they think. There is no magic in this tale, and Bluebeard becomes the victim of his own miscalculations.

Perrault's "Bluebeard" is a tale about male power and calculation based on the instinctual drive for power that misfires, and by viewing Perrault's story and adaptations by male writers, filmmakers, and dramatists from 1697 to the present, I want to argue that readers and viewers have been drawn to the tale because of the manner in which it reveals the miscalculation of male power and, in some cases, male anxiety about the potential encroachment of women on this power. In developing my argument, I want to set limits with regard to my focus first by considering only "Bluebeard tales" and not the variants that stem from the oral tradition of "The Robber Bridegroom," as Tatar has done, and second by exploring "Bluebeard" *variants written only by men*. By doing this, I hope to show a gendered evolution of a fairy tale initiated by a male writer and contested gradually by female writers. By focusing solely on the male perspective, I want to analyze how a meme can be used instinctively by the male gender both to rationalize and critique the putative natural authority that men claim as rightfully theirs.

Numerous studies have linked Perrault's tale to the Greek myth about Pandora, biblical stories of Adam and Eve and Judith of Holofernes, folk tales related to the "Robber Bridegroom" and "Fitcher's Bird" and the history of a known murderer, Gilles de Rais. They are all interesting stories and events that comprise the heterogeneity of this tale. Perhaps they may have influenced Perrault. Yet, there is no conclusive evidence that he used or referenced any of these myths and stories. Instead, it is quite clear that this particular tale is one of the few stories that Perrault did not base on particular literary antecedents. Nor is there clear evidence of an oral tale that served as a model for "Bluebeard." More than likely Perrault took motifs from French folklore and combined them to invent the story of "Bluebeard," a tale that, I shall argue, was created to play a role in the debate about the civilizing process, masculine domination, and the proper roles of men and women during the time of Louis XIV's reign. By limiting my study narrowly to the origin of Perrault's "Bluebeard" and its role in the development of a fairy-tale discourse with a focus on male miscalculation, I hope to open up Bluebeard's secret and trace the manifold ways in which male writers and artists in Europe and North America have continued to view power and calculation. It is an interesting example of how a literary tale forged a memetic tradition within the fairy-tale genre.

When the genre of the literary tale became firmly institutionalized in France at the end of the eighteenth century, two significant features were also established and continue to be spread today through epidemiological dissemination: the plots of very specific tale types such as "Bluebeard," "Little Red Riding Hood," "Cinderella," and so on were transformed into gendered discourses about the mores, norms, and manners of men and women; the specific discourses embodied feminine and masculine dispositions within a larger patriarchal context that can be discerned in variations of themes about power relations and narrative strategies that inform the style of the tales.

PERRAULT AND FAIRY-TALE DISCOURSE

To understand Perrault's "Bluebeard" and its cultural ramifications up to
the present, it is necessary to review the sociohistorical context in which
the tale first appeared. During the 1780s Perrault had been involved
in a long debate about French culture with Nicolas Boileau, a highly
regarded poet and philosopher, and he published four volumes titled
Parallèle des Anciens et des Modernes (1688–97), in which he argued that
France should break with the classical Greek and Roman tradition and
draw upon its own lore and history to produce original and modern
works of art. This debate became famous and is known in English as
The Quarrel of the Ancients and the Moderns, and while this debate is
indeed important, it is little known that Perrault was also involved in
another significant debate with Boileau about women. He published a
long ironical poem *Apologie des Femmes* (*The Vindication of Women*) in
1694 to attack Boileau's poem *Satire X* (1694), which denigrated women.
Though Perrault's defense of women is somewhat dubious because he
still adhered to many conservative and stereotypical notions about
women, it is significant because he basically endeavored to show that
women had a unique role in the lives of men, and he did this through
the voice of a father trying to convince his recalcitrant son to marry.

> Do you not know that all Civility
> Is Born in Women with Propriety?
> That in them all politeness is innate,
> Gentleness, taste and manners delicate?
> Look, if you will, at each uncivil wright
> Who lives alone, from women shut up tight,
> You'll find him filthy, mannerless and wild,
> A boor in manner and in speech defiled.
> To him a finer thought quite strange has grown,
> He only speaks harsh words and sayings well known.
> All good for him is buried and long dead,
> And at our modern ways he jeers instead.
> In testing, all of value must be old,
> Such varied talents form the Pedant's mould,

Most irksome, loathsome and withal purblind
Of any creature known to all mankind.
When foolish women in so light a way
Devote themselves to singing and trifling play,
Are you not sometimes tempted to exclaim
That it is husbands who are oft to blame
By the excess of their rule severe?
Through indolence or the too mild course they steer?[4]

Perrault was not alone in his defense of women, which was more an explication of how to keep them in their place than a celebration of their equality. As Patricia Hannon has pointed out, there were numerous treatises, essays, and books about the nature and place of women published in seventeenth-century France.

> The developing centralized state witnessed a shift in the misogynist attitudes that abandoned diatribes against evil feminine nature for the censure of society women who undermined family values. As legislation strengthened the family unit and diminished in theory women's considerable influence, the domestic woman was idealized by authors ranging from Perrault to Fénelon. However, the unmistakable puritanical tendencies that characterize the early modern state existed in tension with the sexual liberty practiced at both court and salon. And while feminists thought women's household and societal roles compatible, they, like women's detractors, valorized the engendering woman and accepted her subordinate position in the family household. Seventeenth-century fairy tales, written in the last decade of the century, appeared at a time when interest in defining women's "nature" so as to better designate their place in the newly reinforced hierarchy, was at its height.[5]

In fact, Perrault's debates with Boileau about women's place in the family and society figure prominently in the manner in which he incorporated them into the tales that he wrote from 1694 to 1697. In his *Contes du temps passé*, there are eleven tales altogether (including three verse tales), and with the exception of "Riquet with the Tuft," "The Master Cat, or Puss in Boots," "Bluebeard," and "Little Thumbling," all the others ("Cinderella, or The Glass Slipper," "The Sleeping Beauty in the Woods," "Little Red Riding Hood," "Griseldis," "Donkey-Skin," "The Fairies," and "The Foolish Wishes") feature women, in particular, the comportment of women in desperate situations, and how their qualities enable them to triumph and find their proper place in society under masculine domination. Even "Riquet with the Tuft" and "Bluebeard" can be considered tales more concerned about women than men because the focus is on women who, when confronted with difficult choices, prove themselves to be valiant and noble despite maltreatment by powerful men. In fact, more than any of the important male writers of fairy tales before him such as the Italians Giovan Francesco Straparola and Giambattista Basile, Perrault initiated a male discourse about gender relations that became foundational in the rise of the literary fairy tale as genre and cultural institution.

In the case of "Bluebeard," there is a very specific masculine narrative strategy that Perrault developed in defense of arbitrary phallocratic power that he unwittingly shows to be impotent, and this strategy has been cultivated in different ways by most male adapters of the tale. The secret of "Bluebeard" is that there is no secret, as Philip Lewis has so brilliantly explained, but before I comment and elaborate on Lewis's interpretation of the tale, I want to suggest that there is a possible biographical reading of the tale that adds another dimension to the discussion of power—the question of impotence.

The Empty Secret

As we know, Perrault had an intense personal dislike for his rival Boileau, and it is evident, though one can dispute this forever, that the figure of Bluebeard is based somewhat on Boileau, and that the tale is a cruel story of revenge, an exposure of Boileau's lack, and another argument for a modern assessment of the power relations between men and women. In his psychoanalytic study, *Du sang et du sexe dans les contes de Perrault*, Jean-Pierre Mothe recalls that Boileau had to undergo an operation for gallstones when he was about ten years old, that he was tended by Pierre Perrault, a doctor and brother of Charles, and that he was left impotent. Perrault knew a great deal about Boileau's personal life and how he sought to keep his impotency secret, and Mothe suggests that Perrault exposes and kills Boileau in this tale.[6] The blue beard conceals the secret of Boileau's childhood injury to the point that the villainous protagonist of the tale murders the women he marries to protect the discovery of his wound, and yet, because he is impotent, he, also identified with the feminine *la barbe*, cannot defend himself against two potent male aggressors.

All this is speculation, of course. But there is no doubt that Boileau was on Perrault's mind during the period of his writing the fairy tales,[7] and that many barbs of the tales are directed at Boileau to prove the power of Perrault's words in a contest concerning the women question. There was more at stake for Perrault in "Bluebeard" than defeating Boileau, and it is a secret that profoundly disturbs all men.

Lewis puts his finger on this deep secret by hypothesizing what happened when Bluebeard married his first wife and instructed her not to unlock the forbidden chamber. It is a test, a calculated risk, and Bluebeard basically wants his wife to believe that he has a powerful secret that she cannot know. It is a power that is intended to be beyond women's grasp. When she does, however, seek to know what it is, she finds nothing. "Thus," Lewis argues, "the paradoxical core at the origin of his secret had to be its falseness or emptiness: the secret truth of his secret is that there is no secret. In these circumstances, the victim's ordeal was essentially a test of her obedience, while the perpetrator's experience—including, along with the frustration caused by her disobedience, his discovery of the perverse pleasures accessible to killers and undertakers—entailed compensating for his lack of a genuine secret by constituting one after the fact."[8]

Lewis proceeds to argue that the tale is about doubling and difference, and that Bluebeard needs to keep killing women to differentiate himself from his wife/woman as the source of power and to maintain his sense of superiority. Relying heavily on Lacanian theory, Lewis maintains that the disobedience of the wife, represented as a supplemental castration threat, reveals Bluebeard's deficiency or impotence and mars his unique phallocratic role. But it is not just Bluebeard's identity that is threatened, for Lewis believes that the tale reveals a crisis for the phallotocracy in general because Bluebeard, as representative of men, cannot guarantee for himself a satisfactory self-representation by a female. Hence, Lewis explains, Bluebeard's need to murder.

When the tempter who seeks wifely compliance via castrational supple-mentarity turns into the executioner who revels in punishing the non-compliance that he has fostered, what does he accomplish, and to what end? The pattern of reenactment, whereby Bluebeard persists in remar-rying and rekilling, clearly implies that his acts of execution, if they prove his power and provide a certain pleasure, nonetheless fail to sat-isfy him fully. Each sequence of death and burial results in a void to be filled by another woman. While his wife-killing makes retribution for the women's tarnishing resistance to his phallic empire, it also deprives him of the living mirror that reflects and sustains that empire's ground in sexual difference. His violent restoration of the difference his wife has challenged thus reconstitutes, for him, a lack—a renewed need for his double—that he is driven to fill.[9]

If we recall the sociohistorical tendencies in seventeenth-century France—numerous writings by men about women's sexual and social roles, their fears about the prowess of women, growing power of women, especially aristocratic women in the salons, women forging a stronger cultural role in the civilizing process—it is no wonder that Perrault's "Bluebeard" reflects a major crisis for the phallotocracy, and it also pro-vides a template that men will use to reinscribe and to contemplate this crisis time and again up through the present century. But there is more to the template than meets the eye, more about the secret of the un-secret that needs further unraveling.

If it is true, as Lewis has argued, that Bluebeard seeks to hide the fact that there is no secret, he is still hiding something, and that something is his knowledge that he has no power, that he is essentially impotent and not entitled to control women. In other words, Bluebeard, as do all men, knows there is no essential or rational proof of his superior power, nothing to justify male power, no real god or gods who ordain power. Men know and sense that power can only be obtained through calculating manipulation of the other, more often than not, females and their offspring, and by concealing this knowledge of power, storing it away, that power is arbitrarily determined and the male maintains the myth of superior power backed by brute force. Such force and violence must be ritualized and become sacred for males to keep their secret, and women must be kept out and prescribed a place in the symbolic order of things so that they will serve men docilely. For centuries, women have bodily and textually been compelled to undergo a test that turns into a contest mirrored in canonical stories about Adam and Eve, Pandora's Box, Judith of Holofernes, and so on. What is slightly different in "Bluebeard" is that its publication, making the secret public, revealed more fissures and anxieties in the ritual of phallocratic secrecy than ever before in Western history. And perhaps this is why it finds such great resonance in both the print and oral tradition after the first publication of the tale in 1697. Perhaps this is why it sticks.

What disturbed Perrault and other male writers of the seventeenth century still disturbs men today: the deep knowledge that the grounds for their superior power vis-à-vis women, backed by laws and rules, are groundless. It is only through manipulation and calculation that men can convince women to reconcile themselves to domesticity and inferiority. In Perrault's tale, he frames the actions of the young wife within the parameters of male power. Placed in the hands of Bluebeard, she moves within his house and must be saved by other men. In the end she marries again and goes to another male house where she is to forget what happened. And Perrault even suggests in his second moral that times have changed, and she has nothing about which to worry:

> No longer are husbands so terrible,
> Or insist on having the impossible.
> Though he may be jealous and dissatisfied,
> He tries to do as he's obliged.
> And whatever color his beard may be,
> It's difficult to know who the master be.[10]

Bluebeard miscalculated his power, and Perrault sought to explain why, and why male attitudes toward women had to change while still rationalizing male superiority. According to Perrault, Bluebeard is the exception, and normal men are not criminal. Yet as we know, the exception not only makes the rule, it also conceals normative behavior, for force and violence (physically and psychologically) continue to be "justifiable" if not effective means employed by men to secure their power. Only if women do not differentiate themselves from men will they be secure in the male symbolic order. From a male viewpoint women must either gloss over their discovery of male impotence and accept their civil role of domesticity (placate the beast within the man) or they must calculate how to act to save themselves when the male miscalculates his power.

BLUEBEARD ADAPTATIONS

It is virtually impossible to provide a full sociohistorical account of how male writers and artists have used Perrault's fairy tale of "Bluebeard" to ruminate discursively about the protagonist's profound secret that all men share, women know, and both sexes debate as to whether they should continue to hide—the secret of the nonsecret. There is no clear evolution in the use of "Bluebeard" in the fairy-tale discourse about the miscalculation of power. If anything, one could say that it is a messy unresolved discourse that must be examined within its genericity. However, there is, as I have stated at the beginning, a certain male predisposition in the employment of "Bluebeard" in fairy-tale discourse, and I want to discuss some literary markers before I turn to particular cinematic representations that, perhaps, indicate a shift or heightening in the crisis of phallotocracy.

When I speak about the male disposition, which, I believe, stems from what Pierre Bourdieu defines as the male *habitus*, I am specifically relying on the critique developed by Bourdieu in his book, *Masculine Domination*, in which he argues:

> [T]he strength of the masculine order is seen in the fact that it dispenses with justification: the androcentric vision imposes itself as neutral and has no need to spell itself out in discourses aimed at legitimating it. The social order functions as an immense symbolic machine tending to ratify the masculine domination on which it is founded: it is the sexual division of labour, a very strict distribution of the activities assigned to each sex, of their place, time and instruments; it is the structure of space, with the opposition between the place of assembly or the market, reserved for men, and the house reserved for women, or, within the house, between the male part, the hearth, and the female part—the stable, the water and vegetable stores; it is the structure of time, the day and the farming year, or the cycle of life, with its male moments of rupture and the long

female periods of gestation. The social world constructs the body as a sexually defined reality and as the depository of sexually defining principles of vision and division.[11]

Bourdieu makes clear that we tend to view the world as being organized according to the division into relational genders, male and female, with the male arbitrarily designated as superior to the female. "The particular strength of the masculine sociodicy comes from the fact that it combines and condenses two operations: *it legitimates a relationship of domination by embedding it in a biological nature that is itself a naturalized social construction.*"[12] Throughout history this relationship has been reinforced through the social ordering of the family, work, education, government, and cultural institutions. The continuous socialization of "distinctive identities instituted by the cultural arbitrary are embodied in habitus that are clearly differentiated according to the dominant principle of division and capable of perceiving the world according to this principle."[13] The habitus is a complex of customary behavior, dress, attitudes, beliefs, and postures that we assume to distinguish our roles in society and that become integral to our identities and appear to be natural. They are articulated, formed, and reformed in our everyday activities that tend toward maintaining the status of male domination. In writing, males will develop and use narrative strategies to position themselves vis-à-vis females to guarantee that their arbitrary power will be respected and obeyed. Within the parameters of the Bluebeard discourse that has evolved during the past three hundred years, the vital aspect of the story concerns the legitimacy of male power that has no legitimacy.

Knowing this, whether it be through some kind of rational investigation or clear intuition, male writers, dramatists, musicians, and filmmakers, who have consciously chosen to revise Bluebeard tales, devise strategies to question Bluebeard's power and secret, to conceal them, joke about them, or to propose more equitable ways to conduct gender relations. They respond to their times and societies, to the shifts in male and female power, and to their own desires either to retain or abandon power. Perrault's classic Bluebeard fairy tale becomes an experiment in which male writers and filmmakers play out, explore, and grapple with a secret that undermines that arbitrary social status or what Bourdieu might call "habitus." Since there are so many male experiments with the Bluebeard tale, I want to focus chronologically on some of the more interesting variants from different countries before turning to comment on the key films of the twentieth century.

THE POLITICIZATION OF BLUEBEARD AND THE INCULPATION OF HIS WIFE

By the end of the eighteenth century, "Bluebeard" had become widely known in England, France, and Germany, thanks to translations of Perrault's tales and individual adaptations of his tale in chapbooks. Bluebeard was a popular figure, so popular that he became the subject of some important operas, plays, and stories that saw him "anointed" either a count, duke, or king, and his wife depicted as a young woman who marries for money and who foolishly sins out of her innate female curiosity in seeking to determine Bluebeard's notorious secret. The key adaptation of Perrault's work was the opera *Raoul Barbe-bleue* first performed in 1789 with music by Andrè Modeste Grétry and a libretto by Michael-Jean Sedaine. This opera represented a politicization of Perrault's tale. Bluebeard is transformed into a ruthless medieval prince who is overthrown by middle-class protagonists, while his wife is a bourgeois figure who must be rescued to save herself from her own curiosity. The transformation of the plot and the use of Gothic motifs made Perrault's tale into one of the most classical "rescue operas" of this period, and these operas were widespread in France, England, and Germany. As Diane Hoeveler and Sarah Cordova have explained:

> "Rescue operas" are not simply a politically conservative discourse system as has generally been argued, but rather they intend to present something like an anarchistic warning by constructing a distant past that the opera reshapes as redeemable through the elimination of corrupt aristocrats. Each opera presents a political and social warning to the monarchy: reform or be overthrown by violence, which certainly would seem to constitute something of an anarchist message. The specter of the French Revolution hangs over each of these works and all of them introduce middle-class characters who embody the best of what Britain and France must become if they are to avoid violent and chaotic fates.

The operas clearly are attempting to mediate between classes, races, and genders that saw themselves as being at odds over the shape and power structure of the newly evolving bourgeois society.[14]

Although there was a politically radical and nationalist side to these operas with regard to class conflict, there was an evident tendency by male writers and musicians to heighten the helplessness and foolishness of Bluebeard's wife. Thus, when George Colman the younger adapted the Grétry/Sedaine opera for the Haymarket in 1789 with music by Michael Kelly, he changed the setting to the Middle East and made Bluebeard into a tyrannical Turk, and his wife has to escape from his harem. This rescue opera with the title *Blue-Beard, or Female Curiosity* became a popular spectacle and was staged sixty-three times in 1798 and reproduced in the early nineteenth century, leading to James Robinson Planché's *Blue Beard*, subtitled *A Grand Musical, Comi-Tragical, Melo-Dramatic, Burlesque Burletta*. Planché brings the action back to Brittany, and though his play is a light musical farce—his Bluebeard is named Baron Abomelique, a crude rich aristocrat who has been married nineteen times—there is a demeaning depiction of his young bride-to-be, Fleurette, who readily gives up her loyal fiancé Joli Coeur when she visits the Baron's castle:

> Ab. How do you like my castle, madam, say?
> It's furnished to your taste? Be candid, pray.
> Fleur. I find your castle, sir, the truth to tell,
> Superb! Enchanting! Marches!—pretty well!
> (*aside*) I'm dazzled quite with all I round me view,
> I wish his beard was not so very blue.
> Ab. Madam you flatter me by your approval,
> I trust you'll think no longer of removal,
> But make yourself at home—my house, my grounds,
> My servants, coaches, horses, hawks, and hounds,
> Are yours, if you will have their master too.
> Fleur. (*aside*) I really think his beard is not so blue.
> Ab. My wealth's enormous—I've rent roll clear
> Of forty millions—I'm a potent peer!
> Likely to die before you, a great point sure—

> A youthful peeress, with a thumping jointure!
> The king himself might at your feet then fall.
> Fleur. (*aside*) I'm quite convinced his beard's not blue
>   at all;
> Besides, if he's so very much my slave,
> He'd be polite enough, perhaps to shave.
> A peeress! 'twould be cheap at any cost![15]

Of course, it is she who becomes his "slave," so to speak, and only through the intervention of her brothers can she be rescued—rescued from herself and her curiosity.

This is clearly the case in another play that may have been influenced by the Sedaine/Grétry opera, which had also been performed in Germany. This drama, *Ritter Blaubart. Ein Ammenmärchen*, published in 1797 by Ludwig Tieck, who also wrote a prose version, is more a serious medieval melodrama than a rescue opera. While Tieck, too, transforms Bluebeard into a ruthless aristocratic knight named Peter Werner, he does not contrast him with a bourgeois hero. The conflict in Tieck's drama, which is often long-winded and philosophical, is one that involves noblemen and the comportment of the feuding medieval lords reflecting the debates about the nobility in Tieck's own times. Here, the so-called heroine Agnes, an aristocratic young woman, who marries the ruthless Peter Werner, is childish and somewhat flighty. Yet, she knows what she wants, and it is the arranged marriage with Bluebeard because she is very materialistic and curious. Her behavior is contrasted with her more demure and modest sister Anne, and when she finally has the golden key to her husband's secret chamber, she is at first torn by doubts and begins speaking to herself:

> Agnes! Agnes! Be careful. You're just being tormented now by that notorious women's curiosity.—And why shouldn't I be allowed to be a woman like all the others?—Mere curiosity is not a sin.—I'd like to see the person who wouldn't be curious in my place.—My sister would be just like me if she weren't totally in love. But if the idea occurred to her that her Reinhold might be in that chamber, then she would get down on her knees and plead with me for the key.—People are always making excuses for their own weaknesses.—And ultimately it's not even a weakness of me. There might be a secret hidden in the chamber, and my fate may

depend upon it. I can almost sense it.—So I'm going inside.—What's to
tell him that I've been in there?[16]

Of course, the key will tell, and it is the key that also keeps telling
in other German versions during the nineteenth century such as the
Brother Grimms' "Blaubart" (1815), Ludwig Bechstein's "Das Märchen
von Ritter Blaubart" (1845), and numerous other slightly modified versions of Perrault's tale. The repetition of this particular tale in chapbooks,
popular literature, and also illustrated books for children reinforced the
message of Perrault's plot that focused on women's precarious situation
in an arranged marriage to a tyrant and the necessity of curbing her
curiosity and concealing her calculation.

There were already some humorous parodies and experimental versions in prose throughout the nineteenth century in England, France,
and Germany that suggested that women might be less curious and
calculating than they seem, such as Frederick William Naylor Bayley's
delightful poem "Bluebeard" (1842) and William Makepeace Thackeray's "Bluebeard's Ghost" (1843). Two of the more important works are
the opera Barbe-bleue by Jacques Offenbach and the very short story,
"La volupteuse" by Marcel Schwob. Offenbach's comic opera was composed with a libretto by Henri Meilhac and Lodovic Halévy and was
first performed in 1866. It is highly significant because it was a huge success in Paris and was also performed in French, German, and Yiddish in
New York and other cities in Europe. That is, it touched a chord in the
Bluebeard reception that signaled a new sensitivity about the desire and
intelligence of women that undermined the ruthless quest of men to
maintain power at all costs. Aside from Offenbach's usual vigorous and
delightful music, the story line of the opera indicated that many male
writers were beginning to reconsider how to deal with the knowledge of
their nonsecret. In this farce Bluebeard, a wealthy nobleman, is looking
for a sixth wife after his fifth one has disappeared. He marries a buxom
peasant woman named Boulotte, a Rose Queen in the village, but then
he falls in love with a shepherdess, Fleurette, who is actually the Princess
Hermia, who eventually becomes engaged to a shepherd, who is actually
Prince Saphir. Despite their love, Bluebeard pursues Hermia and turns
Boulotte over to his astrologist Popolani to be killed. However, Popolani
takes pity on her, and thanks to him, she discovers that Bluebeard has

never killed any of his wives. Rather, Popolani has been guarding them in his dungeon, and the cunning Boulotte plans revenge. By this time, Hermia is about to marry Prince Saphir at court, and Bluebeard arrives with an army and threatens to kill everyone there unless he can have her for his seventh wife. He challenges Prince Saphir to a duel and supposedly kills him. Now Hermia must marry Bluebeard, but right before the wedding, a band of masked gypsies arrives. As they start telling the fortunes of the king and Bluebeard, they reveal that they are the five former wives of Bluebeard and five courtiers whom the king had suspected of having relations with his wife and had ordered to be killed. At the same time, Prince Saphir reveals that he has not been killed. Both the king and Bluebeard are shamed in front of the entire court. So the king pardons the courtiers, and Bluebeard promises to change his behavior and returns to Boulotte, while Hermia and Saphir are wed, and the five wives are also joined with the courtiers in a grand finale.

Although perhaps not intended, this farce fully ridicules the power of men, especially Bluebeard. The women are not helpless; rather, they assume control of their lives. Nor is Bluebeard killed. His "punishment," so to speak, is Boulotte; that is, he is sentenced to spend his life in a real marriage with a strong and smart peasant woman. Whether he will be controlled remains an open question, but it is clear that Offenbach's opera marks a shift in narrative strategies that treat the gender conflict in Bluebeard tales.

But not all the innovative versions of "Bluebeard" reflect the optimism of Offenbach's opera. In Schwob's brilliantly disturbing tale of 1894, he employs a little boy and girl to explore the meaning of Bluebeard in the imaginative games they play in a garden. At one point, the little girl suggests that they play "Bluebeard." She wants to be the wife, and her friend is to be Bluebeard. Then she proceeds to dictate the entire story. As they move toward the end of the tale, the girl tells him that he is to slit her throat because she doesn't want to replicate what happened in the canonical tale. She explains to the boy that she doesn't have a sister Anne and that her brothers wouldn't come to rescue her. Therefore, she insists, he must kill her.

> She kneeled down. He grabbed her hair and pulled it forwards. Then he raised his hand. Casually, with closed eyes and trembling eyelids,

a nervous smile on her lips, she held her bare neck and her sensually slumped shoulders ready for the terrible blow of Bluebeard's sword.

"Oh ... Oww!" she cried. "This will hurt!"[17]

It is clear that the girl wants to be hurt, that is, the masochistic desire of women is played out by the young girl in this game. Schwob provocatively asks whether women want to be violated and killed, for he has the girl manipulate the boy to the point that he must hurt her. This narrative strategy is a common one used in many works of the nineteenth century to rationalize the brutal behavior of men. Here the boy appears totally innocent. He has nothing to hide, nor does he apparently want to play the game the way she wants it played. In the end, it is the woman who is responsible for abuse by men.

In the nineteenth century, the majority of the works, almost all written by men, tended to stigmatize the female protagonist as the curious woman, who cannot help but sin because it is part of her nature. In other words, women are driven by curiosity and cannot save themselves from themselves, for they are indeed weak and need governance. In some cases, they are masochistic. Men in the "Bluebeard" tales, plays, and operas tend to be divided into two stereotypical roles: the mysterious, powerful, and wealthy killer, who seemingly murders to protect the murders he has committed and never fully reveals his real secret; or the honorable rescuer, generally a devoted brother, who represents noblesse oblige. From the male writers' point of view, no matter how different their plots may be, the onus for the crime falls upon the woman—not unlike the situation in "Little Red Riding Hood"—for nothing would have happened to Bluebeard's wife if she knew how to tame herself and thus maintain a code of civility that calls for female subservience without legitimacy. Bayley makes this quite clear in part of his funny moral:

> Next,—let all beautiful ladies beware
> How they marry a man with a bunch of blue hair,
> Or if they so marry—or marry at all,—
> Be discreet in their actions whatever befall;
> And should your spouse give you a key, and say,
>   "There;
> Go and open my gallery door if you dare!"

Don't let Miss Curiosity drag you up to it,
But tell her point blank, "Get along, I won't do it;"
Lest he come home in a mighty big passion,
And settle your hash in the Blue Beard fashion:
But if you're obedient, loving, and true,
You'll manage his beard, if ever so blue![18]

Yet, as I have already stated, this message begins to lose its validity toward the end of the nineteenth century and the beginning of the twentieth in large part due to the rise of the suffragette movement and the changing role of the women within the family, social institutions, and workplace. If men had been fearful and opposed to women's questioning of their arbitrary power, many men, as we have seen in the Meilhac and Halévy libretto of *Bluebeard* in 1866, began to be more open to these questions and began exploring what it might mean to reveal their secret of the nonsecret.

It is not by chance that the first three decades of the twentieth century, a period of great social and political turmoil, saw some of the most significant variations of the Bluebeard constellation. To be sure, plays, poems, and stories for children and adults based on Perrault's traditional tale continued to be published, but as the power of men throughout the West began to be challenged, the traditional tale that basically perpetuated conventional notions of gender was seriously questioned by men themselves. As soon as films could be made, George Méliès, the great French pioneer, produced a remarkable short film, *Barbe-bleue* (1901), which along with the operas by Paul Dukas, *Ariane et Barbe-bleue* (1907) and Béla Bartók, *Bluebeard's Castle* (1911), and the short story, "The Seven Wives of Bluebeard" (1909) by Anatole France, reflected greater sophistication and self-reflection on the part of male artists with regard to gender conflict and male power.

Although Méliès's film does not depart much from the traditional plot of the Perrault tale, it is a brilliant work cinematically because of its technical invention, imaginative sets, elaborate costumes, and humorous critique of a tyrannical count. Méliès's Bluebeard has already married and killed seven women. In his old age he seeks to wed yet another young woman, but this time he miscalculates his own power and is killed by his young wife's two brothers. Interestingly, Méliès has her father force his daughter to marry because of Bluebeard's fabulous wealth. In addition, the figure of curiosity is a male demon who jumps out of a book to prompt her to yield to her curiosity. In other words, her fate is framed by men who manipulate her or save her. Even the fairy's role is minimal within the male struggle over her body. There are comic touches in each one of Méliès's scenes such as the very first one in which Bluebeard refuses to pay the notary for the marriage contract and kicks him out of his hall. In the very next scene Bluebeard's young wife is led through the kitchen, and the cooks begin fighting with one another as they prepare the marriage banquet, and one of the cooks becomes lost in the kettle of stew. When the young wife dreams, she envisions the dead bodies of Bluebeard's former wives and oversized keys dancing above her. Méliès also used montage and surreal effects to create tension, and the final scene in which Bluebeard is pinned to a stake by a sword while he watches his former wives come to life is worthy of the best kind of operatic melodrama.

Clearly, Méliès did not alter the stereotypical gender roles of Perrault's tale very much. Bluebeard's young wife, however, does not marry for money and is not calculating. Rather, she is a victim—also a victim of her own curiosity when she gives in to curiosity and is reprimanded by the fairy. Bluebeard's power is represented by enlarged keys and other the phallic symbols such as the swords throughout the film. Knowing how to use the keys and swords will determine the fate of women. Yet, Méliès's critique of arbitrary power and oppression is clear. His comic play subverts the pomposity and pretension of the wealthy classes in almost all his films, and the possibility for transformation is mediated by the magic. In many respects, Méliès followed in the burlesque tradition of Bluebeard interpretations and kept the door open through his comedy for other artists to grapple with the serious implications of how men defiantly sought to maintain the secret of their unfounded power through violence.

It was left to the great Belgian writer Maurice Maeterlinck to be the first at the beginning of the twentieth century to explore the social, political, and philosophical meanings of the "Bluebeard" tale in great depth. He wrote the three-act play *Ariane et Barbe-bleue* with the important subtitle *La deliverance inutile* as an opera libretto for his mistress Georgette

Leblanc, an acclaimed French singer. Originally, Maeterlinck had hoped that Edvard Grieg would write the music for the libretto, but Grieg was not interested. Instead, it was Paul Dukas who fortunately decided to compose the music for what is one of the most extraordinary operas of the twentieth century, but unfortunately also one of the most neglected.

Maeterlinck's play was the first to cast Bluebeard's last wife as a fearless, independent woman, who seeks to liberate Bluebeard's five former wives who are living in fear in an underground dungeon of his castle. Maeterlinck incorporated elements of the Greek myth about Ariane and the Minotaur and an old French verse, "The Seven Maidens of Orlamonde" into his play to endow his version of "Bluebeard" with multiple layers of meaning. In act one Ariane arrives with her nurse in the large hall of Bluebeard's castle while outside the peasants yell and warn her about Bluebeard's bloodthirsty acts. However, she does not at first believe what she considers to be rumors about her husband, who has placed six silver keys and one gold one in her care. Not interested in Bluebeard's wealth, she allows her nurse to open the first six doors that lead to vast treasures. The seventh door, opened by Ariane herself with the gold key, leads to a dark dungeon down below where she hears the song of the daughters of the fairy Orlamonde, who yearn for light. All of a sudden, Bluebeard arrives, and he tries to prevent Ariane from descending into the dungeon. At the same time peasants pursue him to protect Ariane. When Bluebeard draws his sword, Ariane intervenes and assures the peasants that she has not been harmed, and they leave. In the second act, Ariane has already entered the dungeon with her nurse, and they discover the five wretched former wives of Bluebeard who are terrified by light. Eventually, Ariane persuades them not to be afraid of the light. She smashes an underground window and encourages the women to come and glimpse the beauty of the countryside and sea. Finally, she leads them up into the hall of Bluebeard's castle.

In act three Ariane and the five wives celebrate their freedom, but the nurse warns them that Bluebeard is returning to the castle. They rush to a window, where they watch as the peasants attack Bluebeard with their pitchforks. Eventually, they capture him and bring him into the hall, bound hand and foot. Convinced that Ariane and the other wives will now kill him, the peasants leave. However, the wives begin to take pity on him and tend his wounds. After Ariane unties him, she decides to leave and calls upon the other women to depart with her. They refuse, and Ariane goes off by herself.

Dukas's original music for the libretto was influenced by Wagner, French folk songs, and Debussy. He varies the major theme of the music using different keys and tones as the doors to the chambers are opened. Folk melodies are heard throughout the opera, and the pitch is raised when the former wives cry out for light. The theme of liberation is, of course, pronounced through the voice of Ariane, who carries the action and yet fails in her mission, if one can call it a failure. Both Maeterlinck and Dukas bring out a deep psychological problem inherent in the "Bluebeard" tale. Rather than viewing the drama in light of feminism, Dukas wrote that the play concerns freedom. He maintained that no one wants to be liberated. Liberation is costly because it is the unknown, and men and women will always prefer a familiar bondage to the awesome uncertainty that constitutes the burden of liberty. Indeed, he felt that one cannot liberate anyone.

Of course, this was Dukas's interpretation of Maeterlinck's libretto that does not exactly correspond to the action of the play. In fact, the peasants do liberate themselves and provide the opportunity for others to do the same. Ariane, from the beginning, is represented as a confident, strong woman, who does not prefer bondage to liberty. Once she realizes that Bluebeard's power is negligible, she knowingly leaves his house so she can be on her own. There is no need for killing, because the act of murder would make her into the same kind of tyrant that her husband is. Enlightened, she leaves, so it is hoped, to start a new life.

Her fate is, of course, just the opposite of Béla Bartók and Béla Balázs' Judith in *Bluebeard's Castle*, which may even be considered a response to the Maeterlinck/Dukas opera. Both Bartók and Balázs may have been familiar with *Ariane et Barbe-bleue*, and both Bartók's unconventional music and Balázs's libretto depart greatly from the work of Maeterlinck and Dukas. First of all, the play is one act and takes place in the huge circular hall of Bluebeard's castle that is in darkness. Judith, Bluebeard's seventh wife, has arrived with the intention of brightening her husband's life. She has married against the wishes of her family, and she is clearly passionately in love with Bluebeard and wants to know all she can about him. When she sees the seven doors in the hall, she insists on unlocking them. Bluebeard hesitantly gives her the keys, and with each door that she opens she discovers something about her husband's life, always tainted with blood. He constantly asks her whether she is frightened, and she dismisses his questions. In the final door three of Bluebeard's former wives, representing dawn, noon, and sunset and more beautiful than Judith, appear. Bluebeard now bestows upon Judith a diamond crown, cloak, and jewels from the third door, and she realizes that she will be his midnight wife and disappears into the seventh chamber. As her door closes, Bluebeard is left in darkness alone in the castle hall.

This disturbing psychological drama is filled with dread and was conceived as a mystery play by Balázs. In the prologue, Balázs implies that the action may be taking place in our minds, and it has an eerie mystical quality to it. During this point in his life, Balázs was intrigued by what he called the aesthetics of death that brought about an intensified consciousness of life. The fairy tale was the medium of a condition of consciousness and of being suspended in a world of the imagination that is not a transcendental world but opens up right in the middle of the daily world. In his diary, as Hanno Loewy notes, he writes about "visions of a new forthcoming medium: 'New forms of drama: the inner images must also be shown. The struggles are internal dialogues. The effects that are seen in the internal images sometimes produce visions, and they must be played out externally and made visible.'"[19] The fairy tale of Bluebeard was turned by him into a kind of rite of passage, and Judith is brought to the brink of death and suspended in a world that will apparently raise her consciousness of life. But Balázs's story is disturbing and haunting, for on another level it is about love buried alive and about the impossibility of enlightening another person. Judith is to be incarcerated in darkness, and Bluebeard is to live on in dark solitude. She is punished for wanting to know and share his past, which is too bloody for Bluebeard to be willing to share. The taciturn Bluebeard is left locked up as well. He has not killed anyone, but he has certainly cut himself off from love and buried his wives.

Balázs, who had been studying folklore with Bartók, used the traditional eight-syllable metric line of a folk song that Bartók effectively reinforced with melodic passages that recalled Hungarian folk music. With each door that opens and each shift of mood, Bartók created a blend of music recalling Debussy and subtle folk songs that create a harmonic arch paralleling the course of action and setting on stage. The circle is closed at the end, and the hopelessness is a striking but perhaps more realistic understanding of the relations between men and women in Europe right before the outbreak of World War I.

If Balázs and Bartók are pessimistic and basically depict how women in the figure of Judith fail to bring light to men, that is, incriminate them because they in some strange way fail men, Anatole France went in another direction in "The Seven Wives of Bluebeard," to show how women cannot be trusted. To be sure, France's tale is told tongue-in-cheek. His narrator is a historian, who had always been disturbed by many of the contradictions in Perrault's tale. Therefore, he uncovers the so-called true tale of a wealthy nobleman named Bernard de Montragoux, who is timid, kind, and generous. However, each time he marries—and he marries six times—his wife turns out to be demented, weird, or foolish and dies in an accident. The seventh time he marries, he is blind to the fact that his young beautiful wife, Jeanne de Lespoisse, is having an affair with a young chevalier and decides to murder Bluebeard for his money. Her lover, mother, sister, and brothers are part of the plot, and they successfully carry it out.

By no means is France's delightful horror story impossible, and his conclusion could certainly have been drawn from Perrault's tale. After all, Bluebeard's wife did marry him for money. But in his desire to create a parody of Perrault's story, France depicts Bluebeard as a victim, thereby minimizing or even discounting his well-known literary acts as a killer. This is not to say that France is not serious in his treatment of the Bluebeard material. Rather, perhaps in response to the growing suffragette movement at the beginning of the twentieth century, he unwittingly contributes to a notion of powerful conniving women who do not appreciate the kindness and generosity of men, who only desire the best for their wives. And we know what happens to "ungrateful wives."

Though it is always dangerous to speculate and generalize why certain fairy tales suddenly become a popular topic at a certain point in history and then are forgotten for a while until they once again become significantly fashionable and memorable, I want to suggest that the "Bluebeard" tales did seem to strike a chord among serious and popular writers during the early part of the twentieth century, when the roles of women and men in Western society were undergoing a change and revolutions and war erupted. Therefore, there was a tendency to produce more and think more about the paradigm of gender relations in that tale in light of social changes that brought greater emancipation to women in Europe and North America. As a result, the narrative that questioned the absolute authority of men became more public and was displayed and mediated through different art forms. The second important phase in the popularity of the "Bluebeard" tales occurs in the post-1945 period in response to World War II, which brought about major changes in the relations between men and women and a transformation of the bourgeois nuclear family. This is not to say that the period from 1919 to 1945 did not see the publication and performance of "Bluebeard" tales and poems and plays. But it does appear that the Bluebeard topic was repressed during a violent period of fascism and war when a critique or questioning of arbitrary male power would have been perhaps regarded as subversive.

BLUEBEARDS AFTER WORLD WAR II

In the post–World War II period up to the present, many writers, filmmakers, artists, and musicians have attempted to use the Bluebeard constellation as a means to comment on social and political transformations that have affected male identity. In the case of male writers and artists, the doubts about their social status and their feelings about women as a threat to their dominant role in the family and society appear to have increased. Maria Tatar astutely comments:

> [T]he Bluebeard story, with its heroine who lives with a sinister stranger in a remote castle, provided the perfect plot apparatus for working through material crises experienced by men and women whose lives had been unsettled by the war experience. Like *Beauty and the Beast* (filmed in the immediate post–World War II period by Jean Cocteau), "Bluebeard" became a kind of foundational story, a point of departure

for thinking about courtship and romance for a generation healing itself from the wounds of war. As we shall see, it was explicitly framed as an alternative to "Cinderella" and "Sleeping Beauty," which were discarded as dated narrative models for reflecting on love and marriage.[20]

Yet, it was not only a foundational story for thinking about love and marriage, it was also, for men particularly, a means by which they could address their fears of women's encroachment on their power and their concerns about the essence of male identity. For example, in her important study about American men in postwar America, Susan Falludi argues that men were "stiffed" or "shafted" after World War II, and this betrayal may account for many of the violent acts by men or what seems to be their violent nature. She argues that there were two prevailing models of American manhood in the nineteenth and early part of the twentieth centuries: Daniel Boone, the nurturer, who saw his role as contributing to the welfare of society and caring for the environment; Davy Crockett, the virile killer, who wanted absolute control over everything and did not care who or what he would have to destroy to demonstrate his talents. Needless to say, it was the image of Davy Crockett that has basically triumphed in the imagination of American men, and men still strive to meet the ideal of the untouchable and immutable hero who can conquer anything to which he sets his mind, even though it has become apparent that he has less control over his life than he realizes. In fact, if men feel insecure, they generally have blamed women for undermining them and prying, perhaps even stealing their secret power. As Falludi has perceptively explained:

Today it is men who cling more tightly to their illusions. They would rather see themselves as battered by feminism than shaped by the larger culture. Feminism can be demonized as just an "unnatural" force trying to wrest men's natural power and control from their grasp. Culture, by contrast, is the whole environment we live in; to acknowledge its sway is to admit that men never had the power they imagined. To say that men are embedded in the culture is to say, by the current standards of masculinity, that they are not men. By casting feminism as the villain that must be defeated to validate the central conceit of modern manhood, men avoid confronting powerful cultural and social expectations that have a lot more to do with their unhappiness than the latest sexual harassment ruling.[21]

It is clear that, in the postwar period, men throughout the world had to adjust to social and economic changes that saw a limitation of their power, and to a large extent the loss of this power has quite often been attributed to women, who then become the targets of men's misdirected rage. As Falludi warns, one must be careful and cautious when discussing images of manhood and male behavior, for they are "contingent on the times and the culture."[22] Yet, there are many parallels that one can draw between the situation of American and European men from 1945 to the present: men serving their countries in war, seeking to be heroes, returning to societies in which women had taken many of their jobs, the adjustment to the changes in the family and economy, the recuperation of the manly national image constantly challenged and undercut by political wars and economic transformations that has disempowered most men up to the present. It is part of the male secret that to be a man, a true man cannot admit that he has no power, and this is what lies at the bottom of most Bluebeard variants. What is revealing about these "Bluebeard" variants is how they portray men killing or attacking the wrong object or cause for their failures, weaknesses, and frustrations. If we try to understand the male viewpoint expressed through postwar Bluebeard representations in different cultures at different times up through the present, we can trace the inner conflicts that men have suffered and rarely resolved—one of the reasons they continue to revisit the "Bluebeard" story.

Among the important works in the post-1945 period that I want to discuss are the films, *Bluebeard* (1944) directed by Edgar L. Ulmer, *Monsieur Verdoux* (1947) directed by Charlie Chaplin, *Landrou* (1963) directed by Claude Chabrol, and *Bluebeard* (1972) directed by Edward Dmytryk; the novels, *Blaubart* (*Bluebeard*, 1982) by Max Frisch, *Bluebeard* by Kurt Vonnegut, and *Fitcher's Brides* (2002) by Gregory Frost; and the stories, Peter Rühmkorf's "Blaubarts letzte Reise" ("Bluebeard's Last Trip," 1983) and John Updike's "Bluebeard in Ireland" (1994). There are, in fact, many other "Bluebeard" versions, and those written by women are especially telling about the female perspective regarding

Bluebeard's secret. But I am more concerned about why men continue to cling to this secret rather than tell it.

The four films by Ulmer, Chaplin, Chabrol, and Dmytryk are only the tip of the iceberg when it comes to cinematic representations of Bluebeard. Tatar has done a more comprehensive study of such other important films as Alfred Hitchcock's *Rebecca* (1940), *Suspicion* (1941), *Shadow of a Doubt* (1943), and *Spellbound* (1948), George Cukor's *Gaslight* (1944), Fritz Lang's *Secret beyond the Door* (1948), and Max Ophuls's *Caught* (1949) with a sharp focus on marital illusions and disillusionment. I want to shift the focus somewhat to view how the male protagonists use and abuse women to prevent themselves from understanding why they are so desperate and caught in a situation that undermines their power.

Ulmer's *Bluebeard* was produced just as World War II was coming to an end, and it recalls an ethical problem that began haunting men, and would continue to haunt them, ever since Perrault wrote his tale: how to maintain godlike power when women seek to be real, equal, and intimate without killing to defend one's illusions. Set in Paris during the nineteenth century, Ulmer's film is a study of a pathological artist named Gaston Morrell. The reason for his demented mind and behavior is, according to him, a woman. Morrell, whose ambition was to become a great painter, had found a sick woman named Jeannette on the streets of Paris, and as he was nursing her back to health, he painted her portrait, and his work became a masterpiece. But when Jeannette recovered and left him, he searched for her, only to discover that she had become a prostitute. Morrell thought she had defiled his work, and therefore, killed her and sold the painting through a well-known art dealer named Lamarté. Now it is only through killing women that Morrell discovers he can continue painting extraordinary works and making money through Lamarté. All of Paris becomes terrified of Morrell, now known as Bluebeard; however, he falls in love with a young costume maker named Lucille and desperately seeks to mend his ways by not painting her and working primarily as a puppeteer. But Lamarté continues to put pressure on him to paint portraits for profit, and Morrell accidentally murders Lucille's sister while she is working for the police in order to capture the notorious Bluebeard. Lucille bravely seeks him out when she suspects that he has killed her sister, and when he confesses his crimes, he expects her to continue to love him. She is repulsed and is almost murdered. However, the police rescue her, and Morrell drowns in the dark waters of the Seine as he attempts to escape the police.

Ulmer, a Czech director who had studied under Max Reinhardt in Vienna and also worked under Fritz Murnau and other talented European directors, came to America in the 1930s and quickly made a name for himself as a young director of morality films. Steeped in European culture and influenced by socialist ideas and the New Deal, Ulmer began making all kinds of films about different ethnic groups as well as documentaries, film noirs, and morality films. *Bluebeard* was a combination of the morality play with film noir, and it is particularly interesting because Ulmer intended to expose the misogynous nature in men who seem to idealize pure women. Morel appears to be contradictory: a murderer but a haunted romantic artist who, like the hero of E. T. A. Hoffmann's brilliant tale "Madame Scudèry," which also takes place in Paris, kills to preserve the genuine nature of art and his own soul. But as Erik Ulman points out, Morel's contradictory character is not really contradictory at all because that idealization is only the other side of misogyny, and "Ulmer demonstrates Morel's propensity for murder not only with his normal desires, but with something self-willed in his economic condition as well."[23]

Morel is not a victim of uncontrollable and irrational forces. Rather, he makes choices based on economic profit and kills for profit. Although it might be an exaggeration to argue that Ulmer saw in this Bluebeard figure a prototype of the fascist killer, there is no doubt that he abhorred war and the rise of fascism in Europe and spoke out against murder in the name of idealism or any kind of -ism. His representation of manhood in the figure of Bluebeard at the close of World War II reflects a condemnation of men who violate women, live for their illusions, and thus represent a danger to civil society.

There is no self-deception in Charles Chaplin's brilliant dark comedy *Monsieur Verdoux*, which cynically suggests that society is more a danger to humankind than men are to society. In fact, this film is highly relevant today because it concerns a man, who is "stiffed" and resigns himself to the overwhelming economic and military forces that are about to bring about the mass murders of World War II. On trial for having murdered over twelve women, Monsieur Verdoux bitterly defends himself by explaining that he was only carrying on the same ruthless business that individuals within organizations constantly conduct, and that in comparison with the contemporary world that is "building weapons of mass destruction for the sole purpose of mass killing," he is only an amateur.

Chaplin made this film in 1946 after the atomic bombs had been dropped in Nagasaki and Hiroshima and during the hearings of the House Committee on Un-American Activities. In fact, he purposely had one of the first showings of the film in 1947 take place in Washington, D.C., to stir controversy and to support one of his friends, the communist musician Hanns Eisler, who was about to be deported from the United States. The film makes a blunt didactic statement to support freedom of speech and small people exploited by the government and big business, and thus it was banned in many states and received unjust if not hypocritical treatment by the press.

Chaplin set the film in Paris right after the Great Depression, and it begins in a cemetery. In the first frame the camera glides by the gravestone of Henri Verdoux, born 1880, died 1937, and it is his voice that we hear, explaining that he had once been an honest bank clerk, who had worked hard for thirty years, until he was suddenly fired by the bank in 1930 soon after the Depression started. To support his invalid wife and young son, he tells us, he had to go into business by killing wealthy women. But he ironically adds that the career of a Bluebeard is not profitable, and he proceeds to narrate his history to demonstrate why he failed in his business. The very next clip shifts to the crude, somewhat revolting, members of the Corvais family in northern France who argue about what they should do about their missing sister Thelma. Though they are concerned that her new husband is a gold-digger and might have harmed her, they are obviously vulgar people and represent the greedy merchants who are part of what is wrong in society.

Right after we are introduced to them, we are brought to southern France, where Monsieur Verdoux is in a luscious flower garden clipping roses. Just as he has finished, he almost steps on a caterpillar, but he daintily avoids it and places it in a safe place. As he enters his villa, there is black smoke coming from an outside incinerator, and we can easily surmise what has happened to poor Thelma. Though Monsieur Verdoux appears to be a refined, gracious, and amiable man, he is only playing a role to conceal the ferocious anger that has driven him to become a mass murderer.

Chaplin makes no excuse for Verdoux. This is not a film that justifies male brutality toward women. Rather, it is a film about a man who has lost his identity as an honest worker and falls in and out of his role as a misfit murderer, who eventually—after his wife and son die—abandons the business of murdering because he doesn't see how anyone can set a moral "example in these immoral times," as he himself puts it. What makes this film so exceptionally poignant is that Verdoux is depicted clearly as a cog in the wheel of an economy and society that drive people to death, while the comic touches and interludes reveal the touching human side of Verdoux that he cannot help but express. Not only does he stumble about as he woos and kills his wives, plays the stock market, and races by train from place to place to expedite his calculating plans, but he also visits his invalid wife and son, helps poor animals, and takes in a young woman in distress, who ironically marries a munitions manufacturer by the end of the film. If Verdoux has a secret, he does not keep it from himself, nor can he keep it from others. He is the shafted man, the man who has no power, and he does not attribute his loss to women. They are unfortunately easy victims, objectified and convertible. Even here, the women are not simply passive and obedient but represent different types like the outrageous Annabella Bonheur and dignified Mme. Grogney, whom Verdoux fails to trap.

In the end it is Verdoux, who is trapped. But stripped of his disguises, he becomes more noble than ever before, and in the last frame we watch as Verdoux walks toward the guillotine and recalls the figure of Chaplin's tramp, defeated but aware of what the forces are that have taken away his manhood.

Claude Chabrol was very familiar with Chaplin's Verdoux and his fate, and thus his decision to make an entirely different film in 1963 about the historical Landru was somewhat of a corrective to Chaplin's portrait—and it was perhaps a bitter reflection of what was happening to the image of men in France in the 1960s. Instead of portraying Landru as a philosophical murder, Chabrol depicted him as a merciless trickster who supports a nasty family that he detested as much as they despised him. Instead of using the Great Depression as his backdrop, Chabrol has the action take place during World War I, when the real Landru committed most of his crimes.

Chabrol has stated that he doesn't "like stories which attempt to demythify a myth. But Landru ... is he a myth or is he a man? A man transformed into a myth. So when one makes a film about Landru does one transform the myth into a man, or must one transform the man into myth? That's the question! So there are both in this film. For the first time in world cinema, we see before our very eyes the metamorphosis from man into myth!"[24] The difficulty is that Chabrol is unable to capture the personality of Landru or the compelling motives for his gruesome acts. Landru was a common crook who evaded the police in 1914 and went on to murder more than twelve women. Chabrol shows how he would place ads in the personal sections of newspapers, lure wealthy middle-aged women to a villa, kill them, chop their bodies into pieces, and then burn them. As his crimes became known between 1914 and 1919, Chabrol interweaves shots of the battlefields and unpleasant visits that Landru made to his family. In the meantime the mass media have made him into a mass murderer and have bestowed the name of Bluebeard upon him. However, after he is arrested and put on trial, Landru insists that he is innocent and not a pathological killer. He shows no remorse for his crimes and goes to the guillotine in February 1922.

If there is a value to Chabrol's film, it resides in his resistance to portray Landru as a "mythic" and compelling figure, something that Chaplin's film tends to do. Chabrol's Landru is banal. He kills solely for money and for survival. He is petty and unlikable, never concerned about other people, the war, or the immorality of his acts. He is a non-reflective man who does not bother himself to probe the meaning of his vicious acts and clings to his secret even when it is exposed. It is this intransigent position, the murderer who believes that he has not murdered, and his illusion of innocence that are most frightening in this film.

There is nothing, however, frightening about Edward Dmytryk's *Bluebeard* (1972), a film so stupid, ridiculous, and insulting that it cannot even be designated as "camp." In a pithy review of the film, Chris

Kirkham writes: "An odd duck of a movie, *Bluebeard* doesn't fit neatly into any one cinematic category. It isn't a horror film, although there are certain horror elements in it. It's not a comedy, black, bedroom or otherwise. It doesn't even quite qualify as exploitation, although there's plenty of skin to be sure. If forced to do so, the best three word description I could come with would be 'fantasy suspense misfire.'"[25]

The grim, stoic Bluebeard, played by the illustrious British actor Richard Burton, is Baron von Sepper, an Austrian aristocrat and ex–World War I flying ace, whose face was burned in a crash, and thus he sports a strange blue beard. Moreover, he may have lost more than skin in the crash because he is clearly impotent, something we learn later during the course of action in the film. Most of the events take place near his castle during the 1930s, when he has become a ruthless fascist leader of some kind. (Curiously Dmytryk has the Baron and his friends don black uniforms and wear armbands with symbols that seem like the swastika but are some other insignia.) Flashbacks enable us to see how he destroyed Jewish homes and businesses and how afterward he is pursued by a Jewish violinist whose family the baron had destroyed. But the film centers on his relationship with his seventh wife, a spirited American dancer and singer, who discovers the Baron's former wives frozen in a secret chamber while he is absent from the castle. Of course, he returns and catches her. But she is clever and pretends to be concerned and caring and convinces him to tell her what happened to the other six wives. What follows are six ludicrous flashbacks in which six international actresses, Raquel Welch, Virna Lisi, Nathalie Delon, Marilù Tolo, Karin Schubert, and Agostina Belli, known for their sex appeal, are murdered by the Baron in comical horrific ways: they are shot, guillotined, stabbed by the tusk of a rhinoceros, clawed to death by a falcon either because they ridiculed him or betrayed him. For instance, one of his wives is kinky and has sex with another woman. All the sex scenes are gratuitous exploitation of the star actresses, obviously to guarantee the film some commercial success. Predictably, after the Baron tells these ghastly revolting tales, he is killed by the Jewish violinist, who also rescues Anne from the refrigerated chamber in which she would have died.

Dmytryk had been blacklisted in the 1940s as one of the famous Hollywood Ten and had emigrated for a short time to England. Then he returned to America in 1951, only to reveal the names of members of left-wing groups in Hollywood so he could work there again, and he obviously intended this film to be taken seriously. Also, at the beginning of the 1970s, he probably wanted to make some kind of statement about women's liberation and the threat it posed to seemingly potent men. It is insulting, however, that he transformed Bluebeard into an impotent "Nazi" and implied that fascism can somehow be connected to male impotency and impotent men can be held responsible for the Holocaust. As Klaus Theweleit has demonstrated in his significant study, *Male Fantasies*, long ago, the psychological problems of men who fought for Nazi Germany were much more complex and connected to an idealization of a particular female type who had to be protected, saved, and kept pure at all costs. Nevertheless, Dmytryk's film does mark a turning point in male attitudes toward women. Bluebeard's confusion and anxiety that his lack of power might be discovered reflect the troubled minds of many men from the 1970s to the present, and male troubles were not only visible in films.

For instance, the short stories by Rühmkorf and Updike are interesting speculations about male identity, how it is formed, and why relationships with women are disturbed. Rühmkorf's tale of 1982 takes place some time in the distant past in France and continues the tradition of parodying Bluebeard's lack of power. In this instance, his dominating mother controls him almost from birth, deprives him of any sexual or sensual contact, and has him educated by strict monks. When the time comes for him to marry, his mother chooses different prospective brides for him and advises him to test whether his wives will be absolutely obedient to him, otherwise they are to be killed. His lust for killing is a result of sexual deprivation, and after murdering several women, he inadvertently slaughters his own mother when his clever new wife, Anna von Calvados, tricks her into entering the dark chamber that was to be her own fate. In the end Bluebeard, during a celebration at his court, appears gray and dreary so that he is barely recognizable.

This dark comic story is an eerie psychological exploration of the "Bluebeard" syndrome. Though one might criticize Rühmkorf for shifting the blame to Bluebeard's mother for causing her son to become a mass murderer, it is clear that he also wants to demythicize Bluebeard, somewhat in the manner that Chabrol did with Landru, so his Bluebeard is a petty, impotent, and ignorant young man whose secret is revealed in his final gray appearance. His power has been reduced to what he is—a gray nothing.

Updike's short story, "Bluebeard in Ireland," on the other hand, provides a more realistic picture of contemporary men, perhaps more typical of many married men, who do not kill but have murderous thoughts. In this case, George Allenson is married to Vivian, his third wife, twenty years younger than he is. While visiting Ireland, they take a hike into the countryside, quarrel, and seemingly become lost. During their walk, George keeps thinking about his previous wives and how they might have acted differently in the same situation. He feels guilty about not having a child with Vivian, but he also contemplates finding and marrying a new wife. Toward the end of the hike, when their differences appear to have been somewhat resolved in his mind, she surprises him by reading his mind, something that he denies, and they are back where they had started.

Updike's tale implies that men need not rid themselves of inquiring wives in the late twentieth century to prevent them from becoming too intimate; one just has to divorce them. George has apparently switched wives a few times and contemplates another such move. The predominant atmosphere in this short story is one of guilt and nostalgia. As George ruminates, he tries to come to terms with his mistakes and manipulation of Vivian. In the end, it appears as though he has gone in a circle that has led to nothingness.

Nothingness is also the major theme in a short but boring novel by the renowned Swiss novelist Max Frisch, who was married a few times himself. His Bluebeard, who is named Felix Schaad, is on trial for having murdered his seventh wife. During the trial he keeps a diary and plays billiards to distract himself. What is revealed in public testimony—and all his former wives bear witness to his character—is that he has been a jealous husband and somewhat apathetic. In fact, it is his apathy that led to his many divorces and his inability to communicate with the outside world. There is no reason, it seems, to place Schaad on trial because he is not a killer, and yet, he confesses to the crime that someone else had committed. His diaries are filled with comments that reveal that he has lost contact with the outer world; and the outer world, with the exception of the trial, has little interest in him. Frisch, who has always been interested in problems of identity in such works as *Andorra* and *Stiller*, appears to be arguing that there is no need to fear Bluebeard, a serial monogamist, for he is more a danger to himself than he is to society. If Bluebeard, indeed, does not exist, and if he, in this case Schaad, cannot create a new identity for himself, then he might as well be dead for all times.

Frisch was always concerned with the manner in which society labeled people and imposed identities on them, and he often wrote about how the individual helplessly fought against society to mold his or her own identity. Schaad as Bluebeard has no identity in the end, no raison d'être, and perhaps this can be viewed positively. If Frisch is arguing that the patriarchal tradition is hopeless and dead at the end of the twentieth century, that men are not violent and abuse their power, there may be something positive in the endless dialogues and stream of consciousness in his novel. On the other hand, given the continued violation of women by men and the resistance of men to reflect upon the grounds for power relations in the home and public sphere, the novel conceals more than it reveals about Bluebeard's secret.

More poignant and more revealing, Kurt Vonnegut's novel, *Bluebeard*, written about the same time as Frisch's work, concerns an Armenian painter, Rabo Karabekian, who was once famous as an abstract painter and mixed with famous artists such as Jackson Pollock. However, he had been using a paint that dissolved and led to the effacement not only of his paintings but also his career. Therefore, he moves to a farm on East Hampton, Long Island, and he writes a diary that he may make into a book about the struggles of his life. On this farm he has a locked barn that contains his greatest secret that he refuses to reveal to anyone. That is, until Circe Berman, a writer, appears and begins to spend much of the summer with him. Their relationship is the basis of the novel, for she wants to pry the secrets of his life from him, especially the secret in the barn. Though Karabekian had been married twice and though he had more or less killed his own paintings, he is not a murderer. Rather he is an artist who desperately wants to represent the most crucial aspects and secrets of life to the world through his art. But until Circe comes along, he has been unwilling to trust anyone with whom he might share his vision. Finally, Karabekian does show her his work in the barn, which she has inspired. It is called *Now It's the Women's Turn*, a huge canvas that depicts the horrors of World War II with the sun rising as the war has come to an end. Though this picture may not have a direct connection to the traditional Bluebeard tale, Maria Tatar explains its significance with regard to the male Bluebeard identity:

> In the potato barn, Rabo Karabekian has housed a new identity, one that declares itself prepared for a different representational regime. Bluebeard's secret turns out to hinge on a decision to abandon violence and to embrace a true renaissance, a rebirth that will avoid the sterile solipsism of Abstract Expressionism and the banal pathos of mimetic art. In the end, this artistic Bluebeard has found his soul, and with a "happy heart," he has decided that the time has come for women to generate new paintings that tell new stories about the figures of lived experience and about the wonders of an imagined world.[26]

Although at times somewhat self-indulgent, Vonnegut's novel does point in a new direction that women writers had already taken in their rewriting of "Bluebeard" tales, and it has prepared the way for other male writers such as Gregory Frost, whose recent work, *Fitcher's Brides* (2002), brings together the literary tradition of Bluebeard with the more subversive oral tradition of "The Robber Bridegroom." The action in this historical horror novel takes place in 1843 when John Charter moves to the town of Jekyll's Glen with his second wife, Lavinia, and his three teenage daughters, Vernelia, Amy, and Catherine. He had lost his first wife and all his money in Boston during the market crash of 1837, and Lavinia, a follower of the cult preacher Elias Fitcher, convinces him to settle in the Finger Lakes district of New York to join the utopian community of Harbinger House and to serve Fitcher. However, it soon becomes clear that Fitcher, who has been preaching that the end of the world will occur in 1843, is a demented sadist, who has been using his charisma and the words of the Bible to deceive hundreds of people. Not only does he exploit them, but he also murders anyone who stands in his way and takes great sadistic pleasure in torturing and slaughtering his wives. With the help of the nasty stepmother Lavinia, Fitcher manages to persuade the Charter to give his daughters to him as brides, one after the other, but the youngest named Kate manages to outwit the gruesome and delirious Fitcher, brings her sisters back to life, and burns down the large mansion of Harbinger House.

The novel is overly filled with traditional motifs from fairy tales and horror stories such as the magic key, potent egg, torture chambers, sadistic whippings, gruesome murders, and miraculous resurrections, and the characters tend to be stereotypes that recall Perrault's "Bluebeard" and the Grimms' "Fitcher's Bird." In addition, the plot is clearly predictable. Nevertheless, Foster's work does raise some interesting questions about the charismatic character of a religious fanatic, who is a murderer, and the people who are readily swayed by him. If Fitcher is a false representative of God on earth and if God does not exist, then Fitcher as a religious leader has amassed his power based on lies and stories. The political implications of Frost's novel are clear, especially at the beginning of the twenty-first century when political and religious leaders are creating mass hysteria and leading millions of people into "holy" wars. Frost's Bluebeard figure promises salvation while bringing about destruction. But his problem is not an individual one: Frost exposes a certain type of manliness that cannot exist without the complicity of enormous numbers of followers. If indeed Bluebeard is not just a murderer of women, but also of children and men, his crimes are no longer totally related to the women's question and gender conflict but to the entire question of masculine domination.

Male violence that may be connected to a genetic disposition in men cannot be explained simply by studying how certain genes have evolved, enabling men to become physically more aggressive and stronger than women. Nor can it be fully grasped by analyzing how the social organization of power propels and mobilizes men to use brute force in competition to assert their dominance. Both biological and cultural factors must be studied historically if we are to learn more about serial murderers and why men are more prone to use brute force to assert their dominance over women. The Bluebeard tales became relevant in Western society because they open up an unresolved discourse about the men's question closely connected to the debate about the women's question. This is why I have focused primarily on how men view Bluebeard and his crimes. The fairy tales about Bluebeard take different forms that range from legitimation and justification of male power to exposure of the faulty premises and condemnation of male power. There never should have been a debate about women's rights in the seventeenth century, nor should there be one now. The key to understanding why there has been such a debate that continues into the twenty-first century can be found in Perrault's original text of "Bluebeard" and the circumstances that have given rise to a memetic discourse within the genre of the fairy tale.

"Hansel and Gretel"
Illustrator: Arthur Rackham

Chapter 6

Hansel and Gretel: On Translating Abandonment, Fear, and Hunger

Nothing but poverty did they know.
Caught while stealing.
Locked up.
Made their escape:
Killed the attendant watching over them.
And do you really think
that something can become
of them once again?

Josef Wittmann, *Hänsel und Gretel*[1]

espite all its sweetness and seemingly comforting happy ending, "Hansel and Gretel" is a very problematical fairy tale. It raises problems that pertain to the consequences of hunger in poor families, the trauma of abandonment, the depiction of women as nasty stepmothers and witches, survival, and the sanctification of paternal rule that were, in fact, glossed over by the Brothers Grimm. The readers of their tales in the nineteenth century and early part of the twentieth century were faced with these problems to one degree or another, but they did not question their depiction and treatment by the Grimms. In fact, they tended to agree with the patronizingly Christian way that the Grimms dealt with the hunger, abandonment, and survival of two small children. Certainly the promotion of the tale to classical status would make it seem so: "Hansel and Gretel" is one of the most popular tales in the world today. Yet many post-1945 writers, illustrators, and filmmakers—those who have not just insipidly replicated the Grimms' tale without questioning their work—have not been completely satisfied with the narrative mode and contents of "Hansel and Gretel" and have interrogated the original Grimms' text in an endeavor to grasp the underlying reasons for the abandonment of two children by their parents and for their return to a weeping father who is rewarded with pearls and jewels.

Since I have already written an essay[2] that deals at length with the manner in which the tale was collected by the Brothers Grimm and constantly revised to rationalize the actions of the parents, in particular, the father, who is forgiven by his children, while the stepmother, associated with the witch, is punished by death, I shall not dwell too much on the theme of abandonment in examining how contemporary writers, illustrators, and filmmakers have approached this classical Grimms' tale. Instead, I want to explore how we have translated and transformed "Hansel and Gretel" in a highly productive fairy-tale discourse and why this particular tale has stuck with us as a meme ever since its publication in 1812 and become classical in some form or other. Such an exploration demands questions. For instance, how did the Grimms translate this tale from the oral tradition and why did they keep altering it until the seventh edition of *Kinder- und Hausmärchen* (*Children's and Household Tales*) in 1857? What is the impact of their translation on other translations? Finally, how can translations and adaptations of "Hansel and Gretel" enable us to comprehend malnourishment and come to terms with the material and intellectual deprivation of children from poor families—and there are millions of such families in the world today?

Translating Hansel and Gretel

To talk about "Hansel and Gretel"—and to talk about any of the Grimms' fairy tales for that matter—is to talk first and foremost about translation. When most children and adults hear or read "Hansel and Gretel," they rarely think that they are reading or listening to a translation, no matter what language is being used, even German. Let us recall that the Grimms first heard this tale told by Dortchen Wild[3] some time between 1808 and 1810 and wrote it down in the Ölenberg manuscript of 1810 under the title "Das Brüderchen und das Schwesterchen" ("The Little Brother and the Little Sister").[4] It was very short and much different from the text that they published in the first edition of the *Children and Household Tales* in 1812. For instance, in the Ölenberg manuscript, the children are not named; their mother is their biological mother; there are no references to God; the children survive on their own, manage to kill the witch, find jewels, and do not need a dainty duck to carry them anywhere. In a recent essay on the romantic fairy tale, Gabrielle Brandstetter and Gerhard Neumann examine "Hansel and Gretel" as exemplary for the special genre of fairy tale that the Grimms created, and that has become world renowned, namely a socialization fairy tale of reality, typical of most of the tales in the Grimms' collection.[5] They argue that Hansel and Gretel leave their home to undergo a psychological socialization in which they must realize that their mother and home are ambivalent, loving, and cruel, and they must learn to come to terms with this ambivalence and their own sexuality and aggression in order to survive. Though it is interesting to study the Grimms' tales with regard to the formation of a bourgeois socialization process in the nineteenth century, Brandstetter and Neumann generalize too much, for it is not true that most of the Grimms' tales contain a clear socialization process as they outline it. Moreover, they misread the textual and intertexual development of "Hansel and Gretel" and thus overlook important issues of poverty, abandonment, and patriarchy. If there is an initiation and socialization in this tale, these processes have to be read within the context of genericity, and one of the major concerns must focus on textual changes that the Grimms made to minimize the role of the father as victimizer and to depict a *stepmother* as aligned with a witch who wants to devour the children. The reading must also take into consideration that the father benefits from the children at the end of the tale and symbolically represents a safe home, something that it never was and may never become, especially if the father marries again! Furthermore, we must also remember that the text was not the Grimms' own work and reflected attitudes regarding poverty and famine that were shared by many people at the time, especially poor people, not the bourgeoisie.

Over the course of forty-seven years the Grimms, in particular Wilhelm, kept changing "Hansel and Gretel," adding some important motifs and incidents from an Alsatian tale collected by August Stöber. Today the 1857 version is considered to be the most definitive and "authentic." But how can any text that was first told by Dortchen Wild, a middle-class young woman and Wilhelm's future wife, that was written down, translated from the Grimms' perspective, and then edited and revised numerous times, be considered "authentic," "definitive," or "original"? How did the Grimms claim ownership to a tale in the name of the German "folk," and why should we accord them ownership of this text when they took it from a storyteller and did not acknowledge that she had previously "owned" the tale and told it with her own gestures, voice, and emphases? What right did they have to "translate" this tale in their own manner? But what does translation have to do with the way we (adults and children) read the text and regard illustrations and film adaptations in our own day and age? Who cares about translation?

This last question, of course, reveals a major problem—our non-recognition of translation. We do not pay enough attention to translation when we study fairy tales, especially the canonical ones by Charles Perrault, the Brothers Grimm, Hans Christian Andersen, and Walt Disney. But translation is vital in the history of the oral folk tale and the literary fairy tale as genre. To translate is to take someone else's words, interpret them as faithfully as possible according to the original writer/speaker's intention, find the appropriate terms in one's own language that will make sense to an implied readership, and move readers to empathize, perhaps identify, and grasp a text and context with which they are not familiar. Translation is a process of familiarization, an appropriation of someone else's language, making it familiar so that you and others who share your language and values will feel at home while reading the translated text. In some ways, it is the overcoming of what Freud calls "das Unheimliche," the uncanny in life, so that which is strange becomes familiar and we feel comfortable with it. The adjective "*heimlich*" means homey taken from the noun "*Heimat*," which means home. The translator takes that which is "un-*heimlich*," not homey, and transforms it into something "*heimlich*," so that we are not threatened by what we otherwise cannot understand. But translation is not only the practice of mediating and interpreting a "strange" foreign language with unfamiliar contents and passing it on in one's own native language so that a narrative can become familiar. It can also function negatively to colonize a text, rob it of its "original" meaning, and deaden it. More positively the translation process can involve the interrogation and reiteration of a text spoken or written in one's own language. There are also philosophical, psychological, and political dimensions to translation that are crucial to comprehend if we are to develop the tradition of fairy tales, that is, the trading and commerce of fairy tales, in an innovative manner relevant to our times, but also relevant to the very nature of storytelling.[6]

In his incisive and highly stimulating essay, "On Translating a Person," Adam Philips, the renowned British psychoanalyst, draws an analogy between the art of translation and the art of psychoanalysis, and at one point he suggests that when it is at its most useful and interesting, psychoanalysis can be

> a consciousness of history, a consciousness of alternatives, a consciousness of aspirations and possibilities: a wish for translation. But adding to this an acknowledgment of the unconsciousness of these things, and what that might involve. Without translation in its familiar sense of transferring from one language into another, and in its more metaphorical sense of moving across, or removing to another place, there can be no sense of history, of alternatives, of aspirations, or of possibilities. And contemporary so-called multi-cultural societies depend for their viability on their members' enthusiasm, however ambivalent for translation. Our relationship to translation has become a virtual synonym for our relationship to ourselves.[7]

Philips places the emphasis in his essay on how psychoanalysts are always translating their patients, how they often mistranslate, why people complain about being mistranslated, not only by psychoanalysts, but by friends and relatives, and whether it is possible to create social relations in which people feel at ease to translate and be translated. I want to change his emphasis somewhat, to translate Philips, if you will, to focus on aspects of his essay that reflect upon how translation is vital to the historical survival of fairy tales and the human species because it enables the tales to become consciousness-raising narratives that offer us alternatives to a social world not of our making.

Philips makes the interesting comment that "the translator uses the text to reveal something about himself; but it depends upon there being something there to be faithful to. The comfort of the text is that it is there, and that it is as it is. The words themselves don't change around."[8] Obviously, there are many different questions one can ask about the translator to determine what his or her relationship is to the text, whether the text be fictitious, historical, religious, and so on. In the case of the fairy tale, the text can actually be the spoken word, a folk tale, or it might be a literary tale written down a few hundred years ago or a few years ago. The first question to ask is why a translator chooses to translate a particular tale or collection of tales. Why does a teller of fairy tales replicate or re-create a tale? For the love of art? For money? To make the tale more available to audiences unfamiliar with the tale? Out of personal desire because the tale appeals to the translator and says something relevant about him or her that the translator wants to communicate to other people? Does the translator ever know his or her real motive? Is there an unconscious element of appeal that needs exploring and arises through translation? For instance, in the case of the Brothers Grimm, they began collecting the tales to help the poet Clemens Brentano, who wanted to produce a collection of folk tales after he had published a book of folk songs with his friend Achim von Arnim. Only after they began collecting and translating the tales and only after Brentano lost interest in the project did they realize the historical value of the tales that said something about themselves and their attachment to German culture.

Translation is always concerned with our conscious and unconscious ties to the past and the present. However, the past is problematical because we both need it and need to transcend it. We must recognize its anachronistic features that may weigh upon us, and we must work through them and their ramifications to start anew. The present has no essential meaning without our conscious reflection and knowledge of the past. Without dealing with the past we cannot move forward. Philips cites both Karl Marx and Sigmund Freud, who believed that the past weighs like a nightmare on the minds of the living.

> Clearly the dead are never quite dead enough, but a nightmare, of course, wakes the sleeper up. Freud would say, it wakes the dreamer up with something from the past, the representation of which—the language of which—the dreamer cannot bear. He needs to return to so-called reality in order not to be overwhelmed himself; in order not to die. For Freud, in a sense, as for Marx, the past is both a nightmare from which we must awaken, but it is also our only resource. It is literally where we get our language from, where we learn it. To learn a language is to learn a history, and to acquire a medium from the past in which to reconstruct the past.[9]

Indeed, dreams need translation just as the past needs it. Translation can be an awakening and a means to make use of the past for a better life. The translator is compelled to step back into the past and step away from it. He or she appropriates a past text or tale of times past so it can be presented anew and readers can have a new look at what has occurred. In discussing what makes for a relevant translation, the French philosopher Jacques Derrida notes that a key to understanding the process of translation is the Hegelian notion of sublation or *Aufhebung*, which he translates in French as *relève*.

> Without plunging us deeply into the issues, I must at least recall that the movement of *Aufhebung*, the process of establishing relevance, is always in Hegel a dialectical movement of interiorization, interiorizing memory (*Erinnerung*) and sublimating spiritualization. It is also translation. ... What the translation with the word "relevant" also demonstrates, in an exemplary fashion, is that every translation should be relevant by vocation. It would thus guarantee the survival of the body of the original (survival in the double sense that Benjamin gives it in "The Task of the Translator," *fortleben* and *überleben*: prolonged life, continuous life, *living on*, but also life after death.[10]

Understanding a relevant translation as sublation or *Aufhebung* is crucial if we are to grasp how the process of translation works and what distinguishes a translation that brings about a relative understanding between source text and implied reader and a translation that prevents any understanding whatsoever and is self-serving. A relevant translation can provide a different perspective on history and on one's relationship to it in the present because it both negates certain anachronistic aspects of the source text and maintains usable aspects while forming a synthetic work that will endure as long as people in a particular culture need it. In some respects, translation is connected to evolution: translating is the process of adapting something and making it fit, and we shall retranslate something when older translations no longer fit.

The Grimms' process of translating is most revealing because they collected tales—many originally told in some kind of dialect—throughout their lives and constantly reexamined different versions of the same tale, added new translations, and revised their own texts in high German with the purpose of making them culturally relevant, that is, they retranslated them in keeping with their changing views of the history, politics, and customs of their own day. They constantly dealt with the variants of tales, tales that were repeated to them, or tales they repeated to one another to capture the natural essence they wanted to replicate. But repetition can be dangerous if that is all we do. Even repetition of the same texts as variants reveals a certain lack of progress or our inability to overcome difficulties that continue to bother us. Marx argued that history will keep repeating itself unless we grasp it by its roots, and Freud insisted that repetitions need to be analyzed and translated so they could be grasped, worked through, and surmounted, allowing an individual to move onward without being hampered by the past. The translation of repetition must involve transformation, otherwise our lives will be spent by reliving the past, being dependent on the past. In this sense, a good translation is always an adaptation. It is a re-creation, or what Walter Benjamin in "The Task of the Translator" called a "free" translation:

> [F]or the sake of pure language, a free translation bases the text on its own language. It is the task of the translator to release in his own language that pure language which is under the spell of another, to liberate the language imprisoned in a work in his re-creation of that work. For the sake of pure language he breaks through decayed barriers in his own language ... a translation touches the original lightly and only at the infinitely small point of the sense, thereupon pursuing its own course according to the laws of fidelity in the freedom of linguistic fidelity.[11]

If we repeat, replicate, and adapt "Hansel and Gretel" today, there are good reasons for doing so. We use the language of the text to communicate an equivalent experience of the past as effectively as possible so that we can deal with the present. "Hansel and Gretel" sticks with us, in our minds, because it relates a story in as concise and relevant a manner as possible about starvation, abandonment, and survival. If we simply repeat and literally translate the Grimms' text as it was, however, we remain bound by the past, or our repetition reflects that we are bound by the past. We do not overcome the past to start a new approach to similar experiences of starvation, abandonment, and survival. We copy it, imitate it, and fall back into the past because we have not understood it. To translate "Hansel and Gretel" freely for contemporary readers and spectators entails a careful historical reexamination of the German text's origins and a conscious decision to alter the past text somewhat to make people's experiences of need and want more accessible to contemporary audiences and to show a link between the causes of pauperization in the past and its consequences today. A literal translation of the Grimms' text with illustrations that reinforces its message serves a very limited purpose except to misrepresent the past and keep readers in a state of historical oblivion, even if the illustrators set their images in the past.

Mind you, I am not arguing against literal or literary translations of the Grimms' tales, or endeavors by illustrators to approximate the past through their drawings and paintings. There are occasional needs for such translations as points of reference. For instance, I translated *The Complete Fairy Tales of the Brothers Grimm* in 1987 with an introduction and notes because I felt that it would basically serve an educated community of readers, and because I felt that most of the translations up to that point were either incompetent or lacked a context that would explain the origins of the Grimms' texts. I tried to be as faithful to the Grimms' translations as I could be (fully cognizant that I was writing in American English of the late twentieth century) and even included texts that they had deleted or placed in their notes. I also wanted Johnny Gruelle's quaint black-and-white ink drawings to be used because they recalled nineteenth-century images. Finally, there was a political motif to my translation, for my introduction and notes sought to reveal that the tales were not genuine folk tales and had a very strong patriarchal bias. In this regard I wanted somehow to suggest that we could use these historical tales to move forward and that we needed to create new tales to address our present situation. One can debate the merits of my translation and others that have appeared in the past twenty years or so. But one thing that one cannot debate is the lack of merit of the hundreds if not thousands of texts and picture books that employ pirated translations or sweetened-down adaptations to repeat the story of "Hansel and Gretel" without critical reflection and with the intent to infantilize children and adults and make money at the same time.

In her recent book, *Comparative Children's Literature*, Emer O'Sullivan comments:

> [M]ultinational media and companies manufacturing mass-produced goods for children coordinate their strategies beyond the borders of individual countries, further changing and globalizing what were once regionally contained children's cultures. … Multinational media conglomerates are perceived to encourage cultural leveling out, plundering mass culture as a whole and taking what they want from various genres, cultural circles and periods. This, it is said, has led both to an internationalization of children's culture and to the technologically equipped childhood world of the 1990s, an event-led society of heavily marketed merriment and instant consumption.[12]

Indeed, I can think only of a few choice adjectives to describe the so-called fairy-tale goods of this world market—banal, tedious, artificial, pernicious, sentimental, nauseating, fallacious, stupid, stereotypical, saccharine, putrid, and just plain ignorant and redundant. It is not worth discussing them unless one wants to explore notions of repetition and regression within the culture industry of our present-day consumer society. What is worth discussing, however, are the works by writers, illustrators, and filmmakers since 1945 who have actively sought to translate the Grimms' "Hansel and Gretel" in an effort to provide alternatives to poverty, the trauma of abandonment, and its disastrous effect on families.

MYRIAD HANSELS AND GRETELS

To translate "Hansel and Gretel" means reexamining the plight of two young children and their poor parents who are compelled by famine and poverty to abandon their children. It means revisiting the social conditions that make poor people desperate and that induce storytellers and writers to place part of the blame for the situation, if not all of it, ignorantly on women. It consists of choosing and using one's own words imaginatively and carefully to suggest alternatives to a tale that sentences two children to return to a victimizer and to forget their traumatic history by bringing home a stolen treasure, indicating that the acquisition of riches or money will solve their problems. Furthermore, to translate "Hansel and Gretel" demands that we deal with the question of translation.

It is only since the late 1970s and 1980s that translation studies began to be instituted at universities in North America and Europe, and it is only since the 1990s that some scholars, indeed, very few, began examining the translations of children's literature.[13] Some of the important issues at stake in the discussions that focus on translating for children are how to make the texts accessible to children and whether to change names and places, to delete, alter, or adapt passages. One of the leading theoreticians of translations created specifically for children is Riitta Oittinen, who has used Bakhtin's category of dialogics to explain how translators should address the young reader:

> Translation is in many ways a covenant. The translator of children's literature should reach out to the children of her/his culture. The translator should dive into the carnivalistic children's world, reexperience it. Even if she/he cannot, being an adult, succeed, she/he should try to reach into the realm of childhood, the children around her/him, the child in her/himself. This reaching into the carnivalistic world of children, this reaching out to children without the fear of relinquishing one's own authority, is dialogics. When translating for children, we should listen to the child, the child in the neighborhood and the child within ourselves.[14]

The difficulty with Oittinen's idealistic position is its lack of specificity: it is impossible to know the "realm of childhood" or even the child within oneself. Moreover, she does not discuss the social class and cultural and ethnic differences of children. In contrast, Emer O'Sullivan offers a more sensible approach to translating not just for children but for adults as well by using a communicative model of translation that connects the theoretical fields of narratology and translation studies and by focusing on the importance of the translator as the implied reader of the text. She argues that "the implied reader of a text is thus a time specific and culture-specific entity. In translation, the translator acts in the first instance as the real reader of the source text. As someone familiar with the source language and culture, the translator is in a position to assume the role of the implied reader of the source text and, above and beyond that, to try to identify the natures of the implied author and the implied readers(s)."[15]

O'Sullivan maintains that the translator becomes the counterpart of the real author of the source text, and through his or her intervention and mediation the translator interprets the source text according to new norms and creates a different implied reader from the one in the source text. "The implied reader can be equated with the implied reader of the source text to varying degrees, but they are not identical. The implied reader of the translation will always be a different entity from the implied reader of the source text. This statement applies to all translated fictional texts."[16]

Though there are different demands placed on translators of texts for young readers by publishers, educational institutions, governments, and adult censors, the process through which a translator must go as implied reader of any text is basically the same but results in a translated text that creates a new relationship with readers and can possibly offer new perspectives on the source text. Therefore, to discuss "Hansel and Gretel" as a children's story, part of children's literature, is to distort if not obfuscate its historical origins and its reception up to the present. As we know, "Hansel and Gretel" was appropriated from an oral tradition that included the entire family and was a cultural form of entertainment determined by adults. The tale that the Grimms heard was edited by them many times, printed, and read to adults and children. It is a tale about children viewed from an adult perspective, basically from a male adult perspective, because the Grimms were the ones who changed it and made it popular. It has never been a children's story and never will be, despite efforts by publishers, writers, and illustrators to dumb it down and encase it with categories. This is a tale that has always crossed boundaries—age and cultural boundaries.

In the English language it has had a very curious development. The very first translation of "Hansel and Gretel" appeared in Edgar Taylor's *German Popular Stories* in 1823, and it begins:

> Hansel one day took his sister Grettel by the hand, and said, "Since our poor mother died we have had no happy days; for our new mother beats us all day long, and when we go near her, she pushes us away. We have nothing but poor crusts to eat; and the little dog that lies by the fire is better off than we; for he sometimes has a nice piece of meat thrown to him. Heaven have mercy on us! O if our poor mother knew how we are used! Come, we will go and travel over the wide world." They went the whole day walking over the fields, till in the evening they came to a great wood; and then they were so tired and hungry that they sat down in a hollow tree and went to sleep.[17]

Anyone familiar with a literal translation of the Grimms' 1819 or 1857 "Hansel and Gretel" would recognize immediately that this is not a translation, but a free adaptation. Indeed, in Taylor's version, Gretel eventually marries a prince at the end of the tale, and in Taylor's revision of his original work, *Gammer Grethel; or German Fairy Tales, and Popular Stories, From the Collection of* MM. *Grimm* (1839),[18] he rewrote his original translation entirely, and there are more surprises: he combines "Hansel and Gretel" with "Brother and Sister," "Foundling," and "Sweetheart Roland" and marries off Gretel to Hansel. Lest fears about incest be raised, it should be noted that Hansel and Gretel are not brother and sister in this compilation. Gretel is found in a high tree by a poor woodman, who takes her home to be raised with his son Hansel. They form an intimate relationship, and after he is transformed into a fawn, Gretel is taken in by a prince, who wants to marry her, but she rejects him in favor of Hansel.

What are we to make of Taylor's unusual translations? I use the term "translation" because Taylor honestly believed that he was translating the text by the Brothers Grimm, with whom he was in contact. And Wilhelm actually approved of the first edition of *German Popular Stories* when Taylor wrote to him in 1823 to explain his method and intentions: "In compiling our little volume we had the amusement of some young friends principally in view, and were therefore compelled sometimes to conciliate local feelings and deviate a little from strict translation."[19] By the time Taylor published his second book, *Gammer Gretel*, in 1838, he was more interested in catering to the tastes and expectations of an English reading public than in providing a strict translation. Moreover, both of Taylor's translations were made while Wilhelm was reworking the 1819 text and continued to alter "Hansel and Gretel" until the last edition of *Children's and Household Tales* appeared in 1857. In other words, Taylor used the 1819 edition as the basis for both his translations of "Hansel and Gretel," and the English audience did not have a clue about the final Grimm version until after 1869—and even then the translations were faulty.

What is interesting about Taylor's two versions of "Hansel and Gretel" is that he obviously regarded translation as a means to capturing the essence of a story and passing it on to his readers in a manner that they might grasp the feelings of the characters and understand their situation. So, to a certain degree, the beginning of "Hansel and Gretel" in the 1823 *German Popular Stories* does seek to translate or convey the desperation of two poor children, beaten and starving, and it does this perhaps in starker tones than the Grimms did and alludes to the way that children were treated in England at that time.

I refer to Taylor's translations not because I want to discuss their accuracy and quality, but because they reveal how vital and relative the process of translation was and is when we talk about classical fairy tales. Taylor's versions of the Grimms' tales and, in particular, his versions of "Hansel and Gretel," were widely distributed and well known in Great Britain and North America well into the twentieth century. They helped stamp our notion of a classical fairy tale, and they demonstrate how a translator struggled from the very beginning to make an unfamiliar text familiar and accessible to his intended and implied readership of children and adults. As Jennifer Schacker remarks in *National Dreams: The Remaking of Fairy Tales in Nineteenth-Century England*:

> [T]he seamlessness of the translated tales not only made for an easier
> reading experience; it also allowed for interpretation of these written

versions of German popular tales as unclouded windows onto cultural difference and earlier points in social and literary development. ... In fact, familiarization is only part of the story. Closer examination suggests that Edgar Taylor's editorial choices reflect another impulse, one more oriented toward *defamiliarization* or exoticization. While undoubtedly an heir to English translation strategies, Taylor also demonstrates some indebtedness to the "foreignizing" approach, which had recently emerged in Germany. Like his German counterparts, Taylor seems to use his translation of the imported text "not so much to introduce the foreign" to English readers but to "use the foreign to confirm and develop sameness, a process of fashioning an ideal cultural self on the basis of an other."[20]

Without consciously endeavoring to establish a theory or proper method of translation, Taylor's introductions to his works demonstrate that he was highly conscious of the need not only for a literal translation but also how necessary it was to understand the original texts as representations of experiences that had to be altered if the intended audience was to relate to the narrative. The transformation depended on his choice, on his personal philosophy, on the publishers' wishes, and on the social conditions of his time.

These key factors have also influenced the translations of the Grimms' 1857 version of "Hansel and Gretel" in English-language countries in the post-1945 period, and though there has been an abundance of variation and experimentation, most of the picture books and translations of this tale tend to be tedious, repetitive, and useless—largely because they fail to translate the Grimms' work for the present in terms that convey some of the deplorable conditions in American and British societies and fail to suggest ways to change them, for that was also the didactic intention of the Grimms. Since it would be difficult to discuss individually the many translations that have appeared in the past sixty years, I want briefly to summarize some of the negative tendencies in the republishing of "Hansel and Gretel" that trivialize its contents, namely the hardship of two abandoned children, who lack both spiritual and material nourishment. Then I want to address selected works by writers and illustrators who have sought to redress or adapt the problems of the Grimms' "Hansel and Gretel" with the obvious intention to reflect upon the past in order to surmount it.

The Publishing Syndrome

Let us begin with the policies of publishers and editors, and we must bear in mind that there is no one set policy in the United States and United Kingdom, and that policies keep changing. Nevertheless, there are clear tendencies that allow us to see the norms of publishing houses that play a major role in the dissemination of the fairy tale and are part of its genericity.

First, almost all publishers have categorized "Hansel and Gretel" as a children's tale, and consequently, their attitudes toward its representation tend to reflect a one-dimensional attitude toward the tale that must be made "appropriate" for children. This means that they guarantee that it is not too frightening, that the children are charming, usually blond, that the images are sweet if not comic, and that the language is simplified so that most picture books, especially the cheapest products, are dumbed-down versions in language and image.

Second, to save money and to make money, publishers have generally appropriated translations in the public domain from the nineteenth and early part of the twentieth centuries. They have hired hack writers and illustrators to touch up the texts and to draw attractive pictures to capitalize on the classical status of "Hansel and Gretel." Since every child should know this tale, every publisher wants or has wanted part of the action, and, therefore, we have myriad cheap and thoughtless picture books with vapid texts and images.

Third, many publishers, however, have been interested in quality reproductions of "Hansel and Gretel" and have hired competent translators and skilled illustrators to produce picture books, which tend to be lavish and in the higher price category, banking on the reputation of the illustrators to attract buyers. However, there is an astonishing similarity in almost all of the picture books, even when the illustrations appear to be unique and reveal great artistry.

Let us take Anthony Browne's *Hansel and Gretel* (1981) as an example. If we disregard the translation, which is very basic and inaccurate, the images constitute what is significant in this book. There are fourteen full-page illustrations that reflect conditions of an impoverished family living somewhere in England during the 1980s. Yet, despite the stark neorealistic images that capture the drab existence and desperate circumstances of the family, Browne's composition is very traditional: instead of questioning or challenging the text with his images, his pictures only reinforce the conventional message that the stepmother, a smoker dressed in a fine imitation leopard overcoat and leather boots, is responsible for the abandonment of the children. Indeed, she leads the way into the woods and appears in another image to be the warden of their home depicted as a jail with bars. Finally, Browne makes it clear in portraying the witch behind the lattice of her cottage, that she is an older version of the stepmother. The witch has the exact same expression as the stepmother and bears the very same mole. The final scene, in which the children embrace their father, indicates that he is their savior and protector, though he had been complicit in the crime of abandonment and had not gone in search of his children. It is stunning, no matter how different or artistic the illustrations seem to be, that most picture books portray the same scenes time and again and end with the warm embrace that implies trust in a duplicitous and passive father.

The books illustrated by such gifted illustrators as Lisbeth Zwerger, Paul Zelinsky, Antonella Bolliger-Savelli, Arnold Lobel, James Marshall, Mercer Mayer, Sandro Nardini, and others leave no doubt in their final illustration, which I call the "treacherous embrace," that the children should only be with their father to whom they bring their pearls and gems. Some of the illustrated books by Marshall and Mayer are offensive in the lighthearted manner in which they treat the serious subject of child abuse. Others tend to be melodramatic and sentimental. None of them offer a new perspective on the causes of poverty and child abandonment.

Fourth, the publishers and editors in charge of picture books do not dictate how "Hansel and Gretel" should be translated through texts and images. They merely set the parameters. In each instance, it is important to explore the final product to ask why the illustrator decided to interpret the text in a particular manner. For instance, one might ask Browne why he associated the stepmother and witch so closely. Or one could ask him why there are so many contradictions in his images. Why didn't the parents, who may actually own their house and have a television and many articles of clothing, sell some of their possessions to keep their children? There tends to be a slavish conformity to an anachronistic text on the part of most illustrators, no matter how diligent they are in their attempts to recapture the mood, atmosphere, costumes, and settings of the Grimms' nineteenth-century text. The desire to be authentic as an illustrator leads to a certain inauthenticity. If one wants to convey what it means to be poor and live in desperate circumstances, very few of the illustrators have managed to grasp the conditions or the despair.

Finally, the despair of "Hansel and Gretel" calls for a critical analysis of what it means to be down and out in contemporary America and Great Britain. Translating "Hansel and Gretel" demands that the writer and artist focus on what the classical tale might have meant in the past, what the Grimms did to the oral tale, and how reappropriation might be made to clear the way for innovation so that the tale speaks to the readers and spectators, old and young, in the late twentieth and early twenty-first centuries. In this regard, translation calls for adaptation, experimentation, re-elaboration, and self-reflection.

ALTERNATIVE HANSELS AND GRETELS

As we have seen, "Hansel and Gretel" was freely adapted as an English translation from the very beginning. In fact, there have been numerous parodies, didactic revisions, and serious elaborations from the nineteenth century to the present. For instance, in recent times there are such versions as Mike Thaler's *Hanzel and Pretzel* (1997), in which two disobedient but clever children manage to outsmart the witch and eat her cottage, while she ends up becoming a vegetarian and opening a health food store. In Karin Law's *The Truth about Hansel and Gretel* (2002), a harmless old lady tells how Hansel and Gretel spread rumors about her so that she became regarded as a nasty witch. In Kees Moerbeek's pop-up book, *The Diary of Hansel and Gretel* (2002), we have a different perspective, namely the amusing viewpoint of a spunky Gretel and scraps of drawings, found objects, and newspaper articles that show how Gretel saved Hansel's life. Finally, Gregory Maguire has transformed the fairy tale into a contemporary animal fairy tale in "Hamster and Gerbil" (2004), which has a multicultural cast and focuses on problems caused by a skunk stepmother. Aside from these experiments in stories published largely for children, there have been many other poems,[21] novels, short stories, and films for children and adults that seek to challenge the traditional versions or notions that readers and viewers may have about this classical tale. I want to focus on some of the more unusual endeavors that reflect critically on the Grimms' narrative and seek through adaptation to address contemporary social issues.

One of the more exemplary revisions of "Hansel and Gretel" is Gianni Rodari's "Nino and Nina" (1969), a story that is set in Milan during the 1960s. This was the period in Italy following World War II, when there was still widespread poverty, and Rodari, the most renowned writer for children in Italy during the twentieth century, transforms all the motifs in the traditional "Hansel and Gretel" tale to bring out the economic causes underlying poverty and how solidarity among brother and sister and among people from the working class can provide an alternative to a desperate situation. The mother of Hansel and Gretel is not accused of a crime. The father is largely responsible for his actions and is active in his pursuit of the children. The ending, while happy, is not closed and indicates how the father has learned a lesson from his children. In another European version, "Hansel and Gretel" (1979) by German writer Otto Gmelin, the author presents an interesting twist from the beginning: the children decide to go into the forest by themselves to seek food. The parents do not abandon them. Lost in the woods, they are captured by a gluttonous witch, who wants to enslave the children, just as she as done with her cat, the dogs, and the gate that take pity on the generous children and enable them to escape. Gmelin borrows motifs from other folk tales to show how Gretel uses magic articles to create obstacles that prevent the witch from capturing them. The witch is not killed but simply frustrated. The children find their way home without a duck or bird. Their story is about survival and family solidarity, how children want to help their parents in dire circumstances and learn that the world is treacherous and that, though they may be courageous, they may not be ready to provide the help that the family needs.

What makes Rodari's and Gmelin's translations significant is that they use their own experience and knowledge of child abuse, sexism, deprivation, and poverty to build on and go beyond the Grimms' "Hansel and

Gretel." They do not speak down to children but explore alternatives to the traumatic childhood experiences. In the case of Rodari's story it is desertion by the parents who feel helpless; in Gmelin's tale it is the frightening experience of childhood abuse by a stranger. In each case, the family is reunited with a greater consciousness of the dangers of despair and how a family can be torn apart by poverty. Moreover, in both tales, the reader is left with a sense of optimism and hope that the children can become agents of their own destiny without succumbing to male domination.

In Tony Kushner's *Brundibar* (2003), illustrated by Maurice Sendak, the optimism and joy of a desperate brother and sister, who are living with their single mother, are contagious. This picture book is a good example of a narrative that recalls "Hansel and Gretel" and the Holocaust at the same time to suggest ways to overcome the barbarism of tyranny. Based on an opera written by Adolf Hoffmeister with music by Hans Krása, performed by children the Nazi concentration camp Terezin, it is set in a village during the late 1930s and deals with two poor Christian children named Aninku and Pepicek, who want to save their sick mother. They leave home to fetch some milk and do battle with a monstrous figure named Brundibar, who resembles Hitler. With the aid of some animals and other children from the village, they manage to procure the milk they need, and a Jewish doctor gleefully heals their mother. As U. C. Knoepflmacher points out, "[I]t is the children, Aninku and Pepicek, rather than a paralyzed or debilitated parental figure who boldly initiate the journey away from the family home. This sister/brother pair thus is much closer to rebellious escapists such as Max or Mickey or Jenny and to the heroic Ida of *Outside Over There* than to Hansel and Gretel, children deprived of the agency they require in order to survive parental desertion."[22]

Kushner's quaint and sprightly narrative and Sendak's colorful and complex electrical images that recall the bizarre Breughelian peasant world in Czechoslovakia during the Nazi period convey the courage of the children who indict dictators like Hitler. Interestingly, Brundibar incarnates the concrete evil of the times and replaces the female witch of the "Hansel and Gretel" stories. Though he is vanquished and the Jewish doctor heals the mother and departs saying "Mazel Tov," leaving the home that has a crucifix on the wall over his shoulder, Brundibar has the last word and warns that he will return. "Nothing ever works out neatly—Bullies don't ever give up completely." This open ending is not pessimistic, rather a reminder that the forces that contributed to the creation of the Shoah are still with us, and we must learn to live with this knowledge with the hope that children can join in solidarity to combat those forces. Life does indeed entail adapting to difficult conditions and involves moral altruism and reciprocity.

Donna Jo Napoli's *The Magic Circle* (1993), a novella, clearly intended for somewhat older readers, provides another fascinating perspective on hope with a somewhat different depiction of the witch and the meaning of evil. A gripping, tragic story, it is also a narrative that reveals how adults can struggle against demonic forces that drive people to pedophilia, infanticide, and self-destruction. Told in the first person by a humpbacked midwife called the Ugly One and set some time in the Middle Ages, the novella recounts how a woman, devoted to her young daughter and to helping people in her community, succumbs to pride: after she becomes a healer, she believes that she can control all the forces of evil. Instead, they take control of her life, and she is driven deep into the forest, where she builds a hut covered with candy that will protect her from Baal and other wicked creatures. Separated from her daughter and other human beings, she is grateful when Hansel and Gretel appear, fleeing their nasty stepmother. They live together in harmony for a few weeks until Gretel discovers the jewels the Ugly One had brought with her and inadvertently allows evil forces to enter the house. Once this occurs, the old woman is possessed by demons and intends to eat Hansel. Yet, her good conscience prevents her from following the commands of the demonic forces, and she more or less commits suicide by enabling Gretel to push her into the oven. Her death sets her free.

Napoli's profound psychological narrative is one of the few versions that enables readers to understand that witches are not always what they appear to be. Nor is any story straightforward and simple. Texts like people and people like texts need to be placed in a sociohistorical context in order to be interpreted and translated. Here Napoli uses the first person so that the putative witch can have her say. It is not the "definitive" story about her experiences with Hansel and Gretel, but it does provoke readers to contemplate many factors lacking in the Grimms' version by trying to get at some underlying truths.

This is also the ostensible purpose of Louise Murphy's novel, *The True Story of Hansel and Gretel* (2003), which takes place in Poland during World War II. It is not the first novel that uses the Holocaust as the backdrop for a contemporary fairy tale to reflect upon the horrors of the Nazi period. Peter Rushforth, Jane Yolen, Roberto Innocenti, Edgar Hilsenrath, Maurice Sendak, and other writers and illustrators have alluded to the Holocaust in their fantasy and fairy-tale works. But Murphy's work is one of the more successful narratives that manages to translate the traumatic effects of abandonment from the Grimms' tale to contemporary readers because she adds the dimension of wartime atrocities and seeks to convey how well-intentioned human beings can be driven to commit barbaric acts. Not only does Murphy manage to draw parallels to the Grimms' story, but she constantly questions it, critiques it, and reveals alternative behaviors and courses of action.

The narrative concerns two Jewish children, who are forced to change their given names to Hansel and Gretel when they are separated from their parents while fleeing the Nazis. Lost in a forest, they are eventually taken in by an old Polish gypsy woman named Magda, who is a wise midwife and an outsider because of her Gypsy blood. She and her friends and relatives risk their lives to save the children. However, they cannot prevent Gretel from being raped in a forest by two Polish stragglers. In fact, the girl is almost killed, but Gretel's stepmother, who is fighting with a Polish resistance group, appears in time to save her but loses her own life in the process. Gretel survives only to lose her mind and may be in danger of being transported to a camp by the Nazis. Thanks to Magda, who is deported to a concentration camp and burned to death in an oven, she and her brother survive the war and are eventually reunited with their father, called the Mechanik, in Bialystock.

This short summary does not do justice to Murphy's work, which is not only a riveting account of the effects of Nazi occupation on a small village in Poland during 1943, based on meticulous research, but also a radical translation and interpretation of the Grimms' "Hansel and Gretel." Murphy has stated, "[T]his is the fairy tale that scared me most when I was a child. It mirrors my worst adult fears about what the abandonment and blind violence of war does to children all over the world. ... Stereotypes are always lies. It was the idea of the 'witch' that began my struggle to understand Magda and then all the other characters. Our culture denigrates older women, yet they are often the ones who protect and nurture everyone in the family."[23]

In fact, all the stereotypes or so-called Jungian archetypes have no relevance in this novel. The children's stepmother becomes a resistance fighter and saves Gretel from murder. Magda constantly finds ways to combat the prejudices of the villagers and the actions of the Nazis with the help of her son and brother. The children's father, Mechanik, because of his technical skills, joins the resistance and actively seeks out his children. We never learn the Jewish names of Hansel and Gretel, yet we comprehend who they are as they learn how to survive and assume new identities after the war. They will discard the imposed names of Hansel and Gretel and resume living under their old names, but not in old ways. Even though they have been traumatized, there is hope for them because they are conscious of the barbarism that can destroy them. They help capture the S.S. officer responsible for crimes in the Polish village. They are aware of why their father had to abandon them and return to him not with a material treasure, but with survival skills. "History is the bookkeeping of murderers,"[24] Magda says before her death, but fiction, and the transformation of the Grimms' "Hansel and Gretel" in Murphy's subversive and critical narrative voice and style provides us with truths that might enable us to write a different kind of history.

CINEMATIC ADAPTATIONS

It is not just through prose fairy-tale narratives and poetry, however, that "Hansel and Gretel" is being translated, revised, and represented, but also through the mediation of film. Strange to say, "Hansel and Gretel" is one of the few fairy tales that Walt Disney and the Disney Corporation has not transformed into a feature-length animated film. But given its thematic relevance and stature as a classical fairy tale, numerous filmmakers have made a stab at adapting the fairy tale for the screen. I am using the word "stab" purposely because many of the films, especially those designed for adult audiences, have cut and slashed the text and pasted it back into a horror film intended to play upon our anxieties for affect more than anything else. For instance, *Whoever Slew Auntie Roo?* (1971) stars Shelly Winters as a psychotic American mother and ex-vaudeville star, living in England in the 1920s, who plunders an orphanage and is burned to death in her mansion. She is so ridiculous and comical as a would-be witch that the film is more camp than horror film. More recently, François Ozon, a French filmmaker, produced *Criminal Lovers* (1999), in which two teenagers kill an Arab schoolmate and flee to a forest, where they are captured by a lonely hunter who treats them in brutal and sadistic ways, until the girl is killed by the police and her friend and hunter are arrested. Here the arbitrary violent acts are to be taken more seriously because they are horrific representations of how common the random acts of violence among teenagers have become.

There are, of course, more cheerful versions of "Hansel and Gretel" such as James Frawley's *Hansel and Gretel* (1982), part of Shelly Duvall's Faerie Tale Theatre. In this short film filled with Hollywood celebrities showing off their talents, Joan Collins takes delight in starring as both the evil stepmother and the even more evil witch, who is, of course, sent to her death by the brother and sister in a typical imitative interpretation of the Grimms' "Hansel and Gretel," backed by melodic music reminiscent of Engelbert Humperdinck's opera. If the Grimms' text is not used for cinematic adaptation, it is often Humperdinck's opera with a sentimental Christian libretto written by his sister Adehelheid Wette. This was the basis of the Canon Movies production, *Hansel and Gretel* (1988), directed by Len Talan, a hastily made film that drips with sentimentality even if it represents a more realistic picture of the children's mother. Just as the Faerie Tale Theatre films always wink at adults to make preposterous jokes and gain their approval for "harmless" retellings of fairy tales, this film, too, is filled with sentimental scenes and pathetic humor.

The most stupid of all the comic versions, however, is Gary Tunnicliffe's *Hansel & Gretel* (2002), which resembles more a fractured fairy tale that turns all the traditional motifs inside out. This film is framed by a concerned father reading a musty magic book to his two children who have recently lost their mother, and he changes the tale therapeutically to help his children overcome their trauma. In his version of "Hansel and Gretel," a bossy and bumbling stepmother takes two children, clearly contemporary American kids, who are spunky, witty, and powerful, into a magic forest. Abandoned, the children meet a gay sandman, a sexy wood fairy, and a dumb troll, and then *à la Wizard of Oz*, the children manage to defeat the British actress Lynn Redgrave, whose parody of a witch only makes a mockery of her own choice to be in the film, one of the most cinematic insipid adaptations of "Hansel and Gretel" to date.

None of the above films, except for *Criminal Lovers*, makes a serious endeavor to address the profound themes of "Hansel and Gretel" and to translate them into meaningful artworks for the present. Perhaps the only filmmaker to do this thus far in America is Tom Davenport in his very short Appalachian version of 1975. This was Davenport's first educational film, and he set the story in the 1930s during the Depression. Though well intended, the film is flawed. Like most of the writers, illustrators, and filmmakers, he sticks too closely to the Grimms' version in his adaptation and associates the stepmother with the evil witch—the same actress almost always plays the stepmother and the witch—thereby obfuscating the real causes of evil and stereotyping all the characters in the film. To his credit, Davenport does capture some of the misery, despair, and poverty of the people in Appalachia during the Great Depression, but there is no hint of rethinking and re-creating the tale so that viewers might reflect about the possibilities for transformation. This film, like many picture books, ends with the father's embrace of his children, a loving but deadly embrace of closure.

THE RELEVANCE OF RETELLING "HANSEL AND GRETEL"

"Hansel and Gretel," despite its closure in the Grimms' version and despite all its irrelevant imitations, is a never-ending story that has become memetic. It is never-ending because the problems raised by the discourse in this tale have not been resolved in reality: poverty, conflict with stepparents, the trauma of abandonment, child abuse, and male domination. In a recent article in *Harper's* magazine titled "The Christian Paradox," Bill McKibben points out that recent statistics show that the United States is a most unchristian Christian nation when it comes to helping the poor. Not only did we rank second to last in giving aid to foreign countries, but in 2004, nearly 18 percent of American children lived in poverty (compared with, say, 8 percent in Sweden). In fact, by pretty much any measure of caring for the least among us you want to propose—childhood nutrition, infant mortality, access to preschool— we come in nearly last among the rich nations, and often by a wide margin. The point is not just that (as everyone knows) the American nation trails badly in all these categories; it's that the overwhelmingly Christian American nation trails badly in all these categories, categories to which the Bible tells us Jesus paid particular attention. And it's not just as if the numbers were getting better; the U.S. Department of Agriculture reported last year that the number of households that were 'food insecure with hunger' had climbed more than 26 percent between 1999 and 2003."[25]

It is, of course, not just in America where children are poor, malnourished, neglected, and maltreated. But America is one of the richest countries in the world, and like other rich countries contributes to the impoverishment of children through the social and economic policies of state and federal governments. Given these facts and statistics, one must ask, I believe, how they can be translated through a tale about "Hansel and Gretel," which originated out of a concern for impoverished and abused children and which became a classic fairy tale in Western culture precisely because it developed a relevant discourse that made a marked impression on listeners, readers, and viewers and caused them to ponder solutions to the dilemma of abused and abandoned children. Money and a return to a caring father have not turned out to be much of a solution, no matter how many times we may repeat the tale.

To make it more relevant than it is, writers and illustrators, if they are conscientious and conscious, must seek to take the ostensible problem of malnutrition and poverty and find the concise and effective linguistic and illustrative compositions that will speak to people's concerns in the contemporary world. This is the ethical imperative for writers of fairy tales that I addressed in Chapter 1. To reprint and republish tales that adhere mindlessly to the Grimms' version of "Hansel and Gretel" is to do the brothers a disservice and ignore deep social and political problems that threaten to shove our children into the witch's oven. Their survival is always at stake in each and every version of "Hansel and Gretel" published throughout the world.

"Iron Hans"
Illustrator: Jiri Trnka

Chapter 7

To Be or Not to Be Eaten: The Survival of Traditional Storytelling

The tradition of sacrificing children is deeply oriented in most cultures and religions. For this reason it is also tolerated, and indeed commended, in our western civilization. Naturally, we no longer sacrifice our sons and daughters on the altar of God, as in the biblical story of Abraham and Isaac. But at birth and throughout their later upbringing, we instill in them the necessity to love, honor, and respect us, to do their best for us, to satisfy our ambitions — in short to give us everything our parents denied us. We call this decency and morality. Children rarely have any choice in the matter. All their lives, they will force themselves to offer parents something that they neither possess nor have any knowledge of, quite simply because they have never been given it: genuine, unconditional love that does not merely serve to gratify the needs of the recipient.

Alice Miller, *The Body Never Lies*[1]

One of the great storytellers of the twentieth century, Bertolt Brecht, once wrote a story about a father who wanted to teach his little son a lesson by placing him on the top of a six-foot wall and commanding him to jump.

"Jump into my arms!" cried the father. "I'll catch you."

"No, no," the son responded. "I'm afraid."

"Jump, I said. There's nothing to fear," the father reassured him.

"No, no! I can't. I won't. You won't catch me," shrieked the shivering child.

"Of course, I'll catch you. What do you think I am, a monster?"

"You promise?" the son sobbed.

"I promise."

So, the boy leapt from the wall. The father took a step back, and the child crashed to the ground in pain.

Brecht told this tale as part of the Herr Keuner series of stories, intended as political parables about survival under capitalist conditions. In a dog-eat-dog world, you can't even trust your father, nor should you. But it is not necessarily capitalism that fosters such a tenuous, if not ruthless, relationship between father and son. If we recall, Cronos, the great Greek god, devoured his children and had to be forced to regurgitate them. Abraham was no better. Though he did not eat his sons, he banished Ishmael to the desert and was prepared to kill Isaac to prove his loyalty to God. Some stories even relate that Abraham did indeed kill both Ishmael and Isaac, and other narratives about the origins of the world involve bitter conflicts between a stern authoritarian father, who refuses to have his power and laws questioned, and his children, who are compelled to obey him or face death or banishment. More to the point, folklore is filled with tales of fathers, giants, ogres, monsters, sorcerers, cannibals, bogeymen, fiends, and devils who eat or beat young children. And men are not the only danger for children. There is also a fair share of mothers, grannies, witches, ogresses, sorceresses, and female demons who lust after children, punish them, and destroy them. Even those allegedly good fairies who have absolute control over children can be wicked. But they generally don't eat their own. Human beings are the ones projected as monsters who eat and destroy their own. Why?

In her thought-provoking and comprehensive study of horror stories and horrific creatures, *No Go the Bogeyman: Scaring, Lulling and Making Mock*, Marina Warner comments:

> The question "Who eats and who gets eaten?" reverberates in the material of bogeydom. How cannibalistic impulses beat in the cultural imagination and what significance they carry can still be heard in the tread

of the flesh-eating ogre and his progeny, whether he rattles his bones or strides in seven-league boots or comes whiffling through the tulgey wood. Control of food lies at the heart of the first werewolf story, the transformation of Lycaon, of famous fairy tales, like "Hansel and Gretel" and less familiar ones that feature ogres and ogresses like Baba Yaga. Vampires and the undead progeny of Bram Stoker's *Dracula* (1897), who walk abroad in the shadows of our culture, form part of the larger family of fatal monsters who cannibalize humans. Food—procuring it, preparing it, cooking it, eating it—dominates the material as the overriding image of survival; consuming it offers contradictory metaphors of life and civilization as well as barbarity and extinction.[2]

Though food—the lust for it and lack of it—may be a dominant motif in folklore, Warner makes clear that there is no one exclusive reason for the unsavory and uncontrollable appetite of adults, often represented metaphorically as monsters, who abuse their power over children. The causes are numerous: famine, starvation, disobedience of the young, fear of losing power, jealousy, sensual pleasure, and so on. Often it is difficult to discover any reason whatsoever. The adult as ogre or witch arbitrarily eats children, lives off children, is obsessed by children, and devouring the young is his or her way of life. The appetite rules.

> Fee-fi-fo-fum,
> I smell the blood of an Englishman.
> Be he alive, or be he dead
> I'll have his bones to grind my bread.[3]

But it's not only young Jack who is often in danger of being devoured by a cannibalistic giant. Tom Thumb and his brothers in Perrault's tale, based on French folklore, are threatened by an ogre, who unintentionally slits the throats of his own daughters, because he thinks they are the boys whom he wants to eat. The witch in "Hansel and Gretel" intends to bake and eat Hansel, and we never know why, unless she is indeed a projection of the stepmother or mother. Even then her reason is murky. She is pure appetite.

We live in a world filled with vampires, demons, aliens, sinister robots run amuck, demented scientists, serial killers, nasty pedophiles, and barbarous politicians, indifferent to the murder of innocent children that they cause. No story, however grotesque, should surprise us. We live in a world clouded by hysteria and hypocrisy in which child abuse and poverty are rampant. We live in a world torn apart by political and religious forces that shred us and make us feel so threatened and desperate that we seek an overall arching narrative to provide us with security. But as we pursue this narrative that has numerous variants—and not everyone seeks an overall narrative related to some kind of intelligent design—I believe we must first recognize that there is a common thread running from ancient times to the very present that underlies many of our tales: we eat our young, and if we don't succeed, we confront them with the question, to be or not to be eaten.

We also nurture our young, but our nurturing is somewhat like the witch in "Hansel and Gretel," who wants to fatten Hansel before she eats him. Do we nurture our young so we can eat them? Is this tradition? Do we nurture and cultivate them to transform them into cannibals and cutthroat barbarians who will eat their young? Do we tell fictional stories and maintain illusory traditions that foster intolerance, ignorance, racism, sexism, and wars? Why should we respect and maintain traditional storytelling and classical fairy tales as memes if traditions based on different religions and nationalisms are responsible for much of the misunderstandings and conflicts in our world today? Why should we be concerned whether traditional storytelling and fairy tales can survive or whether we are using the appropriate means to transmit customs, mores, and language when they may be anachronistic and deadly for our children and ourselves? Aren't the religious narratives of every living religion today intended to be taken as the gospel truth, somewhat responsible in their literal and fundamental interpretations for crimes against children and humanity? How do we find truth in untruthful tales and believe traditional storytellers—priests, ministers, rabbis, tribal leaders, shamen, imams, gurus, teachers, politicians, actors, and so on—who often blur our view of the world to rationalize their own power?

The only way we can do justice to traditional tales and storytelling, in my opinion, is to problematize the value of these tales and to question the purpose of tradition and the role of the storyteller. Not all traditional tales are religious and demand belief in and obedience to the strictures of the tale. Not all traditional storytellers are holy people who call for blind faith in the putative truths of their tales. There are hundreds of types of traditional tales and many diverse traditional ways of telling tales. They will continue to exist and to be transmitted. Some will be discarded, but the ones that become memetic have an impact on our behavior and the way we view the world. So we must ask these questions about traditional tales and their survival: What are the traditional tales that reoccur and are repeated in traditional storytelling and why? And I am not talking solely about fairy tales, although we shall see that they overlap with other genres. Is it realistically possible to convey a sense of the past about one's culture to people in the present through traditional storytelling? How is it possible to tell a tale from another culture through traditional storytelling? Is it worth the effort to use storytelling to bring about greater intercultural understanding? If a great deal of traditional storytelling pertains to the question "to be or not to be eaten," how can we use the same storytelling to feed listeners and tellers alike so that they will not have to fear abuse, abandonment, and betrayal?

THE TRADITIONAL CANON OF TALES

Clearly, the tales that become canonical in a society are those that have generally been fostered by religious ritual, pedagogical standards, practical custom, and social communication. What we call canon formation began in the fourth century A.D. when, as John Guillory explains, the word canon "was used to signify a list of texts or authors, specifically the books of the Bible and of the early theologians of Christianity. In this context 'canon' suggested to its users a principle of selection by which some authors or texts were deemed worthier of preservation than others."[4] The formation of canons was primarily developed through modes of orality and the writings of early religious and education establishments until the invention of the printing press in the fifteenth century. At that point it became important in Western civilization to set standards of literacy through published works, schools, and churches that fostered the memorization and rote learning of religious and didactic stories, national legends, and codes. R. A. Houston points out that "the early modern period saw much greater intervention by governments in the interests of regulation, systematization and even provision. During the sixteenth century the principal drive to control, extend and structure the provision of education came from a desire for religious conformity whether in the bounds of a nation state or within a principality or even a single town."⁵ Of course, it was very difficult to control the diverse modes of storytelling—one of the reasons why the early oral wonder tales and other folk tales were not looked upon with approval by the upper classes. Competing canons of stories arose, and it is difficult to trace or even insist that there is a definitive canon of storytelling in any one society or nation. What is written down as traditional is always challenged by the spoken word and daily practice. Nevertheless, religions and nation-states have derived their authority and power from traditional canons of literature and storytelling. The Christian, Jewish, Islamic, and Buddhist religions and many others have made their mark in the world and organized manifold forms of storytelling so that their belief systems are spread not only from the pulpit but through the mass media and through people themselves—through word of mouth abetted by print. Political leaders and states have also fostered stories about their histories, heroes, events, and incidents that have helped construct a sense of community or nation. Schools and universities are sites where canonical tales and traditions are evaluated and debated. History, as we know, is not only written by the victors, but also told by them and spread by victorious peoples from all walks of life. What becomes traditional and canonical often becomes memetic and is also relevant for survival and the maintenance of identity and community determined by dominant social groups in what Norbert Elias has called the "civilizing process."⁶

Most important for traditions of storytelling and canon formation is the interaction between literacy and orality as mediated through educational systems. Guillory remarks:

> [T]he fact that in our time the teaching of how to read and write, and the teaching of how to interpret literary works, are divided between the lower and the higher levels of the educational system has perhaps blinded us to the real historical motives of canon formation, and to the relations among literature, language, and the social structure. Most important, we have yet to acknowledge or explain fully the relation between literature

and society, a relation mediated by the school, as the institution of linguistic control. Literature and language have marched through history in tandem with one another, and yesterday's literature has become today's grammar. The language of societies with written literatures has thus tended to become internally stratified according to which groups among the population have access to the school, and how much access each has.[7]

Yet, not all the tales that become canonical through the processes of oral and literary traditions reinforce the dominant groups of a particular society. Indeed, there are thousands if not millions of tales that people tell time and again, such as many of Aesop's fables, or fables similar to those he allegedly told, that bring people together and expose the contradictions of the powerful and suggest ways in which the oppressed can survive. Many of the classical fairy tales, while reinforcing the social organization and mentality of patriarchal cultures, also open up a discourse about instinctual drives and civilization that is relevant for the survival of the species as societies change. One can perhaps talk about counter-canonical traditions or modes of storytelling. That is, tradition always engenders subversion in a dialectical process. For instance, many legends question the authoritarianism of authority figures. Robin Hood takes from the rich and gives to the poor and tries to pave the way for a just ruler in England. Barbarossa will rise from the dead to revive the fortunes of Germany. Emiliano Zapata, the revolutionary peasant, is celebrated as a hero in numerous Mexican legends. Many fairy tales have mutated so that Red Riding Hoods and Cinderellas take destiny into their own hands. Canonical tales are not static and stable; their many transformations are worth studying because they reflect changing values, morals, and politics in a given society. Here we must keep in mind that there are multiple canons throughout the world that are shared and contested among multiple groups and social forces. The stories themselves are resilient precisely because they open themselves to multiple layers of identification and interpretation. Not everyone is exposed to canonized storytelling or canonical tales.

Nevertheless, we must bear in mind that, to become literate today, to function as a world citizen and attain power in a constantly changing civilizing process, an individual must know how to read and write and be able to reference standard traditional stories to prove his or her membership in a particular community. It is not necessary for an individual to believe in a traditional story that has become canonized. In our day and age when it is almost impossible to avoid the mass media, we tend to be exposed to homogenized traditional stories, and canonical tales tend to condition our thinking even in the form of lies and misinformation. The canonical tale as selfish meme brings about a proclivity to listen to a particular story time and again so that a certain tradition will be reinforced. The tale becomes registered in our brains almost by osmosis. Once registered by the brain, tales have a memetic function. As I have pointed out in Chapter 1, Richard Dawkins, the renowned biologist, has argued that there may be memes in our brains that are replicators and function somewhat like genes. Recall the quote from Dawkins:

> Examples of memes are tunes, ideas, catch phrases, clothes fashions, ways of making pots or of building arches. Just as genes propagate themselves in the meme pool by leaping from body to body via sperms or eggs, so memes propagate themselves in the meme pool by leaping from brain to brain via a process which, in the broad sense, can be called imitation. If a scientist hears, or reads about, a good idea he passes it on to his colleagues and students. He mentions it in his articles and his lectures. If the idea catches on, it can be said to propagate itself, spreading from brain to brain.[8]

Though the theory of memetics is controversial,[9] as I have said and as memeticists themselves admit, one thing is clear: a culture of a particular group is established linguistically through narrative exchanges, repetition, imitation, and socialization. These exchanges enact and embody the belief systems that hold people together. As a group of people survives in a particular region, it continually cultivates its own relevant customs through different modes of storytelling to stabilize the lives of those in the group and to transmit their values to the young so the belief system will continue. Whoever controls the transmission, that is, the mediations of established values, mores, and customs, will have a powerful influence on the substance of thought and the manner in which people view their lives. Traditional storytelling that becomes canonized is thus essentially conservative, tends to conserve the interests of the status quo, but the canon cannot exclude counter-traditional tales, for it cannot totally govern word of mouth. Nevertheless, the dominant tendency in Western societies, as represented by states, churches, governments, schools, and corporations, is to place words in our mouths through all sorts of technological means so that we will repeat, memorize, and, through conditioning, imitate. Instead of gaining a sense of tradition through personal experience and experimentation, we are to learn, often by rote, what our traditions are and how we can come to know ourselves through mass-mediated and manipulated stories. We are also—at least in America—expected to uproot ourselves, become mobile, adaptable, and replaceable like the spare parts of a machine set up to operate automatically.

Even traditions are calculated, configured, and streamlined to become automatic, that is, official traditions intended to celebrate nation-states, religions, legal systems, and local customs and to keep them functioning. Paradoxically, they are set up to remain stable and eternal, while people are conditioned to become flexible and expendable to serve the needs of the advanced capitalist economic system now called globalization. To become world citizens or even citizens of our own nation-states, it is necessary to abandon our particular identities and to assume what Pierre Bourdieu calls a social *Habitus*, while paying respect to automatic traditions wherever we may be placed. Paradoxically we are expected to be multicultural as languages and cultures are gradually being eliminated throughout the world. We are expected to hold ourselves together and to be held together through artificial theme parks that make fakelore out of folklore; through churches, synagogues, and mosques that have become entertainment and social centers; through schools that foster rote learning and positivist testing; through storytellers who espouse the value of traditional tales without critically examining what tales they are telling and why; through television programs that promote history and news as spectacle; and through political speeches that use false patriotic appeals to tradition so that the young will sacrifice their minds and bodies for their alleged native country, as though national identity were essential and innate.

How can we know traditions, gain a sense of traditions, when they have become elusive and are employed in the interests of groups that pretend to speak for us when they are speaking at us and not enabling the young to speak for themselves? Why are we so intent on baking and eating our young or beating traditions into them?

THE PROBLEMATIC ROLE OF THE CULTURAL TRANSMISSION OF TRADITION

On September 12, 2004, I was driving my car and listening, as is my wont, to Public Radio, and by chance, I happened to tune into the program "Speaking of Faith," and though I am not religious and avoid programs with ponderous sermons and weighty deliberations about church issues, faith, and God, I was immediately drawn to an ongoing discussion about the story of Abraham. The moderator, Krista Tippett, was interviewing Bruce Feiler, who had written a book titled *Abraham: A Journey to the Heart of Three Faiths*. He was presenting background material about Abraham and why he was impelled to write his book after September 11, 2001. Indeed, Feiler, a journalist, who had witnessed the collapse of the twin towers in New York, had begun research in hopes of understanding Abraham's legacy as the common father of Jews, Christians, and Muslims. He wanted to grasp the story of Abraham in a more profound way, and in particular, he sought to depict Abraham as a unifying symbol in troubled times. Although I had come to know Abraham in my youth as the father of the Jews, who was willing to sacrifice his son Isaac to prove his loyalty to God, I was not conversant with Abraham's role in the Muslim and Christian religions, nor did I know that there were thousands if not millions of competing stories about Abraham that have been passed down through word of mouth and print throughout the world over centuries. The more I listened, the more I became intrigued not only by the role that Abraham apparently played in founding all three religions, but by Feiler's glowingly positive interpretation of Abraham in contrast to Søren Kierkegaard's much more critical and philosophical exposition of the tale in *Fear and Trembling*.[10] Interestingly, both Kierkegaard and Feiler make a leap of faith and assume that what is pure story may be true and should affect our reality, the way we think and pass on stories.

Yet, according to Feiler, there is no archaeological evidence that Abraham ever existed, and in the stories that were created, Abraham was a man of violence who willingly sacrificed his two sons or was ready to sacrifice his two sons in the name of God or because he heard the voice of God demanding that he do this. Who created the stories and how they were spread until they were written down in the Old Testament and the Koran remains a mystery. We only know that they emerged from an oral tradition, from the imagination of storytellers, and that the various tales gathered momentum until they attained something like gospel truth and have been passed on as gospel truth ever since they assumed their written form in the Bible and the Koran. Yet, even in so-called definitive form, they are not fixed stories, for there have been many variants and apocryphal stories printed about Abraham, and who knows how many millions of oral versions told by common people. How, I asked myself, did a man, who subscribed to infanticide and may never have even existed, become an exemplary if not *the* exemplary figure in three world religions?

As I was listening to Feiler, I felt almost as if this program had been "purposely" sent to me, that I was not listening to it by chance, for I had already been taking notes on a talk about traditional storytelling that I was to give at the University of Wisconsin in Madison the beginning of November 2004. I also knew that I was going to focus on the connection between tradition and infanticide. But even more important, I was puzzled by Feiler's almost indifferent attitude toward the element of child abuse. How could he praise and treat Abraham with so much reverence and offer him as a symbol of unity and, even worse, of humanity?

When the program ended, I realized that it represented an unusually poignant example of problems involved in the cultural transmission of tradition today. It demonstrated vividly how tradition represses (or inadvertently reveals) how we bake and eat our children, or if we keep them alive, how we beat stories into them that will make them willing subjects of forces to whom they grant control over their destinies. No matter how one interprets the story, there are some fundamental threads that hold it together, and they are all tied to patriarchal notions: that there is a male God, that believers in this God are bound to obey his every word, and that they must be ready to kill their own sons and daughters in his name. Over the centuries, these notions have been used in myriad ways, somewhat like memes, to rationalize thousands of wars, and all the murders and deaths that have resulted from these conflicts stem from people's belief in these traditional stories that have no verifiable foundation. Such is the power of storytelling, or rather such is the power of traditional storytelling.

Neither Feiler nor his moderator Krista Tippett was prepared to discuss this disturbing element of the Abraham tradition, and to make sure that I heard correctly, I went to the Internet a couple of days later to read the transcript of the program. To my surprise, I discovered that Feiler had also been interviewed earlier by Neil Conan in 2002 on "Talk of the Nation," another Public Radio program. Fortunately, I was able to read the transcript of this program as well, and I came across an exchange that struck me as highly significant. Conan opened the line for callers, and the very first one was Mimi from Van Nuys, California, who said:

> I do think that Abraham unifies all three religions and in a very timely way in that he thought God demanded the sacrifice of his son in order for him to prove his love and loyalty to God above all else. And he did not have to sacrifice his son, and I think that we should remember all three religions need to outgrow this idea that they need to shed blood and sacrifice their sons and daughters in order to prove their loyalty to their god, the god that they imagine is asking this.

> Conan: Hmmm.

> Mr. Feiler: What's interesting about this is this story of the sacrifice, which everybody remembers from when they were a child—you think that the story would be so barbaric that it would have died out over time. Instead, this story is read in the holiest week of the Jewish year, at Rosh Hashana. It's read in the holiest week of the Christian year, at Easter. It's read in the holiest week—the same story—the holiest week in the Muslim year, at the end of the pilgrimage. And I think it's that question we hope never to ask: Would I kill for God? And as we all …

> Mimi: And the answer should be no. I think Sarah, the mother, might have had a different answer. And a wonderful psychologist named Alice Miller wrote in a book that in looking for a painting to put on the cover of the book about child abuse, she could not find one in which Abraham

was looking at his child. He was always looking up to sacrifice and kill. And she said, "If he looked in the eyes of his child, he would have seen the answer, 'Why are you doing this? Please don't kill me.'"

Mr. Feiler: It's interesting. As you may know, Abraham is on the cover of *Time* magazine this week because of this topical issue we're discussing. And they lay out all of these portraits of Abraham over the generations, and by far and away, the action from Abraham's life that's most frequently depicted in the history of art is this sacrifice.

Mimi: Well, let us look to our children's eyes for God from now on, instead of to the skies where we imagine he is. And that's my comment. Thank you.

It is obvious from this conversation that both Feiler and Conan either did not want to engage Mimi in a discussion about child abuse, or that they did not want to reflect on how the Abraham tales further human sacrifice for an imaginary god, bloodshed, and war. They were bent on seeing Abraham as a kind of unifier, whereas Mimi was asking why should we pay homage to a child abuser and an imaginary deity. She referenced Alice Miller's book, *The Drama of the Gifted Child,* which is perhaps one of the most significant psychological studies in the twentieth century about the power relations between adults and children and how adults are disposed to use their power to control if not warp the lives of children.[11] Whereas Mimi wanted to challenge and open the frame in which Feiler and Conan discussed the tradition of Abraham, they quickly and blithely closed it to conceal some bitter truths. The modus operandi in the mass media, the public sphere, and most of our institutions will only tolerate benign questioning of established traditions. We insist on conserving and building on traditional narratives as though our canons were sacred.

THE UTOPIAN VALUE
OF THE REUTILIZATION OF TRADITION

If we accept the premise that tradition feeds off the young to maintain itself and will do anything to preserve itself, including the sacrifice of the young, storytellers who have a deep concern in preserving their different traditions are in a quandary, especially since there are currents and counter-currents of tradition that foster the autonomy of young and old alike as well as tolerance and respect for difference. Perhaps quandary is the wrong word. Perhaps we must discuss the choices and responsibilities of storytellers and how traditions can be "reutilized" to reconstitute a deeper awareness of their meanings and their impact on our lives.

In his thought-provoking book, *The Past in Ruins*, David Gross argues that the "otherness" of tradition could be used more effectively for a radical critique of present-day capitalism in all its postmodern and postindustrialist forms. What is necessary is a critical appropriation of tradition, and here he relies on a key idea of *Umfunktionierung* (reutilization or refunctioning) developed by the German writers and intellectuals Ernst Bloch, Bertolt Brecht, and Walter Benjamin during the 1920s in their critique of fascism. Gross defines reutilization as "extracting and rearranging elements from within the capitalist system in order to set them against capitalism itself, a process Bloch referred to as salvaging 'that which is true in false consciousness.'" Then Gross adds, "as it turned out, however, the real masters of the art of refunctioning were not Weimar's left-wing intellectuals but the modern state and the modern economy. And the greatest successes of refunctioning have not been those that subverted bourgeois values, but those that transformed many of the old traditions, forcing them to serve ends for which they were not initially intended."[12]

According to Gross, there were at least two types of refunctioning or reutilizing: the first kind takes charge of a certain current of tradition and maintains it by appending new meanings; the second kind takes possession of an entire tradition and imbues it with new layers of signification and social tasks. However, what is one to do, Gross asks, when the radical concept and practice of reutilization are instrumentalized by the market and state to create a false sense of harmony or to manipulate desire by using new inventions and technology to maintain old power structures and traditional hierarchies?

His answer is: we must employ a "subversive genealogy" that would address the exploitative refunctioning of tradition first, by analyzing what is closest at hand—i.e., the instrumentalized and commodified traditions that surround us—and would then move backward in time in order to chart their origin and development. It would do this by breaking down contemporary refunctionings into their parts, showing what role each part now plays and what new meanings have been assigned to each artificially sustained tradition. This amounts to the synchronic first step of a subversive genealogy. But second this kind of genealogy would need to shift into a diachronic dimension by tracing each reworked facet of a tradition back in time in order to locate the point where an apparently authentic tradition, or part of one, becomes inauthentic: the point, that is, where it began to be pulled from its context and refunctioned politically or economically.[13]

The practice of subversive genealogy is not to recuperate traditions that have been marginalized, suppressed, or occluded but to "reconsider what might be called the refuse of the dialectic, not in order to increase social cohesion or promote a *resitutio in integrum*, but in order to acquire a vantage point on modernity based in what modernity has banished or repressed."[14] A critique of tradition is therefore valuable only if it creates a new sense of tradition by revealing how fruitless it is to reclaim or recuperate tradition. By seeing tradition as "the Other," we gain a sense of what was unfulfilled and still needs to be fulfilled.

Certainly, Gross's critique of how the authority of tradition is maintained is valid, but he tends to view the problems of the transmission of tradition too much from the viewpoint of the manipulators. Instead, we must ask what role did and do the majority of people or the *Volk* play? And I do not mean folk in the romantic and nostalgic sense of the word, as those rural people close to nature and living in a noncommodified community. I mean the majority of people in different societies who define themselves through communal associations and cultural references, whether they interact in groups of long or short duration. Gross is apparently so concerned about how traditions are viewed and manipulated from above that his major concern is with the exposure of such manipulation and the development of theoretical analysis that has little basis in history. Unfortunately, he does not seek to understand how people of different classes and creeds come together to create customs, art forms, and social codes to give themselves a sense of identity and cohesion. What good is critical appropriation if it does not enable

people to sustain their life worlds and give their endeavors some sense
of meaning through story or history? Or, put another way, how have
people from different classes and creeds been using their traditions? In
light of the instrumentalization of their traditions by religions, schools,
and market forces, how have they made use of all kinds of traditional
tales to endow their existence on this planet with meaning?

To begin to answer these questions even partially, it is helpful to
return to Bloch, Brecht, and Benjamin because they raised the question
of *Umfunktionierung* not as an intellectual one, but to address political
and cultural practice during the 1920s and 1930s. That is, each one of
these writers was concerned that the *Volk* might become *völkisch*, the
people might become popularist in a reactionary sense. Indeed, their
traditions were being filled by Nazi-reutilized myths that corresponded
to an aestheticization of politics and culture that concealed manipulation. (Today we might use the term social construct and discuss how
culture is socially constructed and controlled.) For Bloch, Brecht, and
Benjamin, the reutilization of tradition through theater and storytelling
was to be a political practice that would use montage and discontinuity
to alienate audiences so that they could gain distance from their situation, think, deliberate, and decide for themselves what they wanted
to do with their lives. Bloch wrote about this political reutilization
in various essays during the 1920s and later in *Heritage of Our Times*
(1934);[15] Benjamin presented his views about this in his famous essay
"The Storyteller" and in other essays on Brecht and epic theater in the
1930s;[16] and Brecht practiced reutilization through his epic theater and
Verfremdungseffekt during the 1930s and until his death in 1956. The
utopian *telos* of reutilization as practice was to foster deeper understanding of contradictions in tradition through open-ended stories and plays
that audiences (namely the people) were encouraged to resolve. Such
resolution necessitates cohesion, coming together, forming an identity
through interests that could be maintained and continually transformed. In this way tradition would be constantly re-created through
critical appropriation.

It is not by chance that Bloch, Brecht, and Benjamin were attracted to
folklore, that is folk tales, fairy tales, and popular culture. If "authentic"
culture was to be passed on, to be *tradiert*, then it was best done through

trading and exchanging stories, for the best of storytellers took their material from the life experiences of the people. They returned this material to the people to keep alive a certain hope that powerless folk could overcome obstacles, determine their own destinies, outwit giants, and prevent ogres and witches from eating them. The listeners of these tales reshaped them, responded, made changes, and interacted with the tellers in a way that enabled them to share in the production of the tales.

Benjamin tended to glorify the so-called true storyteller, and Bloch idealized fairy tales, arguing that they shed light on the potential of humankind to form democratically determined societies or concrete utopias that could be gleaned from the indestructible vestiges of surplus value of tradition. Though Bloch and Benjamin (not so much Brecht) idealized the function of storytelling, they nevertheless addressed the question of nurturing and cultivating "authentic" tradition or tradition appropriate to the material needs of the people in ways other intellectuals of their day did not. And they did this to demonstrate a very common way that people were actually trying to resist or could resist the inauthentic manipulation and exploitation of tradition exemplified by the Nazis' expropriation of tradition. Bloch, Brecht, and Benjamin were concerned with developing strategies that the people (the *Volk*) could use to maintain their autonomy, and they tried to show how the Nazis were appropriating terms of folk traditions and creating their own false traditional symbols and narratives. To tell tales was to govern and navigate tradition, and Bloch, Brecht, and Benjamin were determined in the 1930s to underscore the cultural necessity of telling tales to deflate the myths of Nazism and to reutilize tradition to grasp historical manipulation. Of course, there was no "free" storytelling under the Nazis, but the clandestine telling of tales was a way in which resistance was formed by different groups of people and traditions maintained in Germany and throughout Europe during fascism.

Although some people would maintain that fascism has resurfaced in different forms in America and other parts of the world, we are not living in a totalitarian society. As long as we have freedom of speech in the public sphere, storytelling can play a vital role to enable us to grasp the positive and negative values of traditions. Ever since the 1970s in

America, professional storytellers and storytellers who represent ethnic minority groups and the feminist movement have realized more than ever before that there is something amiss in the way traditions and traditional stories are being passed down through the generations, and that many traditions are missing or endangered. This awareness of a lack of preservation of traditions and a distorted manner of using traditional tales have led to a resurgence of storytelling not only throughout the United States but also in the United Kingdom and Western Europe. Nevertheless, too often there is a sacred regard for traditional folk tales, as if they were authentic remnants from the past that must be treated in a reverent manner—an attitude that one can also find among anthropologists, ethnologists, and folklorists who collect and write about traditional customs and tales. Certainly, the tales, for example, deserve to be documented, treated with care, and preserved so we can know more about the history of different groups. But there is no way that we can "authentically" pass them on to future generations, and there is no reason why we should choose to tell tales just for the sake of these traditions, which, as I have stressed, often involve *the eating of children* or forms of individual or communal madness. Indeed, much of tradition is often romanticized in compelling tales that are twisted into chauvinistic, biased, sexist, and racist tales that storytellers without thinking, like to present for tradition's sake.

In 1993 Roger Abrahams called upon folklorists to shake off the phantoms of romantic nationalism and address the complex process in which tradition is simultaneously preserved and changed in new communal forms:

> Rather than regarding vernacular languages and procedures as systems in place, our altered view regards communication of any sort as an accomplishment carried out in common by members of a speech community, a performance-community, an interpretive-community. But clearly we must bring such ideas of community into line with the ways in which increasingly voluntaristic and plural societies are organizing themselves experientially and practically. It has been clear in the West for some time that forms of popular culture organized around high-intensity experiences (such as festivals or marches) and around stylized and technique-driven activities (such as dancing, sky-diving, camping, sports

spectating, or collecting of any sort) create the possibilities for communities that seldom meet face-to-face. Moreover, we must not regard instant communities as simple outgrowths of the pop-culture industries, for their developed vernacular forms often contain elements that are, in fact, resistant to the mechanical reproduction techniques that originally brought them into being. Processes such as customization and the construction of the pastiche makes this self-evident.[17]

Whereas many folkorists and storytellers have tended to glorify the past now in ruins in their work until the 1970s, there has also been a more recent and strong tendency to reflect critically upon the past, as the "lore" they recover is being used to mark out a future than can lead to a new sense of community. No matter what position we take with regard to tradition, it is clear that the past can devour us, as we devour our children, if our position is not critical and transformative.

TRANSFORMING TRADITION

The great writers and storytellers have always been transformers and translators. One could perhaps argue they never had a choice because there is no such thing as an original or authentic tale. They all have had to build on the past, on tradition, on stories handed down over the ages. They have had to translate from different tongues to facilitate understanding and create meaning. But what distinguishes the great writers and storytellers is that they write and tell with a conscious effort to grab hold of tradition as if it were a piece of clay and to mold it and remold it to see what they can make out of it for the present. They don't view tradition as iron-clad, static, or settled, but as supple and changeable. Nothing is inanimate in their hands and mouths. They are animators, breathing life into all things and all beings. They don't worship the past and tradition, but demand that the past and tradition justify themselves in the present. In turn, they ask that their remolding of the past and tradition be questioned.

It is the emotional and critical engagement with traditional tales that determines the quality of the contemporary storyteller's work as animator and transformer. Whether it is in a performance or pedagogical mode in front of a large audience, in families and tribes, or in intimate settings with children and adults in institutions such as schools, universities, hospitals, old age homes, and so on, the storyteller must reveal that he or she is engaged in the preservation of tradition while standing outside it and transforming it from a personal and ideological viewpoint. The storyteller is never the tradition, never represents authentic tradition. The storyteller is an actor, an agent, a translator, an animator, and as I have argued elsewhere, a thief who robs treasures to give something substantive to the poor.[18]

Most of all, the storyteller who is interested in the past and in preserving tradition must be curious and follow hints that interest him or her. In his highly stimulating book *The Beast in the Nursery*, Adam Phillips remarks, "If curiosity, and what I am calling interest, is always in the service of the new, of the old renewed, then it is always revisionary, making futures out of the past, turning orders into hints and following them up, these orders being both the instructions involved in growing up and their source in the available traditions and canons the culture provides."[19] The difficulty in our society and in most societies in the world is that tradition is used to combat curiosity and to deaden it, just as children's curiosity must be tamed, and if not deadened if they are to be acculturated. Clearly, children have something to do with the unconscious wishes and urges that were never fulfilled or realized by adults and therefore need to be repressed as potential threats to adults. It is perhaps not so much food, then, but children's curiosity that gives rise to stories in which children are eaten or devastated. These tales about bogeymen, monsters, and ogres expose the contradictions of patriarchal rule and both reinforce and subvert tradition at the same time, for they alert children to what they must do if they don't want to be eaten, and they also warn them what to expect and how they might subvert prescriptive and arbitrary rule.

The only way that children (and adults) can be reared into tradition with stories that do not involve scaring them and encouraging them to submit to monsters and arbitrary deities is by transforming our notion of children, childhood, and curiosity, and understanding more sensitively if not sensibly the conflictual nature of civilization and its discontents. Phillips notes:

[I]t is a paradox of some interest that nurture always involves compliance; the child must submit to the fact that some things are too hot to touch, that the parents have a history, and so on. But joining the group is not solely a matter of forced agreements; the child, like the psychoanalyst, also undoes and recombines the connections the culture wants her to make (you handle it because it's too hot to handle). So the ideal of adaptation is always matched—at least in posttraditional societies—by the ideal of improvisation: the child and the adult's relative freedom to transform, according to their unconscious desire, the cultural givens. This often involves changing the rules (the importance of one thing replaces the importance of another, and those who like the new thing call it progress). So there is what might be called a commonsense struggle for survival, and a struggle for the survival of imaginative vision.[20]

How we foster a tale-telling tradition that does not involve devouring children is not a question to be taken lightly, for it concerns the transformation of child-rearing practices, education, and the treatment of our young. It involves the preservation of the imaginative vision. If we do not question and undo dominant traditional storytelling, we risk not only losing the imaginative vision, but we also place our children at risk, as we already have. Their survival depends on our continual engagement with cultural traditions, opening them up, and opening ourselves in the process.

Notes

PREFACE

1. I revised this book in 2005 and added two new chapters and a preface. The new edition was published by Routledge in Spring 2006.
2. Luigi Luca Cavalli-Sforza, *L'evoluzione della cultura: Proposte concreti per studi future* (Turin: Codice, 2004), 68.
3. Susan Blackmore, *The Meme Machine* (Oxford: Oxford University Press, 1999), 17.

CHAPTER 1

1. New York: Norton, 2001.
2. See Dan Sperber and Deirdre Wilson, *Relevance: Communication and Cognition* (London: Blackwell, 1986; updated in 2002). See also Dan Sperber, *Explaining Culture: A Naturalistic Approach* (London: Blackwell, 1996).
3. Two of the best books on this topic are Susan Blackmore, *The Meme Machine* (Oxford: Oxford University Press, 1999) and Robert Aunger, *The Electric Meme: A New Theory of How We Think* (New York: Free Press, 2002).

4. Dan Sperber, "An Objection to the Memetic Approach to Culture," in *Darwinizing Culture: The Status of Memetics as a Science*, ed. Robert Aunger (Oxford: Oxford University Press, 2000), 163–73.

5. Richard Dawkins, *The Selfish Gene* (Oxford: Oxford University Press, 1976), 192.

6. Ibid.

7. For some of the more significant books on this topic, see Daniel Dennett, *Darwin's Dangerous Idea* (London: Penguin 1995); Richard Brodie, *Virus of the Mind: The New Science of the Meme* (Seattle: Inegral Press, 1996); Aaron Lynch, *Thought Contagion: How Belief Spreads through Society* (New York: Basic Books, 1996); Susan Blackmore, *The Meme Machine* (Oxford: Oxford University Press, 1999); Robert Aunger, ed., *Darwinizing Culture: The Status of Memetics as a Science* (Oxford: Oxford University Press, 2000) and *The Electric Meme: A New Theory of How We Think* (New York: Free Press, 2002). There is also an electronic journal, *Journal of Memetics*, http://jom-emit.cfpm.org, and numerous websites with important information and essays such as "Papers on Memetics," http://pespmc1.vub.ac.be.

8. Blackmore, *The Meme Machine*, 7.

9. See Robert Aunger, "A Report on the Conference 'Do Memes Account for Culture?' Held at King's College, Cambridge," *Journal of Memetics* 3 (1999): 1–9. See also the book that derived from the conference, Aunger, *Darwinizing Culture: The Status of Memetics as a Science*.

10. Sandra Beckett, *Recycling Red Riding Hood* (New York: Routledge, 2002); Catherine Orenstein, *Little Red Riding Hood Uncloaked: Sex, Morality, and the Evolution of a Fairy Tale* (New York: Basic Books, 2003); Allesandra Levorato, *Language and Gender in the Fairy Tale Tradition: A Linguistic Analysis of Old and New Story Telling* (New York: Palgrave Macmillan, 2003); Anne-Marie Garat, *Une faim de loup: Lecture du Petit Chaperon rouge* (Arles, France: Actes Sud, 2004); and Walter Fochesato, *Lupus in fabula* (Pisa, Italy: Titivillus, 2004). See also the special section on "Little Red Riding Hood," which I edited for *The Norton Anthology of Children's Literature: The Traditions in English*, eds. Jack Zipes, Lissa Paul, Lynne Vallone, Peter Hunt, and Gillian Avery (New York: W. W. Norton, 2005), 338–87.

11. See Dan Sperber and Lawrence Hirschfeld, "Culture and Modularity," in *The Innate Mind: Culture and Cognition*, ed. Peter Carruthers (Oxford: Oxford University Press, forthcoming); "Why a Deep Understanding of Cultural Evolution Is Incompatible with Shallow Psychology," in *Roots of Human Sociality: Culture, Cognition and Interaction*, eds. Nick Enfield and Stephen Levinson (Gorgonsville, VA: Berg Publishers, 2006), Forthcoming; and Gloria Origgi and Dan Sperber, "Evolution, Communication, and the Proper Function of Language," in *Evolution and the Human*

Mind: Modularity, Language and Mega-Cognition, eds. Peter Carruthers and Andrew Chamberlain (Cambridge: Cambridge University Press, 2000), 140–69.

12. Sperber and Hirschfeld, "Culture and Modularity," in *The Innate Mind: Culture and Cognition*, eds. Tom Simpson, Peter Carruthers, Stephen Laurence, and Stephen Stich (Oxford: Oxford University Press, forthcoming). See also Sperber's website: http://dan.sperber.com/mitecs.htm "Culture and Modularity," p. 1. Italics are in the original.

13. Deirdre Wilson and Dan Sperber, "Relevance Theory," in *Handbook of Pragmatics* (Oxford: Blackwell, 2004), 608.

14. Francis Heylighen, "What Makes a Meme Successful? Selection Criteria for Cultural Revolution." Available at http//pespmc1.vub.ac.be/Papers/MemeticsNamur.html. The italics are in the original text.

15. Cristiano Castelfranchi, "Towards a Cognitive Memetics: Socio-Cognitive Mechanisms for Memes Selection and Spreading," *Journal of Memetics* 5 (2001): 1–20. Available at http//jom-emit.cfpm.org/2001/vol5/castellfranchi_c.html.

16. Ibid., 4.

17. Ellen Dissanayake, *What Is Art For?* (Seattle: University of Washington Press, 1988), 92.

18. Ibid. The italics are in the original text.

19. Jack Zipes, *Fairy Tales and the Art of Subversion: The Classical Genre for Children and the Process of Civilization* (London: Heinemann, 1983), 1–11. Revised 2nd edition published by Routledge in 2006.

20. Frederic Jameson, *The Political Unconscious: Narrative as a Socially Symbolic Act* (Ithaca: Cornell University Press, 1981), 77.

21. Jean Aitchison, *The Seeds of Speech: Language Origin and Evolution* (Cambridge: Cambridge University Press, 1996), 148. The italics are in the original text.

22. For a thorough discussion of the module and how it operates, see Steven Pinker, "Mind Design," in *The Language Instinct* (London: Penguin, 1994): 404–30; Jerry Fodor, *The Modularity of Mind* (Cambridge, MA: MIT Press, 1983); and Noam Chomsky, *Language and Problems of Knowledge* (Cambridge, MA: MIT Press, 1988).

23. Sperber and Hirschfeld, "Culture and Modularity," 7.

24. Ibid., 10.

25. Ibid., 12.

26. Jean-Michel Adam and Ute Heidmann, "Des genres à la généricité: L'exemple des contes (Perrault et les Grimm)," *Languages* 153 (2004), 62–72.

27. M. M. Bakhtin, *Speech Genres and Other Late Essays* (Austin, TX: University of Texas Press, 1986), 60. The italics are in the original text.

28. Ibid., 62.

29. See Cristina Lavinio, "La Fiaba tra oralità e scrittura: aspetti linguistici e stilistici" and Giovanna Cerina, "La fiaba tra oralità e scrittura: aspetti semiotici" in *Oralità e Scrittura nel sistema letterario*, eds. Giovana Cerina, Cristina Lavinio, and Luisa Mulas (Rome: Bulzoni, 1982), 91–114; 115–32.

30. Ibid., 62.

31. Ibid., 98.

32. Stephen Benson, *Cycles of Influence: Fiction, Folktale, Theory* (Detroit: Wayne State University Press, 2003), 65.

33. Ibid., 76–77.

34. Ibid., 78. The italics are in the original text.

35. Tzvetan Todorov, "L'origine des genres," in *La notion de littérature et autres essays* (Paris: Seuil, 1987), 27–46.

36. Ibid., 30–31.

37. Ibid., 35.

38. Ibid., 36.

39. Brian Stock, *Listening for the Text: On the Uses of the Past* (Baltimore: Johns Hopkins University Press, 1990), 23. The italics are in the original text.

40. Dawkins, *The Selfish Gene*, 199.

41. Ibid., 199–200. The italics are in the original text.

42. Jean-Michel Adam and Ute Heidmann, "Des genres à la généricité: L'exemple des contes (Perrault et les Grimm), *Languages* 153 (2004), 62–72. See also their essay, "Du théâtre de Coppet aux contes des Grimm: les mutations génériques d'un étrange récit," in *Les Textes comme aventure* (Carouge-Genève: Editions Zoe, 2003), 174–84.

43. Adam and Heidmann, "Des genres," 62. The italics are in the original text.

44. See Gérard Genette, *Palimpsestes* (Paris: Seuil, 1982); translated as *Palimpsests: Literature in the Second Degree* (Lincoln, NE: University of Nebraska Press, 1997).

45. Jean-Michel-Adam and Ute Heidmann, "Discursivité et (Trans)textualité: La comparison pour méthode. L'exemple du conte," in *L'Analyse du discours*, eds. Ruth Amossy and Dominque Maingueneau (Paris: Presses Universitaires du Mirail, 2003), 49.

46. Ute Heidmann and Jean-Michel Adam, "Text Linguistics and Comparative Literature: Toward an Interdisciplinary Approach to Written Tales. Angela Carter's Translations of Perrault," in *Language and Verbal Art Revisited: Linguistic Approaches to the Literature Text*, eds. Donna Miller and Monica Turci (London: Equinox, 2006), 5. The italics are in the original text.

47. Graham Anderson, *Fairy Tale in the Ancient World* (London: Routledge, 2000), 96.

48. Ibid., 13.

49. For a full account of the significance of this Latin verse tale, see Jacques Berlioz, Claude Bremond, and Catherine Velay-Vallantin, trans., *Formes médiévales du conte merveilleux* (Paris: Stock, 1989), 133–39; Jacques Berlioz, "Un Petit Chaperon rouge medieval? 'La petite fille épagnée par les loups dans la Fecunda ratis d'Egbert de liege (début du XIe siècle),'" *Merveilles et Contes* 5 (Winter 1991): 246–63; Gunter Lontzen, "Das Gedicht 'De puella a lupellis servata' von Egbert von Lüttich—Eine Parabel zum Thema der Taufe," *Merveilles et Contes* 6 (1992): 20–44; Jan Ziolkowski, "A Fairy Tale from Before Fairy Tales: Egbert of Liège's 'De puellis a lupellis seruata' and the Medieval Background of 'Little Red Riding Hood,'" *Speculum* (1992): 549–75.

50. Jan Ziolkowski, *Fairy Tales* from *Before Fairy Tales: The Medieval Latin Past of Wonderful Lies* (Ann Arbor: University of Michigan Press, forthcoming), manuscript page 208.

51. Ziolkowski, *Fairy Tales from Before Fairy Tales*, manuscript page 211.

52. Ibid., manuscript page 232.

53. Cf. Dorothy Thelander, "Mother Goose and Her Goslings: The France of Louis XIV as Seen through the Fairy Tale," *Journal of Modern History* 54 (September 1982): 467–96; and my chapter "Setting Standards for Civilization through Fairy Tales," in *Fairy Tales and the Art of Subversion* (New York: Routledge, 1983), 47–96.

54. Jack Zipes, *The Trials and Tribulations of Little Red Riding Hood*, 2nd ed. (New York: Routledge, 1993), 5–6.

55. See Yvonne Verdier, "Grand-mères, si vous saviez: le Petit Chaperon Rouge dans la tradition orale," *Cahiers de literature orale* 4 (1978): 17–55.

56. There are numerous theories about the *chaperon rouge*. One of the more interesting interpretations is to be found in Hans T. Siepe's article "Rotkäppchen einmal anders. Ein Märchen für den Französischunterricht," *Der fremdsprachliche Unterricht* 65 (1983): 1–9. Siepe points out that the term *grand chaperon* designated an older woman who was supposed to escort young girls from the upper class, much as chaperon in the English sense of the word. The fact that Little Red Riding Hood only has a "little chaperon" indicates that she did not have enough protection. Whatever the case may be, the chaperon transforms the peasant girl into a bourgeois type, and the color red, which may suggest menstruation, was a clear symbol of her sin. See also Bernadette Bricout, "L'aiguille et l'epingle," in *La 'Bibliotheque bleue' nel Seicento o della Letteratura per il popolo*, eds. P. A. Jannini, G. Dotoli, and P. Carile (Bari, Italy: Adriatica, 1981), 45–58.

57. Steven Pinker, *The Blank Slate: The Modern Denial of Human Nature* (London: Penguin, 2002), 364; Randy Thornhill and Craig T. Palmer, *A Natural History of Rape: Biological Bases of Sexual Coercion* (Cambridge, MA: MIT Press, 2000).

58. Pinker, 363. The italics are in the original text.

Chapter 2

1. For informative discussions about this development see Giuseppe Cocchiara, *The History of Folklore in Europe*, trans. John N. McDaniel (Philadelphia: Institute for the Study of Human Issues, 1981), originally published in Italian as *Storia del folklore in Europa* (Turin: Editore Borghinghieri, 1952); and Richard Dorson, *The British Folklorists: A History* (Chicago: University of Chicago Press, 1968).

2. See Graham Anderson's book, *Fairy Tale in the Ancient World* (London: Routledge, 2000) and his more recent essay, "Old Tales for New: Finding the First Fairy Tales," in *The Companion to Fairy Tale*, eds. Hilda Ellis Davidson and Anna Chaudhri (Cambridge: D. S. Brewer, 2003), 85–98.

3. See J. E. Hanauer, *Folklore of the Holy Land: Moslem, Christian and Jewish* (Mineola, NY: Dover, 2002), first published in 1907 and revised in 1935; Alan Dundes, *Holy Writ: The Bible as Folklore* (Lanham, MD: Rowman & Littlefield, 1999); and Manfred Fuhrmann, "Mythen, Fabeln, Legenden und Märchen in der antiken Tradition," in *Metamorphosen des Märchens*, eds. Gundel Mattenklott and Kristin Wardetzky (Hohengehren: Schneider, 2005), 6–22.

4. Derek Brewer, "The Interpretation of Fairy Tales," in *The Companion to the Fairy Tale*, eds. Hilda Ellis Davidson and Anna Chaudrhi (Cambridge: D. S. Brewer, 2003), 27.

5. See Jean-Claude Schmitt, *Religione, folklore e società nell Occidente medievale* (Bari: Laterza, 1988); Rudolf Schenda, *Von Mund zu Ohr: Bausteine zu einer Kulturgeschichte volkstümlichen Erzählens in Europa* (Göttingen: Vandenhoeck and Ruprecht, 1993); and Jan Ziolkowski, *Fairy Tales from Before Fairy Tales: The Medieval Latin Past of Wonderful Lies* (Ann Arbor, MI: University of Michigan Press, forthcoming).

6. See Schmitt, *Religione, folklore e società*; Rosmarie Thee Morewedge, "Orality, Literacy, and the Medieval Folktale" and Donald Ward, "Do Märchensingverse Indicate Orality?" in *Varieties and Consequences of Literacy and Orality*, eds. Ursula Schaefer and Edda Spielmann (Gunter Narr: Tübingen, 2001), 85–106; 125–48; Ziolkowski, *Fairy Tales*.

7. In particular see Herman Pleij, *Dreaming of Cockaigne: Medieval Fantasies of the Perfect Life*, trans. Diane Webb (New York: Columbia University Press, 2001).

8. Ibid., 283.

9. See Richard Dorson, *The British Folklorists: A History* (Chicago: University of Chicago Press, 1968) and Giuseppe Cocchiara, *Storia del folklore in Europa* (Turin: Editore Borginghieri, 1952), trans. John N. McDaniel, as *The History of Folklore in Europe* (Philadelphia: Institute for the Study of Human Issues, 1981).

10. See Detlev Fehling, *Amor und Psyche. Die Schöpfung des Apuleius und ihre Einwirkung auf das Märchen. Eine Kritik der romantischen Märchentheorie* (Wiesbaden: Steiner, 1977), and Dietz Rüdiger Moser, "Altersbestimmung des Märchens," in *Enzyklopädie des Märchens*, vol. 1, ed. Rolf Wilhelm Brednich (Berlin: Walter de Gruyter, 1977), 407–19. For a lucid discussion of this debate, see Donald Ward, "Do Märchensingverse Indicate Orality?" in *Varieties and Consequences of Literacy and Orality: Formen und Folgen von Schriftlichkeit und Mündlichkeit*, eds. Ursula Schaefer and Edda Spielmann (Tübingen: Narr, 2001), 125–45.

11. Ruth Bottigheimer, "The Ultimate Fairy Tale: Oral Transmission in a Literate Word," in *The Companion to the Fairy Tale*, eds. Hilda Ellis Davidson and Anna Chaudrhi (Cambridge: D. S. Brewer, 2003), 57–70.

12. See Hans-Joachim Griep, *Geschichte des Lesens: Von den Anfängen bis Gutenberg* (Darmstadt: Wissenschaftliche Buchgesellschaft, 2005).

13. Jan Ziolkowski, *Fairy Tales from Before Fairy Tales: The Medieval Latin Past of Wonderful Lies* (Ann Arbor, MI: University of Michigan Press, forthcoming), manuscript page 65.

14. See André Jolles, *Einfache Formen* (Tübingen: Niemeyer, 1958).

15. In fairness to Propp, he did move away from his structural approach in a later very important work. See *Theory and History of Folklore*, trans. Adriadna Y. Martin and Richard P. Martin, ed. Anatoly Liberman (Minneapolis: University of Minnesota Press, 1984). The American translation is incomplete and inadequate, as is the introduction. For a better translation and discussion of Propp's significance, see Vladimir Propp, *Die historischen Wurzeln des Zaubermärchens* (Munich: Hanser, 1987).

16. See Pierre Bourdieu, *Distinction: A Social Critique of the Judgment of Taste* (Cambridge, MA: Harvard University Press, 1984). Bourdieu argues that, out of necessity, we must learn to position ourselves and internalize sets of tastes, codes, and values, if we want to assume a particular role or function in a social institution, class, or group. We must dispose of ourselves to take on a position. We adjust our customs and life styles in accordance with the systematic practices of larger associations, and we form a habitus

that identifies us just as much as we try to identify ourselves. This habitus is constituted by our acts, speech, choices, and tastes in our daily interaction with other people, and it distinguishes us from others.

17. See Marina Warner's admirable study on this topic, *From the Beast to the Blonde: On Fairy Tales and Their Tellers* (London: Chatto & Windus, 1994). In her introduction she states: "Prejudices against women, especially old women and their chatter, belong in the history of fairy tale's changing status, for the pejorative image of the gossip was sweetened by influences from the tradition of Sibyls and the cult of St. Anne, until the archetypal crone by the hearth could emerge as a mouthpiece of homespun wisdom" (xx).

18. See the important studies by Stephen Wilson, *The Magical Universe: Everyday Ritual and Magic in Pre-Modern Europe* (London: Hambledon and London, 2000); and Darren Oldrige, *Strange Histories: The Trial of the Pig, the Walking Dead, and Other Matters of Fact from the Medieval and Renaissance Worlds* (London: Routledge, 2005).

19. See Alberto Manguel, *A History of Reading* (New York: Viking Penguin, 1996); and Hans-Joachim Griep, *Geschichte des Lesens: Von den Anfängen bis Gutenberg* (Darmstadt: Wissenschaftliche Buchgesellschaft, 2005).

20. See Harvey J. Graff, *The Legacies of Literacy: Continuities and Contradictions in Western Culture and Society* (Bloomington, IN: University of Indiana Press, 1987); and R. A. Houston, *Literacy in Early Modern Europe: Culture and Education*, 2nd ed. (London: Pearson Education Limited/Longman, 2002).

21. Morewedge, "Orality, Literacy, and the Medieval Folktale," 89.

22. See Walter Raiz, *Zur Soziogenese des bürgerlichen Romans. Eine literatursoziologische Analyse des "Fortunatus"* (Düsseldorf: Bertelsmann, 1973); and Helmut Scheuer, "Das 'Volksbuch' Fortunatus (1509). Zwischen feudaler Anpassung und bürgerlicher Selbstverwirklichung," in *Literatursoziologie, II, Beiträge zur Praxis*, ed. Joachim Bark (Stuttgart: Kohlhammer, 1974), 99–117.

23. Luisa Rubini, "Fortunatus in Italy: A History between Translations, Chapbooks and Fairy Tales," *Fabula* 44.1/2 (2003): 25–54. See also Stephen L. Wailes, "Potency in Fortunatus," *German Quarterly* 59.1 (Winter, 1986): 5–18.

24. The book was translated by W. G. Waters as *The Facetious Nights* (London: Society of Bibliophiles, 1898), and the title could also be translated as *The Pleasant Nights* or *The Delectable Nights*. For the best contemporary scholarly edition, see Giovan Francesco Straparola, *Le piacevoli notti*, ed. Donato Pirovano, 2 vols. (Rome: Salerno Editrice, 2000).

25. The most reliable information about Straparola is Donato Pirovano's "Nota Biografica," in Giovan Francesco Straparola, *Le piacevoli notti*, vol. 1, ed. Donato Pirovani (Rome: Salerno Editrice, 2000), 51–54.

26. The book was condemned by the ecclesiastical authorities in 1604 and placed on the *Index librorum prohibitorum*.

27. See Charles Diehl, *La République de Venise* (Paris: Flammarion, 1986).

28. See Dieter Richter, "Die Märchen des Basile und ihre Metamorphosen," in *Metamorphosen des Märchens* (Hohengehren: Schneider, 2005), 29.

29. In fact, Jacob Grimm wrote the preface to *Giambattista Basile, Der Pentamerone oder: Das Märchen aller Märchen*, trans. Felix Liebrecht (Breslau: Max und Komp, 1846). The Brothers Grimm probably knew about Basile's work as early as 1806 through their contact with Clemens Brentano, who was already adapting Basile. At the very latest, they were familiar with Straparola's work in 1817, when the first extensive translation appeared: *Die Märchen des Straparola*, trans. Friedrich Wilhelm Schmidt (Berlin: Duncker und Humlot, 1817).

30. For more recent works on Basile, see the excellent studies by Barbara Broggini, *"Lo cunto de li cunti" von Giambattista Basile: Ein Ständepoet in Streit mit der Plebs, Fortuna, und der höfischen Korruption* (Frankfurt am Main; Lang, 1990); Nancy Canepa, *From Court to Forest: Giambattista Basile's Lo cunto de li cunti and the Birth of the Literary Fairy Tale* (Detroit: Wayne State University Press, 1999); Michelangelo Piccone and Alfred Messerli, eds., *Giovan Battista Basile e l'Invenzione della Fiaba* (Ravenna: A Longo, 2004).

31. For a full account of Basile's life, see Canepa, *From Court to Forest*.

32. See Charles Speroni, "Proverbs and Proverbial Phases in Basile's Pentameron," *University of California Publications in Modern Philology* 24, no. 2 (1941): 181–288.

33. Michele Rak, ed., *Fiabe campane*, trans. Domenico Rea (Milan: Mondadori, 1984), 25.

34. Michele Rak, *Logica della fiaba: Fate, orchid, gioco, corte, fortuna, viaggio capriccio, metamorfosi, corpo* (Milan: Bruno Mondari, 2005), 3.

35. Ibid., 79–80.

36. For a thorough examination of the Italian influence, see Charlotte Trinquet, "La Petite Histoire des Contes de Fées Littéraires en France (1690–1705)," dissertation, University of North Carolina, Chapel Hill, 2001.

37. There have been several excellent studies about this vogue: Mary Elizabeth Storer, *Un Episode littéraire de la fin du XVIIe siècle: la mode des contes de fées, 1685–1700* (Paris: Champion, 1928); Jacques Barchilon, *Le Conte merveilleux français de 1690 à 1790: cent ans de féerie et de poésie ignorées de l'histoire littéraire* (Paris: Champion, 1975); Teresa Di Scanno,

Les Contes de fées à l'époque classique, 1680–1715 (Naples: Liguori, 1975); Raymonde Robert, *Le Conte de fées littéraire en France, de la fin du XVIIe à la fin du XVIIIe siècle* (Nancy: Presses Universitaires de Nancy, 1982); and Olivier Piffault, *Il était une fois ... les contes de fées* (Paris: Seuil/Bibliothèque nationale de France, 2001).

38. Patricia Hannon, *Fabulous Identities: Women's Fairy Tales in Seventeenth Century France* (Amsterdam: Rodopi, 1998), 172. Other pertinent books that deal with this topic and are also important for understanding the vogue are: Erica Harth, *Cartesian Women: Versions and Subversions of Rational Discourse in the Old Regime* (Ithaca: Cornell University Press, 1992); Linda Timmermans, *L'Accès des femmes à la culture, 1598–1715. Un débat d'idées de Saint François à la Marquise de Lambert* (Paris: Champion, 1993); and Lewis Seifert, *Fairy Tales, Sexuality and Gender in France, 1690–1715: Nostalgic Utopias* (Cambridge: Cambridge University Press, 1996). For a more recent significant publication with an exhaustive bibliography see Holly Tucker, ed., "Reframing the Early French Fairy Tale," special issue of *Marvels & Tales* 19/1 (2005).

39. See Timmermans, *L'Accès des femmes à la culture*.

40. Hannon, *Fabulous Identities*, 177.

41. It is interesting to note that three of the important male writers of this vogue were marginalized types. Perrault was retired from his governmental position and had lost the support of the king. Mailly was an illegitimate son of an aristocrat and did not find favor at court. Le Noble was a libertine, who had served some time in prison.

42. Lewis Seifert, "Marvelous Realities: Reading the Merveilleux in the Seventeenth-Century French Fairy Tale," in *Out of the Woods: The Origins of the Literary Fairy Tale in Italy and France*, ed. Nancy Canepa (Detroit: Wayne State University Press, 1997), 138–39.

43. For two excellent accounts of this development, see Robert Mandrou, *De la culture populaire aux XVIIe et XVIIIe siècles. La Bibliothèque bleue* (Paris: Stock, 1965); and Geneviève Bollème, *La Bibliothèque bleue* (Paris: Juillard, 1971).

44. Mary Louise Ennis, "Fractured Fairy Tales: Parodies for the Salon and Foire," in *Out of the Woods: The Origins of the Literary Fairy Tale in Italy and France*, ed. Nancy Canepa (Detroit: Wayne State University Press, 1997), 223.

45. Manfred Graetz, *Das Märchen in der deutschen Aufklärung* (Stuttgart: Metzler, 1988). The one drawback of Graetz's work is that he discounts the influence of the oral tradition without adequately dealing with the diverse manner in which tales circulated in the medieval period up through the Enlightenment. Nor does he deal adequately with the concept of the "Volk" or people as oral transmitters of tales.

46. This fascinating fairy-tale novel was translated into French and included in the *Cabinet des Fées*. Wieland had an ambivalent attitude toward the fairy tale. In this novel he depicts how a young man is too easily carried away by his imagination and warns against having too much fantasy. At the same time, Wieland incorporates a highly unusual fairy tale into the novel and employs fairy-tale motifs in highly innovative ways. After writing this novel, he did not abandon the fairy tale, and it is interesting from the viewpoint of cultural interconnections that his novel, influenced by the French, should then be translated into French as part of the *Cabinet des Fées*.

47. The most important edition is Heinz Rölleke, ed., *Die älteste Märchensammlung der Brüder Grimm* (Cologny-Geneva: Fondation Martin Bodmer, 1975). Rölleke's thorough scholarship enables us to trace the sources of the tales and to see the great changes in style and content that the Grimms made in preparing them for publication.

48. For a comprehensive essay about the Grimms' editorial work, see David Blamires, "A Workshop of Editorial Practice: The Grimms' *Kinder- und Hausmärchen*," in *A Companion to the Fairy Tale*, eds. Hilda Ellis Davidson and Anna Chaudhri (London: D. S. Brewer, 2003), 71–83.

49. See the recent work by Isamitsu Murayama, *Poesie—Natur—Kinder: Die Brüder Grimm und ihre Idee einer "natürlichen Bildung" in den Kinder- und Hausmärchen* (Heidelberg: Universitätsverlag, 2005).

50. Edgar Taylor, ed., *German Popular Stories*, introduction by John Ruskin (London: John Camden Hotten, 1868), ix–x.

51. See Jack Zipes, *Hans Christian Andersen: The Misunderstood Storyteller* (New York: Routledge, 2005).

CHAPTER 3

1. Friedmar Apel, *Die Zaubergärten der Phantasie: Zur Theorie und Geschichte des Kunstmärchens* (Heidelberg: Carl Winter Universitätsverlag, 1978), 273.

2. Ibid., 274.

3. See the postface in Dan Sperber and Deidre Wilson, *Relevance: Communication and Cognition*, 2nd ed. (London: Blackwell, 1995), 255–79. I am using the second edition because Sperber and Wilson made many important changes and updated their terms and categories based on critiques of their work.

4. Ibid., 260.

5. Ibid., 261.

6. Dan Sperber, *Explaining Culture: A Naturalistic Approach* (London: Blackwell, 1996), 25–26.

7. See Jack Zipes, "Introduction," in *The Great Fairy Tale Tradition: From Straparola and Basile to the Brothers Grimm* (New York: Norton, 2001), xi–xiv.

8. Sperber, *Explaining Culture*, 29.

9. Ibid., 83.

10. It should be understood that these theses can be applied to other cultures as well. I am focusing on the United States and the United Kingdom as examples because I am more familiar with cultural conditions in these countries than in others.

11. See Ernst Bloch, *The Utopian Function of Art and Literature: Selected Essays*, trans. Jack Zipes and Frank Mecklenburg (Cambridge, MA: MIT Press, 1988).

12. See Jean-Michel Adam and Ute Heidmann, "Des genres à la génércité: L'exemple des contes (Perrault et les Grimm)," *Languages* 152 (2004): 62–72, and my discussion of their work in Chapter 1.

13. Ellen Datlow and Terri Windling, eds., *Black Heart, Ivory Bones* (New York: Avon, 2000), 2.

14. "Cinderella and the Public Domain," *Storytelling World* (November 2000): 21–29.

15. Joanna Kiernan, "Cabinet of Spells: Cinderella. Application Narrative," National Endowment for the Humanities Proposal (January 10, 2000): 1–2.

16. Joellyn Rock, "The Vasalisa Project: An Experiment in Multiform Storytelling," thesis proposal for the degree of master of fine arts/graphic design, University of Minnesota, Duluth, September 2000, p. 1.

17. Joellyn Rock, "Barebones," *Marvels & Tales* 16.2 (2002): 234–35.

18. Colette Dowling, *The Cinderella Complex: Women's Hidden Fear of Independence* (New York: Pocket Books, 1981), 21.

19. See Jean Godwin, Catherine G. Cauthorne, and Richard T. Rada, "Cinderella Syndrome: Children Who Simulate Neglect," *American Journal of Psychiatry* 137 (October 1980): 1223–25. I have discussed the importance of this essay in the introduction to *Don't Bet on the Prince: Contemporary Feminist Fairy Tales in North America and England* (London: Methuen, 1986), 31.

20. Martin Daly and Margo Wilson, *The Truth about Cinderella: A Darwinian View of Parental Love* (New Haven: Yale University Press, 1998), 2.

21. Ibid., 6.

22. Ibid., 38–39.

23. Vivian Sathre, *Slender Ella and Her Fairy Hogfather* (New York: Bantam, 1999), 6–7.

24. Alan Schroeder, *Smoky Mountain: An Appalachian Cinderella* (New York: Dial, 1977), 1.

25. Joanne Compton, *Ashpet: An Appalachian Tale* (New York: Holiday, 1994), 2–3.
26. Sheila Hébert Collins, *Cendrillon: A Cajun Cinderella* (Gretna, LA: Pelican, 2000), 1–2.
27. Jewell Reinhart Coburn, *Angkat: The Cambodian Cinderella* (Auburn, CA: Shen 1998), 1.
28. Rebecca Hickox, *The Golden Sandal: A Middle Eastern Cinderella Story* (New York: Holiday House, 1998), 2, 4.
29. Susan Lowell, *Cindy Ellen: A Wild Western Cinderella* (New York: HarperCollins Children's Books, 2001), 2–3.
30. Marianna Mayer, *Baba Yaga and Vasilisa the Brave* (New York: Morrow Junior Books, 1994), 3.
31. Philip Pullman, *I Was a Rat!* (New York: Knopf, 1999), 165.
32. Patricia Galloway, "The Prince," *Truly Grim Tales* (New York: Bantam Doubleday Dell, 1995), 124.
33. Emma Donoghue, "The Tale of the Shoe," in *Kissing the Witch: Old Tales in New Skins* (New York: HarperCollins, 1997), 2.
34. Francesca Lia Block, "Glass," in *The Rose and the Beast* (New York: HarperCollins, 2000), 60–61.

CHAPTER 4

1. See Antti Aarne, *The Types of the Folktales. A Classification and Bibliography*, rev. and enlarged by Stith Thompson (Helsinki: Suomalainen Tiedeakatemia, 1961).
2. See "Kay Vandergrift's Snow White Page," http://www/scils.rutgers.edu/special/Kay/snow white.html.
3. Sandra M. Gilbert and Susan Gubar, *Madwoman in the Attic: The Woman Writer and the Nineteenth-Century Literary Imagination* (New Haven: Yale University Press, 1979), 36. Maria Tatar quotes this passage in her fine book, *The Classic Fairy Tales* (New York: Norton, 1999), 74, and her introductory remarks to "Snow White," pp. 74–80, provide important background material for setting it in a historical context.
4. Robert Wright, *The Moral Animal: Evolutionary Psychology and Everyday Life* (New York: Pantheon, 1994), 63.
5. Tanith Lee, *White as Snow* (New York: TOR, 2000), 38.
6. Ibid., 319.
7. See Jack Zipes, "The Origins of the Fairy Tale," in *Fairy Tale as Myth/Myth as Fairy Tale* (Lexington: University Press of Kentucky, 1994), 17–48.
8. Donna Jo Napoli, *Beast* (New York: Atheneum, 2000), 190.

9. Robert Wright, "The Accidental Creationist," *New Yorker* (December 13, 1999): 63.

10. Matt Ridley, *The Origins of Virtue* (London: Penguin, 1996), 147.

11. Russell Schroeder, *Disney's Mulan* (New York: Disney Press, 1998), 30.

12. See Catherine Velay-Vallantin, *La fille en garçon* (Carcassone: Garae/Hesiode, 1992), which contains examples only from the French tradition. But there are also similar tales in English, German, and Italian.

13. Jack Zipes, ed., *Beauties, Beasts and Enchantment: Classic French Fairy Tales* (New York: NAL, 1989), 568.

14. Bradford W. Wright, *Comic Book Nation: The Transformation of Youth Culture in America* (Baltimore: Johns Hopkins University Press, 2001), 205–7.

15. Kristin Kathryn Rusch and Dean Wesley Smith, *X-Men* (New York: Del Rey, 2000), 23–24.

16. See Ernst Bloch, *The Utopian Function of Art and Literature*, trans. Jack Zipes and Frank Mecklenburg (Cambridge: MIT Press, 1987).

Chapter 5

1. Charles Perrault, "Bluebeard," in *Beauties, Beasts and Enchantment: Classic French Fairy Tales*, ed. and trans., Jack Zipes (New York: Meridian, 1989), 35.

2. Maria Tatar, *Secrets beyond the Door: The Story of Bluebeard and His Wives* (Princeton: Princeton University Press, 2004), 173.

3. Ibid., 53.

4. Charles Perrault, *The Vindication of Wives*, trans. Roland Gant (London: Rodale Books, 1954), 20.

5. Patricia Hannon, *Fabulous Identities: Women's Fairy Tales in Seventeenth-Century France* (Amsterdam: Rodopi, 1994), 22.

6. See Jean-Pierre Mothe, *Du sang et du sexe dans les contes de Perrault* (Paris: L'Harmattan, 1999).

7. See Marc Soriano, *Les Contes de Perrault: culture savante et traditions populaires* (Paris: Gallimard, 1968), 443–45.

8. Philip Lewis, *Seeing Through the Mother Goose Tales: Visual Turns in the Writings of Charles Perrault* (Stanford, CA: Stanford University Press, 1996), 208.

9. Lewis, *Seeing Through the Mother Goose Tales*, 236–37.

10. Perrault, "Bluebeard," in *Beauties, Beasts and Enchantment*, 35.

11. Pierre Bourdieu, *Masculine Domination* (Stanford, CA: Stanford University Press, 2001), 9–11.

12. Ibid., 23. The italics are in the original text.

13. Ibid.
14. Diane Long Hoeveler and Sarah Davies Cordova, "Gothic Opera in Britain and France, Genre, Nationalism, and Trans-Cultural Angst," *érudite* (May–August 2004): 2, electronic version. Available at: http//www.erudit.org/revue/ron/2004/v/n34-35/009435ar.html
15. James Robinson Planché, *Bluebeard* (London: 1845), 48.
16. Ludwig Tieck, Blaubart: Ein Ammenmärchen," in *Ludwig Tiecks Schriften*, Vol. 5 (Berlin: Reimer, 1828), 65.
17. Marcel Schwob, "La Volupteuse," in *Le Livre de Monelle* (Paris: Éditions Allia, 2005), 37. The story was first published in 1894.
18. F. W. N. Bayley, *Blue Beard* (London: William S. Orr, 1842), 46.
19. Hanno Loewy, *Béla Balázs—Märchen, Ritual und Film* (Berlin: Vorwerk 8, 2003), 35.
20. Tatar, *Secrets beyond the Door*, 90.
21. Susan Faludi, *Stiffed: The Betrayal of the American Man* (New York: William Morrow, 1999), 14.
22. Ibid., 15.
23. Erik Ulman, "Edgar G. Ulmer" Senses of Cinema. Available at http://www.sensesofcinema.com/contents/directors/03/ulmer.html, p. 4.
24. Mark Shivas, "An Interview with Claude Chabrol." Available at http://home.comecast.net/~chabrol/Chabrol-interviews.html, p. 6.
25. Chris Kirkham, "Bluebeard (1972): A Euro-trashy Review." Available at http://alansmithee.5u.com/junkdrawer/danning/bluebeard/bluebeard.html, p. 1.
26. Tatar, *Secrets beyond the Door*, 159.

Chapter 6

1. "Hänsel und Gretel," in *Daumesdick. Neuer Märchenschatz mit vielen Bildern*, ed. Hans-Joachim Gelberg (Weinheim: Beltz & Gelberg), 297.

Nichts als die Not gekannt.
  Beim Stehlen erwischt.
    Eingesperrt.
    Ausgebrochen:
Den Aufseher umgebracht.

    Und aus so was,
      Meinst du,
Soll noch mal was werden?

2. "The Rationalization of Abandonment and Abuse in Fairy Tales: The Case of Hansel and Gretel," in *Happily Ever After: Fairy Tales, Children, and the Culture Industry* (New York: Routledge, 1997), 39–60.

3. See Regina Böhm-Korff, *Deutung und Bedeutung von "Hänsel und Gretel"* (Frankfurt am Main: Peter Lang, 1991), 19–20.

4. See Heinz Rölleke, ed., *Die älteste Märchensammlung der Brüder Grimm* (Cologny-Genève: Fondation Martin Bodmer, 1975), 70–83.

5. Gabrielle Brandstetter and Gerhard Neumann, "Gaben. Märchen der Romantik," in *Romantik und Exil*, eds. Claudia Christophersen and Ursula Hudson-Wiedenmann (Würzburg: Königshausen und Neumann, 2004), 17–38.

6. For the most comprehensive compilation of important essays about the different approaches to translations, see Lawrence Venuti, *The Translation Studies Reader*, 2nd ed. (New York: Routledge, 2004).

7. Adam Phillips, *Promises, Promises* (London: Faber and Faber, 2000), 128.

8. Ibid., 141.

9. Ibid., 134.

10. Jacques Derrida, "What Is a 'Relevant' Translation?" in *The Translation Studies Reader*, 2nd ed., ed. Lawrence Venuti (New York: Routledge, 2004), 443.

11. Walter Benjamin, "The Task of the Translator: An Introduction to the Translation of Baudelaire's *Tableaux Parisien*," in *The Translation Studies Reader*, 2nd ed., ed. Lawrence Venuti (New York: Routledge, 2004), 82. This essay, translated by Harry Zohn, has been changed somewhat by Steven Rendall, who has corrected various flaws in Zohn's work and thus provides a more accurate account of Benjamin's views on translation.

12. Emer O'Sullivan, *Comparative Children's Literature*, trans. Anthea Bell (London: Routledge, 2005), 150.

13. See Göte Klingberg, *Children's Fiction in the Hands of Translators* (Lund: Gleerup, 1986); Zohar Shavit, *The Poetics of Children's Literature* (Athens, GA: University of Georgia Press, 1986); Riitta Oiittinen, *Translating for Children* (New York: Garland, 2000); O'Sullivan, *Comparative Children's Literature*, 74–129.

14. Riitta Oittinen, *Translating for Children* (New York: Garland, 2000), 183.

15. O'Sullivan, *Comparative Children's Literature*, 105.

16. Ibid.

17. Edgar Taylor, ed. *German Popular Stories*, intro. John Ruskin, illustr. George Cruikshank (London: Hotten, 1869), 130. This edition is based on the 1823 and 1826 editions.

18. For an excellent discussion of Taylor's two translations of "Hansel and Gretel," see Martin Sutton, *The Sin-Complex: A Critical Study of English Versions of the Grimms' Kinder- und Hausmärchen in the Nineteenth Century* (Kassel: Brüder-Grimm Gesellschaft, 1996), 79–110.

19. Otto Hartwig, "Zur ersten englischen Übersetzung der KHM der Brüder Grimm," *Centralblatt für Bibliothekswesen* 15 (1898): 1–16. Quoted in Sutton in his translation, 84.

20. Jennifer Schacker, *National Dreams: The Remaking of Fairy Tales in Nineteenth-Century England* (Philadelphia: University of Pennsylvania Press, 2003), 30.

21. There are some extraordinary poems in Wolfgang Mieder, *Disenchantments: An Anthology of Modern Fairy Tale Poetry* (Hanover, NH: University Press of New England, 1985) and in Jeanne Marie Beaumont and Claudia Carlson, *The Poets' Grimm: 20th Century Poems from Grimm Fairy Tales* (Ashland, OR: Story Line Press, 2003).

22. U. C. Knoepflmacher, "The Hansel and Gretel Syndrome: Survivorship Fantasies and Parental Desertion," *Children's Literature* 33 (2005): 177.

23. Louise Murphy, "A Conversation with Louise Murphy," in *The True Story of Hansel and Gretel* (New York: Viking, 2003), 4.

24. Ibid., 249.

25. Bill McKibben, "The Christian Paradox: How a Faithful Nation Gets Jesus Wrong," *Harper's* (August 2005): 32.

CHAPTER 7

1. Alice Miller, *The Body Never Lies: The Lingering Effects of Cruel Parenting*, trans. Andrew Jenkins (New York: W. W. Norton, 2005).

2. Marina Warner, *No Go the Bogeyman: Scaring, Lulling, and Making Mock* (London: Chatto & Windus, 1998), 12–13.

3. Joseph Jacobs, *English Fairy Tales*, illustr. John Batten (New York: Knopf, 1993). Reprint of 1890 edition.

4. John Guillory, "Canon," in *Critical Terms for Literary Study*, 2nd ed., eds. Frank Lentricchia and Thomas McLaughlin (Chicago: University of Chicago Press, 1995), 233.

5. R. A. Houston, *Literacy in Early Modern Europe: Culture and Education 1500–1800*, 2nd ed. (London: Longman, 2002), 43. See also Harvey J. Graff, *The Legacies of Literacy: Continuities and Contradictions in Western Culture and Society* (Bloomington, IN: Indiana University Press, 1987).

6. See Norbert Elias, *The Civilizing Process: The History of Manners*, trans. Edmund Jephcott (New York: Urizen, 1978) and Johan Goudsblom and Stephen Mennell, eds., *The Norbert Elias Reader* (London: Blackwell, 1998).

7. Guillory, "Canon," 242.

8. Richard Dawkins, *The Selfish Gene* (Oxford: Oxford University Press, 1978), 192. See also Susan Blackmore, *The Meme Machine* (Oxford: Oxford University Press, 1998) and Robert Aunger, *The Electric Meme: A New Theory of How We Think* (New York: Free Press, 2002).

9. For diverse opinions, see the essays in Robert Aunger, ed., *Darwinizing Culture: The Status of Memetics as a Science* (Oxford: Oxford University Press, 2000).

10. See Søren Kierkegaard, *Fear and Trembling*, trans. Alastair Hannay (London: Penguin Books, 2003) with an interesting introduction by Hannay.

11. Miller, *The Body Never Lies*.

12. David Gross, *The Past in Ruins: Tradition and the Critique of Modernity* (Amherst, MA: University of Massachusetts Press, 1992), 108.

13. Ibid., 117.

14. Ibid., 135.

15. See Ernst Bloch, *Heritage of Our Times*, trans. Neville and Stephen Plaice (Berkeley, CA: University of California Press, 1990) and *Literary Essays*, trans. Andrew Joron and Others (Stanford, CA: Stanford University Press, 1998).

16. See Walter Benjamin, *Illuminations*, ed. Hannah Arendt, trans. Harry Zohn (New York: Harcourt, Brace & World, 1968).

17. Roger Abrahams, "Phantoms of Romantic Nationalism in Folkloristics," *Journal of American Folklore*, 106 (winter 1993): 29–30.

18. See "How Storytellers Can Change Education in Changing Times: Stealing from the Rich to Build Community Bridges," in *Speaking Out: Storytelling and Creative Drama for Children* (New York: Routledge, 2004), 35–59.

19. Adam Phillips, *The Beast in the Nursery: On Curiosity and Other Appetites* (New York: Pantheon, 1998), 113.

20. Ibid., 116.

Bibliography

CRITICISM

Aarne, Antti. *The Types of the Folktales. A Classification and Bibliography*. Rev. and enlarged by Stith Thompson. 2nd rev. ed. FF Communications Nr. 3. Helsinki: Suomalainen Tiedeakatemia, 1961.

Abrahams, Roger. "Phantoms of Romantic Nationalism in Folkloristics." *Journal of American Folklore* 106 (winter 1993): 3–37.

Adam, Jean-Michel, and Ute Heidmann. "Du théâtre de Coppet aux contes des Grimm: les mutations génériques d'un étrange récit." In *Les textes comme aventure*. Carouge-Genève: Zoé, 2003. 174–84.

———. "Discursivité et (trans)textualité. La comparaison pour méthode. L'exemple du conte." In *L'analyse du discours dans les études littéraires*, eds. R. Amossy and D. Maingueneau. Mirail: Presses Universitaires du Mirail, 2003. 27–49.

———. "Des genres ã la généricité: L'exemple des contes (Perrault et les Grimm). *Languages* 153 (March 2004): 62–72.

———. "Text Linguistics and Comparative Literature: Towards an Interdisciplinary Approach to Written Tales. Angela Carter's Translations of Perrault." In *Language and Verbal Art Revisited. Linguistic Approaches to the Literature Text*, eds. Donna R. Miller and Monica Turci. London: Equinix, forthcoming. Chap. 7.

Aitchison, Jean. *The Seeds of Speech: Language Origin and Evolution*. Cambridge: Cambridge University Press, 1996.

Anderson, Graham. *Fairy Tale in the Ancient World*. London: Routledge, 2000.

———. "Old Tales for New: Finding the First Fairy Tales." In *A Companion to the Fairy Tale*, eds. Hilda Ellis Davidson and Anna Chaudrhi. Cambridge: D. S. Brewer, 2003. 85–98.

Apel, Friedmar. *Die Zaubergärten der Phantasie: Zur Theorie und Geschichte des Kunstmärchens.* Heidelberg: Carl Winter Universitätsverlag, 1978.

Ashman, Mike. "Around the Bluebeard Myth." In *The Stage Works of Béla Bartók.* English National Opera Guide. London: John Calder, 1991. 35–44.

Aunger, Robert, ed. *Darwinizing Culture: The Status of Memetics as a Science.* Oxford: Oxford University Press, 2000.

———. *The Electric Meme: A New Theory of How We Think.* New York: Free Press, 2002.

Azzara, Claudio. *Le civiltà del Medioevo.* Bologna: Mulino, 2004.

Bacchilega, Cristina. "'Writing' and 'Voice': The Articulation of Gender in Folklore and Literature." In *Folklore, Literature, and Cultural Theory.* Ed. Cathy Lynn Preston. New York: Garland, 1995. 83–101.

Bakhtin, M. M. *Speech Genres and Other Late Essays.* Austin, TX: University of Texas Press, 1986.

Barchilon, Jacques. *Le Conte merveilleux français de 1690 à 1790.* Paris: Champion, 1975.

Barchilon, Jacques, and Peter Flinders. *Charles Perrault.* Boston: Twayne, 1981.

Barzilai, Shuli. "The Bluebeard Barometer: Charles Dickens and Captain Murderer." *Victorian Literature and Culture* (2004): 505–24.

Bausinger, Hermann. "'Historisierende' Tendenzen im deutschen Märchen seit der Romantik. Requisitenverschiebung und Requisitenerstarrung." *Wirkendes Wort* 10 (1960): 279–86.

———. *Märchen, Phantasie und Wirklichkeit.* Frankfurt am Main: Dipa-Verlag, 1987.

Bédier, Joseph. *Les fabiliaux, études de littérature populaire et d'histoire littéraire du moyen age.* Paris: Bouillon, 1895.

Belcher, Stephen. "Framed Tales in the Oral Tradition: An Exploration." *Fabula* 36 (1994): 1–19.

Belmont, Nicole. "De Cendrillon à La Cenerentola: transformation ou avatar?" *Ethnologie française* 28 (1998): 167–74.

Bendix, Regina. *In Search of Authenticity: The Formation of Folklore Studies.* Madison: University of Wisconsin Press, 1997.

Benjamin, Walter. *Illuminations.* Ed. Hannah Arendt. Trans. Harry Zohn. New York: Harcourt, Brace & World, 1968.

Benson, Stephen. *Folklore, Literature, and Cultural Theory.* New York: Garland, 1995.

———. "The Afterlife of 'Bluebeard.'" *Marvels and Tales* 14 (2000): 244–67.

———. *Cycles of Influence: Fiction, Folktale, Theory.* Detroit: Wayne State University Press, 2003.

Berlioz, Jacques, Claude Bremond, and Catherine Velay-Vallentin, eds. *Formes médievales du conte merveilleux.* Paris: Stock, 1989.

Bertheimer, Kate, ed. *Mirror, Mirror on the Wall.* New York: Anchor, 1998.

Blackmore, Susan. *The Meme Machine*. Oxford: Oxford University Press, 1999.

Blamires, David. "A Workshop of Editorial Practice: The Grimms' *Kinder- und Hausmärchen*." In *A Companion to the Fairy Tale*, eds. Hilda Ellis Davidson and Anna Chaudrhi. Cambridge: D. S. Brewer, 2003. 71–83.

Blatt, Gloria T., ed. *Once Upon a Folktale: Capturing the Folklore Process with Children*. New York: Teachers College Press, 1993.

Bloch, Ernst. *The Utopian Function of Art and Literature*. Trans. Jack Zipes and Frank Mecklenburg. Cambridge, MA: MIT Press, 1987.

———. *Heritage of Our Times*. Trans. Neville Plaice and Stephen Plaice. Berkeley, CA: University of California Press, 1991.

———. *Literary Essays*. Trans. Andrew Joron and Others. Stanford, CA: Stanford University Press, 1998.

Böhm-Korff, Regina. *Deutung und Bedeutung von "Hänsel und Gretel."* Frankfurt am Main: Peter Lang, 1991.

Bolte, Johannes, and Lutz Mackensen. *Handworterbuch des deutschen Marchens*. Berlin: W. de Gruyter, 1931.

Bolte, Johannes, and George Polivka. *Anmerkungen zu den "Kinder- und Hausmärchen."* 5 vols. Leipzig: 1913–32. Reprint: Hildesheim: Georg Olms, 1963.

Boswell, John. *The Kindness of Strangers: The Abandonment of Children in Western Europe from Late Antiquity to the Renaissance*. New York: Pantheon, 1988.

Bottigheimer, Ruth. "The Ultimate Fairy Tale: Oral Transmission in a Literate World." In *A Companion to the Fairy Tale*, eds. Hilda Ellis Davidson and Anna Chaudhri. Cambridge: D. S. Brewer, 2003. 57–70.

Bourdieu, Pierre. *Distinction: A Social Critique of the Judgment of Taste*. Cambridge, MA: Harvard University Press, 1984.

———. *Masculine Domination*. Trans. Richard Nice. Stanford, CA: Stanford University Press, 2001.

Brackert, Helmut. "Hansel und Gretel, oder Möglichkeiten und Grenzen der Märchendeutung." In *Und wenn sie nicht gestorben sind*, ed. Helmut Brackert. Frankfurt am Main: Suhrkamp, 1980. 223–39.

Brandstetter, Gabrielle, and Gerhard Neumann. "Gaben. Märchen in der Romantik." In *Romantik und Exil*, eds. Claudia Christophersen and Ursula Hudson-Wiedenmann. Würzburg: Königshausen und Newmann, 2004. 17–38.

Brednich, Rolf Wilhelm, ed. *Enzyklopädie des Märchens*. 15 vols. Berlin: Walter de Gruyter, 1977–2006.

Brewer, Derek. "The Interpretation of Fairy Tales." In *A Companion to the Fairy Tale*, eds. Hilda Ellis Davidson and Anna Chaudrhi. Cambridge: D. S. Brewer, 2003. 15–37.

Bricout, Bernadette. "L'aiguille et l'epingle." In *La 'Bibliothèque bleue' nel seicento o della letteratura per il popolo*, eds. P. A. Jannini, G. Dotoli, and P. Carile. Bari, Italy: Adriatica, 1981. 45–58.

Brodie, Richard. *Virus of the Mind: The New Science of the Meme*. Seattle: Integral Press, 1996.

Burkert, Walter. *Structure and History in Greek Mythology*. Berkeley, CA: University of California Press, 1979.

———. *Creation of the Sacred: Tracks of Biology in Early Religions*. Cambridge, MA: Harvard University Press, 1996.

Byatt, A. S. *On Histories and Stories: Selected Essays*. Cambridge, MA: Harvard University Press, 2000.

Calame-Griaule, Geneviève, Veronika Görög-Karady, and Michèle Chiche, eds. *Le conte pourquoi? Comment? Folktales, Why and How*. Paris: Éditions du Centre National de la Recherche Scientifique, 1984.

Camporesi, Piero, ed. *Rustici e buffoni: Cultura popolare e cultura d'elite fra medioevo ed età moderna*. Torino: Einaudi, 1991.

———. *The Magic Harvest: Food, Folklore and Society*. Trans. Joan Krakover Hall. Cambridge: MA: Polity Press, 1993.

Canepa, Nancy, ed. *Out of the Woods: The Literary Fairy Tale in Italy and France*. Detroit: Wayne State University Press, 1997.

———. *From Court to Forest: Giambattista Basile's "Lo cunto de li cunti" and the Birth of the Literary Fairy Tale*. Detroit: Wayne State University Press, 1999.

Carroll, Joseph. *Evolution and Literary Criticism*. Columbia, MO: University of Missouri Press, 1995.

———. *Literary Darwinism: Evolution, Human Nature, and Literature*. New York: Routledge, 2004.

Carruthers, Peter, Stephen Laurence, and Stephen P. Stich, eds. *The Innate Mind: Structure and Contents*. New York: Oxford University Press, 2005.

Castelfranchi, Cristiano. "Towards a Cognitive Memetics: Socio-Cognitive Mechanisms for Memes Selection and Spreading." *Journal of Memetics* 5 (2001): 1–20.

Cavalli-Sforza, Luigi Luca. *L'evoluzione della cultura*. Turin: Codice, 2004.

Cavalli-Sforza, Luigi Luca, and Marcus Feldman. *Cultural Transmission and Evolution: A Quantitative Approach*. Princeton, NJ: Princeton University Press, 1981.

Cerina, Giovanna. "La fiaba tra oralità e scrittura: aspetti semiotici." In *Oralità e Scrittura nel Sistema Letterario*, eds. Giovanna Cerina, Cristina Lavinio, and Luisa Mulas. Rome: Bulzoni, 1982. 115–32.

Cerina, Giovanna, Cristina Lavinio, and Luisa Mulas. *Oralità e Scrittura nel Sistema Letterario*. Rome: Bulzoni, 1982.

Chessman, Jacqueline. "Hansel and Gretel and the Impoverished Stepmother." In *The Step Mother in Fairy Tales: Bereavement and the Feminine Shadow*. Boston: Sigo Press, 1993. 51–78.

Chestnutt, Michael, ed. *Telling Reality: Folklore Studies in Memory of Bengt Holbek*. Copenhagen & Turku: NIF Publications, 1993.

Chraïbi, Aboubakr, ed. *Les Mille et une nuits en partage*. Arles: Actes Sud, 2004.

"Cinderella and the Public Domain." *Storytelling World* (November 2000): 21–29.

Clark, William R., and Michael Grunstein. *Are We Hardwired? The Role of Human Genes in Human Behavior*. Oxford: Oxford University Press, 2000.

Clausen-Stolzenburg, Maren. *Märchen und mittelalterliche Literaturtradition*. Heidelberg: Universitätsverlag C. Winter, 1995.

Cocchiara, Giuseppe. *Storia del folklore in Europa*. Turin: Editore Borginghieri, 1952. Translated by John N. McDaniel, as *The History of Folklore in Europe*. Philadelphia: Institute for the Study of Human Issues, 1981.

Coe, Kathryn. "Art: The Repliable Unit. An Inquiry into the Possible Origin of Art as a Social Behavior." In *Biopetics: Evolutionary Explorations in the Arts*, eds. Brett Cooke and Frederick Turner. Lexington, KY: ICUS, 1999. 263–92.

Cooke, Brett, and Frederick Turner, eds. *Biopoetics: Evolutionary Explorations in the Arts*. Lexington, KY: ICUS, 1999.

Costa Fontes, Manuel da. *Folklore and Literature: Studies in the Portuguese, Brazilian, Sephardic, and Hispanic Oral Traditions*. Albany: State University of New York Press, 2000.

Crago, Hugo. "What Are Fairy Tales?" *Signal* 100 (September 2003): 8–26.

Crain, Caleb. "The Artistic Animal." *Lingua Franca* 11 (October 2001): 28–37.

Craveri, Benedetta. *La civiltà della conversazione*. Milan: Adelphi, 2001.

Daly, Martin, and Margo Wilson. *The Truth about Cinderella: A Darwinian View of Love*. New Haven, CT: Yale University Press, 1998.

Davidson, Hilda Ellis, and Anna Chaudhri, eds. *A Companion to the Fairy Tale*. Cambridge: D. S. Brewer, 2003.

Davies, Mererid Puw. *The Tale of Bluebeard in German Literature: From the Eighteenth Century to the Present*. Oxford: Clarendon Press, 2001.

Dawkins, Richard. *The Selfish Gene*. Oxford: Oxford University Press, 1989.

———. *The Extended Phenotype*. Oxford: Oxford University Press, 1992.

———. *Unweaving the Rainbow: Science, Delusion and the Appetite for Wonder*. New York: Houghton Mifflin, 1998.

Dennett, Daniel. *Consciousness Explained*. Boston: Little, Brown, 1991.

———. *Darwin's Dangerous Idea*. London: Penguin, 1995.

Derungs, Kurt. *Der psychologische Mythos. Frauen, Märchen und Sexismus*. Bern: Amalia, 1996.

———. *Die ursprünglichen Märchen der Brüder Grimm: Handschriften, Urfassung und Texte zur Kulturgeschichte*. Bern: Amalia, 1999.

Detlor, Theda. *A Fresh Look at Fairy Tales: A Thematic Unit Exploring Gender Bias in Classic Stories*. New York: Scholastic, 1995.

De Vos, Gail and Anna Altmann. *New Tales for Old: Folktales as Literary Fictions for Young Adults*. Englewood, CO: Libraries Limited, 1996.

Diehl, Charles. *La République de Venise*. Paris: Flammarion, 1985.

Dissanayake, Ellen. *What Is Art For?* Seattle: University of Washington Press, 1988.

———. *Homo Aestheticus: Where Art Comes From and Why*. Seattle: University of Washington Press, 1992.

———. *Art and Intimacy How the Arts Began*. Seattle: University of Washington Press, 2000.

Dorson, Richard. *The British Folklorists: A History*. Chicago: University of Chicago Press, 1968.

Dowling, Colette. *The Cinderella Complex: Women's Hidden Fear of Independence*. New York: Pocket Books, 1981.

Drasce, Daniel. "'Simsala Grimm': Zur Adaptation und Modernisierung der Märchenwelt." *Schweizerisches Archiv für Volkskunde* 97 (2001): 70–89.

Dresang, Eliza T. *Radical Change: Books for Youth in a Digital Age*. New York: H. W. Wilson, 1999.

Duggan, Anne. *Salonnières, Furies, and Fairies: The Politics of Gender and Cultural Change in Absolutist France*. Newark, DE: University of Delaware Press, 2005.

Dundes, Alan, ed. *Cinderella: A Casebook*. Madison: University of Wisconsin Press, 1988.

Dyson, Anne Haas. *Writing Superheroes: Contemporary Childhood, Popular Culture, and Classroom Literacy*. New York: Teachers College Press, 1997.

Edinger, Monica. *Fantasy Literature in the Elementary Classroom: Strategies for Reading, Writing, and Responding*. New York: Scholastic, 1995.

Elias, Norbert. *The Civilizing Process: The History of Manners*. Trans. Edmund Jephcott. New York: Urizen, 1978.

Enders, Jody. *Death by Drama and Other Medieval Urban Legends*. Chicago: University of Chicago Press, 2002.

Eschenbach, Ursula. *Hänsel und Gretel: Das geheime Wissen der Kinder*. Stuttgart: Kreuz Verlag, 1986.

Evans, Dylan. *Introducing Evolutionary Psychology*. Cambridge: Icon, 1999.

Faludi, Susan. *Stiffed: The Betrayal of the American Man*. New York: William Morrow, 1999.

Fehling, Detlev. *Amor und Psyche. Die Schöpfung des Apuleius und ihre Entwicklung auf das Märchen. Eine Kritik der romantischen Märchentheorie*. Wiesbaden: Steiner, 1977.

Feiler, Bruce. *Abraham: A Journey to the Heart of Three Faiths*. New York: William and Morrow, 2002.

Fludernik, Monika. *Towards a "Natural" Narratology*. London: Routledge, 1996.

Fox, Adam. *Oral and Literate Culture in England 1500–1700*. Oxford: Oxford University Press, 2000.

Franz, Kurt, and Walter Kahn, eds. *Märchen—Kinder—Medien*. Hohengehren: Schneider, 2000.

Frazer, James. *The Golden Bough: A Study in Comparative Religion*. 2 vols. London: Macmillan, 1890.

Fuhrmann, Manfred. "Mythen, Fabeln, Legenden und Märchen in der antiken Tradition." In *Metamorphosen des Märchens*, eds. Gundel Mattenklott and Kristin Wardetzky. Hohengehren: Schneider, 2005. 6–22.

Genette, Gérard. *The Architext: An Introduction*. Trans. Jane E. Lewin. Berkeley, CA: University of California Press, 1979.

Gerould, Gordon Hall. *The Grateful Dead: The History of a Folk Story*. Introduction by Norman Cohen. Urbana, IL: University of Illinois Press, 2000. First published in London by David Nutt in 1908.

Gilbert, Sandra M., and Susan Gubar. *The Madwoman in the Attic: The Woman Writer and the Nineteenth Century Literary Imagination*. New Haven, CT: Yale University Press, 1979.

Godwin, Jean, Catherine G. Cauthorne, and Richard T. Rada. "Cinderella Syndrome: Children Who Simulate Neglect." *American Journal of Psychiatry* 137 (October 1980): 1223–5.

Goforth, Frances S., and Carolyn V. Spillman. *Using Folk Literature in the Classroom: Encouraging Children to Read and Write*. Phoenix: Oryx, 1994.

Goldberg, Christine. "Folktale." In *Folklore: An Encyclopedia of Beliefs, Customs, Tales, Music, and Art*, ed. Thomas A. Green. Santa Barbara, CA: ABC-CLIO, 1997. 356–66.

Görög-Karady, Veronika, ed. *D'un conte … à l'autre. La Variabilité dans la littérature orale. From one Tale … to other. The Variability in Oral Literature*. Paris: Éditions du Centre National de la Recherche Scientifique, 1990.

Gorp, Hendrik van, and Ulla Musarra-Schroeder, eds. *Genres as Repositories of Cultural Memory*. Amsterdam: Rodopi, 2000.

Goudsblom, Johan, and Stephen Mennell, eds. *The Norbert Elias Reader*. London: Blackwell, 1998.

Gould, Steven Jay. "OPUS 200." *Natural History* 8 (August 1991): 18–20.

Graff, Harvey. *The Legacies of Literacy: Continuities and Contradictions in Western Culture and Society*. Bloomington, IN: University of Indiana Press, 1987.

Green, Thomas A., ed. *Folklore: An Encyclopedia of Beliefs, Customs, Tales, Music, and Art*. Santa Barbara, CA: ABC-CLIO, 1997.

Griep, Hans-Joachim. *Geschichte des Lesens: Von den Anfängen bis Gutenberg*. Darmstadt: Wissenschaftliche Buchgesellschaft, 2005.

Gross, David. *The Past in Ruins: Tradition and the Critique of Morality*. Amherst, MA: University of Massachusetts Press, 1992.

Guillory, John. "Canon." In *Critical Terms for Literary Study*, 2nd ed., eds. Frank Lentricchia and Thomas McLaughlin. Chicago: University of Chicago Press, 1995. 232–45.

Hanauer, J. E. *Folklore of the Holy Land: Moslem, Christian, and Jewish.* Mineola, NY: Dover, 2002.

Hannon, Patricia. *Fabulous Identities: Women's Fairy Tales in Seventeenth-Century France.* Amsterdam: Rodopi, 1998.

Hartwig, Otto. "Zur ersten englischen Übersetzung der KHM der Brüder Grimm." *Centralblatt für Bibliothekwesen* 15 (1898): 1–16.

Hayes, Kevin J. *Folklore and Book Culture.* Knoxville: University of Tennessee Press, 1997.

Heidmann, Ute. "L'invention des contes: transformations ou détournement?" *Parole* 50 (2001): 3–9.

Heindrichs, Ursula. *Es war einmal—es wird eines Tages sein: Zur Aktualität der Volksmärchen.* Baltmannseiler: Schneider, 2001.

Hermansson, Casie. *Reading Feminist Intertextuality through Bluebeard Stories.* Lewiston, NY: Edward Mellen, 2001.

Heylighen, Francis. "What Makes a Meme Successful? Selection Criteria for Cultural Evolution." In *Proceedings of the 15th International Congress on Cybernetics,* 2006. Available at http:pespmc1.vub.ac.be/Papers/Memetics-Namur.html.

Hippolyte, Jean-Louis. "Étude compare du *Petit Poucet* de Perrault et de *Hänsel et Gretel* des Frères Grimm." *Marvels & Tales* 5.2 (December 1991): 390–402.

Holbek, Bengt. *Interpretation of Fairy Tales: Danish Folklore in a European Perspective.* Helsinki: Academia Scientarium Fennica, 1987.

Houston, R. H. *Literacy in Early Modern Europe: Culture and Education 1500–1800.* 2nd ed. London: Pearson Education Limited/Longman, 2002.

Humperdinck, Engelbert, and Adelheid Wette. *Hänsel und Gretel.* Ed. Wolfram Humperdinck. Stuttgart: Reclam, 1952.

Irwin, Bonnie. D. "What's in a Frame? The Medieval Textualization of Traditional Storytelling." *Oral Tradition* 10 (1995): 27–53.

Jakobson, Roman. "On Russian Fairy Tales." In Aleksandr Afanas'ev, *Russian Fairy Tales.* Trans. Norbert Guterman. New York: Pantheon, 1945. 631–56.

Jannini, P. A. et al, eds. *La Bibliothèque Bleue nel seicento o della letteratura per il popolo.* Bari, Italy: Adriatica, 1981.

Jason, Heda, and Aharon Kempiniski. "How Old Are Folktales?" *Fabula* 24 (1983): 1–27.

Jolles, André. *Einfache Formen.* Tübingen: Niemeyer, 1958.

Keller, Evelyn Fox. *The Century of the Gene.* Cambridge, MA: Harvard University Press, 2000.

Keller, Evelyn Fox, and Elisabeth A. Lloyd, eds. *Keywords in Evolutionary Biology.* Cambridge, MA: Harvard University Press, 1992.

Kiefer, Emma Emily. *Albert Wesselski and Recent Folktale Theories.* Bloomington, IN: Indiana University Press, 1947.

Kierkegaard, Søren. *Fear and Trembling.* Trans. and ed. Alastair Hannay. London: Penguin Books, 2003.

Knoepflmacher, U. C. "The Hansel and Gretel Syndrome: Survivorship Fantasies and Parental Desertion." *Children's Literature* 33 (2005): 171–84.

Kroeber, Karl. *Retelling/Rereading: The Fate of Storytelling in Modern Times.* New Brunswick, NJ: Rutgers University Press, 1992.

Kryzanowski, Julian. "The Cultural Background of Folk Tales." *Literature Studies in Poland* 8 (1981): 15–28.

Kudszus, Winfried. *Terrors of Childhood in Grimms' Fairy Tales.* New York: Peter Lang, 2005.

Labatut, Jean-Pierre. *Les nonoblesses européenes de la fin du XVe à la fin d XVIIIe siècle.* Paris: Presses Universitaires de France, 1978.

Lahire, Bernard. *La culture des individus: dissonances culturelles et distinction de soi.* Paris: Éditions la Découverte, 2004.

Lang, Andrew. *Custom and Myth.* London: Longmans, Green, 1884.

Lange, Günter, ed. *Märchen—Märchenforschung—Märchendidaktik.* Hohengehren: Schneider, 2004.

Lavinio, Cristina. "La fiaba tra oralità e scrittura: aspetti linguistici e stilistici." In *Oralità e Scrittura nel Sistema Letterario*, eds. Giovanna Cerina, Cristina Lavinio, and Luisa Mulinas. Rome: Bulzoni, 1982. 91–114.

———. *La magia della fiaba tra oralità e scrittura.* Florence: La Nuova Italia, 1993.

Lawrence, John, and Robert Jewett. *The Myth of the American Superhero.* Grand Rapids, MI: Eerdmans, 2002.

Le Goff, Jacques. "Clerical Culture and Folklore Traditions in Merovingian Civilization." In *Time, Work, and Culture in the Middle Ages*, trans. Arthur Goldhammer. Chicago: University of Chicago Press, 1980. 153–58.

Leafstedt, Carl. *Inside Bluebeard's Castle: Music and Drama in Béla Bartók's Opera.* New York: Oxford University Press, 1999.

Levins, Richard, and Richard Lewontin. *The Dialectical Biologist.* Cambridge, MA: Harvard University Press, 1985.

Lewis, Philip. *Seeing Through the Mother Goose Tales: Visual Turns in the Writings of Charles Perrault.* Stanford, CA: Stanford University Press, 1996.

Lewontin, Richard C. *Biology as Ideology: The Doctrine of DNA.* New York: Harper, 1991.

Lindahl, Carl. "Folktale." In *Medieval Folklore: An Encyclopedia of Myths, Legends, Tales, Beliefs, and Customs*, eds. Carl Lindahl, John McNamara, and John Lindow. New York: Oxford University Press, 2002. 142–48.

Lindahl, Carl, John McNamara, and John Lindow, eds. *Medieval Folklore: An Encyclopedia of Myths, Legends, Tales, Beliefs, and Customs.* 2 vols. Santa Barbara, CA: ABC-CLIO, 2000.

Lipp, Carola, ed. *Medien popularer Kultur: Erzählung, Bild und Objekt in der volkskündlichen Forschung.* Frankfurt am Main: Campus, 1995.

Loewy, Hanno. *Béla Balázs—Märchen, Ritual und Film*. Berlin: Vorwerk 8, 2003.

Lynch, Aaron. *Thought Contagion: How Belief Spreads through Society*. New York: Basic Books, 1996.

Maaz, Wolfgang. "Märchen und Märchenmotive im MA." In *Lexikon des Mittelalters*, eds. Charlotte Bretsche-Gisiger, Bettina Marquis, and Thomas Meier, Vol. 6. Stuttgart: Metzler, 1999. 224–26.

Manguel, Alberto. *A History of Reading*. New York: Viking Penguin, 1996.

Mattenklott, Gundel, and Kristin Wardetzky, eds. *Metamorphosen des Märchens*. Hohengehren: Schneider, 2005.

Mayr, Ernst. *Toward a New Philosophy of Biology: Observations of an Evolutionist*. Cambridge, MA: Harvard University Press, 1988.

McClary Susan. "Introduction: A Material Girl in Bluebeard's Castle." In *Feminine Endings: Music, Gender, and Sexuality*. Ed. Susan McClary. Minneapolis: University of Minnesota Press, 1991. 3–34.

McKibben, Bill. "The Christian Paradox: How a Faithful Nation Gets Jesus Wrong." *Harper's* (August 2005): 31–37.

Menninghaus, Winfried. *In Praise of Nonsense: Kant and Bluebeard*. Trans. Henry Pickford. Stanford, CA: Stanford University Press, 1999.

Miller, Alice. *The Drama of the Gifted Child*. Trans. Ruth Ward. New York: Basic Books, 1981.

———. *For Your Own Good: Hidden Cruelty in Child-Rearing and the Roots of Violence*. New York: Basic Books, 1983.

———. *The Body Never Lies: The Lingering Effects of Cruel Parenting*. New York: W. W. Norton, 2005.

Miller, Geoffrey. *The Mating Mind*. New York: Doubleday, 2000.

Morewedge, Rosmarie Thee. "Orality, Literacy, and the Medieval Folktale." In *Varieties and Consequences of Literacy and Orality*, eds. Ursula Schaefer and Edda Spielmann. Tübingen: Narr, 2001. 85–106.

Moser, Dietz-Rüdiger. "Gedanken zur historischen Erzählforschung." *Zeitschrift für Volkskunde* 69 (1973): 61–81.

———. "Altersbestimmung des Märchens." In *Enzyklopädie des Märchens*, Vol. 1, ed. Rolf Wilhelm Brednich. Berlin: Walter der Gruyter, 1977. 407–19.

Mothe, Jean-Pierre. *Du sang et du sexe dans les contes de Perrault*. Paris: L'Harmattan, 1999.

Mulvey, Laura. *Fetishism and Curiosity*. Bloomington, IN: Indiana University Press, 1996.

Murayama, Isamitsu. *Poesie—Natur—Kinder: Die Brüder Grimm und ihre Idee einer "natürlichen Bildung" in den Kinder- und Hausmärchen*. Heidelberg: Universitätsverlag, 2005.

Nières, Isabelle. "Une planche d'Épinal: Histoire de la Barbe bleue; NE 1102." In *Tricentenaire Charles Perrault: Les grands contes du XVIIe Siècle et leur fortune littéraire*, ed. Jean Perrot. Paris: In Press Éditions, 1998. 75–84.

Niles, John D. *Homo Narrans: The Poetics and Anthropology of Oral Literature.* Philadelphia: University of Pennsylvania Press, 1999.

Oberfeld, Charlotte, ed. *Wie alt sind unsere Märchen.* Regensburg: Röth, 1990.

Oittinen, Riitta. *Translating for Children.* New York: Garland, 2000.

Oldrige, Darren. *Strange Histories: The Trial of the Pig, the Walking Dead, and Other Matters of Fact from the Medieval and Renaissance Worlds.* London: Routledge, 2005.

Ong, Walter. *Orality and Literacy: The Technologizing of the Word.* London: Methuen, 1982.

Origgi, Gloria, and Dan Sperber, "Evolution, Communication, and the Proper Function of Language." In *Evolution and the Human Mind: Language, Modularity and Social Cognition*, eds. Peter Carruthers and Andrew Chamberlain. Cambridge: Cambridge University Press, 2000. 140–69.

O'Sullivan, Emer. *Comparative Children's Literature.* Trans. Anthea Bell. London: Routledge, 2005.

Parsons, Linda T. "Ella Evolving: Cinderella Stories and the Construction of Gender Appropriate Behavior." *Children's Literature in Education* 35.2 (2004): 134–54.

Petzoldt, Leander, Siegfried de Rachewiltz, and Petra Streng, eds. *Studien zur Stoff-und Motivgeschichte der Volkserzählung.* Frankfurt am Main: Peter Lang, 1995.

Philip, Neil, ed. *The Cinderella Story.* New York: Viking, 1989.

———. "Creativity and Tradition in the Fairy Tale." In *A Companion to the Fairy Tale*, eds. Hilda Ellis Davidson and Anna Chaudhri. Cambridge: D. S. Brewer, 2003. 39–55.

Phillips, Adam. *The Beast in the Nursery: On Curiosity and Other Appetites.* New York: Pantheon, 1998.

———. "On Translating a Person." In *Promises, Promises:* London: Faber and Faber, 2000. 125–47.

Picone Michelangelo, and Alfred Messerli, eds. *Giovan Battista Basile e l'invenzione della fiaba.* Ravenna: Longo Editore, 2004.

Piffault, Olivier, ed. *Il était une fois … les contes de fees.* Paris: Seuil/Bibliothèque nationale de France, 2001.

Pinker, Steven. *The Language Instinct.* London: Penguin, 1994.

———. *The Blank Slate: The Modern Denial of Human Nature.* New York: Viking Penguin, 2002.

Pirovano, Donato, ed. "Introduzione." In Giovan Francesco Straparola, *Le piacevoli Notti.* Rome: Salerno Editrice, 2000. 9–50.

————. "Nota Biografica." In Giovan Francesco Straparola, *Le piacevoli Notti*, ed. Donato Pirovano. Rome: Salerno Editrice, 2000. 51–54.

Pleij, Herman. *Dreaming of Cockaigne: Medieval Fantasies of the Perfect Life*. New York: Columbia University Press, 2001.

Plotkin, Henry. *Evolution in Mind: An Introduction to Evolutionary Psychology*. Cambridge, MA: Harvard University Press, 1998.

Pöge-Alder, Kathrin. Märchen als mündlich tradierte Erzählungen des Volkes? Zur Wissenschaftsgeschichte der Entstehungs- und Verbreitungstheorien von Volksmärchen. Frankfurt am Main: Peter Lang, 1994.

Propp, Vladimir. *Morphology of the Folktale*. 2nd rev. ed. Eds. Louis Wagner and Alan Dundes. Trans. Laurence Scott. Austin: University of Texas Press, 1968.

————. "Les Transformations des Contes Fantastiques." In *Théorie de la littérature*, ed. Tzvetan Todorov. Paris: Seuil, 1965. 234–62.

————. *Theory and History of Folklore*. Trans. Adriadna Y. Martin and Richard P. Martin. Ed. Anatoly Liberman. Minneapolis: University of Minnesota Press, 1984.

————. *Die historischen Wurzeln des Zaubermärchens*. Trans. Martin Pfeiffer. Munich: Hanser, 1987.

Raitz, Walter. *Zur Soziogenese des bürgerlichen Romans: Eine literatursoziologische Analyse des "Fortunatus."* Düsseldorf: Bertelsmann, 1973.

Rak, Michele. *Logica della fiaba: Fate. orchi, gioco, corte, fortuna, viaggio capriccio, metamorfosi, corpo*. Milan: Bruno Mondadori, 2005.

Rancour-Laferriere, Daniel. "Preliminary Remarks on Literary Memetics." In *Biopoetics: Evolutionary Explorations in the Arts*, eds. Brett Cooke and Frederick Turner. Lexington, KY: ICUS, 1999. 59–70.

Richter, Dieter. "Die Märchen des Basile und ihre Metamorphosen." In *Metamorphosen des Märchens*, eds. Gundel Mattenklott and Kristin Wardetzky. Hohengehren: Schneider, 2005. 23–35.

Ridley, Matt. *Evolution*. 2nd ed. Oxford: Blackwell, 1996.

————. *The Origins of Virtue*. London: Penguin, 1996.

Robinson, Orrin W. "Rhymes and Reasons in the Grimms' *Kinder- und Hausmärchen*." *German Quarterly* 77.1 (Winter 2004): 47–58.

Roest, Bert, and Herman Vanstiphout, eds. *Aspects of Genre and Type in Pre-Modern Literary Cultures*. Groningen: Styx, 1999.

Röhrich, Lutz. *"Und weil sie nicht gestorben sind ...": Anthropologie, Kulturgeschichte und Deutung von Märchen*. Cologne: Böhlau, 2002.

Rölleke, Heinz, ed. *Die älteste Märchensammlung der Brüder Grimm*. Cologny-Genève: Fondation Martin Bodmer, 1975.

————. *Wo das Wünschen noch geholfen hat*. Bonn: Bouvier, 1985.

Rosenberg, Bruce. *Folklore and Literature: Rival Siblings*. Knoxville: University of Tennessee Press, 1991.

Rubini, Luisa. "Il sale della Fiaba: Alimentazione e Gastromonia nei *Kinder- und Hausmärchen* de Fratelli Grimm." In *La Fiaba d'Area Germanica: Studi tipologici e tematici*, ed. Enza Gini. Florence: La Nuova Italia, 1990. 35–55.

————. "Fortunatus in Italy: A History between Translations, Chapbooks and Fairy Tales." *Fabula* 44 1.2 (2001): 25–54.

Ruddick, Nicholas. "Another Key to Bluebeard's Chamber: Ideal and Fundamentalist Masculinity in the Literature of Fantasy." In *Images of Masculinity in Fantasy Fiction*, eds. Susanne Fendler and Ulrike Horstmann. Lewiston, NY: Edwin Mellen, 2003. 1–17.

Rusch-Feja, Diann. *The Portrayal of the Maturation Process of Girl Figures in Selected Tales of the Brothers Grimm*. New York: Peter Lang, 1995.

Sahar, Shulamith. *Childhood in the Middle Ages*. London: Routledge, 1990.

Sahr, Michael. *Zeit für Märchen: Kreativer und medienorienterter Umgang mit einer epischen Kurzform*. Baltmannsweiler: Schneider, 2002.

Samuelson, David. "The Experience of Cinderella." *College English* 37.8 (1976): 767–79.

Sanga, Glauco. Odi di produzione e forme di tradizione: dall'oralità feudale alla scrittura capitalistica." In *Oralità e Scrittura nel Sistema Letterario*, eds. Giovanna Cerina, Cristina Lavinio, and Luisa Mulinas. Rome: Bulzoni, 1982. 31–48.

Sautman, Francesca Canadé, Diana Conchado, and Giuseppe Carlo Di Scipio, eds. *Telling Tales: Medieval Narratives and the Folk Tradition*. New York: St. Martin's Press, 1998.

Schacker, Jennifer. *National Dreams: The Remaking of Fairy Tales in Nineteenth-Century England*. Philadelphia: University of Pennsylvania Press, 2003.

Schaefer, Ursula. *Mündlichkeit, Schriftlichkeit, Weltbildwandel: literarische Kommunikation und Deutungsschemata von Wirklichkeit in der Literatur des Mittelalters und der frühen Neuzeit*. Tübingen: Narr, 1996.

Schaefer, Ursula, and Edda Spielmann, eds. *Varieties and Consequences of Literacy and Orality*. Tübingen: Narr, 2001.

Scheuer, Helmut. "Das 'Volksbuch' *Fortunatus* (1509). Zwischen feudaler Anpassung und bürgerlicher Selbstverwirklichung." In *Literatursoziologie, II, Beiträge zur Praxis*, ed. Joachim Bark. Stuttgart: Kohlhammer, 1974. 99–117.

Schmitt, Jean-Claude. *Religione, folklore e società nell'Occidente medievale*. Rome-Bari: Laterza, 1988.

Schroeder, Russell. *Disney's Mulan*. New York: Disney Press, 1998.

Scobie, Alex. *Apuleius and Folklore: Toward a History of ML3045, AaTh567, 449A*. London: 1983.

Sexton, Ed. *Dawkins and the Selfish Gene*. Cambridge: Icon, 2001.

Shattuck, Roger. *Forbidden Knowledge: A Landmark Exploration of the Dark Side of Human Ingenuity and Imagination*. San Diego: Harcourt Brace, 1996.

Siepe, Hans. "Rotkäppchen einmal anders. Ein Märchen für den Märchenunterricht." *Der fremdsprachliche Unterricht* 65 (1983): 1–9.

Shippey, Tom. "Rewriting the Core: Transformations of the Fairy Tale in Contemporary Writing." In *A Companion to the Fairy Tale*, eds. Hilda Ellis Davidson and Anna Chaudrhi. Cambridge: D. S. Brewer, 2003. 253–74.

Simons, Elizabeth. *Student Worlds Student Words: Teaching Writing Through Folklore*. Portsmouth, NH: Heinemann, 1990.

Soriano, Marc. *Les Contes de Perrault*. Paris: Gallimard, 1968.

———. *Le Dossier Charles Perrault*. Paris: Hachette, 1972.

Sperber, Dan. *Explaining Culture: A Naturalistic Approach*. London: Blackwell, 1996.

———. "An Objection to the Memetic Approach to Culture." In *Darwinizing Culture: The Status of Memetics as a Science*, ed. Robert Aunger. Oxford: Oxford University Press, 2000. 163–73.

Sperber, Dan, and Lawrence Hirschfeld. "Culture, Cognition, and Evolution." In *MIT Encyclopedia of the Cognitive Sciences*, eds. Robert Wilson and Frank Keil. Cambridge, MA: MIT Press, 1999. 111–32.

Sperber, Dan, and Deirdre Wilson. *Relevance: Communication and Cognition*. 2nd ed. London: Blackwell, 1995.

Stock, Brian. *Listening for the Text: On the Uses of the Past*. Baltimore: Johns Hopkins University Press, 1990.

Storey, Robert. *Mimesis and the Human Animal: On the Biogenetic Foundations of Literary Representation*. Evanston, IL: Northwestern University Press, 1996.

Suhrbier, Hartwig. *Blaubarts Geheimnis*. Cologne: Diederichs, 1984.

Sutton, Marin. *The Sin-Complex: A Critical Study of English Versions of the Grimms Kinder- und Hausmärchen in the Nineteenth Century*. Kassel: Brüder-Grimm Gesellschaft, 1996.

Tatar, Maria. *Secrets Beyond the Door: The Story of Bluebeard and His Wives*. Princeton, NJ: Princeton University Press, 2004.

Teitelbam, Michael. *The Story of the X-Men: How It All Began*. New York: Dorling Kindersley, 2000.

Thelander, Dorothy. "Mother Goose and Her Goslings: The France of Louis XIV as Seen through the Fairy Tale." *Journal of Modern History* 54 (September 1982): 467–96.

Thornhill, Randy, and Craig T. Palmer. *A Natural History of Rape: Biological Bases of Sexual Coercion*. Cambridge, MA: MIT Press, 2000.

Todorov, Tzvetan. "L'origine des genres." In *La notion de littérature et autres essaies*. Paris: Seuil, 1987. 27–46.

Tooby, John. *The Adapted Mind: Evolutionary Psychology and the Generation of Culture*. Oxford: Oxford University Press, 1992.

Trinquet, Charlotte. "La Petite Histoire des Contes de Fées Littéraires en France (1690–1705)." Diss. University of North Carolina, Chapel Hill, 2001.

Tucker, Holly, ed. *Reframing the Early French Fairy Tale. Marvels & Tales* 19/1 (special issue, 2005).

Turner, Frederick, ed. *Biopoetics: Evolutionary Explorations in the Arts*. New York: Paragon House, 1999.

Tylor, Edward. *Primitive Culture: Researches into the Development of Mythology, Philosophy, Religion, Language, Art and Custom*. London: Murray, 1871.

Vàvaro, Albert. *Apparizioni fantastiche. Tradizioni folkloriche e letteratura nel medioevo: Walter Map*. Bologna: Il Mulino, 1994.

Vaz da Silva, Francisco. *Metamorphosis: The Dynamics of Symbolism in European Fairy Tales*. New York: Peter Lang, 2002.

Velay-Vallantin, Catherine. *La fille en garçon*. Caracassonne: Garae Hesiode, 1992.

———. "From 'Little Red Riding Hood' to the 'Beast of Gévaudan': The Tale in the Long Term Continuum." In *Telling Tales: Medieval Narratives and the Folk Tradition*, eds. Francesca Canadé Sautman, Diana Conchado, and Giuseppe Carlo Di Scipio. New York: St. Martin's Press, 1998. 269–95.

Venuti, Lawrence, ed. *The Translation Studies Reader*. 2nd ed. New York: Routledge, 2004.

Verdier, Yvonne. "Grand-mères, si vous saviez: le Petit Chaperon Rouge dans la tradition orale." *Cahiers de littérature orale* 4 (1978): 17–55.

Vos Gail de, and Anna Altmann. *New Tales for Old: Folk Tales as Literary Fictions*. Englewood, CO: Libraries Unlimited, 1996.

Wailes, Stephen. "Potency in *Fortunatus*." *German Quarterly* 59.1 (Winter 1986): 5–18.

Wanke, Matilde Dillon, ed. *La voce scritta: Laboratorio sulle strutture della fiaba e della letteratura infantile fra tradizione e modernità*. Bergamo: Bergamo University Press/Edizioni Sestante, 2002.

Ward, Donald. "Do *Märchensingverse* Indicate Orality?" In *Varieties and Consequences of Literacy and Orality*, eds. Ursula Schaefer and Edda Spielmann. Tübingen: Narr, 2001. 125–48.

Warner, Marina. *From the Beast to the Blonde: On Fairytales and Their Tellers*. London: Chatto and Windus, 1994.

———. *No Go the Bogeyman: Scaring, Lulling, and Making Mock*. London: Chatto and Windus, 1998.

Wesselski, Albert. *Versuch einer Theorie des Märchens*. Reichenberg: Prager Deutsche Studien 45, 1931.

———. *Märchen des Mittelalters*. Berlin: Stubenrauch, 1942.

Wilson, Deirdre, and Dan Sperber. "Relevance Theory." In *Handbook of Pragmatics*, eds. G. Ward and L. Horn. Oxford: Blackwell, 2004. 607–32.

Wilson, Edward O. *Consilience: The Unity of Knowledge*. New York: Knopf, 1998.

Wilson, Stephen. *The Magical Universe: Everyday Ritual and Magic in Pre-Modern Europe*. London: Hambledon and London, 2000.

Windling, Terri. "Introduction." In *Fitcher's Brides*, ed. Gregory Frost. New York: TOR, 2002. 11–29.

Wright, Bradford W. *Comic Book Nation: The Transformation of Youth Culture in America*. Baltimore: Johns Hopkins University Press, 2001.

Wright, Robert. *The Moral Animal: Evolutionary Psychology and Everyday Life*. New York: New York: Pantheon, 1994.

———. "The Accidental Creationist." *New Yorker* (December 13, 1999): 56–65.

Ziolkowski, Jan. "A Fairy Tale Before Fairy Tales: Egbert of Liège's 'De puellis a lupellis seruata' and the Medieval Background of 'Little Red Riding Hood.'" *Speculum* (1992): 549–75.

———, ed. *Obscenity: Social Control and Artistic Creation in the European Middle Ages*. Leiden: Brill, 1998.

———. "Old Wives' Tales: Classicism and Anticlassicism from Apuleius to Chaucer." *Journal of Medieval Latin* 12 (2002): 90–113.

———. *Fairy Tales from Before Fairy Tales: The Medieval Latin Past of Wonderful Lies*. Ann Arbor, MI: University of Michigan Press, forthcoming.

Zipes, Jack, ed. *Don't Bet on the Prince: Contemporary Feminist Fairy Tales in North America and England*. London: Methuen, 1986.

———. *The Trials and Tribulations of Little Red Riding Hood*. 2nd ed. New York: Routledge, 1993.

———. *Happily Ever After: Fairy Tales, Children, and the Culture Industry*. New York: Routledge, 1997.

———, ed. *The Oxford Companion to Fairy Tales: The Western Fairy Tale Tradition from Medieval to Modern*. Oxford: Oxford University Press, 2000.

———. *Hans Christian Andersen: The Misunderstood Storyteller*. New York: Routledge, 2005.

———. *Fairy Tales and the Art of Subversion: The Classical Genre for Children and the Process of Civilization*. 2nd rev. ed. New York: Routledge, 2006.

Fairy-Tale Collections and Related Literature, 1500–1900

Almanni, Luigi. "Bianca, Figliuola del Conte di Tolosa" (1531). In *Novelle del Cinquecento*, ed. Giambattista Salinari. 2 vols. Turin: Unione Tipografico-Editrice Tornese, 1955.

Al-Mas'udi. *Al-Mas'udi's Historical Encyclopedia, Entitled Meadows of Gold and Mines of Gems*. London: Oriental Translation Fund of Great Britain and Ireland, 1841.

Andersen, Hans Christian. *Wonderful Stories for Children*. Trans. Mary Botham Howitt. 1st English ed. London: Chapman and Hall, 1846.

———. *Danish Fairy Legends and Tales*. Trans. Caroline Peachey. 2nd ed., with a memoir of the author. London: Addey, 1852.

———. *The Complete Fairy Tales and Stories*. Trans. Erik Christian Haugaard. New York: Doubleday, 1974.

Appelbaum, Stanley. *Medieval Tales and Stories*. Mineola, NY: Dover, 2000.

Arnim, Friedmund von. *Hundert neue Mährchen im Gebirge gesammelt*. 1844.

———. *Hundert neue Mährchen im Gebirge gesammelt*. Ed. Heinz Rölleke. Cologne: Eugen Diederichs, 1986.

Asbjørnsen, Peter Christen. *Norske huldreeventyr of folkesagn*. Christiania: C. A. Oybwad, 1848.

———. *Round the Yule. Norwegian Folk and Fairy Tales*. Trans. H. L. Braekstad. London: Sampson Low, Marston, Searle, and Irvington, 1881.

Asbjørnsen, Peter Christen, and Jorgen Møe. *Norske folke-eventyr*. Christiania: J. Dahl, 1852.

———. *Popular Tales from the Norse*. Intro. George Dasent. Edinburgh: Edmonstron and Douglas, 1859.

Aubailly, Jean-Claude, ed. *Fabliaux et contes moraux du Moyen Age*. Preface by Jean Joubert. Paris: Livre de Poche, 1987.

Aulnoy, Marie-Catherine, with Baronne de Jumel de Barneville. *Les Contes de fées*. 4 vols. 1st ed. Paris: Claude Barbin, 1697.

———. *Contes Nouveaux ou les Fées à la mode*. 2 vols. Paris: Veuve de Théodore Girard, 1698.

———. *Suite des Contes Nouveaux ou des Fées à la mode*. 2 vols. Paris: Veuve de Théodore Girard, 1698.

———. *The Fairy Tales of Madame d'Aulnoy*. Trans. Anne Macdonell. Intro. Anne Thackeray Ritchie. London: Lawrence and Bullen, 1895.

———. *Contes*. Ed. Philippe Houcade. Intro. Jacques Barchilon. 2 vols. Paris: Société des Textes Français Modernes, 1997–98.

Barchilon, Jacques, ed. *Nouveau Cabinet des fées*. 18 vols. Geneva: Slatkine Reprints, 1978. Partial reprint of *Le Cabinet des fées*, ed. Charles-Joseph Mayer.

Basile, Giambattista. *Lo cunto de li cunti overo Lo trattenemiento de peccerille*. De Gian Alessio Abbattutis. 5 vols. Naples: Ottavio Beltrano, .1634–36.

———. *The Pentamerone of Giambattista Basile*. Trans. and ed. N. M. Penzer. 2 vols. London: John Lane and the Bodley Head, 1932.

———. *Lo cunto de li Cunti*. Ed. Michele Rak. Milan: Garazanti, 1986.

———. *Il racconto dei racconti*. Ed. Alessandra Burani and Ruggero Guarini. Trans. Ruggero Guarini. Milan: Adelphi Edizioni, 1994.

———. *The Pentamerone*. Trans. Richard Burton. London: Spring, n.d.

Bebel, Heinrich. *Facetiarum ... libri tres, a mendis repurgati, & in lucem rursus redditi*. Tübingen: Morhard, 1542.

Bechstein, Ludwig. *Deutsches Märchenbuch*. Leipzig: Wigand, 1845.

———. *Ludwig Bechsteins Märchenbuch*. Leipzig: Wigand, 1853.

———. *Neues Deutsches Märchenbuch*. Vienna: Hartleben, 1856.

———. *Sämtliche Märchen*. Ed. Walter Scherf. Munich: Winkler, 1968.

Benfey, Theodor. *Pantschatantra: Fünf Bücher indischer Fabeln, Märchen und Erzählungen*. Leipzig: Brockhaus, 1859.

Bernard, Catherine. *Inès de Cardoue, nouvelle espagnole*. Paris: Jouvenol, 1696; Geneva: Slatkine Reprints, 1979.

Bierling, Friedrich Immanuel, ed. *Cabinet der Feen*. 9 vols. Nürnberg: Raspe, 1761–66.

Bignon, Abbé Jean-Paul. *Les Aventures d'Abdalla, fils d'Hani, envoyé par le sultan des Indes à la découverte de l'ile de Borico*. Paris: P. Witte, 1710–14.

Blackwell, Jeannine, and Susanne Zantop, eds. *Bitter Healing: German Women Writers 1700–1830. An Anthology*. Lincoln: University of Nebraska Press, 1990.

Calvi, Francois de. *Histoire Générale des Larrons*. Paris: Martin Collet, 1623.

Calvino, Italo, ed. *Fiabe*. Torino: Einaudi, 1970.

———, ed. *Italian Folktales*. Trans. George Martin. New York: Harcourt Brace Jovanovich, 1980.

Cambell of Islay, John Francis, ed. *Popular Tales of the West Highlands*. 4 vols. Orally collected translated. 3rd ed. Hounslow, Middlesex: Wildwood House, 1983–84.

Ciccuto, Marcello, ed. *Novelle italiene: Il Cinquecento*. Milan: Garzanti, 1982.

Crane, Thomas Frederick. *Italian Popular Tales*. Boston: Houghton, Mifflin, 1889.

Curtin, Jeremiah. *Myths and Folk-lore of Ireland*. Boston: Little Brown, 1890.

Daudet, Alphonse. "Les huit pendules de Barbe-Bleue. Moralité." In *Le Roman Chaperon Rouge. Scenes et Fantaisies*. Paris: J. Tardieu: 1862. 129–51.

Delarue, Paul, and Marie-Louise Tenèze. *Le Conte populaire français. Un catalogue raisonné des versions de France et des pays de langue française et d'Outre-mer*. 4 vols. Paris: Maisonneuve et Larose, 1957–76.

Delarue, Paul, ed. *French Fairy Tales*. Illus. Warren Chappell. New York: Knopf, 1968.

Deulin, Charles. *Les Contes de ma Mère l'Oye avant Perrault*. Paris: Dentu, 1878.

Egerton, Francis, Earl of Ellesmere. *Bluebeard; or, Dangerous Curiosity and Justifiable Homicide*. London: T. Brettell, 1841.

Ehrismann, Otfrid, ed. *Der Stricker: Erzählungen, Fabeln, Reden*. Stuttgart: Philipp Reclam, 1992.

Ey, Karl August Eduard, ed. *Harzmärchenbuch. Oder Sagen und Märchen aus der Oberharze*. 4th ed. Leipzig: Stade, F. Strudel, 1862.

Fatini, Guiseppe, ed. *Novelle del Cinquecento*. Turin: Unione Tipografico-Editrice Tornese, 1930.

Fiorentino, Ser Giovanni. *Il Pecorone*. Milan: Giovanni Antonio, 1554; reprinted and edited by Enzo Esposito, Ravena: Longo, 1974.

Galland, Antoine. *Les Milles et une nuit*. 12 vols. Vols. 1–4 Paris: Florentin Delaulne, 1704; Vols. 5–7, ibid., 1706; vol. 8, ibid., 1709; vols. 9–10, Florentin Delaulne, 1712; vols. 11–12, Lyon: Briasson, 1717.

Gonzenbach, Laura. *Sicilianische Märchen*. 2 vols. Leipzig: W. Engelmann, 1870.

Grimm, Albert Ludwig. *Kindermährchen*. Heidelberg: Morhr und Zimmer, 1808.

———. *Lina's Mährchenbuch*. Frankfurt am Main: Wilmans, 1816.

Grimm, Jacob, and Wilhelm Grimm. *Kinder- und Hausmärchen. Gesammelt durch die Brüder Grimm*. Berlin: Realschulbuchhandlung, 1812.

———. "Blaubart." In *Kinder- und Hausmärchen*. Vol. 1. No. 62. Berlin: 1812.

———. *Kinder- und Hausmärchen. Gesammelt durch die Brüder Grimm*. Vol. 2. Berlin: Realschulbuchhandlung, 1815.

———. *German Popular Stories, Translated from the Kinder und Haus Märchen*. Trans. Edgar Taylor. London: C. Baldwin, 1823.

———. *Kinder- und Hausmärchen. Gesammelt durch die Brüder Grimm*. 7th rev. and exp. ed. 2 vols. Göttingen: Dieterich, 1857.

———. *Household Stories from the Collection of the Brothers Grimm*. Trans. Lucy Crane. London: Macmillan, 1882.

———. *The Complete Fairy Tales of the Brothers Grimm*. Ed. and trans. Jack Zipes. New York: Bantam, 1987.

Gueullette, Thomas Simon. *Les Mille et un quarts d'heure, contes tartares*. Paris: 1715.

Guglielminetti, Marziano. *Novelliei del Cinquecento*. Milan: Ricciardi, 1972.

Haltrich, Josef, ed. *Deutsche Volksmärchen aus dem Sachsenlande in Siebenbürgen*. Hermannstadt: Krafft, 1885.

Histoire de la belle Hélène de Constantinople. Troyes: Garnier, 1700.

Husain, Shahrukh. *Handsome Heroines: Women as Men in Folklore*. New York: Doubleday, 1995.

Imbriani, Vittorio. *La Novellaja fiorentina*. Livorno: F. Vigo, 1877.

Jacobs, Joseph. *English Fairy Tales*. Illus. John Batten. New York: Knopf, 1993. Reprint of 1890 edition.

———, ed. *English Fairy Tales*. London: Nutt, 1890.

Jamieson, Robert. *Popular Ballads and Songs from Tradition, Manuscripts and Scarce Editions*. Edinburgh: A. Constable, 1806.

Joisten, Charles. *Contes Populaires du Dauphiné*. Vol. 1. Grenoble: Publications du Musée Dauphinois, 1971.

Karlinger, Felix, ed. *Der abenteuerliche Glückstopf: Märchen des Barock*. Munich: Bruckmann, 1965.

La Force, Charlotte-Rose Caumont de. *Les Contes des contes par Mlle de ****. Paris: S. Bernard, 1697.

———. *Les Jeux d'esprit ou la promenade de la Princesse de Conti à Eu par Mademoiselle de la Force*. Ed. M. le Marquis de la Grange. Paris: Auguste Aubry, 1862.

Lang, Andrew, ed. and trans. *Perrault's Popular Tales*. Oxford: Clarendon Press, 1888.

Langosch, Karl. *Waltharius. Ruodlieb. Märchenepen. Lateinische Epik des Mittellaters mit deutschen Versen*. Darmstadt: Wissenschaftliche Buchgesellschaft, 1956.

Lhéritier de Villandon, Marie-Jeanne. *Oeuvres meslées, contenant l'Innocente tromperie, l'Avare puni, les Enchantements de l'éloquence, les Aventures de Finette, nouvelles, et autres ouvrages, en vers et en prose, de Mlle de L'H***—avec le Triomphe de Mme Des-Houlières tel qu'il a été composé par Mlle ****. Paris: J. Guignard, 1696.

———. *La Tour ténébreuse et les jours lumineux, contes anglois, accompagnés d'historiettes et tirés d'une ancienne chronique composée par Richard, surnommé Coeur de Lion, roi d'Angleterre, avec le récit des diverse aventures de ce roi*. Paris: Veuve de Claude Barbin, 1705.

Le Noble, Eustache. *Le Gage touché, histoires galantes*. Amsterdam: Jaques Desbordes, 1700.

Le Prince de Beaumont, Marie. *Magasin des enfans, ou Dialogue d'une sage gouvernante avec ses élèves de la première distinction*. Lyon: Reguilliat, 1756.

Maier, Bruno, ed. *Novelle italiane del Cinquecento*. Milan: Il Club del Libro, 1962.

Mailly, Jean de. *Les Illustres fées, contes galans. Dédié aux dames*. Paris: M.-M. Brunet, 1698.

Martines, Lauro, ed. *An Italian Renaissance Sextet: Six Tales in Historical Context*. Trans. Murtha Baca. New York: Marsilo, 1994.

Massignon, Geneviève, ed. *Folktales of France*. Trans. Jacqueline Hyland. Chicago: University of Chicago Press, 1968.

Masùdi. *The Meadows of Gold. The Abbasids*. London: Kegan Paul, 1989.

Mayer, Charles-Joseph, ed. *Le cabinet des fées; ou Collection choisie des contes des fées, et autres contes merveilleux*. 41 vols. Amsterdam: s.n., 1785.

Mieder, Wolfgang, ed. *Grimms Märchen—modern*. Stuttgart: Reclam, 1979.

Millien, A., and P. Delarue. *Contes du Nivernais et du Morvan*. Paris: Érasme, 1953.

Morlini, Girolamo. *Novellae, fabulae, comoedia*. Naples: Joan. Pasquet de Sallo, 1520.

———. *Hieronimi Morlini Parthenopei Novellae, Fabulae, Comoedia*. Paris: P. Jannet, 1855.

———. *Novelle e favole*. Ed. Giovanni Villani. Rome: Salerno, 1983.

Murat, Henriette Julie de Castelnau, Comtesse de. *Contes de fées dédiez à S. A. S. Madame la princesse douairière de Conty, par Mad, la comtesse de M****. Paris: Claude Barbin, 1698.

———. *Les Nouveaux Contes de fées par Mme de M****. Paris: Claude Barbin, 1698.

———. *Histoires Sublimes et Allégoriques*. Paris: Floentin Delaulne, 1699.

Musäus, Johann Karl August. *Volksmährchen der Deutschen*. 5 vols. Gotha: Ettinger, 1782–87.

Offenbach, Jacques, Jacques Halévy, and Henri Meilhac. *Barbe-Bleue. Opéra bouffe en trois actes*. Paris: E. Gérard, 1866.

Painter, William, trans. *The Palace of Pleasure: Elizabethan Versions of Italian and French Novels from Boccaccio, Bandello, Cinthio, Straparola, Queen Margaret of Navarre, and Others*. 3 vols. 1890. New York: Dover Publications, 1966.

Perrault, Charles. *Histoires ou contes du temps passé*. Paris: Claude Barbin, 1697.

———. *The Vindication of Wives*. Trans. Roland Gant. London: Rodale, 1954.

———. *Perrault's Complete Fairy Tales*. Trans. A. E. Johnson and others. Illus. W. Heath Robinson. New York: Dodd, Mead, 1961.

———. *Contes de Perrault*. Ed. Gilbert Rouger. Paris: Garnier, 1967.

———. *Contes*. Ed. Jean Pierre Collinet. Folio, 1281. Paris: Gallimard, 1981.

———. *Contes*. Ed. Marc Soriano. Paris: Flammarion, 1989.

———. *Contes*. Ed. Catherine Magnien. Paris: Le Livre de Poche, 1990.

Pitré, Giuseppe. *Fiabe e Leggende Popolari Siciliani*. Palermo: L. Pedone Lauriel, 1870.

———. *Fiabe, Novelle e Racconti Popolari Siciliani*. 4 vols. Palermo: L. Pedone Lauriel, 1875.

Planché, James Robinson, and Charles Dance. *Blue Beard: A Grand Musical, Comi-tragical, Melo-dramatic, Burlesque Burletta in One Act*. London: T. H. Lacy, 1839.

Pocci, Franz Graf von. *Blaubart: Ein Märchen*. Munich: Christian Kaiser, 1845.

Rak, Michele, ed. *Fiabe campane*. Milan: Mondadori, 1984.

Ricci, Lucia Battaglia, ed. *Novelle italiene: Il Duecento, Il Trecento*. Milan: Garzanti, 1982.

Ritchie, Anne Thackeray. "Bluebeard's Keys." In *Bluebeard's Keys and Other Stories*. *1871*. *The Works of Miss Thackeray*. Vol. 5. London: Smith and Elder, 1902. 1–118.

Robbins, Rossell Hope, ed. and trans. *The Hundred Tales (Les Cent Nouvelles Nouvelles)*. New York: Crown, 1960.

Robert, Raymonde, ed. *Il était une fois les fées: contes du XVIIe et XVIIIe siècles*. Nancy: Presses Universitaires de Nancy, 1984.

———, ed. *Contes parodiques et licencieux du 18e siècle*. Nancy: Presses Universitaires de Nancy, 1987.

Rölleke, Heinz, ed. *Die älteste Märchensammlung der Brüder Grimm*. Cologny-Geneva: Fondation Martin Bodmer, 1975.

———, ed. *Märchen aus dem Nachlaß der Brüder Grimm*. 3rd rev. ed. Bonn: Bouvier, 1983.

———, ed. *Die wahren Märchen der Brüder Grimm*. Frankfurt am Main: Fischer, 1995.

———, ed. *Grimms Märchen und ihre Quellen: Die literarischen Vorlagen der Grimmschen Märchen synoptisch vorgestellt und kommentiert*. Trier: Wissenschaftlicher Verlag Trier, 1998.

Ryder, Arthur W., trans. *The Panchatantra*. Chicago: University of Chicago Press, 1956.

Saal, Justus Heinrich. *Abendstunden in lehrreichen und anmuthungen Erzählungen*. Breslau: Johann Friedrich Korn, 1767.

Sacchetti, Franco. *Il Trecentonovelle*. Ed. Antonio Lanza. Florence: Sansoni, 1984.

Salinari, Giambattista, ed. *Novelle del Cinquecento*. 2 vols. Turin: Unione Tipografico-Editice Tornese, 1955.

Sarnelli, Pompeo. *Posilecheata*. Naples: Morano, 1684.

Schulz, Friedrich. *Kleine Romane*. 5 vols. Leipzig: Georg Joachim Göschen, 1788–90.

Schwob, Marcel. *Le Livre de Monelle*. Paris: Léon Chailly, 1894.

———. *Le Livre de Monelle*. Paris: Éditions Allia, 2005.

Scrivano, Riccardo, ed. *Cinquecento minore*. Bologne: Zanichelli, 1966.

Somadeva. *The Ocean of Story*. Ed. N. M. Penzer. Trans. Charles H. Tawney. 10 vols. Indian edition. Delhi: Motilal Banarsidass, 1968.

Stahl, Karoline. *Fabeln und Erzählungen für Kinder*. Nuremberg, 1818.

Stephens, George and H. Cavallius. *Old Norse Fairy Tale: Gathered from the Swedish Folk*. Trans. Albert Alberg. London: W. Swann Sonnenschein, 1850–1899.

Stöber, August. *Volksbüchlein: Kinder- und Volksliedchen, Spielreime, Sprüche und Märchen*. Strasburg: G. L. Schuler, 1842.

Straparola, Giovan Francesco. *Le Piacevoli Notti*. 2 vols. Venice: Comin da Trino, 1550–53.

———. *The Facetious Nights of Straparola*. Trans. William G. Waters. Illus. Jules Garnier and E. R. Hughes. 4 vols. London: Lawrence and Bullen, 1894.

———. *Le Piacevoli Notti*. Ed. Donato Pirovano. 2 vols. Rome: Salerno Editrice, 2000.

Sutermeister, Otto. *Kinder- und Hausmärchen aus der Schweiz*. Aarau, Switzerland: Sauerländer, 1873.

Tatar, Maria, ed. *The Classic Fairy Tales*. New York: W. W. Norton, 1999.

Taylor, Edgar, ed. *Gammer Grethel; or German Fairy Tales, and Popular Stories, From the Collection of MM. Grimm*. London: Green, 1839.

———, ed. *German Popular Stories*. Intro. John Ruskin. Illus. George Cruikshank. London: Hotten, 1869.

Thackeray, William Makepeace. "Bluebeard's Ghost." *Frazier's Magazine* (October 1943).

Tieck, Ludwig. "Ritter Blaubart: Ein Ammenmärchen in vier Akten." In *Tiecks Schriften*. Vol. 5. Berlin: Reimer, 1828. 7–152.

Tomkowiak, Ingrid, and Ulrich Marzolph, eds. *Grimms Märchen International*. 2 vols. Paderborn: Schöningh, 1996.

Trimm, Timothée. [Pseudonym for Léo Lespès]. "Madame veuve Barbe-Bleue." In *Les contes de Perrault continues par Timothée Trimm*. Paris: Librairie du Petit Journal, 1865. 67–72.

Uther, Hans-Jörg, ed. *Märchen vor Grimm*. Munich: Eugen Diederichs Verlag, 1990.

Villeneuve, Gabrielle-Suzanne Barbot de. *La jeune Amériquaine et Les Contes marins*. La Haye aux dépes de la Compagnie, 1740.

Wesseleski, Albert, ed. *Deutsche Märchen vor Grimm*. Brünn: Rudolf M. Rohrer, 1938.

Widter, Georg and Adam Wolf. *Volksmärchen aus Venetien. Jahrbuch für romanische und englische Literatur* (Leipzig 1866): Vol. VII, 1–36; 121–154; 249–290.

Windling, Terri, ed. *The Armless Maiden and Other Tales for Childhood's Survivors*. New York: Tor, 1995.

Wolf, Johann Wilhelm, ed. *Deutsche Märchen und Sagen*. Leipzig: F. A. Brockhaus, 1845.

———. *Deutsche Hausmärchen*. Göttingen: Dieterich, 1851.

Zingerele, Ignanz Vinzenz, and Joseph Zingerele. *Tirols Volksdichtungen und Volksbräuche*. Innsbruck: Wagner, 1852.

Zipes, Jack, ed. *Beauties, Beasts, and Enchantment: French Classical Fairy Tales*. New York: New American Library, 1989.

———, ed. *Spells of Enchantment: The Wondrous Fairy Tales of Western Culture*. New York: Viking, 1991.

———, ed. *The Great Fairy Tale Tradition: From Straparola and Basile to the Brothers Grimm*. New York: Norton, 2001.

FAIRY TALES 1900–2005

Ada, Alma Flor. *Jordi's Star*. Illus. Susan Gaber. New York: Putnam, 1996.

———. *Gathering the Sun. An Alphabet in Spanish and English*. Illus. Simon Silva. New York: Lothrop, Lee and Shepard, 1997.

———. *The Malachite Palace*. Illus. Leonard Gore. New York: Atheneum, 1998.

———. *The Three Golden Oranges*. Illus. Reg Cartwright. New York: Atheneum, 1999.

Afanas'ev, Aleksandr. *Russian Fairy Tales*. Trans. Norbert Guterman. New York: Pantheon, 1945.

Alexander, Lloyd. *Time Cat: The Remarkable Journeys of Jason and Gareth*. Illus. Bill Sokol. New York: Holt, Rinehart and Winston, 1963.

———. *The Truthful Harp*. Illus. Evaline Ness. New York: Holt, Rinehart and Winston, 1967.

———. *The King's Fountain*. Illus. Ezra Jack Keats. New York: E. P. Dutton, 1971.

———. *The Four Donkeys*. Illus. Lester Abrams. New York: Holt, Rinehart and Winston, 1972.

———. *The Cat Who Wished to Be a Man*. New York: E.P. Dutton, 1973.

———. *Westmark*. New York: E.P. Dutton, 1981.

———. *The Iron Ring*. New York: Dutton, 1999.

Anthony, Edward, and Joseph Anthony. "Bluebeard's Bathtub." In *The Fairies Up to Date*. Illus. Jean De Bosschère. London: T. Butterworth, c. 1923. 152–69.

Ash, Jutta. *Rapunzel*. New York: Holt, Rinehart and Winston, 1982.

Ashley, Mike, ed. *The Mammoth Book of Fairy Tales*. London: Robinson, 1997.

———. *The Mammoth Book of Comic Fantasy*. London: Robinson, 1998.

———. *The Mammoth Book of Comic Fantasy II*. London: Robinson, 1999.

———. *The Mammoth Book of Seriously Comic Fantasy*. London: Robinson, 1999.

Atwood, Margaret. *Bluebeard's Egg and Other Stories*. New York: Ballantine, Fawcett Cress, 1983. 144–84.

———. *The Robber Bride*. New York: Doubleday, 1993.

———. *Good Bones and Simple Murders*. New York: Doubleday, 1994.

———. *Princess Prunella and the Purple Peanut*. Illus. Maryann Kovalsiki. Toronto: Key Porter Books, 1995.

Avi. *Tom, Babette, & Simon: Three Tales of Transformation*. Illus. Alexi Natchev. New York: Macmillan, 1995.

Bail, Murray. *Eucalyptus*. London: Harvill, 1998.

Barth, John. *Chimera*. New York: Random House, 1972.

Barthelme, Donald. "Bluebeard." In *Forty Stories*. New York: Putnam, 1987. 92–97.

Bayley, F. W. N. *Blue Beard*. London: William Orr, 1842.

Beaumont, Jeanne Marie, and Claudia Carlson. *The Poets' Grimm: 20th Century Poems from Grimm Fairy Tales*. Ashland, OR: Story Line Press, 2003.

Bechstein, Ludwig. "Das Märchen vom Ritter Blaubart." In *Deutsches Märchenbuch*. Illus. Ludwig Richter. Leipzig: Wigand, 1845. 79–83.

Beck, Ian. *Hansel and Gretl*. London: Doubleday, 1999.

Bender, Aimee. *Willful Creatures*. New York: Doubleday, 2005.

Bergen, Lara. *X-Men*. Based on the screenplay by Christopher McQuarrie and Ed Solomon. New York: Dell, 2000.

Berne. Eric. *The Happy Valley*. Illus. Sylvie Selig. New York: Grove Press, 1968.

Bird, Carmel. *Red Shoes*. Sydney: Vintage, 1998.

Biro, Val. *Hansel and Gretel*. Oxford: Oxford University Press, 1997.

Block, Francesca Lia. *Dangerous Angels: The Weetzie Bat Books*. New York: HarperCollins, 1998.

———. *I Was a Teenage Fairy*. New York: HarperCollins, 1998.

———. *The Rose and the Beast: Fairy Tales Retold*. New York: HarperCollins, 2000.

Blundell, Tony. *Beware of Boys*. London: Viking Children's Books, 1991.

Border, Rosemary. *Hansel and Gretel*. Illus. Maxun Tang. Oxford: Oxford University Press, 1995.

Brooke, William J. *A Telling of the Tales: Five Stories*. Illus. Richard Egielski. New York: HarperCollins, 1990.

———. *Untold Tales*. New York: HarperCollins, 1992.

Browne, Anthony, *Hansel and Gretel*. London: Julia MacRae, 1981.

———. *Anthony Browne's King Kong*. London: Julia MacRae, 1994.

Bruna, Dick. *Cinderella*. Chicago: Follett, 1966.

Bryan, Ashley. *The Dancing Granny*. Illus. Ashley Bryan. New York: Atheneum, 1977.

———. *Turtle Knows Your Name*. New York: Atheneum: 1989.

———. *Sh-Ko and His Eight Wicked Brothers*. Illus. Fumio Yoshimura. New York: Atheneum, 1998.

———. *African Tales, Uh-Huh*. New York: Atheneum, 1998.

Buckley, Michael. *The Sisters Grimm: The Fairy-Tale Detectives*. New York: Abrams, 2004.

———. *The Sisters Grimm: The Usual Suspects—Book #2*. New York: Abrams, 2005.

———. *The Sisters Grimm: The Problem Child—Book #3*. New York: Abrams, 2006.

Byatt, A. S. *Possession*. London: Chatto and Windus, 1990.

———. *The Djinn in the Nightingale's Eye*. London: Chatto and Windus, 1994.

———. *Little Black Book of Stories*. New York: Vintage International, 2005.

Calvino, Italo, ed. "Silvernose." In *Italian Folktales*. Trans. George Martin. New York: Harcourt Brace Jovanovich, 1980. 26–30.

Carryl, Guy Wetmore. "How the Helpmate of Blue-Beard Made Free with a Door." In *Grimm Tales Made Gay.* Illus. Albert Levering. Boston: Houghton Mifflin, 1902. 64–71.

Carter, Angela. "The Bloody Chamber." In *The Bloody Chamber and Other Stories*, ed. Angela Carter. New York: Penguin, 1979. 7–41.

Carter, Anne. *Beauty and the Beast.* Illus. Binette Schroeder. New York: Clarkson N. Potter, 1986. First American edition.

Cashorali, Peter. *Fairy Tales: Traditional Stories Retold for Gay Men.* San Francisco: HarperCollins, 1997.

Cave, Emma. *Bluebeard's Room.* London: Coronet, 1995.

Child, Lauren. *Beware of the Storybook Wolves.* New York: Scholastic, 2000.

Chin, Charlie. *China's Bravest Girl: The Legend of Hua Mu Lan.* Illus. Tomie Arai. San Francisco: Children's Book Press, 1993.

Claremont, Chris. *X-Men: Visionaries.* New York: Marvel, 1998.

Clarkson, Atelia, and Gilbert C. Cross, eds. *World Folktales: A Scribner Resource Collection.* New York: Charles Scribner's Sons, 1980.

Claverie, Jean. *Le Petit Chaperon Rouge.* Paris: Albin Michel Jeunesse, 1997.

Climo, Shirley. *The Egyptian Cinderella.* Illus. Ruth Heller. New York: Thomas Y. Crowell, 1989.

———. *The Irish Cinderlad.* Illus. Loretta Krupinski. New York: HarperCollins, 1996.

———. *The Persian Cinderella.* Illus. Robert Florczak. New York: HarperCollins, 1999.

Coady, Christopher. *Red Riding Hood.* New York: Dutton, 1991.

Coburn, Jewell Reinhart, with Tzexa Cherta Lee. *Jouanah: A Hmong Cinderella.* Illus. Anne Sibley O'Brien. Arcadia, CA: Shen's Books, 1996.

———. *Angkat: The Cambodian Cinderella.* Illus. Eddie Flotte. Auburn, CA: Shen's Books, 1998.

———. *Dormitila: A Cinderella Tale from the Mexican Tradition.* Illus. Connie McLennan. Auburn, CA: Shen's Books, 2000.

Cole, Brock. *Buttons.* New York: Farrar, Straus and Giroux, 2000.

Coleman, Michael. *Top Ten Fairy Stories.* Illus. Michael Tickner. London: Scholastic, 1999.

Colman, George, the Younger. *Blue Beard, or Female Curiosity, a dramatic romance.* London: Cadell and Davies, 1798.

Collins, Sheila Hébert. *Cendrillon: A Cajun Cinderella.* Illus. Patrick Souper. Gretna, LA: Pelican, 2000.

Compton, Joanne. *Ashpet: An Appalachian Girl.* Illus. Kenn Compton. New York: Holiday, 1994.

Cooke, Rose Terry. "Blue-Beard's Closet." 1861. In *American Women Poets of the Nineteenth Century.* New Brunswick, NJ: Rutgers University Press, 1992. 267–69.

Coover, Robert. "The Gingerbread House." In *Pricksongs & Descants: Fictions*. New York: E. P. Dutton, 1969.

———. *Briar Rose*. New York: Grove Press, 1996.

———. *Hansel and Gretel: The Traditional Tale*. Ed. Alison Hedger. London: Golden Apple Productions, 2000.

———. *Stepmother*. Illus. Michael Kupperman. San Francisco: McSweeney's Books, 2004.

———. *A Child Again*. San Francisco: McSweeney's Books, 2005.

Cramer, Heinz von. "Ritter Blaubart." In *Märchen, Sagen und Abenteuer auf alten Bilderbogen neu erzählt von Autoren unserer Zeit*, ed. Jochen Jung. Munich: DTV, 1974. 26–28.

Crowley, John. "Lost and Abandoned." In *Black Swan, White Raven*. Eds. Ellen Datlow and Terri Windling. New York: Avon, 1997.

Crump, Jr., Frederic. *Beauty and the Beast*. Nashville, TN: Winston-Derek, 1992.

Daily, Audry. *Hansel and Gretel: A Traditional Tale*. Illus. Isabella Misso. London: Ladybird, 1999.

Daly, Jude. *Fair, Brown & Trembling: An Irish Cinderella Story*. New York: Farrar, Straus and Giroux, 2000.

Datlow, Ellen, and Terri Windling, eds. *Black Thorn, White Rose*. New York: Avon, 1993.

———. *Snow White, Blood Red*. New York: Avon, 1994.

———. *Ruby Slippers, Golden Tears*. New York: Avon, 1995.

———. *Silver Birch, Blood Moon*. New York: Avon, 1999.

———. *Back Heart, Ivory Bones*. New York: Avon, 2000.

———. *A Wolf at the Door and Other Retold Fairy Tales*. New York: Simon & Schuster, 2000.

———. *The Faery Reel: Tales from the Twilight Realm*. New York: Viking, 2004.

Davis, Kathryn. *The Girl Who Trod on a Loaf*. New York: Knopf, 1993.

De La Mare, Walter. "Bluebeard." In De La Mare, *Told Again. Old Tales Told Again*. London: 1927. 152–65.

Delarue, Paul. *Le conte populaire français: Catalogue raisonné des versions de France et des pays de langue française d'outre-mer*. Vol. 1. Paris: Editions Erasme, 1957.

DeLuise Dom. *King Bob's New Clothes*. Illus. Christopher Santoro. New York: Simon & Schuster, 1996.

———. *Dom DeLuise's Hansel and Gretel*. Illus. Christopher Santoro. New York: Simon & Schuster, 1997.

———. *Dom DeLuise's The Nightingale*. Illus. Christopher Santoro. New York: Simon & Schuster, 1996.

De Régnier, Henri. "Le Sixième mariage de Barbe-Bleue." *Entretiens politiques et Littéraires* 32 (1892): 221–32.

Döblin, Alfred. "Der Ritter Blaubart." In *Die Ermordung einer Butterblume und andere Erzählungen*. Berlin: S. Fischer, 1913. 131–54.

Doherty, Berlie. *Hansel and Gretel*. Illus. Jane Ray. London: Walker, 2000.

Donoghue, Emma. *Kissing the Witch: Old Tales in New Skins*. New York: Harper-Collins, 1997.

Duffy, Carol Ann. *Rumpelstiltskin and Other Grimm Tales*. London: Faber and Faber, 1999.

Dufour, Hortense. *La dernière Femme de Barbe-Bleue*. Paris: Grasset, 1976.

Dunbar, Joyce. *Hansel and Gretel*. Illus. Ian Penney. Hove, England: Macdonald Young Books, 1997.

Edwards, Pamela Duncan, and Henry Cole. *Dinorella: A Prehistoric Fairy Tale*. New York: Hyperion, 1997.

Eisner, Will. *The Princess and the Frog*. New York: Nantier, Beall, Minoustchine, 1999.

Ellesmere, Francis Egerton. *Bluebeard; or, Dangerous Curiosity & Justifiable Homicide*. London: T. Bertell, 1841.

Emberley, Michael. *Ruby*. Boston: Little Brown, 1990.

Ernst, Lisa Campbell. *Little Red Riding Hood: A Newfangled Prairie Tale*. New York: Scholastic, 1995.

Ford, Michael, ed. *Happily Ever After: Erotic Fairy Tales for Men*. New York: Masquerade, 1995.

———. *Once Upon a Time: Erotic Fairy Tales for Women*. New York: Masquerade, 1996.

Foster, Alan Dean, and Martin Harry Greenberg, eds. *Smart Dragons, Foolish Elves*. New York: Ace, 1991.

Fox, Cameron. *Hansel and Gretel*. Harlow: Pearson Education, 2000.

France, Anatole. *Les Sept Femmes de La Barbe-Bleue et Autres Contes Merveilleux*. Paris: Calman-Lévy, 1909.

———. *The Seven Wives of Bluebeard*. Trans. James Lewis May and Bernard Miall. London: John Lane, 1921.

Frédéric II, Roi de Prusse. "Commentaires apostoliques et théologiques sur les saintes prophéties de l'auteur sacré de Barbe-Bleue." In *Ouvres Poétiques de Frédric II Roi de Prusse*, Vol. VI, ed. J. D. E. Preuss. Berlin: R. Decker, 1790. 33–57.

Frisch, Max. *Blaubart: Eine Erzählung*. Frankfurt am Main: Suhrkamp, 1982.

Frost, Gregory. *Fitcher's Brides*. New York: Tom Doherty, 2002.

Froud, Wendy, and Terri Windling. *Midsummer Night's Faery Tale*. New York: Simon & Schuster, 1999.

Gaiman, Neil. "Snow, Glass, Apples" [1994]. In *Smoke and Mirrors: Short Fictions and Illusions*. New York: Avon, 1998.

———. *Smoke and Mirrors: Short Fictions and Illusions*. New York: Avon, 1998.

—. *The Dream Hunters*. Illus. Yoshitaka Amano. New York: DC Comics, 1999.

Galloway, Priscilla. *Truly Grim Tales*. New York: Bantam, 1995.

Gardner, Martin. *Visitors from Oz: The Wild Adventures of Dorothy, the Scarecrow, and the Tin Woodman*. New York: St. Martin's Press, 1998.

Gardner, Sally. *I, Coriander*. New York: Dial, 2005.

Gelberg, Hans-Joachim, ed. *Daumesdick. Neuer Märchenschatz mit vielen Bildern*. Weinheim: Beltz and Gelberg, 1990.

Geras, Adèle. *The Tower Room*. London: Hamish Hamilton, 1990.

—. *Watching the Roses*. London: Hamish Hamilton, 1991.

—. *Pictures of the Night*. London: Hamish Hamilton, 1992.

—. *Cinderella*. Illus. Gwen Tourret. London: Macdonald Young Books, 1996.

Gill-Brown, Vanessa and Mandy Stanley. *Rufferella*. New York: Scholastic, 2000.

Goldstein, Lisa. "Breadcrumbs and Stones." In *Snow White, Blood Red*, eds. Ellen Datlow and Terri Windling. New York: Avon, 1995.

Goodall, John G. *Puss in Boots*. New York: Macmillan, 1990.

Goode, Diane. *Cinderella: The Dog and Her Little Glass Slipper*. New York: Scholastic, 2000.

Gordon, Karen Elizabeth. *The Red Shoes and Other Tattered Tales*. Normal, IL: Dalkey Archive Press, 1996.

Gorman, Ed, and Martin H. Greenberg, eds. *Once Upon a Crime*. New York: Berkley Prime Crime, 1998.

Granowsky, Alvin. *A Deal Is a Deal!* Illus. Tom Newbury. Austin, TX: Steck-Vaughn, 1993.

—. *That Awful Cinderella*. Illus. Rhonda Childress. Austin, TX: Steck-Vaughn, 1993.

—. *The UnFairest of Them All*. Illus. Mike Krone. Austin, TX: Steck-Vaughn, 1993.

Greenberg, Martin H., and Janet Pack, eds. *Magic Tails*. New York: Daw, 2005.

Greenway, Shirley. *Hansel and Gretel*. Illus. Peter Richardson. London: Pan, 1981.

Grimm, The Brothers. *Hansel and Gretel*. Illus. Arnold Lobel. New York: Delacorte, 1971.

—. *Hansel and Gretel*. Illus. Susan Jeffers. Trans. Mrs. Edgar Lucas. New York: Dial, 1980.

—. *Hansel and Gretel*. Illus. Anthony Browne. Adapt. from the translation by Eleanor Quarrie. London: Julia MacRae, 1981.

Grimm, Gebrüder. *Hänsel and Gretel*. Illus. Lisbeth Zwerger. Basel, Switzerland: Neugebauer, 1978; English edition: The Brothers Grimm, *Hansel and Gretel*. New York: William Morrow, 1979.

Grimm, Jacob. *Hansel and Gretel*. Illus. Antonella Bolliger-Savelli. New York: Oxford University Press, 1981.

Grimm, Jacob, and Wilhelm Grimm. *The Six Servants*. Trans. Anthea Bell. Illus. Sergei Goloshapov. New York: North-South Books, 1996.

————. *The Brave Little Tailor*. Trans. Anthea Bell. Illus. Sergei Goloshapov. New York: North-South Books, 1997.

Grimm, Jacob, and William Grimm. *Hansel and Gretel*. Illus. Erika Weihs. New York: Simon & Schuster/A Little Golden Book, 1943.

Grimm, Jakob, and Wilhelm Grimm. *Hansel & Grettel*. Illus. Monique Felix. Mankato, MN: Creative Education, 1983.

Hale, Shannon. *The Goose Girl*. New York: Bloomsbury, 2003.

Hamilton, Virginia. *The People Could Fly: American Black Folk Tales*. Illus. Leo Dillon and Diane Dillon. New York: Alfred A. Knopf, 1985.

————. *Her Stories: African American Folktales, Fairy Tales, and True Tales*. New York: Blue Sky Press, 1995.

————. *The Girl Who Spun Gold*. Illus. Leo Dillon and Diane Dillon. New York: Blue Sky Press, 2000.

Hargreaves, Georgina. *Hansel and Gretel*. London: Dean, 1976.

Haumont, Marie. *Drôle de conte*. Paris: Editions Thierry Magnier, 2000.

Hay, Sara Henderson. *Story Hour*. Illus. Jim McMullan. Garden City: Doubleday, 1963.

Hayes, Sarah. *Hansel and Gretel*. London: Walker, 1985.

Helprin, Mark. *A City in Winter*. Illus. Chris Van Allsburg. New York: Viking, 1996.

Hickox, Rebecca. *The Golden Sandal: A Middle Eastern Cinderella Story*. New York: Holiday House, 1998.

Hine, Daryl. *Bluebeard's Wife*. Illus. Virgil Burnett, 1968. Toronto: Coach House, 1975.

Holland, Sarah. *Bluebeard's Bride*. Toronto: Harlequin, 1985.

Hooks, William. *Moss Gown*. Illus. Donald Carrick. New York: Clarion, 1987.

Huck, Charlotte. *Toads and Diamonds*. Illus. Anita Lobel. New York: Greenwillow, 1996.

Humperdinck, Engelbert. *Hansel and Gretel*. Illus. Yoshitaro Isaka. Adapt. Eriko Kishida. Trans. Ann Brannen. Tokyo: Gakken, 1971.

Hunia, Fran. *Hansel and Gretel*. London: Ladybird, 1999.

Husain, Shahrukh. *Women Who Wear Breeches*. London: Virago, 1995.

Impey, Rose. *Hansel and Gretel and the Princess and the Pea*. Illus. Peter Bailey. London, Orchard, 2001.

Irish, William. *Bluebeard's Seventh Wife*. New York: Popular Library, 1952.

Jackson, Ellen. *Cinder Edna*. Illus. Kevin O' Malley. New York: Lothrop, Lee & Shepard, 1994.

Jacobs, A. J. *Fractured Fairy Tales*. New York: Bantam, 1997.

Jaffe, Nina. *The Way Meat Loves Salt: A Cinderella Tale from the Jewish Tradition*. Illus. Louise August. New York: Henry Holt, 1998.

Jarrell, Randall, ed. and trans. *The Golden Bird and Other Fairy Tales of the Brothers Grimm*. Illus. Sandro Nardini. New York: Macmillan, 1962.

———, ed. and trans. *The Rabbit Catcher and Other Fairy Tales of Ludwig Bechstein*. New York: Macmillan, 1962.

Jiang, Wei, and Cheng An Jiang. *The Legend of Mu Lan: A Heroine of Ancient China*. Monterey, CA: Victory Press, 1992.

Joyce, Graham. *The Tooth Fairy*. New York: Tor, 1996.

Jukes, Mavis. *Cinderella 2000: Looking Back*. New York: Dell Yearling, 1999.

Jungman, Ann. *Cinderella and the Hot Air Balloon*. Illus. Russell Ayto. London: Frances Lincoln, 1992.

Keene, Carolyn. *The Bluebeard Room*. Nancy Drew Mystery 77. New York: Minstel, 1988.

Kelly, Mave. *Alice in Thunderland: A Feminist Fairytale*. Dublin: Attic Press, 1993.

Kerr, Peg. *The Wild Swans*. New York: Warner, 1999.

Kilmer, Alice. "The Case of Bluebeard." In *Hunting a Hair Shirt and Other Spiritual Adventures*. New York: Doran, 1923. 93–98.

Kilworth, Garry. "The Trial of Hansel and Gretel." In *Black Swan, White Raven*, eds. Ellen Datlow and Terri Windling. New York: Avon, 1997.

Kincaid, Lucy. *Hansel and Gretel*. Illus. Eric Kincaid. Newmarket, England: Brimax, 1990.

Kirsten, Lincoln. *Puss in Boots*. Illus. Alain Vaës. Boston: Little Brown, 1992.

Kraft, Kinuko Y. *Cinderella*. New York: Sea Star, 2000.

Kushner, Tony. *Brundibar*. Illus. Maurice Sendak. New York: Hyperion, 2003.

Lacapa, Michael. *The Flute Player: An Apache Folktale*. Flagstaff, AZ: Northland, 1990.

———. *Antelope Woman: An Apache Folktale*. Flagstaff, AZ: Northland, 1992.

Lackey, Mercedes. *The River's Gift*. New York: ROC, 1999.

Langley, Jonathan. *Rumpelstiltskin*. New York: HarperCollins, 1991.

Lardner, Ring. "Bluebeard." In *What of It?* New York: Doran, Scribner, 1925. 70–73.

Lattimore, Deborah Nourse. *Cinderhazel: The Cinderella of Halloween*. New York: Blue Sky Press, 1997.

Law, Karina. *The Truth About Hansel and Gretel*. Illus. Elke Counsell. Minneapolis: Picture Window Books, 2002.

Lee, Tanith. "Red as Blood." In *Red as Blood or Tales from the Sisters Grimmer*. New York: Avon, 1983. 18–28.

———. "Snow Drop." In *Snow White, Blood Red*, eds. Ellen Datlow and Terri Windling. New York: William Morrow, 1993. 106–29.

———. *White as Snow*. New York: Tor, 2000.

Leichman, Seymour. *The Wicked Wizard and the Wicked Witch*. New York: Harcourt Brace Jovanovich, 1972.

Levine, Gail Carson. *Ella Enchanted*. New York: HarperCollins, 1997.

————. *The Princess Test*. Illus. Mark Elliott. New York: HarperCollins, 1999.

————. *The Fairy's Test*. Illus. Mark Elliott. New York: HarperCollins, 1999.

————. *Princess Sonora and the Long Sleep*. Illus. Mark Elliott. New York: HarperCollins, 1999.

————. *Cinderellis and the Glass Hill*. Illus. Mark Elliott. New York: HarperCollins, 2000.

Little, Denise, ed. *Twice Upon a Time*. New York: DAW, 1999.

Loher, Dea. *Manhattan Medea: Blaubart—Hoffnung der Frauen*. Frankfurt am Main: Verlag der Autoren (Theaterbibliotek), 1999.

Louie, Ai-Ling. *Yeh Shen: A Cinderella Story from China*. New York: Philomel, 1982.

Lowell, Susan. *Little Red Cowboy Hat*. Illus. Randy Cecil. New York: Henry Holt, 1997.

————. *Cindy Ellen: A Wild Western Cinderella*. New York: HarperCollins Children's Books, 2001.

Ludlam, Charles. *Bluebeard: A Melodrama in Three Acts. 1970*. In *The Complete Plays of Charles Ludlam*. New York: Harper & Row, 1989. 116–41.

Macchio, Ralph. *X-Men: The Movie Adaptation*. New York: Marvel, 2000.

Maeterlinck, Maurcie. *Sister Beatrice and Ardiane & Barbe Bleue*. Trans. Bernard Miall. New York: Dodd Mead, 1913.

Maguire, Gregory. *Wicked*. Illus. Douglas Smith. New York: Regan Books, 1995.

————. *Confessions of an Ugly Stepsister*. Illus. Bill Sanderson. New York: Regan Books, 1999.

————. *Mirror Mirror*. New York: Regan Books, 2003.

————. "Hamster and Gerbil." In *Leaping Beauty and Other Animal Fairy Tales*. New York: HarperCollins, 2004.

Mah, Adeline Yen. *Chinese Cinderella and the Secret Dragon Society*. New York: HarperCollins, 2005.

Mahy, Margaret. *17 Kings and 42 Elephants*. Illus. Patricia MacCarthy. New York: Dial, 1987.

————. *The Seven Chinese Brothers*. Illus. Jean and Mou-sien Tseng. New York: Scholastic, 1990.

Mains, David, and Karen Mains. *Tales of the Resistance*. Illus. Jack Stockman. Elgin, IL: Chariot Books, 1986.

Marcantonio, Patricia Santos. *Red Ridin' in the Hood and Other Cuentos*. Illus. Renato Alarcão. New York: Farrar, Straus, and Giroux, 2005.

Marshall, James. *Hansel and Gretel*. New York: Dial, 1990.

Marsoli, Lisa Ann. *Disney's Mulan*. Illus. Judith Holmes Clarke, Brent Ford, Denies Shimabukuro, Scott Tilley, Lori Tyminski, and Atelier Philippe Harchy. New York: Disney Enterprises, 1998.

Martin, Rafe. *The Rough-Face Girl*. Illus. David Shannon. New York: G. P. Putnam's Sons, 1992.

Mayer, Gloria Gilbert, and Thomas Mayer. *Goldilocks on Management: 27 Revisionist Fairy Tales for Serious Managers*. Illus. Michael Zaharuk. New York: American Management Association, 1999.

Mayer, Marianna. *Baba Yaga and Vasalissa the Brave*. Illus. K. Y. Craft. New York: Morrow Junior Books, 1994.

———. *Iron John*. Illus. Winslow Pels. New York: Morrow Junior Books, 1999.

Mayer, Mercer. *One Monster after Another*. New York: Golden Press, 1974.

———. *Favorite Tales from Grimm*. Retold by Nancy Garden. Illus. Mercer Mayer. New York: Four Winds Press, 1982.

Mayo, Margaret. *Hansel and Gretel*. Illus. Philip Norman. London: Orchard, 2002.

McCallum, Phyllis. *Hansel and Gretel and the Golden Petticoat*. Denver, CO: Denver Pioneer Service, 1971.

McClintock, Barbara. *Cinderella*. London: Scholastic, 2005.

McKinley, Robin. *Deerskin*. New York: Ace, 1993.

———. *Spindle's End*. New York: G. P. Putnam's Sons, 2000.

Mieder, Wolfgang, ed. *Disenchantments. An Anthology of Modern Fairy Tale Poetry*. Hanover, NH: University Press of New England, 1985.

Millar, Mark. *Ultimate X-Men: Issues 1, 2 3*. New York: Marvel Comics, 2001.

Millay, Edna St. Vincent. [Bluebeard Sonnet.] In *Collected Poems*. Ed. Normal Millay. New York: Harper, 1956.

Minters, Frances. *Cinder-Elly*. Illus. G. Brian Karas. New York: Viking, 1994.

———. *Sleepless Beauty*. Illus. G. Brian Karas. New York: Viking, 1996.

Mitchell, Stephen. *The Frog Prince: A Fairy Tale for Consenting Adults*. New York: Harmony Books, 1999.

Mizuno, Junko. *Junko Mizuno's Hansel & Gretel*. San Francisco: Viz Communications, 2003.

Moerbeek, Kees. *The Diary of Hansel and Gretel*. New York: Simon & Schuster, 2002.

Mollel, Tololwa M. *The Princess Who Lost Her Hair: An Akamba Legend*. New York: Troll Associates, 1993.

Mongredien, Sue. *Master Hansel and Miss Gretel*. Oxford: Oxford University Press, 2001.

Montgomery, L. M. *The Blue Castle*. New York: Bantam, 1988.

Montresor, Beni. *The Nightingale*. Adapt. Alan Benjamin. New York: Crown, 1985.

———. *The Witches of Venice*. New York: Doubleday, 1989.

Myers, Bernice. *Sidney Rella and the Glass Sneaker*. Boston: Houghton Mifflin, 1996.

Murphy, Louise. *The True Story of Hansel and Gretel*. New York: Penguin, 2003.

Napoli, Donna Jo. *The Prince of the Pond*. Illus. Judith Byron Schachner. New York: Dutton, 1992.

———. *The Magic Circle*. New York: Dutton, 1993.

————. *Jimmy, The Pickpocket of the Palace*. New York: Dutton, 1995.

————. *Zel*. New York: Dutton, 1998.

————. *Sirena*. New York: Scholastic, 1998.

————. *Crazy Jack*. New York: Delacorte, 1999.

————. *Beast*. New York: Atheneum, 2000.

Napoli, Donna Jo, and Richard Tchen. *Spinners*. New York: Dutton, 1999.

Narayan, R. K. *The Grandmother's Tale*. London: William Heinemann, 1993.

Nardini. *My Book of Hansel and Gretel*. New York: Maxton, 1960.

Nix, Garth. "Hansel Eyes." In *A Wolf at the Door*, eds. Ellen Datlow and Terri Windling. New York: Simon & Schuster, 2000.

Oates, Joyce Carol. "Blue-Bearded Lover." In *The Assignation: Stories*, ed. Joyce Carol Oates. New York: Ecco, 1988. 184–86.

Paterson, Katherine. *The Tale of the Mandarin Ducks*. Illus. Leo Dillon and Diane Dillon. New York: Dutton, 1990.

————. *The Wide-Awake Princess*. Illus. Vladimir Vagin. New York: Clarion, 2000.

Paterson, Stuart. *Hansel and Gretel*. London: Nick Hern, 2000.

Paul, Richard. *Red Riding Hood Races the Big Bad Wolf*. Illus. Eugene Clark. Macomb, MI: Twilight Press, 1999.

Perlman, Janet. *Cinderella Penguin or, The Little Glass Flipper*. New York: Viking, 1992.

Perrault, Charles. *Puss in Boots*. Trans. Anthea Bell. Illus. Giuliano Lunelli. New York: North-South Books, 1999.

Philip, Neil, ed. *American Fairy Tales: From Rip Van Winkle to the Rootabaga Stories*. Illus. Michael McCurdy. New York: Hyperion, 1996.

Plath, Sylvia. "Bluebeard." [pre-1956]. In *The Collected Poems*, ed. Ted Hughes. New York: Harper & Row, 1981. 305.

Pollock, Penny. *The Turkey Girl: A Zuni Cinderella Story*. Illus. Ed Young. Boston: Little Brown, 1996.

Pomerantz, Charlotte. *Mangaboom*. Illus. Anita Lobel. New York: Greenwillow, 1997.

Presencer, Alain. *Hansel and Gretel*. Illus. Ron van deer Meer and Attie van der Meer. London: Methuen Children, 1986.

Pullman, Philip. *I Was a Rat!* New York: Knopf, 1999.

Quindlen, Anna. *Happily Ever After*. Illus. James Stevenson. New York: Viking, 1997.

Ragan, Kathleen, ed. *Fearless Girls, Wise Women and Beloved Sisters: Heroines in Folktales from Around the World*. New York: Norton, 1998.

Ray, Jane. *Hansel and Gretel*. London: Walker, 1997.

Reed, Jeremy. *Count Bluebeard*. Breakish, Scotland: Acquila/the Phaethom Press, 1976.

Regnier, Henri de. "Le sixième Mariage de Barbe-Bleue." *Entretiens politiques et littéraires* (November 1892): 221–223.

Reichart, Elisabeth. "Die Kammer." In *La Valse: Erzählungen*. Salzburg: Otto Müller, 1992. 103–16.

Resnick, Mike, and Martin H. Greenberg, eds. *Aladdin: Master of the Lamp*. New York: DAW, 1992.

Ribbons, Mary. *Hansel and Gretel*. Illus. La Sorgente. London: Purnell, 1967.

Rock, Joellyn. "Barebones." *Marvels & Tales* 16.2 (2002): 233–62.

Rosen, Michael. *Hansel and Gretel*. Illus. Francese Rovira. London: Firefly, 1989.

Ross, Tony. *Hansel and Gretel*. London: Andersen, 1989; New York: Overlok Press, 1994.

Rühmkorf, Peter. "Blaubarts letzte Reise." In *Der Hüter des Misthaufens: Aufgeklärte Märchen*. Reinbek: Rowohlt, 1983. 110–22.

Rusch, Kristin Kathryn, and Dean Wesley Smith. *X-Men*. Based on the movie by Christopher McQuarrie and Ed Solomon. New York: Del Rey, 2000.

Rushforth, Peter. *Kindergarten*. New York: Alfred Knopf, 1980.

Russell, P. Craig. *Fairy Tales of Oscar Wilde*. New York: Nantier, Beall, Minoustchine, 1998.

San Souci, Robert D. *Sootface: An Objibwa Cinderella Story*. Illus. Daniel San Souci. New York: Doubleday, 1994.

———. *Nicholas Pipe*. Illlustr. David Shannon. New York: Dial, 1997.

———. *Cendrillon: A Caribbean Cinderella*. Illus. Brian Pinckney. New York: Simon & Schuster, 1998.

———. *Fa Mulan*. Illus. Jean and Mou-Sien Tseng. New York: Hyperion, 1998.

———. *Cinderella Skeleton*. Illus. David Catrow. New York: Harcourt, 2000.

———. *Peter and the Blue Witch Baby*. Illus. Alexi Natchev. New York: Doubleday, 2000.

———. *Little Gold Star: A Spanish American Cinderella Tale*. Illus. Sergio Martinez. New York: HarperCollins, 2000.

Sanderson, Peter. *Ultimate X-Men*. New York: Dorling Kindersley, 2000.

Sathre, Vivian. *Slender Ella and Her Fairy Hogfather*. Illus. Sally Anne Lambert. New York: Bantam Doubleday Dell, 1999.

Scieszka, Jon. *The Frog Prince Continued*. Illus. Steve Johnson. New York: Viking, 1991.

Schami, Rafik. *Fatima and the Dream Thief*. Trans. Anthea Bell. Illus. Els Cools and Oliver Streich. New York: North-South Books, 1996.

Schlepp, Wayne. "Cinderella in Tibet." *Asian Folklore Studies* 61 (2002): 123–47.

Schmitz, Anthony. *Darkest Desire: The Wolf's Own Tale*. Hopewell, NJ: Ecco Press, 1998.

Schroeder, Alan. *Smoky Mountain Rose: An Appalachian Cinderella*. Illus. Brad Sneed. New York: Dial, 1997.

Schwartz, Susan, ed. *Arabesques: More Tales of the Arabian Nights*. London: Pan, 1988.

Sedaine, Michel-Jeane and André Modeste Gretry. *Raoul Barbe-Bleue*. Vol. 18. *Collection complète des Oeuvres de Grétry publiée par le Gouvernement Belge*. Bruxelles: 1883–1937.

Sharratt, Mary. *Summit Avenue*. Minneapolis: Coffee House, 2000.

Shorto, Russell. *Cinderella*. Illus. T. Lewis. New York: Birch Lane, 1990.

Shute, Evan Vere. [Pseud. Vere Jameson.] "Bluebeard." In *Bluebeard*. London, Ont.: Hunter, 1954. 7.

Sierra, Judy. *The Gift of the Crocodile: A Cinderella Story*. Illus. Reynold Ruffins. New York: Simon & Schuster, 2000.

———, ed. *Cinderella*. Phoenix: Oryx, 1992.

Silverman, Erica. *Raiser's Riddle*. Illus. Susan Gaber. New York: Farrar, Straus and Giroux, 1999.

Simon, Francesca. *Big Class, Little Class*. London: Orion, 1996; republished as *Don't Cook Cinderella*. Illus. Tony Ross. Orion Books, 2005.

Slater, Lauren. *Blue Beyond Blue: Extraordinary Tales for Ordinary Dilemmas*. New York: W. W. Norton, 2005.

Spiegelman, Art, and Françoise Mouly, eds. *Little Lit: Folklore and Fairy Tale Funnies*. New York: HarperCollins, 2000.

Springer, Nancy. *Fair Peril*. New York: Avon, 1997.

Stanley, Diane. *Rumpelstiltskin's Daughter*. New York: William Morrow, 1997.

Stearns, Michael, ed. *A Wizard's Dozen: Stories of the Fantastic*. New York: Harcourt Brace, 1993.

Stehr, Frédéric. *Loupiotte*. Paris: L'école des loisirs, 2000.

Steig, Jeanne. *A Handful of Beans*. Illus. William Steig. New York: Harper-Collins, 1998.

Strauss, Gwen. "Bluebeard." In *Trail of Stones*. Illus. Anthony Browne. New York: Knopf, 1990. 20–21.

Struck, Karin. *Blaubarts Schatten: Roma*. Munich: List, 1991.

Taylor, C. J. *How Two-Feather Was Saved from Loneliness: An Abenaki Legend*. Montreal: Tundra, 1990.

Tchana, Katrin. *The Serpent Slayer and Other Stories of Strong Women*. Illus. Trina Schart Hyman. Boston: Little Brown, 2000.

Tegethoff, Ernst, trans. *Märchen, Schwänke und Fabeln*. Munich: Bruckmann, 1925.

Tepper, Sheri. *Beauty*. New York: 1991.

Thaler, Mike. *Hanzel and Pretzel*. Illus. Jared Lee. New York: Scholastic, 1997.

———. *Schmoe White and the Seven Dorfs*. Illus. Jared Lee. New York: Scholastic, 1997.

———. *Cinderella Bigfoot*. Illus. Jared Lee. New York: Scholastic, 1997.

Thompson, Jill. *The Little Endless Storybook*. New York: DC Comics, 2001.

———. *Scary Godmother: One*. Dover, NJ: Sirius Entertainment, 2001.

Trakl, Georg. *Blaubart: Ein Puppenspiel*. In *Georg Trakl, Dichtungen und Briefe*, Vol. 1, eds. Walter Killy and Hans Szklenar. Salzburg: O. Müller, 1969. 435–45.

Truijens, Hannie. *Hansel and Gretel*. London: Macmillan Education, 1989.

Untermeyer, Louis. "Bluebeard." In *Tales from the Ballet*. Illus. Alice and Martin Provensen. New York: Golden Press, 1968.

Updike, John. "Bluebeard in Ireland." In *The Afterlife and Other Stories*. New York: Knopf, 1994. 154–89.

Velde, Vivian Vande. *Tales from the Brothers Grimm and the Sisters Weird*. New York: Harcourt Brace, 1995.

———. *The Rumpelstiltskin Problem*. Boston: Houghton Mifflin, 2000.

Verschoyle, Teresa. *Hansel and Gretel*. Illus. Pat Oakley. Loughborough, England: Ladybird, 1982.

Walker, Nancy G. *Feminist Fairy Tales*. San Francisco: Harper, 1996.

Warner, Sylvia Townsend. "Bluebeard's Daughter." In *The Cat's Cradle Book*. New York: Viking, 1940. 160–86.

Wegman, William, with Carole Kismaric and Marvin Heiferman. *Cinderella*. New York: Hyperion, 1993.

Welty, Eudora. *The Robber Bridegroom*. New York: Harcourt, 1942.

Wenzel, David, and Douglas Wheeler. *Fairy Tales of the Brothers Grimm*. New York: Nantier, Beall, and Minoustchine, 1995.

Wiesner, William. *Hansel and Gretel*. New York: Seabury, 1971.

Wildsmith, Brian, and Rebecca Wildsmith. *Jack and the Meanstalk*. New York: Knopf, 1994.

Willard, Nancy. *The Mountains of Quilt*. Illus. Tomie de Paola. San Diego: Harcourt Brace Jovanovich, 1987.

———. *The Ballad of Biddy Early*. Illus. Barry Moser. New York: Knopf, 1989.

———. *Firebrat*. Illus. David Wiesner. New York: Knopf, 1989.

———. *East of the Sun & West of the Moon. A Play*. Illus. Barry Moser. New York: Harcourt Brace Jovanovich, 1989.

Williams, Jay. *The Cookie Tree*. Illus. Blake Hampton. New York: Parents' Magazine Press, 1967.

———. *The Reward Worth Having*. New York: Four Winds Press, 1977.

Wilson, David Henry. *The Coachman Rat*. New York: Carroll and Graf, 1989.

Wilson, Gahan. "Hansel and Grettel." In *Ruby Slippers, Golden Tears*, eds. Ellen Datlow and Terri Windling. New York: Avone, 1996.

Windling, Terri, ed. *The Armless Maiden and Other Tales for Childhood's Survivors*. New York: Tor, 1995.

Windling, Terri, and Ellen Steiber. *Voyage of the Basset: The Raven Queen*. New York: Random House, 1999.

Wittmann, Josef. "Hänsel und Gretel." In *Daumesdick. Neuer Märchenschatz mit vielen Bildern,* ed. Hans-Joachim Gelberg. Weinheim: Beltz and Gelberg, 1990. 297.

Wolfe, Gene. "In the House of Gingerbread." In *Endangered Species.* New York: Tor, 1989.

Wrede, Patricia. *Book of Enchantments.* New York: Harcourt Brace, 1996.

Wynne Jones, Diana. *Year of the Griffin.* New York: Greenwillow Books, 2000.

Yep, Lawrence. *Tongues of Jade.* Illus. David Wiesner. New York: HarperCollins, 1991.

Yolen, Jane. *Briar Rose.* New York: Tor, 1992.

———. *Not One Damsel in Distress: World Folktales for Strong Girls.* Illus. Susan Guevara. San Diego: Silver Whistle/Harcourt, 2000.

Yolen, Jane, and Heidi Stemple. *Mirror, Mirror Forty Folktales for Mothers and Daughters to Share.* New York: Viking, 2000.

Yorinks, Arthur. *Ugh.* Illus. Richard Egielski. New York: Farrar, Straus, and Giroux, 1990.

Zelinsky, Paul O. *Rapunzel.* New York: Dutton, 1997.

Zemach, Harve. *Awake and Dreaming.* Illus. Margot Zemach. New York: Farrar, Straus, and Giroux, 1970.

Zemach, Margot. *The Three Sillies.* New York: Holt, Rinehart and Winston, 1963.

———. *The Three Wishes.* New York: Farrar, Straus, and Giroux, 1986.

Zipes, Jack, ed. *The Complete Fairy Tales of the Brothers Grimm.* New York: Bantam, 1987; 3rd rev. ed. 2003.

BRITISH SCHOLASTIC SERIES

Branford, Henrietta. *Hansel and Gretel.* Lesley Harker. London: Scholastic, 1998.

Doherty, Berlie. *The Snow Queen.* Illus. Sin Bailey. London: Scholastic, 1998.

Fine, Anne. *The Twelve Dancing Princesses.* Illus. Debbi Gliori. London: Scholastic, 1998.

Garner, Alan. *Grey Wolf, Prince Jack and the Firebird.* Illus. James Mayhew. London: Scholastic, 1998.

Gates, Susan. *The Three Heads in the Well.* Illus. Sue Heap. London: Scholastic, 1998.

Geras, Adèle. *The Six Swan Brothers.* Illus. Ian Beck. London: Scholastic, 1998.

Morporgo, Michael. *Cockadoodle-doo, Mr. Sultana!* London: Scholastic, 1998.

Pullman, Philip. *Mossycoat.* Illus. Peter Bailey. London: Scholastic, 1998.

Temperley, Alan. *The Simple Giant.* Illus. Mark Edwards. London: Scholastic, 1999.

Wilson, Jacqueline. *Rapunzel.* Illus. Nick Sharratt. London: Scholastic, 1998.

Wilson, Susan. *Beauty.* New York: Simon & Schuster, 1996.

Wright, Kit. *Rumpelstiltskin.* Illus. Ted Dewan. London: Scholastic, 1998.

Wynne Jones, Diana. *Puss in Boots.* Illus. Fanghorn. London: Scholastic, 1999.

WEBSITES

Ashliman, D. L. "Folklore and Mythology Electronic Texts." Available at http://www.pitt.edu/~dash/folktexts.html.

Blais, Joline, Keith Frank, and Jon Ippolito. "Fair e-Tales." Available at http://www.three.org/fairetales/.

Brown, David K. "Cinderella Stories." Available at http://ucalgary.ca/~dkbrown/cinderella.html.

Journal of Memetics. Available at http://www.jom-emit.org/.

Memetics. Available at http://pespmc1.vub.ac.bc/Memes.html.

"SurLaLune Fairy Tale Pages." Available at http://members.aol.com/surlalune/frytales/index.htm.

"The Cinderella Project." Available at http://www-dept.usm.edu/~engdept/cinderella/cinderella.html.

Vandergrift, Kay. "Kay Vandergrift's Snow White Page." Available at http://www/scils.rutgers.edu/special/Kay/snow white.html.

Windling, Terri. "The Endicott Studio of Mythic Arts." Available at http://www.endicott-studio.com/.

FILMOGRAPHY (IN CHRONOLOGICAL ORDER)

Bluebeard Films

Bluebeard (1901)
France, black and white, silent
Director: Georges Méliès

Landru, der Blaubart von Paris (1922)
English title: *Landu, the Bluebeard of Paris*
Austria, black and white
Director: Hans Otto

Love from a Stranger (1937)
UK, black and white
Based on Agatha Christie's novel *Philomel Cottage*
Director: Rowland V. Lee

Bluebeard's Eighth Wife (1938)
USA, black and white
Director: Ernst Lubitsch

Rebecca (1945)
UK, black and white
Director: Alfred Hitchcock

Suspicion (1941)
UK, black and white
Director: Alfred Hitchcock

Shadow of a Doubt (1943)
UK, black and white
Director: Alfred Hitchcock

Bluebeard (1944)
USA, black and white
Director: Edgar Ulmer

Dark Waters (1944)
USA, black and white
Director: André de Toth

Gaslight (1944)
USA, black and white
Director: George Cukor

Jane Eyre (1944)
USA, black and white
Director: Robert Stevenson

Spellbound (1945)
USA, black and white
Director: Alfred Hitchcock

Experiment Perilous (1945)
USA, black and white
Director: Jacques Tourneur

Undercurrent (1946)
USA, black and white
Director: Vincent Minelli

El Moderno Barba Azul (1946)
Also known as *A Modern Bluebeard* and *Born on the Moon*
Mexico, black and white, in English
Director: Jaime Salvador
Features Buster Keaton

The Two Mrs. Carrolls (1947)
USA, black and white
Director: Peter Godfrey

Monsieur Verdoux (1947)
USA, black and white
Director: Charles Chaplin
Screenwriter: Charles Chapin, Orson Welles (idea)

Secret Behind the Door (1948)
USA, black and white
Director: Fritz Lang

Caught (1949)
USA, black and white
Director: Max Orphuls

Landrou (1963)
France, color
English title: *Bluebeard*
Director: Claude Chabrol
Screenwriter: Françoise Sagan

Bluebeard (1972)
USA, color
Director: Edward Dmytryk
Screenplay: Ennio De Concini, Edward Dmytryk

Deutschland, bleiche Mutter (1980)
Germany, color
Director: Elma Sanders-Brahms

Raise the Red Lantern (1991)
China, color
Director: Zhang Yimou

The Piano (1993)
Australia, color
Director: Jane Campion

Hansel and Gretel Films

Hansel and Gretel (1909)
USA, silent, black and white
Director: J. Searle Dawley

Babes in the Woods (1917)
USA, silent, black and white
Director: Chester M. Franklin and Sidney Franklin

Hansel and Gretel (1923)
USA, black and white
Director: Alfred J. Goulding

Hansel and Gretel (1933)
USA, animation
Director: Frank Moser

Hansel and Gretel (1951)
USA, animation
Director: Ray Harryhausen

Hansel and Gretel (1952)
USA, animation
Director: Connie Rasinski

Hansel and Gretel (1954)
Hänsel und Gretel
West Germany, color
Director: Walter Janssen
English version (1965) Childhood Productions
Music: Milton and Anne Delugg
Narrator: Paul Tripp

Hansel and Gretel (1954)
USA animated and in color
An opera fantasy. Electric puppet version of the Humperdinck opera.
Directors: Michael Myerberger/John Paul
Screenplay: Padraic Colum, Adelheid Wette

Hänsel und Gretel (1954)
West Germany, color
Director: Fritz Genschow
Screenplay: Fritz Genschow

Hänsel und Gretel verliefen sich im Walde (1970)
German, color
Director: Franz Josef Gottlieb.
Erotic adventures of Hansel and Gretel

Whoever Slew Auntie Roo? (1971)
UK, color
Director: Curtis Harrington

Hansel and Gretel (1975)
USA, color
Director: Tom Davenport

Hansel and Gretel (1982)
USA, color
Filmed version of Engelbert Humperdinck's opera performed at the Metropolitan Opera House.
Director: Nathaniel Merrill

Hansel and Gretel (1982)
USA, color
Director: James Frawley
Screenplay: Patricia Resnick
Producer: Shelly Duvall

Hansel and Gretel (1987)
USA, color
Director: Len Talan
Screenplay: Len Talan and Nicola Weems

Criminal Lovers (*Les Amants criminels*, 1999)
France, color
Director: François Ozon
Screenplay: François Ozon

Hansel & Gretel (2002)
USA, color
Director: Gary J. Tunnicliffe
Screenplay: Jonathan Bogner and Timothy Dolan

Little Red Riding Hood Films

The Company of Wolves (1984)
UK, color
Director: Neil Jordan
Screenplay: Angela Carter and Neil Jordan

Red Riding Hood (1988)
USA, color
Director: Adam Brooks
Screenplay: Carol Lucia Satrina

Bye Bye Red Riding Hood (1989)
Canada (French), color
Director: Marta Meszaros

Freeway (1996)
USA, color
Director: Matthew Bright
Screenplay: Matthew Bright
Features Reese Witherspoon and Kiefer Sutherland

Hoodwinked (2005)
USA, color, animation
Directors: Cory and Todd Edwards
Screenplay: Cory and Todd Edwards
Voices: Glenn Close, Anne Hathaway, and James Belushi

Index

A

C

D

E

H

I

N

P

Z

Lightning Source UK Ltd.
Milton Keynes UK
UKOW07f0944191114

241838UK00011B/275/P

9 780415 977814